NEW CHALLENGES
FOR DEVELOPMENT AND MODERNIZATION

New Challenges for Development and Modernization

Hong Kong and the Asia-Pacific Region in the New Millennium

Edited by

Yue-man Yeung

The Chinese University Press

New Challenges for Development and Modernization:
Hong Kong and the Asia-Pacific Region in the
New Millennium
Edited by Yue-man Yeung

© **The Chinese University of Hong Kong**, 2002

ISBN 962–996–031–1

THE CHINESE UNIVERSITY PRESS
The Chinese University of Hong Kong
SHA TIN, N.T., HONG KONG
Fax: +852 2603 6692
 +852 2603 7355
E-mail: cup@cuhk.edu.hk
Web-site: www.chineseupress.com

Printed in Hong Kong

Contents

Illustrations

Preface

During April 2000, a three-day conference was held at The Chinese University of Hong Kong to celebrate the tenth anniversary of the founding of the Hong Kong Institute of Asia-Pacific Studies at the University. During the first decade of its existence, the Institute had already made its mark in the region and in Hong Kong through the many research collaborations it had entered into with local and overseas research institutes and universities, a continuous and large flow of research publications, and a growing number of research initiatives. The Institute came into being at a time when Hong Kong was reaching out to the region in the run-up to its handover to China in 1997. There was a greater need to situate Hong Kong's development in the wider regional setting, hence the name of the Institute.

After keeping in mutual focus the development of Hong Kong and the Asia-Pacific region for over a decade, it was necessary to take stock of the rapid physical and socioeconomic transformation that had taken them by storm. It was a period of accelerating globalization, a process that penetrated every nook and corner in the region. Signs of the process having gone awry surfaced rapidly in the second half of 1997, when the whole region was gripped in an unprecedented financial crisis. In fact, the negative impact was felt globally over the next two years as the drama began to unfold with pain and anguish, with a majority of the countries in the region having been drawn in.

The celebratory anniversary conference, held at a critical juncture of a new era, provided a valuable opportunity for scholars not only to learn retrospectively from past failures, but also to anticipate inviting and daunting challenges of a new century and millennium. Many renowned scholars in Hong Kong and the region did indeed accept our invitation to scrutinize the past for possible future lessons. The chapters found in this book represent most of the papers that were presented at the conference, subsequently duly revised.

The conference referred to above was held at a time when the Institute was designated by the SAR government as the official Hong Kong APEC

Study Centre. For this reason, a half-day session was devoted to a discussion of APEC affairs, as evidenced by one of chapters in this volume. Financial assistance from the government on the running of the Centre during the past two years, including partial support for the anniversary conference, is gratefully acknowledged.

A ten-year milestone being an important one in the history of any organization, the conference has had the whole-hearted support of many colleagues in its preparation, organization and follow-up. I wish to thank, in particular, Lau Siu-kai, Timothy Wong, Wan Po-san, Maurice Brosseau and Shum Kwok-cheung. Janet Wong has been her dependable self in helping me to correspond with the contributors and typing the manuscript. Able research assistance has been provided by Chau Po-kok and Dora Tsang, with the latter also having prepared the index. I am indebted to Mr. Lam Kin-chung, Trustee of Shaw College of the University, for providing a special grant in support of the publication of this book. I wish to thank the contributors especially for sharing with us their expertise and our anniversary celebrations. Together, we have responded to the helpful comments from an anonymous referee. For putting the book together, I take full responsibility for any shortcomings and imperfections.

At a juncture we mark our existence of ten years, it is an opportune time to thank many organizations and individuals who have helped us in kind or in spirit to enable us to come to where we are today. During the past decade, many organizations and individuals both in Hong Kong and abroad have provided funding in our research endeavours. Without their financial support, our research profile would certainly not have been as strong and diversified as it has been. Within the University, we have enjoyed heart-warming encouragement and excellent support ranging from the Vice-Chancellor, colleagues in the Faculties of Social Science, Education and Business Administration to central administrators. The support of my colleagues in the Department of Geography and Resource Management has been especially helpful to me. The reputation of the Institute has no doubt been greatly enhanced through research partnerships and collaborations with a large number of research institutes and scholars in Hong Kong, Mainland China and other parts of the world. These networks have enriched our research outputs and ensured the relevance and timeliness of our research activities. It has been a successful ten years. We will count on your continued support in the next ten.

Yue-man Yeung
February 2002

1

Millennial Changes and Challenges for Pacific Asia

Yue-man Yeung

"The Mediterranean is the ocean of the past, the Atlantic the ocean of the present and the Pacific is the ocean of the future." (John Hay, 1900)

"In the late nineteenth century, states and capital were bound together and, in the end, international labor had to bend their will and become national too. In the late twentieth century, states and capital are splitting apart, with capital becoming international. Labor now has greater incentive to become international than at any time in the past." (Hanagan, 2000:84)

The purpose of employing these two opening quotations in this introductory chapter is to highlight two major changes in the twentieth century that are germane to this volume. As the century came to a close, the Asia-Pacific region had become the fastest growth centre in the world, the outcome of half a century of rapid economic growth after World War II. Essentially, the oft-quoted prediction of Hay, the American Secretary of State, made a century ago, has become reality. Indeed, the Pacific Ocean has much increased in relative political and economic importance. Trans-Pacific trade exceeded that across the Atlantic, for the first time, in 1982. The Asia-Pacific region, defined here as that part of Asia rimming the Pacific Ocean, otherwise also known as Pacific Asia, is widely recognized as having accomplished rapid economic transition in recent decades. The second statement, that of Michael Hanagan, underscores the changing relationships between states, capital and labour, with the latter two becoming more international than ever and nation-states finding themselves in a changed operating environment. The new environment in which nation-states, capital and labour have found themselves has been the driving force of globalization characterized by a new international division of labour, the free flow of capital, people, ideas and technologies across national boundaries, and a new political culture grounded on greater participation and transparency.

Globalization has been variously defined, depending on the purpose and circumstances. One definition that is used by the International Monetary Fund (IMF) has a broad enough scope to be commonly accepted. According to the IMF (1997),

> Globalization refers to the growing economic interdependencies of countries worldwide through the increasing volume of and variety of cross-border transactions in goods and services and of international capital flows and also through the rapid and widespread diffusion of technology. (p. 45)

Globalization processes have been especially active during the last two decades of the twentieth century. They have assisted the economic and physical transformation of many countries in the region (Watters and McGee, 1997), notably centred on large cities (McGee and Robinson, 1995; Lo and Yeung, 1996) and the coastal region of China (Yeung and Hu, 1992; Yeung and Chu, 1998, 2000). New forms of sub-regional economic co-operation, often known as growth triangles, have emerged (Thant et al., 1998; Yeung, 2000). However, the euphoric overtones that accompanied many of the earlier statements on the future of the region have become markedly subdued following the financial crisis that rocked a majority of the countries in the region in 1997. Some scholars have undertaken an objective assessment of where the Asian miracle has gone astray (Kim, 2000), but others have lost faith in the East Asian model of economic development (Garran, 1998) and have found attraction in Paul Krugmann's (1994) hypothesis on Asian economic growth.

Many researchers have attempted to speculate on how the future will unfold for Pacific Asia in the new century (McCord, 1993; Yeung, 1993; Pape, 1998). These appraisals were undertaken at a time prior to the region's being convulsed by the financial meltdown. Now that the new century and the new millennium have dawned, it is the object of this book to spotlight three major themes of change and challenge, as the organization of this book will reveal. They are, namely, economic globalization, political and social change, and regional patterns of transformation. Given the nature of the conference for which this book has been conceptualized, the close link between the affairs of Hong Kong and the Asia-Pacific region reflects the very rationale for the founding of the Hong Kong Institute of Asia-Pacific Studies itself.

Many of the chapters in this volume have taken into account the negative impact of the Asian financial crisis on the region's development. However, the catastrophic terrorist attacks in New York and Washington, D.C. occurred after the volume had been prepared and, therefore, could not be assessed in their evident and adverse impact on Asia.

Economic Globalization

During the last two decades of the twentieth century, the world economy had been so structurally interdependent that the use of the word global, as distinct from international, has become justifiable (Dunning and Hamdani, 1997:12). Many scholars, such as Dicken (1998), have observed the global shift of economic production, and the effects it has on people, culture and institutions (Kalb et al., 2000) and on cities (Lo and Yeung, 1998). However, even by the 1990s, it had already become clear that the world economy was intrinsically more fragile and vulnerable than that of 30, 40 or 50 years ago. Economic shocks originating in any one of the five or six leading economies were now electronically and instantaneously transmitted across the globe, with possibly devastating consequences on nations which might have had nothing to do with the causes of the shocks (Dunning and Hamdani, 1997:33). The risks, in fact, are compounded if financial liberalization has not been accompanied by the requisite banking supervision and reforms. What can happen is that unregulated finance capital will end up largely in short-term and speculative ventures which, in the long run, debilitate growth and efforts to eradicate poverty and reduce income inequalities (Shari, 2000).

This is precisely the painful scenario that most countries in the region had to go through when they were quickly engulfed by the Asian financial crisis in 1997, bringing to a halt the rapid economic growth they had enjoyed during previous decades. Although a few nations are yet to fully recover from the financial turmoil, most have been in the process of recovery and rebuilding themselves. With an ironic twist, Frederic Deyo (Chapter 2) employs Thailand's case of small- and medium-sized enterprises to examine how the country that is widely associated with triggering the crisis has been adjusting and restructuring itself. The question of the likely emergence of a new "Asian developmentalism" has been raised. Two important trends are certain. First is the acceleration of market reforms, partly in response to pressures from the IMF, the World Bank and international investors. Second, there has been growing Japanese involvement in regional economic recovery. Elsewhere, Edgington and Hayter (2001) have revealed Japanese firms in Asia as having exhibited a high degree of disinvestment or plant closure and transfer of operations to other countries in the aftermath of the financial crisis. Flows of Japanese foreign direct investment (FDI) into

Asia overall held steady throughout the fiscal year 1997–1998. The evidence pointed to a long-term commitment by Japanese transnational corporations to Asia. Similarly, Poon and Thompson (2001) have found that investment of transnational corporations as a whole has been more spatially immobile. A survey conducted in Hong Kong and Singapore in 1998 revealed that the crisis led to greater embedding of transnational capital in the region in the long run.

Economic globalization and China's adoption of an open policy and economic reforms went hand in hand during the last two decades of the twentieth century. Essentially, China was reincorporated into regional and global markets. This had brought into play a state whose demographic size, abundance of entrepreneurial and labour resources, and growth potential surpassed by a good margin that of all other states operating in the region. China's rise as an economic power has been viewed as part of an on-going East Asian economic renaissance, with China's economic achievements over the past two decades as the preamble to a recentring of the regional and world economies on China as they were in pre-modern times (Arrighi, 2000). Against this background, China's recent accession to the World Trade Organization (WTO) makes critical sense in its trajectory to further growth and opening. Shaoguang Wang (Chapter 3) concentrates on the social and political implications of China's WTO membership. Of special concern is the issue of potential distributive conflicts and growing inequalities, with repercussions on the legitimacy of the Chinese government itself. Indeed, what Dunning and Hamdani (1997) observed in a general situation may well be applicable to China:

> ... the possible Achilles heel of globalization and alliance capitalism [one characterized by greater interdependence of governments] is that they could so easily become dysfunctional if they cannot accommodate the desires of ordinary men and women looking for and willing to work; and, if they fail to equip individuals with the skills and talents necessary for the kind of jobs which are now being created. (p. 32)

In this context, it is easy to understand why some countries and individuals do not welcome globalization because it is seen as a threat to their traditional life. The anti-globalization activists have made their views violently clear during recent major international meetings in Seattle, Prague, Quebec City and Barcelona.

Even if an economy develops extremely well in the era of economic globalization, changed socio-economic circumstances make it imperative for it to adjust if it is to continue to succeed. The case of Hong Kong, as presented by Yun-wing Sung (Chapter 4), is a classic example in which an economy has experienced miracle growth for decades, especially during the period after China opened for development in 1978. The Asian financial crisis has exposed the limitations of Hong Kong's growth strategy based, to a large extent, on outward processing. With the relocation of manufacturing capacity to the mainland almost complete and with Hong Kong's return to China under the "one country, two systems" formula, the Special Administrative Region (SAR) has to rediscover a new magic for growth and development. China's entry to the WTO as well as its new policy of developing the sprawling western region provide new opportunities for Hong Kong. Sung touches on a range of key development domains in which Hong Kong should seek speedy policy co-ordination with the mainland authorities if the SAR is to stay ahead of competition. Indeed, Yeung (2001) has recently focused on the competitiveness between Hong Kong, Shanghai and Singapore as maritime cities, a situation rendered all the more acute and inevitable under economic globalization. Among the many ways these cities have prepared themselves for their perceived more competitive future, policies geared to developing high technology and better education for their youngsters have been actively pursued and supported. All three cities have adopted comparable policies and strategies which vary only in their degree of emphasis and extent of funding.

Hong Kong, Shanghai and Singapore epitomize three vibrant and innovative metropolitan centres along the western Pacific rim. They have helped to add economic clout to the region which has been described by Castells (1998), at the end of the second millennium, as follows:

> … the Asian Pacific has become the main center of capital accumulation in the planet, the largest manufacturing producer, the most competitive trading region, one of the two leading centers of informational technology innovation and production (the other is the US), and the fastest growing market. (p. 206)

While the region has registered an impressive economic transition to date, its economic future is nonetheless contingent on the following factors: peace and stability over a long period of time; the ability to lead and succeed in the global revolution in technologies; effective and vigorous amelioration of North-South relations; the successful implementation of economic adjustment and reform in countries in the region; and stable economic development in Japan and the U.S. (Pei, 1989:382).

To be able to compete in the twenty-first century, Hong Kong must maximize the benefit and importance of technology development. Charles Kao (Chapter 5) traces Hong Kong's technology roadmap which has been shown to have changed several times, with the crucial stages between 1991 and 2000. Curiously for an economy that only paid lip service to developing hi-tech earlier, the Asian financial crisis provided a new impetus in this direction, with the SAR government taking the lead to champion hi-tech development to strengthen Hong Kong's competitive edge. Both the 1991 and 2000 technology roadmaps identified and reconformed four technologies, viz., information technology, biotechnology, materials technology and environmental technology, as having favourable potential in Hong Kong. The first-mentioned technology is especially important in the Information Age, as Castells (1998) has elucidated:

> Information technology became the indispensable tool for the effective implementation of processes of socio-economic restructuring. Particularly important was its role in allowing the development of networking as a dynamic, self-expanding form of organization of human activity. This prevailing networking logic transforms all domains of social and economic life. (pp. 336–37)

There is, however, a downside to technological innovations which must be bounded by the rules of political economy and the global balance of power, and Attali (1991) sounded a caveat:

> These rules must be rooted in an understanding both of the history of civilizations and of the cultural mutation of the future being wrought by radical technological innovations. We cannot permit ours to become an age that pushes, and perhaps fatally transgresses, the limits of the human condition — a condition bounded in all previous civilizations by biological borders ... (p. 17)

The new social structure of the Information Age has been identified by Castells (1998:350) as the network society. It is made up of networks of production, power and experience, which construct a culture of virtuality in the global flows that transcend time and space. Against this backdrop and globalization tendencies that transform the nature and organization of business networks, Henry Wai-chung Yeung (Chapter 6) shows that globalization is both a homogenizing and differentiating agent in Asian business systems. While national business systems tend to be relatively enduring over time, major business firms are major actors in economic change. The latter are more susceptible to changes brought about by globalization tendencies because actors and élites in Asian economies are increasingly enrolled into global actor networks, and vice versa. Accelerating globalization has legitimized the demand of Asian élites' for economic liberalization.

This chapter on changing business networks in Pacific Asia should be read in the context of a rapidly growing arena of Chinese business networks in many parts of the world. These business networks, often embedded in family and kinship links, linguistic and cultural affinities, and historical associations, have enjoyed rapid expansion, given recent and dramatic improvements in communication and transport across the world. The infusion of overseas Chinese capital as a driving force in the development of coastal China (Yeung and Sung, 1996; Yeung and Chu, 1998) and the evident success of Hong Kong transnational corporations in Southeast Asia (Yeung, 1998) are examples of thriving Chinese business networks in the region. In fact, the Chinese diaspora has been expanding globally, with business networks forming part of the essence of the mobility of people, talents, technology and capital across national borders (Ma and Cartier, forthcoming).

Political and Social Change

In the nineteenth century, the dramatic breakthroughs in human communication came with the "Three Ts" (telegraph, telephone, typewriter), but no less startling and revolutionary has been the widespread adoption of computerization with endless applications in the late twentieth century (Browne and Fishwick, 1999:1). While technological innovations led by the use of the computer have facilitated economic globalization and some of the unfolding dramas that have been presented in the preceding section, breathtaking progress in information technology has radically changed patterns of human interaction, work habits and wealth accumulation. Indeed, Castells (1998) has predicted:

> There is no question that the twenty-first century will witness the rise of an extraordinarily productive system by historical standards. Human labor will produce more and better with considerably less effort. Mental work will replace physical effort in the most productive sectors of the economy. However, the sharing of this wealth will depend for individuals on their access to education and, for society as a whole, on social organization, politics, and policies. (p. 354)

In a similar survey of the creative society of the new century, Stevens et al. (2000) maintain that:

> Overall, the consensus view is that the prospects for prosperity and well-being in the 21st century will probably depend on leveraging social diversity in order to encourage technological, economic and social dynamism. A striking confluence of forces over the next twenty years could drive a twofold convergence: first, towards more highly differentiated and complex societies, and second, towards the adoption of a common set of general goals that are conducive to both diversity and social sustainability. (p. 7)

With these prognoses in mind, the study by Jose Abueva (Chapter 7) makes eminent sense of the evolving societal complexity surrounding 23 selected Asian countries when they are analyzed from the standpoints of political freedom and democracy, and economic freedom and development. No clear correlation exists between political freedom and human development, despite positive correlation between the two for Japan, South Korea and Taiwan. The study confirms the emergence and broadening of the middle class and the political awareness and activism of civil society. In part, these developments are due to globalization processes which link markets, political systems and cultures. The impact of the global democratic revolution has been felt in many Asian countries.

In a parallel study by Emma Porio (Chapter 10), civil society has been shown to have captured the imagination of political and other leaders in Asia over the past two decades. Civil society has become part of mainstream political discourse and has been viewed as a key force in the democratization of socio-political life in the region. Civil society, in brief, is the political space between the state and society, occupied and created by the non-profit sector between the state and the market. It is best conceptualized as a political space created by non-governmental organizations (NGOs), community-based organizations (CBOs), professional groups and other voluntary associations allied with broad-based movements. Porio concludes that civil society engagements in the new millennium are fraught with tensions and challenges generated by the globalization of capital and information technology, the devolution of central state powers to local structures of governance, and the rise of identity/resource claims laced with funda-mentalist and nationalist discourse. Dean Forbes (1999:18), for instance, has found evidence of an accelerating search for identity which is interwoven with a more strident nationalism in the region. As an effect of globalization, the growing economic integration and interdependence among nation-states threaten political and cultural sovereignty.

Despite the generally sanguine overtones of these two chapters on the development of democracy and civil society in Asia, one must be alerted to the essentially uneven pattern of development that globalization engenders and the potential perils looming, as Attali (1991) warns:

> In the coming world order, there will be winners and there will be losers. The losers will outnumber the winners by an unimaginable factor. They will yearn for the chance to live decently, and they are likely to be denied that chance. They will encounter rampant prejudice and fear. They will find themselves penned in, asphyxiated by pollution, neglected through indifference. The horrors of the twentieth century will fade by comparison. (p. 84)

This is probably a worst case depiction of the future and hopefully will not materialize in the region. However, Attali (1991:12) further reminds us that the riches of growth in Asia are not assured as the countries move towards democracy. The political and economic freedoms so far won can vanish if market economy does not deliver relatively quickly the consumer goods and basic necessities promised by the bold reforms that have demanded harsh sacrifices.

As an example of a polity struggling to achieve democracy, Siu-kai Lau (Chapter 8) highlights the case of the Hong Kong SAR under the "one country, two systems" formula. Under the provisions of the Basic Law for the SAR, Hong Kong has been able to enjoy partial democracy with an executive-led political system. Lau has found plenty of inherent contradictions, stresses and strains in the system, with the rocky executive-legislative relationship perhaps affecting the performance of the government since the handover. There does not appear to be any immediate solution to the gridlock, but the government has shown a willingness to improve the situation through trial and error.

Underlying much of the socio-political changes in the region in the new millennium are the rapidly evolving demographic structures and the problems they tend to generate. Fanny M. Cheung (Chapter 9) calls attention to the ageing population which is an almost universal problem. Population statistics from the United Nations forecast a steadily ageing population in the world over the next 50 years. For example, in Eastern Asia, the percentage of the population aged 60 years and over will soar from 11 percent in 1999 to 30 percent in 2050. The corresponding figures for China, Hong Kong and Japan in those two years are 10 and 30 percent, 14 and 40 percent, and 23 and 38 percent, respectively (UN, 1999). This is part of the global demographic transition, with developing countries undergoing an active decline in fertility and a corresponding reduction in the proportion of younger people. At the same time, gender issues will become more pronounced because, as women have a longer life expectancy, they will predominate in the elderly population. With discrimination against women and the elderly, Cheung highlights the problem of double jeopardy to the elderly women. There is an urgent need for enlightened and focused policy formulation for the elderly population concerning their medical care, housing, security and other needs in the short and long term. The earlier national governments take the bull by the horns, the better will be the socio-economic well-being of their people.

Regional Patterns of Transformation

Along with the trend towards democratization in the region, many countries have been confronted with the boundary question. Baogang He (Chapter 11) has drawn parallels with experience outside Asia to examine the cases of Indonesia, Taiwan and Mainland China, and Korea. He argues that while democratization itself does not decide peaceful separation, unification or independence, it does play various roles. He explores how democratization affects the likelihood of unification/autonomy, the changing power structure of the country and the choices of peace or war. The conclusion being drawn is that democratization in general favours independence rather than unification. The process of democratization has also involved the expansion of political freedom and an assertive media, enabling people to express their views on the boundary question.

Apart from the boundary question which does have a regional dimension, the really momentous changes on the regional scale have stemmed from new opportunities in the informational global economy. Yue-man Yeung (Chapter 12) underlines the urban century that has just begun and the implications it has for urban-regional change in Pacific Asia. Specifically, world cities, subregional economic co-operation centred on growth triangles, mega-urban regions and urban corridors have emerged and have begun to make their imprint on the way of life and the tempo of development in the region (Lo and Yeung, 1996; Yeung, 1999, 2000). There is also a new urbanism characterized by economic and cultural globalization. The search for cultural explanations in their economic growth has been given heightened importance in cities ranging from Hong Kong, Singapore,

Beijing, Seoul, Tokyo to Hanoi (Kim et al., 1997). These may be viewed as regional responses to globalization forces that have impinged on Pacific Asia.

Globalization and regionalization/localization are often seen as two sides of the same coin, being dialectic as they mutually affect each other. As globalization races ahead and holds sway across the world, regionalization is relied upon as a counter weight to balance the need for closer support and articulation of common interests in the countries and peoples in a smaller geographic area. Although Pacific Asia is not known for its efforts at regional integration, progress during the past two decades has been laudable. Andrew Elek (Chapter 13) examines the growing economic co-operation in the Asia-Pacific region, with the formation of Asia-Pacific Economic Co-operation (APEC) in 1989. In the new century, one of the key issues influencing its sustainability as an international organization is the critical need for capacity building in some countries. However, APEC was predated by the formation of Association of Southeast Asian Nations (ASEAN) in 1967. Curiously, ASEAN's reaction to the Asian financial crisis has been an even stronger commitment to economic openness, to faster and closer economic integration, with ASEAN Vision 2020 firmly in place (Severino, 1999). The Pacific Economic Co-operation Council (PECC) founded in 1980 has been working co-operatively with APEC on many issues facing the region. Both PECC and APEC involve the participation of many countries around the Pacific rim. However, countries within Pacific Asia have also been increasingly linked through growing intra-regional trade, investments and formal/informal contacts, such that an unstructured and de facto trading bloc has been formed through recent decades of rapid economic development (Lo and Yeung, 1996). It is envisaged that, barring any major unforeseen political conflicts and within the basic tripolar global structure of North America, Europe and Pacific Asia that has emerged, regional integration within the Asia-Pacific region will most likely strengthen in the new millennium.

References

Arrighi, Giovanni (2000), "Globalization, State Sovereignty, and the 'Endless' Accumulation of Capital." In Don Kalb et al., *The Ends of Globalization*, pp. 125–48.

Attali, Jacques (1991), *Millennium: Winners and Losers in the Coming World Order.* Translated from French by Leila Conners and Nathan Gardels. New York: Random House.

Browne, Ray B. and Marshall W. Fishwick (eds.) (1991), *The Global Village: Dead or Alive?* Bowling Green: Bowling Green State University Popular Press.

Castells, Manuel (1998), *End of Millennium.* Oxford: Blackwell.

Dicken, Peter (1998), *Global Shift: Transforming the World Economy.* 3rd edition. London: Paul Chapman Publishing.

Dunning, John H. and Khalil A. Hamdani (1997), *The New Globalism and Developing Countries.* Tokyo: United Nations University Press.

Edgington, David and Roher Hayter (2001), "Japanese Direct Foreign Investment and the Asian Financial Crisis," *Geoforum*, 32(1):103–20.

Forbes, Dean (1999), "Imaginative Geography and the Postcolonial Spaces of Pacific Asia." In Wong Tai-Chee and Mohan Singh (eds.), *Development and Challenge: Southeast Asia in the New Millennium.* Singapore: Times Academic Press.

Garran, Robert (1998), *Tigers Tamed: The End of the Asian Miracle.* Honolulu: University of Hawaii Press.

Hanagan, Michael (2000), "States and Capital: Globalization's Past and Present." In Don Kalb et al., *The Ends of Globalization*, pp. 67–86.

Kalb, Don, et al. (2000), *The Ends of Globalization: Bringing Society Back In.* Lanham: Rowman & Littlefield Publishers.

Kim, Samuel S. (ed.) (2000), *East Asia and Globalization.* Lanham: Rowman & Littlefield Publishers.

Kim, Won Bae, et al. (eds.) (1997), *Culture and the City in East Asia.* Oxford: Clarendon Press.

Krugman, Paul (1994), "The Myth of Asia's Miracle," *Foreign Affairs*, 73(6):62–78.

Lo, Fu-chen and Yue-man Yeung (eds.) (1996), *Emerging World Cities in Pacific Asia.* Tokyo: United Nations University Press.

—— (1998), *Globalization and the World of Large Cities.* Tokyo: United Nations University Press.

Ma, Laurence J. C. and Carolyn L. Cartier (eds.) (forthcoming), *Geographic Perspectives on the Chinese Diaspora: Space, Place, Mobility and Identity.* Lanham: Rowman & Littlefield Publishers.

McCord, William (1993), *The Dawn of the Pacific Century: Implications for Three Worlds of Development.* New Brunswick: Transaction Publishers.

McGee, T. G. and Ira M. Robinson (eds.) (1995), *The Mega Urban Regions of Southeast Asia.* Vancouver: University of British Columbia Press.

Pape, Wolfgang (ed.) (1998), *East Asia by the Year 2000 and Beyond: Shaping Factors.* Richmond: Curzon Press.

Pei, Monong (1989), *21st Century: The Pacific Century?* Beijing: World Knowledge Press (in Chinese).

Poon, Jessie P. H. and Edmund R. Thompson (2001), "Effects of the Asian Financial Crisis on Transnational Capital," *Geoforum*, 32(1):121–31.

Severino, Rodolfo C., Jr. (1999), *ASEAN Rises to the Challenge*. Jakarta: The ASEAN Secretariat.

Shari, Ishak (2000), "Globalization and Economic Disparities in East and Southeast Asia: New Dilemmas," *Third World Quarterly*, 21(6):963–75.

Stevens, Barrie, Riel Miller and Wolfgang Michalski (2000), "Social Diversity and the Creative Society of the 21st Century." In *The Creative Society of the 21st Century*. Paris: OECD, pp. 7–24.

Thant, Myo, Min Tang, and Hiroshi Kakazu (eds.) (1998), *Growth Triangles in Asia*. 2nd edition. Hong Kong: Oxford University Press.

United Nations (UN) Population Ageing 1999 (http://www.undp.org/popin/wdtrends/a99/a99pwld.htm)

Watters, R. F. and T. G. McGee (eds.) (1997), *Asia Pacific: New Geographies of the Pacific Rim*. Wellington: Victoria University Press.

Yeung, Henry Wai-chung (1998), *Transnational Corporations and Business Networks: Hong Kong Firms in the ASEAN Region*. London: Routledge.

Yeung, Yue-man (ed.) (1993), *Pacific Asia in the 21st Century: Geographical and Developmental Perspectives*. Hong Kong: The Chinese University Press.

Yeung, Yue-man (1999), *Globalization and Regional Transformation in Pacific Asia*. Occasional Paper No. 103. Hong Kong Institute of Asia-Pacific Studies, The Chinese University of Hong Kong.

—— (2000), *Globalization and Networked Societies*. Honolulu: University of Hawaii Press.

—— (2001), "A Tale of Three Cities: Competitiveness among Hong Kong, Shanghai and Singapore under Globalization." Keynote address presented at the International Conference on Maritime Cities, Hong Kong, 1–3 March.

Yeung, Y. M. and David K. Y. Chu (eds.) (1998), *Guangdong: Survey of a Province Undergoing Rapid Change*. 2nd edition. Hong Kong: The Chinese University Press.

—— (2000), *Fujian: A Coastal Province in Transition and Transformation*. Hong Kong: The Chinese University Press.

Yeung, Yue-man and Xu-wei Hu (eds.) (1992), *China's Coastal Cities: Catalysts for Modernization*. Honolulu: University of Hawaii Press.

Yeung, Y. M. and Sung Yun-wing (eds.) (1996), *Shanghai: Transformation and Modernization under China's Open Policy*. Hong Kong: The Chinese University Press.

2

The "New Developmentalism" in Post-Crisis Asia: The Case of Thailand's SME Sector

Frederic C. Deyo

Introduction

In the context of a gradual abatement of the recent Asian economic crisis in Thailand[1] and elsewhere in the region, attention is now turning to the longer term structural and institutional outcomes of that deep recession. And it is here that new debates over the nature and relevance of "Asian capitalism" have pushed to centre-stage some old questions of state-organized developmentalism that were long dormant under ongoing programmes of structural adjustment and market-augmenting economic reforms. I suggest here the possibility that the process and politics of crisis management may eventuate in a new synthesis of neo-classical and developmentalist models of economic governance in Thailand and elsewhere in the region. Of particular importance are three tentative policy outcomes of the crisis: (1) more forceful insertion of a social agenda into restructuring policy at national and international levels, (2) renewed and externally sanctioned policy efforts to tighten financial and corporate regulatory regimes, and relatedly (3) a still tentative (re-)emergence of state-initiated developmentalism in response to evident problems created by market-oriented structural reforms and crisis.

The first of these outcomes — heightened focus on social protection and economic stimulation in government policy — reflects what some have termed a "leftward" shift in neo-liberal thinking[2] at international as well as national levels, and was reflected in protracted debates within the World Bank and elsewhere regarding the appropriateness of initial of the International Monetary Fund (IMF) responses to the crisis. While this shift in conventional thinking may largely reflect immediate concerns about social and political stability under the privations of the crisis and of IMF-supported austerity and restructuring policies adopted at the time, there is indication of a more enduring concern than before with issues of social protection among multi-lateral organizations.[3] The second shift — towards renewed emphasis on the need for more adequate corporate and financial regulation relating especially to external capital liberalization — moves policy debates to the somewhat deeper level of tighter institutional governance of trade and investment transactions, embracing, for example, the controversial imposition of controls on short-term capital flows into and out of Malaysia.

It is the third policy outcome, hereafter termed the "new developmentalism," which is of greatest interest here. Social protection, expansionary fiscal policy and new financial regulatory structures are easily accommodated within a neo-liberal framework insofar as they are seen as establishing an adequate infrastructure for the stable functioning of a market economy. Asian developmentalism, comprising state-organized policy networks, business associations, vertically organized supplier chains, credit-based financial systems and relational/network-based private-sector governance,[4] goes farther in seeking forcefully to direct, guide and "govern" markets through state institutions (Johnson, 1987; Wade, 1998; Weiss, 1995).

While this reactive reassertion of Asian capitalism has generated increased debate in both policy and academic circles, there has been relatively little empirical research on its actual policy manifestation. Employing a political economy approach, this chapter seeks to address this research gap through a case study of policy change in a country especially hard hit by the crisis (Thailand), and relating specifically to government policy towards domestic small-medium sized enterprises (SMEs). It asks how these firms have been affected by the crisis, how they have sought to influence state policy, and whether SME sectoral policy pressures have discernibly influenced evolving strategies of crisis management. It is argued that while SME assistance programmes have comprised a core element of crisis management efforts, these programmes have not been substantially influenced by domestic SME political pressures. Rather, they derive from the combined influence of (1) the competitive requirements of locally-established foreign firms, (2) internal and external pressures to accelerate economic reforms, (3) a policy commitment to foreign investment based, export-led economic recovery, and (4) political resolve to ensure that domestic Thai firms participate advantageously in that recovery. The evolving strategy of crisis management which has flowed from these various pressures and commitments, and which focuses especially on the critical role of SMEs, has been informed by a dynamic tension between Anglo-American market-focused and Asian developmentalist models of national economic governance. This chapter explores the ways in which these pressures and models have shaped evolving SME policy over the course of the crisis.

Domestic Small-Medium Sized Enterprises

Domestic SMEs, officially defined in the Thai context as firms capitalized at under 50 million baht[5] and employing fewer than 200 workers, comprise a critical sector within which to examine the social and developmental impact of the crisis. The social (and thus political) importance of Thai SMEs follows in part from the large percentage of workers employed and self-employed in this sector, currently estimated at 3 million, or 60–70 percent of all industrial workers. It follows as well from the growing tendency of large firms to outsource production to local suppliers (thus further expanding SME employment), and a corresponding growth in the informal sector resulting from both outsourcing and crisis. Finally, SMEs comprise an important conduit for a broad distribution of the economic gains from industrial and commercial growth, including those to women, minorities and indigenous peoples.

The developmental importance of SMEs derives from their numerical preponderance among industrial firms,[6] their significance in accounting for roughly half of GDP, their role in fostering domestic entrepreneurship, their importance in providing a supplier infrastructure for international firms, and their special role in tapping the economic synergies and resources latent in Thai social organization and culture.

The crisis has taken a devastating toll in the SME sector, especially among domestic market-oriented, simple-technology firms not linked as upper-tier suppliers to international firms. Particularly troublesome has been a liquidity crisis resulting from the reticence of banks to advance capital to a sector which accounts for roughly 90 percent of outstanding non-performing loans.[7] The importance of this problem is heightened by the very high capital dependence of firms on loans, which comprised 88 percent of total capital raised in 1997.[8] As important are high interest rates (a consequence in part of the high risk associated with SME loans), drastically reduced domestic demand, increased competition associated with accelerated trade and investment liberalization[9] and, for the relatively few SMEs with foreign-denominated debt,[10] the initial devaluation and continuing relatively low value of the baht. Kakwani and Pothong, in their very careful National Economic and Social Development Board (NESDB) study of the social impact of the crisis, emphasize the devastating employment consequences initially for very small firms of 6–10 workers, and subsequently for medium-sized firms under the pressure of increasingly tight credit availability (NESDB, 1998).

The probable long-term structural and institutional outcomes of the crisis for Thai SMEs relate to (1) a possible denationalization of key industrial sectors, (2) a reinforcement of largely short-term competitive strategies on the part of SMEs and their corporate customers, (3) an attenuation of network forms of economic governance (a defining characteristic of "Asian" capitalism), and (4) a reactivation of state-focused business associations. It will be argued that changes across these various areas suggest a possible regeneration of an Asian developmentalist model in the face of contrary international pressures to pursue an Anglo-American market-oriented reform programme.

The Threat of Denationalization

The crisis has precipitated renewed ambivalence regarding the role of foreign capital in the Thai economy, and the degree to which domestic firms require and merit special protection and support in a globalizing economy. While Thailand was already one of the most open economies in Southeast Asia, the crisis has greatly augmented the role of foreign investment in several major industrial and agro-industrial sectors. A weakened baht along with high levels of SME debt and bankruptcy[11] have eventuated in acquisitions of domestic firms by foreign companies, increased foreign equity holdings in joint ventures, and debt-equity swaps with both domestic and foreign banks and financial institutions. Further competitive pressures are generated by newly established local SME supplier firms linked to same-nationality (especially Japanese) corporations with which they are already associated in their home country. In this context, government legislative changes to permit 100 percent foreign equity in sectors previously reserved for Thais, to allow foreign land ownership, and more generally to enable foreign firms to participate more fully in the domestic economy[12] have triggered sharp parliamentary and public debates among non-internationalized firms and popular sector groups.

Associated with the partial denationalization of some economic sectors is an increased extroversion of state structures and policy networks. This extroversion refers to a growing critical political mass of domestic financial groups, externally linked businesses, transnational corporations, outwardly-oriented state agencies (especially the Ministries of Finance and Commerce), locally active multilateral agencies (e.g., the World Bank, Asia Development Bank and IMF) and representatives of international business (e.g., Chambers of Commerce), collectively active in national, sectoral and local policy networks.[13] Particularly important has been the emergence of a powerful Japanese voice in Thai economic policy circles. The Japanese Chamber of Commerce in Bangkok now represents over 1,100 companies whose representations to government agencies are reflected in and backed by official Japanese financial and advisory support (see below). As this clustered ensemble of internationally-oriented economic interests becomes ever more dominant, in part as an outcome of the reform policies which it begets, the possibilities of reversion to a more inwardly-focused development strategy become ever more problematic.[14]

Short-Term Competitive Strategies

Thai industrialization since the mid-1980s, especially following the Plaza Accord under which an appreciating Japanese yen encouraged growing Japanese investment in Southeast Asia, has drawn increasing numbers of Thai SMEs into the supplier chains of local subsidiaries of large foreign companies. In this context, SME-MNC (multi-national corporation) business linkages have become an ever more important determinant of the development opportunities for local companies. Thus, the competitive strategies of those large firms, especially relating to their supplier base, have taken on special importance for local SMEs.

An unfortunate consequence of the crisis has been to encourage and reinforce short-term-oriented, cost-focused competitive strategies on the part of dominant companies seeking to respond to severe cost-pressures and market contraction over the past three years.[15] The short-term nature of these strategies, especially during the crisis, is encouraged by volatility in policy environments, markets, interest rates and currency exchange rates as well as by the costliness, risk and immediate competitive disadvantage associated with longer-term investments in research and development (R&D), training and work reorganization. Such competitive strategies have, in turn, been associated with heightened cost pressures on suppliers in lieu of longer-term efforts to upgrade suppliers through technology transfer, training and other developmental assistance. Cost-focused outsourcing and informalization have further increased the market vulnerability of SMEs, thus undercutting their bargaining position vis-à-vis larger firms.

It should be noted, however, that a predominance of short-term coping strategies does not preclude concomitant efforts to preserve skills and innovative capacities within core production processes among first-tier suppliers. Indeed, a primary concern of many larger firms has been to protect these "islands of innovation" from the ravages of the crisis. Such concern is especially heightened by Thailand's very weak knowledge/skill infrastructure.[16]

Thus, a more accurate characterization of corporate responses is one of dualism: low-road strategies pursued across most sectors and activities alongside the protection of skill and technology-intensive enclaves (Deyo, 1996; Deyo and Doner, 2000). Such dualism is explained not only as a residual effect of efforts to maintain innovative capacities in core activities, but also as an effort simultaneously to retain core skilled workers and key suppliers while at the same time cutting costs in other areas in order to compensate for the increasingly burdensome cost of maintaining innovative capabilities in the context of overcapacity and crisis.

The Attenuation of Network Economic Governance

A further blow to local SMEs relates to the impact of the crisis on economic governance. If, as already noted, close "developmental" relations between large firms and their suppliers have emerged largely among upper-tier suppliers, those relations have themselves become ever more exclusionary and restrictive by virtue of an attenuation of the network-like inter-firm relations which are often seen as characterizing Asian capitalism. As uncertainty and financial difficulties have beset supplier SMEs, larger firms have grown less and less willing to extend new lines of credit, to offer long-term training and technology assistance, and in general to nurture local (especially domestic) suppliers. More often, supplier linkages beyond core business and production processes have increasingly been governed by short-term market-like relations, associated in turn with exploitative, cost-focused, rather than developmental linkages.

In addition, insofar as network relations have defined a mode of access to finance from both banks and informal sector lenders, the crisis has further undercut networks by reducing the scope of relationship-based loans[17] while increasing lender requirements for full financial disclosure. In part, such new requirements stem from increased risk avoidance on the part of lenders. Recent initiatives by the Bank of Thailand, for example, stress the need for local banks and other financial institutions to reduce lending risks by introducing corporate and disclosure reforms in their own operations as well as in those of client firms.[18] These initiatives are rooted in part in external pressure from international banks and investors, and from the World Bank and IMF, for greater transparency in corporate accounts and decision-making.[19] In addition, a newly launched SME Board in the Stock Exchange of Thailand (SET), established to provide a new source of capital for small enterprises, imposes strict reporting requirements on member companies.[20] Whatever the merits of such reforms from the standpoint of financial stabilization, one of their effects is to compromise the flows of privileged information that define network relations.

Finally, increased need to establish close relationships with foreign firms either as buyers or as joint-venture partners introduces cultural and relational barriers to a continuance and extension of trust-based network relations, and a corresponding shift towards more contractual, market-governed inter-firm relations. Given the propensity for large Japanese firms to develop deeper working relations with local SME suppliers than their Western counterparts, this consideration applies especially to the new wave of Western direct investment.

Reactivation and Politicization of Business Associations

Lacking the individual policy leverage of larger firms, SMEs have turned in part to reactivated business associations in order to seek government assistance in coping with the crisis. Auto parts suppliers, for example, have utilized their Federation of Thai Industries (FTI) representation along with non-FTI parts associations to push for debt restructuring, reduced interest rates, continued tariff protection and various other forms of government assistance. And indeed, FTI lobbying likely played an important role in the recent moratorium on principal repayments to banks on the part of indebted firms[21] and of increased tariff protection for auto-parts-makers (see below). In addition, domestic SMEs have used their sectoral associations to push an agenda of economic nationalism in recurrent parliamentary debates relating to restrictions on foreign investment and to changes in bankruptcy laws which are widely expected to favour foreign creditors over local lenders and shareholders.[22] Noteworthy in this regard is the recent organization of the Club for the Protection of Bank Debtors' Rights, an association largely of SME debtor firms seeking collectively to press large banks for leniency in loan negotiations with member companies.[23]

Crisis-Management: SME Policy Response

While proposed changes to bankruptcy and foreclosure laws have been passed despite domestic SME opposition, SMEs have enjoyed substantial government assistance in coping with the crisis, including a financial support of 50 billion baht in year 2000 following a similar 35 billion baht assistance package in 1999.[24] This assistance is to be channelled in part through two dedicated SME financial institutions, the Small Industry Credit Guarantee Corporation and the Small Industry Finance Corporation (SIFC).[25] A new SME board has been established in the SET to raise fresh capital for local firms.[26] Significantly, the government will empower the FTI to nominate companies for SET board listing.[27] A two-year grace period on principal repayment of bank loans has been enacted. The Board of Investments has revived a previously moribund tax-incentive-based support programme (BUILD) to encourage local supplier linkages to large firms.[28] Provincial industrial promotion offices are to be expanded, and a new SME institute, located at Thammasat University in Rangsit, has been established to assist in SME quality upgrading. And to compensate for the anticipated competitive pressures flowing from the elimination of domestic content requirements in the auto industry mandated by the World Trade Organization (WTO), tariff protection against imported CKD auto parts increased in year 2000 from 21 percent to 33 percent.[29]

Second, a significant portion of Thailand's share of the Japanese Miyazawa regional recovery fund, announced on 30 March 1999, will be directed to domestic SMEs through an expanded SIFC, to be further funded through SIFC bond purchases by the welfare and pension funds of several government ministries,[30] as well as by increased Bank of Thailand SME loans. The SIFC, established in 1991, was in fact inspired by and modelled after its Japanese counterpart, but was never adequately funded to play its intended role.[31] SIFC loans in 1999 are expected to total 3 billion baht, a significant increase over the 3.6 billion baht lent during the previous seven years in operation.[32] This, along with the other SME programmes, including a newly proposed venture capital fund to be established by the Ministries of Finance and Industry,[33] will be co-ordinated by an SME Supervisory Committee chaired by the Prime Minister.[34]

Third, the World Bank has agreed to co-operate with the FTI in establishing a corporate restructuring centre aimed at strengthening the competitiveness of SMEs.[35] And in part under World Bank urging, SME development assistance has been extended to include rural as well as urban business, in part through fuller access by rural businesses to loans from the Bank of Agriculture and Cooperatives, to date a major source primarily of farm credit.[36] And despite the World Bank's urge to maintain relatively high market-based interest rates reflective of the high risk of such loans,[37] both rural and urban SME loans will be offered at low concessionary rates.[38]

SMEs: Agents or Instruments of National Recovery Policy?

Are these dramatic new SME policy initiatives a political outcome of pressure from domestic firms through reinvigorated political institutions and through local policy networks?[39] Or are they outcomes of the strategies of large corporations and government agencies within which their role is largely instrumental for the attainment of broader national and transnational goals? Available evidence suggests a combination of the two but with somewhat greater weight on the latter.

On the one hand, it is clear that SME associational pressure, especially through the FTI, has been important in articulating and presenting SME interests and demands. But while SME pressure may have contributed to the definition of sectoral support programmes, the policy centrality and scale of those programmes, as well as their accessibility at high levels of government, are more easily understood from the standpoint of the interests of corporate and government élites.

The SME recovery programme has been publicly defended as a critical component of a foreign investment-based, export-led recovery strategy. The lion's share of assistance, including loans, tax incentives and ISO quality certification support has clearly been directed to export-related activities,[40] including most prominently the promotion of closer linkage of local suppliers with large, predominantly foreign, export-oriented firms. Further, SME revival is seen by major foreign companies generally, and by locally established Japanese corporate affiliates more specifically, as crucial for the post-crisis period.[41] Indeed, foreign firms have pushed strongly for local SME assistance programmes, even where such assistance has increased their own costs through continued or increased tariff protection (Monsakul, 2000). This paradox follows from the desire by large export firms to establish flexible, just-in-time supplier networks in order to increase responsiveness to market volatility and to ever shorter product cycles. It is important in this regard to recognize the major investments of these firms in the construction and development of local supplier chains in Thailand and their corresponding concern about the collapse of so many of these associated small local companies. Toyota, for instance, maintains supplier relations with over 100 upper-tier (and 2,000 in total) local suppliers.[42] Similar dependence by large electronics firms on local suppliers has led to a targeting of ceramics and glass suppliers for special assistance along with efforts to increase local content in this industry from the current 10–20 percent.[43] It should be noted as well that a large and growing number of the assisted local suppliers are themselves foreign, a flow-on effect of the predominance of relatively small operations among recent direct investments from Japan and elsewhere. It is thus understandable that Japan has played a significant role in recent SME development programmes. Illustrative of this role is the 220 million baht contribution on the part of the Japan International Cooperation Agency (JICA) towards the establishment of a Tool and Mould Development Centre mandated to assist domestic SME plastics suppliers to electronic, electrical and automobile companies.[44] Similarly, it has been noted that a substantial portion of the Japanese Miyazawa Fund is committed to assisting local supplier companies serving major Japanese industrial subsidiaries in Thailand.

It is in this larger context that one quickly understands the privileged position of Thai SMEs in crisis management programmes as flowing less from SME associational and political pressure than from the critical instrumentality of this sector for the agendas of dominant groups, corporate and governmental, domestic and foreign, which are more centrally placed in national policy networks. Even the role of the FTI in pushing the cause of SME protection and debt restructuring, must in the end be seen at least in part as reflecting the interests of large, internationalized companies.[45]

It is noteworthy that SMEs were very influential in pushing through substantial Japanese government assistance and protection during the economic and political crisis there during the mid-1970s and despite opposition, in that instance, from large companies in retail and other sectors (Calder, 1998, Chapter 7). The somewhat weaker influence of Thai SMEs than their Japanese counterparts under arguably similar circumstances may in part be explained by the crucial position of Japanese SMEs in the 1970s as a swing-vote essential to continue the Liberal Democratic Party (LDP) rule (Calder, 1998), as well as by the relative weakness of Thai domestic capital vis-à-vis foreign companies on the one hand, and within Thailand's internationally "extroverted" industrial policy networks (see above) on the other. It, too, may follow from the declining institutional position of functional ministries relative to that of the Ministry of Finance under the reforms of the 1990s.[46] In this instance, small businesses and their associations, traditionally most strongly networked with officials in units of the Ministry of Industry, have experienced a gradual loss of policy leverage.[47]

Discussion: A New Asian Developmentalism?

There has been much discussion and debate relating to the long-term institutional outcomes of the Asian crisis, particularly between those who foresee a continuance of on-going structural reforms and market liberalization, and others who anticipate an adaptation (rather than displacement) of "Asian" economic governance.[48] These arguments are paralleled by other debates regarding the institutional sources of East Asia's (currently aborted) economic "miracle" (World Bank, 1993; Wade, 1998; Wade and Veneroso, 1998), the developmental efficacy of market-based (vs. hierarchical or network/relational) governance for economic development (Deyo and Doner, 2000), and the relative merits of "global" versus regional models (Hirst and Thompson, 1992) of world economic change.

During early stages of the economic crisis, the pressures towards Western market-governance were clear: IMF/World Bank/foreign investor insistence on monetary stabilization, corporate transparency, economic deregulation, elimination of economic rent-seeking in corporate-government relations, privatization of state enterprise, alignment of interest rates to economic realities (e.g., relating to SME and rural loan regimes), deregulation of international capital flows, a move away from relational lending, and new competitive pressures urging flexibility and cost-reduction in the strategies of business firms.

But as important, the crisis has spawned a number of counter-pressures which urge departures from traditional neo-classical prescriptions. First, as noted earlier, mainstream policy-makers at international and national levels themselves increasingly emphasized the importance of financial regulations, restrictions of short-term international capital flows, expansionary (vs. austerity) government budgets, etc. More fundamental departures from neo-classical orthodoxy have been driven by increasing appeals to economic nationalism among oppositional political parties and popular sector groups,[49] growing anti-Westernism in the wake of the crisis, and the increasing prominence of Japan in national and regional policy institutions. Similarly, Thailand's debt-based financial system has received further reinforcement under various financial assistance programmes,[50] disclosure and other requirements involved in listing with the SET.[51]

The impetus to developmentalist heterodoxy is rooted as well in increasingly close government-business policy collaboration. Responding in part to a new activation and increased participation of SMEs and larger firms in business associations, the government has enhanced and redefined policy networks.[52] During the 1980s, business-government relations were institutionalized through establishment of a Joint Public-Private Consultation Committee, within which three peak business associations, the FTI, the Thai Board of Trade and the Thai Banking Association, consulted with government officials regarding economic policy. The FTI, through its affiliate clubs and sectoral organizations, thus offered a channel for information and presentation of views on the part of SMEs. More recent government policy has shifted the locus of joint consultation from bodies like the FTI, wherein industry associations are afforded a modicum of institutional independence in representing member interests, to more controlled bodies, such as the Automobile Institute wherein auto sector firms participate in a deliberative forum under Ministry of Industry leadership and sponsorship.[53] Whether this somewhat more corporatist mode of interest representation is to be generalized across many sectors is not yet clear.

Further evidence of growing policy developmentalism is seen in new government determination to protect and support domestic enterprise, renewed efforts to encourage closer relations between suppliers and local firms, explicit industrial targeting, commitment to a "developmental" (vs. market-based) interest-rate regime in business loan programmes,[54] increased acceptance of the need for heightened regulation of cross-border currency flows,[55] and an emergence of more coherent, developmentally-focused economic policies relating especially to SMEs.[56]

As significant, and indeed underlying many of these counter-pressures, is a growing Japanese influence in Thailand and elsewhere in the region. This influence, evidenced most clearly in an explicit modelling of Japanese business-government relations in policies of crisis management,[57] as well as in direct involvement by Japanese government officials in national development planning, is based on major financial assistance programmes as well as on increased direct investment by Japanese companies in Thailand.[58] As noted by a former vice-minister of Japan's Ministry of International Trade and Industry, Japan is seeking to establish the yen as a regional currency, and "encompasses a plan to make Japan's yen loans within the region 'tied' loans in which procurement of materials will be conducted in yen with Japanese companies."[59] Japan's Ambassador to Thailand, Hiroshi Ota, has more recently further stressed the importance of Thailand as a production and export base for Japanese companies, noting that Japan is now the largest source of foreign investment in Thailand.[60]

It must be emphasized that the various elements of emergent developmentalism suggested here have been identified by reference to proposals, new programmes and official policy pronouncements gleaned mainly from newspaper accounts. Whether the new paths these pronouncements define will in fact be followed, especially as the crisis and its political pressures abate, is entirely uncertain at the time of writing. Indeed, there are recurrent complaints that SME and other assistance funds are not yet reaching their intended client firms.[61] What is clear, however, is that programmes, policies, political commitments and expectations, and indeed the more general Thai development "discourse" has been at least modestly nudged from its earlier reform trajectory.

Conclusion

The evolving story of crisis-management in Thailand suggests an initial period of acceleration of market reforms partly in response to pressures from the IMF, the World Bank and international investors. Following this first-phase response (lasting perhaps until early 1998), domestic business pressures, parliamentary opposition, and a growing Japanese involvement in regional recovery efforts have encouraged a partial and externally tempered shift towards a somewhat chastened and extroverted model of "Asian" developmentalism. It may also be noted that Thailand and other crisis-affected Asian economies are now poised for a gradual "real" sector recovery, thus suggesting some relaxation in pressures to adopt Western-style economic reforms. Indeed, a recent World Bank report bemoans the possibility that the incipient recovery may damage prospects for continued reforms, thus jeopardizing longer-term growth.[62]

While it is yet unclear how these various competing pressures will influence Thai economic policy regimes in the post-crisis period, it may be suggested at a minimum that those regimes will likely depart to some degree from models urged by the World Bank and IMF. It may further be argued that Thailand's traditional inwardly-focused "bureaucratic polity," never historically describable as a developmental state, may provide a foundation for the construction of a hybrid form of economic governance combining Western and Asian developmentalist elements (Lim, 1999). What is already apparent at the time of writing is the emergence of a developmental regime which seeks through industrial policy to achieve what might best be termed "open developmentalism," the state-sponsored positioning of domestic firms in mid-value niches of international commodity and corporate chains organized by Japanese and other transnational firms.

Acknowledgements

I am grateful to Jillian Green and Luke Coxon for their able research assistance in the preparation of this chapter, to Manusavee Monsakul for sharing interview data gathered for her thesis on the Thai auto industry, and to Nigel Haworth and Rick Doner for their helpful comments on an earlier draft.

Notes

1. See, for example, "Moody's Revises Rating Outlook to 'Positive'," *Bangkok Post/Business*, 5 April 1999. The Bank of Thailand has recently revised its GDP growth projections for 1999 from 1 percent to 1.2 percent. Also see "IMF Sees Clear Recovery," *Bangkok Post*, 18 June 1999.
2. See distinctions among "conservative neo-liberalism," "left-wing neoliberalism" and "structural-institutionalism," in Burkett and Hart-Landsberg (1998).
3. See, for example, "Relief Initiative Stalls," *Bangkok Post*, 9 May 2000.
4. As opposed to more exclusively market-governed inter-firm relations and transactional governance.
5. The Ministry of Industry's Department of Industrial Promotion sets this at 100 million baht, while other agencies now involved in SME assistance programmes have adopted the 50 million baht threshold.
6. Comprising some 90 percent of all industrial firms.
7. As a percentage of all firms with non-performing loans. See "SME Clients Account for up to 90% of Bad Loans," *Bangkok Post/Business*, 26 January 1999.
8. "Steady Development Helps Widen Options," *Bangkok Post*, 12 June 2000.
9. "Small Business Needs State Help to Survive," *Bangkok Post/Business*, 23 November 1998.
10. Larger firms, rather than SMEs, tend to carry large foreign debt.
11. "Optimism Could Lead to New Plants," *Bangkok Post/Business*, 15 December 1998.
12. According to Bruce Darrington, a well-known financial consultant in Bangkok, foreign investment topped US$10 billion during 1998 and the first quarter of 1999 (*Asiaweek*, 14 May 1999, p. 70). Virtually all major auto assemblers and most large electronics firms are foreign.

13. Such extroversion refers as well, though to a far lesser degree, to the influence of representatives of foreign and international labour organizations and non-governmental organizations (NGOs) in those policy networks focused specifically on labour and social policy.

14. Foreign chambers of commerce, for instance, have been influential in pushing for further easing of rules on foreign business entry, an improved investment climate for foreign companies, and closer links between government and foreign investors. See "Chambers Seek Further Improvement in Terms," *Bangkok Post*, 6 July 1999.

15. See, for example, the 1998 Andersen Consulting study as reported in "Optimistic Strategies the New Watchword," *Bangkok Post*, 8 June 1999. This article suggests some improvement in this regard during 1999.

16. NESDB (1998) notes in this regard that almost two-thirds of employed persons have only an elementary education.

17. A recent World Bank survey of 3,700 companies in five crisis-hit countries found that fewer than half needed to produce audited financial statements in applying for loans. Source: *Asiaweek*, 14 May 1999, p. 26.

18. "Stability will need Greater Commitment," *Bangkok Post*, 12 June 2000.

19. The World Bank has insisted on an upgrading of company accounts audits to international standards as a condition for financial assistance. See "Tighter Reins on Executives," *Bangkok Post/Business*, 6 May 1999.

20. See "Steady Development Helps Widen Options," *Bangkok Post*, 12 June 2000.

21. "FTI Chairman Suggests Debt Grace Period for SMEs," *The Nation*, 12 May 1998.

22. In fact, many of the most vocal "nationalists" among recalcitrant members of the Senate are themselves creditors and stockholders of indebted companies.

23. "Debtors form Alliance," *Bangkok Post*, 11 July 1999.

24. "B35bn SMEs Plan Presented," *Bangkok Post/Business*, 21 December 1998. "B35bn Assistance Fund Approved for Sector," *Bangkok Post/Business*, 23 December 1998. Total 1999 government assistance commitments stand at approximately B55bn as reported in "Lifeline Set Up for Small Local Enterprises," *Bangkok Post/Business*, 2 February 1999. "B50 bn SME Support Fund to be Allocated within a Year," *Bangkok Post*, 24 May 2000. The Bank of Thailand is to play a major role here through an augmented SME loan programme.

25. Also see *Bangkok Post*, 24 August 1999.

26. Most Thai SMEs obtain investment capital through accumulated savings and informal lending arrangements. See "Reforms Needed to Assist Small Firms: Study," *Bangkok Post*, 27 July 1998. Also see "Listing Conditions Eased to Help Small Companies," *Bangkok Post/Business*, 10 December 1998. Also "New SET Board Planned for Small Firms," *Bangkok Post/Business*, 7 August 1998.

27. "SET to Open Capital Link for Ailing SMEs," *The Nation*, 2 February 1999. Also see the *Bangkok Post/Business*, 7 August 1998.

28. "Thai Firms Keen to Build Ties with Japanese," *Bangkok Post/Business*, 5 November 1998 and 28 November 1998. Also see "200 Seminars Will Assist Industries," *Bangkok Post*, 6 January 2000.

29. U.S. automobile manufacturers, as more recent investors in Thailand, have pushed for continued downward revision in CBU tariffs. The 1998 decision to raise these tariffs, as well as the more recent increase in CKD tariffs, will likely benefit longer established Japanese companies with well developed local supplier chains and less need to rely on CKD imports. See "U.S. Executives Urge Government to Cut Import Tariffs," *Bangkok Post/Business*, 5 March 1999. For full discussion, see Monsakul, 2000.

30. "Small Industries Will Benefit from Loan Worth B5 Billion," *Bangkok Post/Business*, 26 May 1998. Also see "Refinancing Will Help Cut SIFC Rates," *Bangkok Post/Business*, 8 May 1999.

31. "Agency Wants to Beef up Help for Small Business," *Bangkok Post/Business*, 24 November 1998.

32. "SIFC Plans Loans of 3 Billion Baht for Industry," *Bangkok Post*, 17 July 1999.

33. "B3XXXbn Fund Planned to Help Small, Medium Businesses," *Bangkok Post*, 25 July 1999.

34. *Bangkok Post*, 26 May 1998.

35. "SMEs to Get WB Restructuring Aid," *The Nation*, 2 May 1999.

36. At present, only 8 percent of the Bank of Agriculture and Cooperation (BAAC) loans go to non-farm businesses. See "Reforms Needed to Assist Small Firms: Study," *Bangkok Post/Business*, 27 July 1998.

37. "Long-ignored SMEs Suddenly Find They Are in the Political Spotlight," *Bangkok Post/Business*, 12 November 1998.

38. "Refinancing Will Help Cut SIFC Rates," *Bangkok Post/Business*, 8 May 1999.

39. A possibility heightened by inter-party competition to capture political support from the SME sector (see "Long-ignored SMEs suddenly find they are in the Political Spotlight," *Bangkok Post/Business*, 12 November 1998).

40. Thus, for example, substantial assistance is to be offered for firms to establish ISO certification, a requirement for exporting to Europe. Also, new tax exemptions for imported raw materials will apply only to export production. See "Tax Waivers for More Industries," *Bangkok Post/Business*, 13 May 1999. Also see "SME Master Plan due in October," *Bangkok Post*, 24 August 1999.

41. The chairman of Asian Honda Motor Co. has noted that large car manufacturers outsource roughly 80 percent in parts and components from SME suppliers. "Ex-MITI Expert Helps Boost Status of SMEs," *The Nation/Business*, 15 March 1999.

42. It may be noted in passing that the new CKD auto tariff increase will likely

favour and shelter established Japanese auto assemblers, with their existing deep local supplier chains, vis-á-vis newer foreign assemblers (e.g., General Motors) which will initially have to depend more heavily on imported parts.

43. "Industry Ministry Drafting Plan for Electrical, Electronics Sector," *The Nation*, 25 May 1999. Thai Toshiba Electric Industrial Co., noting the loss of firms and employment in the electrical parts industry, has noted that the major risk in this industry relates less to big firms than to the parts suppliers. "Low Interest Rates Alone Cannot Avert Lay-offs," *The Nation/Business*, 25 February 1999.

44. "Fund Established to Boost Local Plastics Industry," *Bangkok Post*, 6 July 1999.

45. The FTI includes and represents the interests of both foreign and domestic firms.

46. A consequence in part of the channelling of vast international recovery funds through financial institutions such as the Bank of Thailand, the Bank of Agriculture and Cooperatives, the International Development Finance Corporations, and a new SIFC. But note that more recent SME assistance programmes have centred prominently on key Ministry of Industry units.

47. An example of the negative consequences of this shift is the conservative stance of the Finance Ministry's representative on the SIFC relating to SME loan policy. "Quality House Expects Debt Plan Approval Soon." *The Nation/Business*, 12 March 1999.

48. In the current Thai context, "Asian" governance refers largely to a Japanese configuration of politically-insulated, state-organized policy networks, state industry-targeting and assistance, business associations, vertically organized supplier chains, debt-based financial systems and relational/network-based private-sector governance.

49. See, for example, "Good Boy Government Despicable," *Bangkok Post/ Perspective*, 9 May 1999.

50. Cross-national comparative research suggests a relationship between credit-based financial systems (vs. capital market-based systems) on the one hand, and network forms of economic governance on the other. See Zysman (1983: 64–65 and passim).

51. "Action Plan Calls for New Incentives," *Bangkok Post*, 12 June 2000.

52. This section relies in part on Monsakul (2000).

53. Based on interview data provided by Manusavee Monsakul.

54. A recent decision to reduce SIFC lending rates to 12 percent reverses a long-standing policy of lending at rates above those of commercial banks. "Agency's Bt3 bn Loans Back Export Push of SMEs," *The Nation*, 1 May 1999.

55. "Pressures for Controls on Capital Flows," *Bangkok Post*, 18 May 1999.

56. As evidenced by the establishment of an SME development plan overseen by an SME committee chaired by the Prime Minister. Indicative of this new

Japan-centred Asian regional focus is the planned July 1999 meeting of Asian and Japanese leaders in Tokyo to discuss the social impact of the crisis and to produce a joint set of recommendations to propose to APEC forum leaders in New Zealand in September 1999. See "Forum Set to Assess Lessons from Crisis," *Bangkok Post/Business*, 11 May 1999.

57. "Agency Wants to Beef up Help for Small Business," *Bangkok Post/Business*, 24 November 1998. On the role of the Japan External Trade Organization (Jetro) in Thai SMN policy, see "Help SMEs, Jetro Chief Urges Government," *The Nation/Business*, 30 March 1999. Note that a former director-general of Japan's MITI, Shiro Mizutani, has been invited to assist in the development of Thailand's SME development programme. "Ex-MITI Expert Helps Boost Status of SMEs," *The Nation/Business*, 15 March 1999.

58. One consequence of growing Japanese control of auto and other key industrial sectors is the likely requirement that local suppliers will need to adopt Japanese practice.

59. "Region's Fundamentals Better than in Other Developing Areas," *Bangkok Post*, 10 June 1999. Also see "PTT to Seek Other Funding," *Bangkok Post*, 11 June 1999.

60. "From Blight to Blossom: Interview with Ambassador Hiroshi Ota," *Bangkok Post*, 4 July 1999.

61. "Withdrawals of Budget below Target," *Bangkok Post*, 10 June 1999. Also "Securities Market Gets Little Interest," *Bangkok Post*, 17 June 1999.

62. See The World Bank (1999:19).

References

Bangkok Post (various issues). Bangkok.

Burkett, Paul and Martin Hart-Landsberg (1998), "East Asia and the Crisis of Development Theory," *Journal of Contemporary Asia* 28, 14 (October):435–52.

Calder, Kent (1998), *Crisis and Compensation: Public Policy and Political Stability in Japan*. Princeton: Princeton University Press.

Deyo, Frederic C. (1996), "Competition, Flexibility, and Industrial Ascent: The Thai Auto Industry." In Deyo (ed.), *Social Reconstructions of the World Automobile Industry*. Houndsmills: Macmillan Press.

Deyo, Frederic C. and Richard Doner (2000), "Dynamic Flexibility and Sectoral Governance in the Thai Auto Industry: The Enclave Problem." In Frederic C. Deyo, Richard Doner and Eric Hershberg (eds.), *Economic Governance and Flexible Production in East Asia*. New York: Rowman and Littlefield.

Hirst, Paul and G. Thompson (1992), "The Problem of 'Globalization': International Economic Relations, National Economic Management and the Formation of Trading Blocs," *Economy and Society*, 21(4) (November):357–96.

Johnson, Chalmers (1987), "Political Institutions and Economic Performance: The Government-Business Relationship in Japan, South Korea, and Taiwan." In Frederic C. Deyo (ed.), *The Political Economy of the New Asian Industrialism.* Ithaca: Cornell University Press.

Lim, Linda (1999), "The Challenges for Government Policy and Business Practice." In *The Asian Economic Crisis*. New York: The Asia Society.

Lo, Dic (1999), "The East Asian Phenomenon: The Consensus, the Dissent, and the Significance of the Present Crisis," *Capital and Class*, 67:1–23.

Monsakul, Manusavee (2000), *Policy Networks and Thai Industrial Policy during the Economic Crisis: A Case Study of the Thai Automobile Industry.* MA Thesis, Development Studies, University of Auckland.

National Economic and Social Development Board of Thailand (1998), "Impact of the Economic Crisis on the Standard of Living in Thailand," *Indicators of Well-Being and Policy Analysis*, 2(4).

The Nation (various issues). Bangkok.

Wade, Robert (1998), "From 'Miracle' to 'Cronyism': Explaining the Great Asian Slump," *Cambridge Journal of Economics*, 22:693–706.

Wade, Robert and F. Veneroso (1998), "The Asian Crisis: The High Debt Model versus the Wall Street-Treasury-IMF Complex," *New Left Review*, 228:3–23.

World Bank (1993), *The East Asian Miracle*. Oxford: Oxford University Press.

—— (1999), *Thailand: Economic Monitor*. March.

Zysman, John (1983), *Governments, Markets, and Growth: Financial Systems and the Politics of Industrial Change*. Ithaca: Cornell University Press.

3

Openness, Distributive Conflict and Social Insurance: The Social and Political Implications of China's WTO Membership*

Shaoguang Wang

The Social and Political Implications of China's WTO Membership

On 15 November 1999, China and the United States (U.S.) signed a bilateral agreement on China's accession to the World Trade Organization (WTO). Since then, China has reached agreements with more countries, including the European Union, and China's entry to the WTO was officially approved in November 2001.

By making concessions to the U.S. and other countries, China has demonstrated to the world that it is determined to embrace globalization and continue its domestic reform drive. To dispel misgivings about these deals,[1] the Chinese government has gone out of its way to publicize the potential benefits of WTO membership. While acknowledging possible risks and challenges, the government insists that these deals are "win-win" deals satisfactory to all sides.[2]

This chapter does not question the rationale of China's decision to join the WTO. Nor does it challenge the premise that, all in all, the potential benefits from WTO membership outweigh the potential costs, at least in the long term. Rather, it focuses on the social and political implications of China's WTO membership. It is assumed here that even if WTO membership is potentially a productivity-enhancing move for China, the benefits and costs of such a change will not be evenly distributed.

* An earlier version appeared as "The Social and Political Implications of China's WTO Membership," *Journal of Contemporary China*, Vol. 9, Issue 25 (November 2000).

Unless there is a mechanism that can induce or force the winners to compensate the losers, distributive conflicts between the two groups will be inevitable. Such conflicts may weaken or even erode political support for globalization. Thus, to remain committed to globalization, the government of an open economy must play a role in redistributing gains and costs.

The first section elaborates an analytical framework for an open economy. To fully understand the possible impact of WTO membership on Chinese society, it is important to know the current situation in the country, which can serve as a benchmark for our discussion. The second section notes that Chinese reforms have undergone two distinct phases. During the first phase of reform (1978–1992), the distribution of gains and losses was relatively even. Nearly all social groups benefited. It was by and large a win-win game. In the second phase, starting from 1993, Chinese reforms have appeared increasingly like a zero-sum game. Certain segments of Chinese society have benefited a great deal, while others have seen little gain or no gain at all. As a result, China has turned itself from a relatively egalitarian society into one with huge and growing inequalities. What will happen as China has become a WTO member? One thing is certain. Greater openness will entail restructuring of the economy, which will inevitably result in job losses, at least for some social groups in the short run. The third section analyzes who stand to win and lose when China removes more barriers to foreign trade and foreign capital. The findings are not encouraging. It is precisely those social groups that have borne the costs of recent reforms that will be hit hardest. More significantly, those losers happen to be the social groups that have long served as the political bases of the communist regime. Will WTO membership pose a challenge to the legitimacy of the Chinese government? It depends on whether the government is willing and able to reduce the risks associated with a greater degree of openness by redistributing the gains and costs of globalization. The final section discusses the political implications of China's WTO membership. To play the role of a redistributor, the Chinese government has to rebuild its extractive capacity, which is by no means an easy task. The section concludes that only by introducing institutions of voice or participation can the government expect to extract sufficient social resources for adjusting to a globalizing world.

Analytical Framework

Greater Openness and Distributive Conflicts

By joining the WTO, China has committed itself to gradually lowering tariffs, removing non-trade barriers, opening domestic markets to foreign competitors and allowing freer capital mobility across national boundaries. According to the prevailing view in academic and policy circles in today's world, if a country pursues a liberal trade policy, it will eventually achieve higher growth rates.[3] But a recent study that systematically scrutinizes the existing literature and empirical data finds little evidence of open trade policies being significantly associated with economic growth (Rodriguez and Rodrik, 1999). Even if we accept that greater openness is indeed conducive to economic growth, it does not follow that everyone will necessarily gain from liberalization, at least not in the short run. There are two reasons for this. First, greater openness implies specialization in production. Thus, it is inevitable for the national economy to be restructured by the forces of comparative advantage. While some social groups will benefit from opportunities offered by the economic restructuring, others may lose their jobs or become less competitive in the labour market. Second, since a more open economy tends to have a less diversified production structure, it is more likely to expose itself to the risks emanating from turbulence in world markets. Growing external risk means greater volatility in domestic income and consumption, which tends to hurt some social groups much harder than others.

The uneven distribution of the gains and costs of globalization may have two consequences. On the one hand, the hardship caused by globalization may alienate the losers from the economic and social system. With a growing sense of economic insecurity, they may withhold their support for the ongoing liberal reforms. If the situation continues to deteriorate in their view, they may openly oppose such reforms. On the other hand, the inequality and other forms of polarization may trigger distributive conflicts between the winners and losers of globalization. Such conflicts may damage the prospects of economic growth in a number of ways. First, distributive conflicts may divert attention, energy and resources from productive uses to bargaining over the distribution of both rents and burdens of globalization (Rodrik, 1998). Second, by generating uncertainty in the economic environment, such conflicts may lead to sub-optimal investment levels (Alesina and Perotti, 1996). Third, distributive conflicts may make it more difficult to build a consensus when a rapid response to external shocks or the formulation of cohesive developmental goals with clear priorities is necessary.

Distributive Conflicts and State Extractive Capacity

Of course, distributive conflicts are not unavoidable. Were the potential gainers from globalization willing to compensate the losers, such conflicts would not materialize. However, it is not realistic to expect that to happen. Even if the gainers agree to do so *ex ante*, they cannot credibly commit to compensate the losers *ex post*. Another option is for the state to tax the gainers and then to buy off the losers. According to Katzenstein (1985), this was a common practice in small European states like Sweden, Austria and the Netherlands. More recently, in a study of 125 countries, Rodrik identifies a positive correlation between an economy's exposure to international trade and the size of its government.[4] Apparently, in many economies exposed to significant external risk, their governments tried to mitigate risk by taking command of a larger share of the economy's resources and institutionalizing social security, welfare spending, income-transfer programmes and other types of compensatory programmes (Rodrik, forthcoming).

Thus, to reduce distributive conflicts and to remain committed to domestic reform and globalization, the state has to possess risk-reducing instruments and the requisite extractive capability, because people seem to demand an expanded government role as the price for accepting larger doses of internal and external risk. Indeed, it has been established that governments have expanded fastest in the most open economies.[5]

The problem is that in many developing countries, there are serious limitations to the government's ability to tax. Without an effective re-distributive mechanism, even if the aggregate gains of greater openness exceed the aggregate losses for the country as a whole (which means that the potential gainers could compensate the potential losers and still keep some extras), distributive conflicts are bound to happen. In other words, when state extractive capacity is weak, its conflict management capacity cannot be strong. When the state lacks the capacity to manage conflicts and social divisions run deep, it is hard for the state to co-ordinate social interests on stabilization and growth-promoting policies, not to mention enlisting the support of most social groups in making short-run sacrifices at times of exogenous shocks and macro-economic crises.

State Extractive Capacity and Voice

Can governments of developing countries strengthen their extractive capacity? Certainly, they could not impose tax burdens on their population that are heavier than those in industrial countries. After all, the level of economic development is a necessary precondition for a strong extractive capacity. A state could not tax effectively when the economy produced little of value. Yet, it would be wrong to attribute all the variation in state extractive capacity to economic strength alone. Even at the same level of economic development, state extractive capacity may be stronger in certain institutional environments than in others. Then, the next question is what type of institutional environment is more likely to facilitate revenue extraction. Some believe that authoritarian mechanisms are more able than participatory mechanisms to extract resources from society, because, in their view, the former can impose higher tax rates by disregarding protests from the people (Haggard, 1990). However, it is naive to expect that a 100 percent increase in the tax rate would automatically yield a 100 percent increase in the tax returns. There is no necessary correlation between higher tax rates and higher level of revenue collection. In fact, higher tax rates could result in lower tax returns if taxpayers react with massive tax revolt or tax evasion.

This essay argues that participatory mechanisms are more capable of increasing the level of revenue collected by the government, because they can help reduce the costs of taxpayer compliance. Indeed, ultimately, the extractive capacity of a government depends on the extent to which it procures taxpayer compliance. Voluntary compliance would secure the state sufficient revenues. If tax evasion became a national sport, however, the state would find it difficult to make ends meet. There are reasons to believe that, other things being equal, participatory mechanisms would enable the government to create taxpayer compliance at relatively low costs.

Facing tax increases, a taxpayer possesses two alternatives: to "exit" or to give "voice." The "exit" option here refers to tax evasion by various means, and the "voice" option refers to paying taxes while trying to alter tax laws through political action (Hirschman, 1970). Where there are no participatory institutions, the "voice" option is essentially shut out. Then taxpayers are left with only the "exit" option. If citizens are given the right to influence government decision-making, however, compliance with taxation may be expected to increase. This is so because in such an institutional environment, the government cannot tax and spend without consent from those whose interests are affected. When citizens vest the government with the right to tax and spend on their behalf, they are more likely to be compliant (Bates and Lien, 1984). Of course, this is not to say that a government with legitimacy can eliminate the free-riding problem. A person who supports his government may still want to receive benefits without incurring costs. Nevertheless, when given a greater voice over the policy choice of governments, taxpayers are definitely more willing to pay taxes. With reduced enforcement costs, the level of revenue the government is able to collect must be higher (Levi, 1988).

The argument that participation induces a greater willingness to pay taxes is supported by both historical and contemporary cases. A study of the political and fiscal history of early modern Europe (1450–1789) finds that:

> In the absolutist states, Spain and France, taxation was relatively light. It is rather in the states with strong representative institutions, the Netherlands and eighteenth-century England, that taxation was extraordinarily heavy. (Hoffman and Norberg, 1994:259)

Such contrast is still visible in today's world. Over the period from 1970 to 1990, it has been noted that countries with representative institutions tended to collect more taxes than those without: on the average, 26.7 percent of the GDP in the former and 17.8 percent in the latter. Even after controlling for other factors that also affect taxation, such as per capita income, taxes are still higher in the former than in the latter (Cheibub, 1998).

Even China itself presents the evidence that participation can help minimize the costs of enforcement associated with taxation. Anyone who studies rural China knows that complaints about "exorbitant local levies" (*tanpai*) are heard everywhere. However, there are exceptions. Wherever grassroots democracy is firmly institutionalized and "voice" really counts, villagers are often willing to pay more. Where forceful participatory institutions were still absent, though, fiscal paralysis was almost inevitably the result. "Voice" matters because it sanctions fiscal demands and subjects the government's performance to popular scrutiny (Wang, 1997).

In sum, a country seeking greater openness should not ignore the economic insecurities and distributive conflicts generated by globalization. Were it to do so, the prospects of maintaining global free trade would be very poor. Distributive conflicts are easier to mediate when compensation is built into the system. However, only when the government possesses a strong extractive capacity can it play the redistributive role. But it is unlikely that the government will possess such a strong extractive capacity unless it institutionalizes mechanisms of "voice." In China, the government's extractive capacity is rather weak and participatory institutions remain underdeveloped. These are the political challenges China will face since it has become a member of the WTO.

From a Win-Win Game to a Zero-Sum Game

The social impact of WTO membership will to some extent be conditioned by the current situation in China. Obviously, if globalization were to generate restructuring and external shocks at all, such changes would have a much worse impact on a country with large inequality and social conflict than on an egalitarian society. Therefore, before trying to figure out who stands to gain and who to lose from China's WTO deal, this section examines to what extent the benefits and costs of the Chinese reforms have been evenly distributed.

In retrospect, it can be said that the Chinese reforms have benefited everyone. There is hardly any household whose welfare has not improved since 1978. However, a careful review of recent history reveals that Chinese reform has actually gone through two distinct phases. The first phase started in 1978 and ended around 1993. During this period, the game of reform was truly a win-win game. All social groups gained. The only difference was that some social groups might have gained relatively more than others.[6] Starting from around 1994, the Chinese reforms entered the second phase, which was characterized by worsening unemployment and growing inequality. To be sure, there were still social groups that profited from the latest round of reforms. However, for the first time, some segments of society became real losers, losers not only in a relative sense, but also in an absolute sense. Their welfare suffered real decline. To the extent that some gained at the expense of others, the new game of reform has become a zero-sum one.

Both the Chinese élite and ordinary citizens are aware of this observation. Since 1997, the Chinese Academy of Social Sciences has conducted surveys among government officials and ordinary urban residents every year. One standard question is: Which social groups in their view have benefited most or least from recent reforms? Table 3.1 presents the results. Although discrepancies exist between the élite and popular views, there is a broad consensus that farmers (including those who work in urban areas as migrants) and the workers of state-owned enterprises (SOEs) are big losers.

Table 3.1   Winners and Losers in Recent Reforms

Question: In your opinion, which social groups have benefited most/least from recent reforms?

(A) Élite View

Survey of Party Officials, October 1997

	Benefit Most		Benefit Least
1	Private business owners	1	SOE workers
2	FDI employees	2	Farmers
3	Farmers	3	Government employees

Survey of Party Officials, October 1998

	Benefit Most		Benefit Least
1	Private business owners	1	SOE workers
2	Artists	2	Farmers
3	FDI employees	3	Government employees

Survey of Party Officials, November 1999

	Benefit Most		Benefit Least
1	Private business owners	1	Unemployed workers
2	Artists	2	Farmers
3	FDI employees	3	SOE workers

(B) Popular View

Survey of Urbanites, November 1997

	Benefit Most		Benefit Least
1	Private business owners	1	SOE workers
2	Artists	2	Farmers
3	Bank employees	3	Migrants

Survey of Urbanites, December 1998

	Benefit Most		Benefit Least
1	Artists	1	SOE workers
2	Corrupt officials	2	Farmers
3	Private business owners	3	Migrants

Survey of Urbanites, August 1999

	Benefit Most		Benefit Least
1	Artists	1	SOE workers
2	Corrupt officials	2	Farmers
3	Private business owners	3	Migrants

Source: Ru Xing et al. (1998, 1999, 2000),

Rural Polarization

The farmers' misfortune has to do with rural underemployment. Rural under-employment has always been a problem in China. In the 1980s and early 1990s, township and village enterprises (TVEs) created millions of jobs for rural residents, thus helping alleviate the underemployment problem. According to Hu Angang's estimate, in 1995, of the 500 million able-bodied labourers in rural China, only 325 million were actually needed. The other 175 million were redundant (Hu, 1999). In other words, if rural labourers were to work to their potential, more than one-third of Chinese farmers would have become unemployed. What is worse, as Figure 3.1 shows, starting from 1993, TVEs seem to have lost their job creation power. In 1997, China changed its definition of TVE. Therefore, data before and after this change are not quite comparable. However, the change of definition cannot conceal a fact: TVE employment has been declining, 4.8 percent in 1997 and 18.7 percent in 1998. In 1999, the trend continued. Such a sharp slump has never occurred before.

Partly due to the waning of the TVEs, the growth of farmers' income has slowed down since 1996. This is clearly demonstrated in Figure 3.2. It needs to be noted that what Figure 3.2 presents is the national average.

Figure 3.1   TVE Employment, 1978–1998

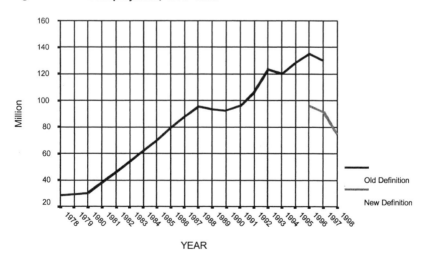

YEAR

Source: State Statistical Bureau (1999). *China Statistical Yearbook, 1999.* Beijing: China Statistical Press, p. 388.

Figure 3.2   Per Capita Income in Rural China

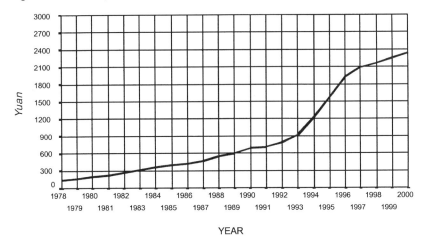

Source: State Statistical Bureau (various years). *Statistical Yearbook of China.*

Surveys have found that, for 80 percent of Chinese farmers, their income is below the national average. In other words, the top 20 percent of rural residents have much higher income than the rest of rural residents. And the gaps between low-income and high-income groups have been widening (Fan, 2000). The trend was already unmistakable before 1995, but has become more visible after 1995. Unfortunately, we only have data on rural Gini coefficients prior to 1995,[7] and these are shown in Figure 3.3. Clearly, not all rural residents are losers. But it is safe to say that a large percentage of them are.

Urban Polarization

While rural underemployment is worsening, urban unemployment is also on the rise. Although the rate increased from 1.8 percent in 1985 to 3.1 percent in 1999, only 5.8 million urban residents were unemployed in 1999 (Yang, 2000). But even the government admits that such statistics are misleading, because "unemployment" is very narrowly defined and does not include millions of *xiagang* workers. *Xiagang* is a peculiar concept. It is different from outright unemployment in that *xiagang* workers maintain some sort of employment contract with their enterprises. In theory, they can return to their posts once their enterprises begin to hire again. Before

Figure 3.3   Gini Coefficients of Rural Income

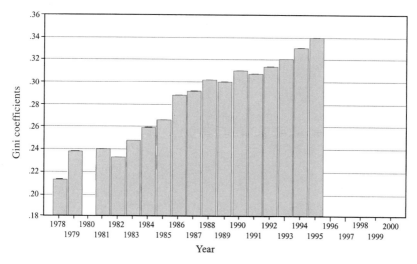

Source: Kang Xiaoguang (2000).

they are rehired, which is not unlikely in most cases, however, they are to all intents and purposes unemployed. By June 1999, there were around 10 million *xiagang* workers (7.42 million from SOEs and 2.4 million from collective enterprises) (Yang, 2000). Even the official statistics on *xiagang* workers may not be very accurate. According to Hu Angang's calculation, in 1998, total SOE employment dropped by 10.27 million and total urban collective employment by another 4.74 million. Together, around 15 million SOE and collective employees no longer worked in their firms. This figure included those who had reached the retirement age and those who found employment elsewhere. In any case, if we add the numbers of *xiagang* workers to those who officially registered as unemployed, the total number of the unemployed probably amounted to 15–16 million in 1998 and 18–19 million in 1999 (Hu, 1999). Figure 3.4 compares the official unemployment rates to Hu's estimates of real rates. Whether we adopt the lower or the higher estimate, one thing is unmistakable: Starting from 1993, urban unemployment has become a serious problem.

The situation is unlikely to improve any time soon, because economic growth in China has increasingly become a sort of "jobless growth." This trend is vividly demonstrated in Figure 3.5. In the 1980s, every additional percentage of GDP growth brought about 0.32 percent increase in

Figure 3.4   **Urban Unemployment in China**

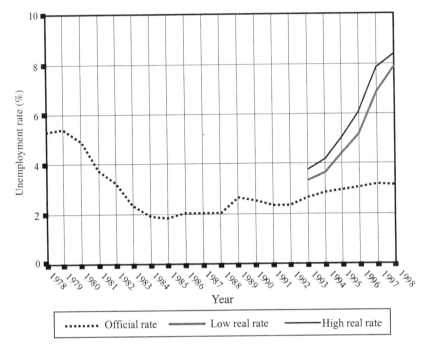

Source: Hu Angang (1999).

Figure 3.5   **Employment Elasticity of Output Growth**

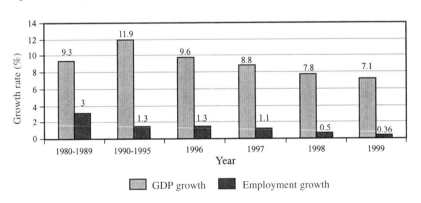

Source: Hu Angang (1999).

employment opportunities. At that time, growth might be seen as creating jobs. By the mid-1990s, the mode of growth had changed, and when GDP grew by an additional percentage point, employment opportunities increased only 0.14 percent. The late 1990s saw the employment elasticity of output growth continue to fall. In 1999, GDP grew 7.1 percent, while employment increased barely 0.36 percent, which meant that every additional percentage of GDP growth brought about only 0.05 percent increase in employment. If the current trend were to continue, even if annual GDP growth rate were to rebound to the level of 8–9 percent in the coming years, China would still not be able to create enough jobs for those newly entering the labour market (about 10 million every year), not to mention absorbing all those who lose their jobs due to SOE reform and economic restructuring.

Unemployment has a regional dimension. Figure 3.6 presents data on both official and real unemployment rates in China's 31 provincial units in 1998. In the national capital, Beijing, barely 2 percent of the labour force was unemployed. However, in three Northeast provinces (Liaoning, Jilin and Heilongjiang), real unemployment rates ranged from 12.8 percent to 15.5 percent. Unemployment was also rather serious in Jiangxi, Hubei, Hunan, Sichuan, Shaanxi and Hainan provinces (above 10 percent), all but Hainan being interior provinces. Coastal provinces in general had much lower unemployment rates than their inland counterparts. For instance, Fujian's rate was as low as 3.1 percent. Guangdong, Shandong, Zhejiang, Jiangsu, Hebei and Shanghai also saw relatively low unemployment rates.

Due to unemployment and other factors, many urban households have experienced declines in their real income. In 1996, about 40 percent of urban households suffered such a bitter experience. The next year was no better: Those with reduced incomes constituted 39 percent of total urban households, hardly any change from a year before. It was the poor who were hit hardest. Of the bottom 20 percent of households, nearly two-thirds found themselves earning less. The second 20 percent of households were also in very bad shape with one out of every two families falling into this category. Although some of the top 20 percent of urban households also suffered income losses, most of them were actually able to increase their income (Table 3.2). When the poor become poorer and the rich become richer, the gaps between them, of course, widen. In 1990, the average income of the top 20 percent of households was only 4.2 times higher than that of the bottom 20 percent. By 1998, the ratio had jumped to 9.6 times, which was an unmistakable sign of polarization. Indeed, the richest 10 percent of households were the biggest winners in the recent reforms. Their share of

Figure 3.6 Unemployment Rates in Provinces, 1998 (%)

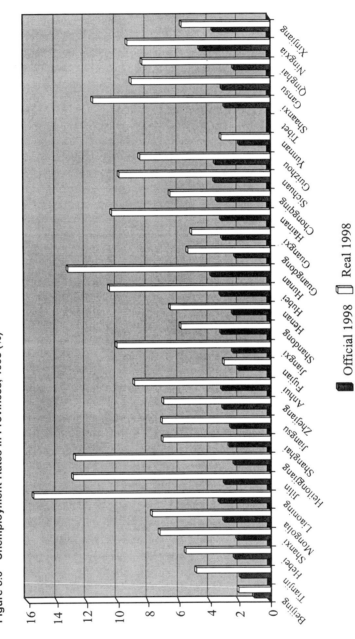

Beijing, Tianjin, Hebei, Shanxi, Mongolia, Liaoning, Jilin, Heilongjiang, Shanghai, Jiangsu, Zhejiang, Anhui, Fujian, Jiangxi, Shandong, Henan, Hubei, Hunan, Guangdong, Guangxi, Hainan, Chongqing, Sichuan, Guizhou, Yunnan, Tibet, Shaanxi, Gansu, Qinghai, Ningxia, Xinjiang

■ Official 1998   ▯ Real 1998

Source: Hu Angang (2000).

Table 3.2   **Urban Population Groups with Reduced Incomes, 1997, by Quintile of Income Distribution (%)**

	Total (100%)	Low income group (20%)	Relatively low income (20%)	Middle income group (20%)	Relatively high income (20%)	High income group (20%)
Percentage of families with lower incomes	39	60	53	33	39	20

Source: State Statistical Bureau (1998), p. 9.

Table 3.3   **Growing Inequality in Urban China, 1990–1998**

Year	Income of top 20%/ income of bottom 20%	Bottom 20%'s share of total income	Top 20%'s share of total income	Top 10%'s share of total income
1990	4.2 times	9.0%	38.1%	23.6%
1993	6.9 times	6.3%	43.5%	29.3%
1998	9.6 times	5.5%	52.3%	38.4%

Source: Xu Xinxin and Li Peilin (1999).

total income increased from 23.6 percent in 1990 to 38.4 percent in 1998. On the other hand, the bottom 20 percent of households were major losers: Their share of total income declined from 9 percent in 1990 to 5.5 percent in 1998 (Table 3.3). Now about 30 million urban residents are living in poverty. Their incomes are no more than one-third of the national average (Ying et al., 1998).

Urban-Rural Divide

Like other Third World countries, China has a dual economy. Economists tend to expect that the expansion of the modern sector will "trickle down" to bring equal prosperity to the traditional sector. But even the originator of the dual-sector model, Arthur Lewis, warns: "There is no reason to expect the traditional always to benefit from expansion of the modern," because "there are forces working for benefit and forces working for loss; the net result will vary from case to case" (Lewis, 1979). Perhaps we should add that, even in a single country, the expansion of the modern sector might produce different outcomes in different periods.

When China launched its reform initiative in 1978, the urban-rural divide was already rather deep: The per capita income of the urban resident was 2.6 times higher than that of the rural resident. In the early years of reform, the urban-rural gap shrank. Starting from 1984, however, the gap began to widen again. Nevertheless, before 1992, the gap was still somewhat smaller than that of 1978. The immediate impact of Deng Xiaoping's famous southern tour was the polarization of growth between China's modern and traditional sectors. Thanks to price increases of state procurement of grains, the polarization was temporarily arrested in 1996 and 1997. But, given that China's grain prices were already higher than those in international markets, it was not realistic for the government to support the agricultural sector by handing out subsidies on a regular basis. Therefore, after 1998, the urban-rural gap began to widen once again. By 1999, the urban-rural divide was as deep as it had been in 1978. All the gains of earlier years had been lost.

Figure 3.8 presents data on the absolute gap, which has been growing. While a typical urban resident earned about 200 *yuan* more than his urban counterpart in 1978, by 1997, the difference amounted to more than 3,000 *yuan*.

Compared to other countries, China's rural-urban gap is unusually large. In other countries, the ratio of urban-to-rural incomes is normally below 1.5 and rarely exceeds 2.0. But, in China, real urban incomes are as much as four times real rural incomes, if urban residents' welfare benefits of various kinds are included (World Bank, 1997).

Figure 3.7   Per Capita Income in Rural and Urban China

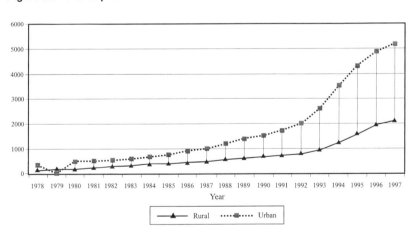

Source: Kang Xiaoguang (2000).

Figure 3.8 Changes of CVw, with and without B.T.S., 1978–1994

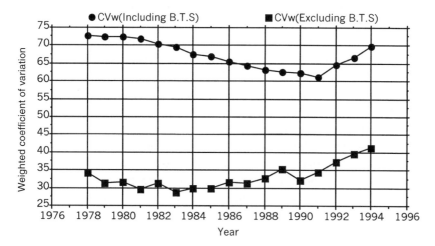

Source: Wang Shaoguang and Hu Angang (1997), p. 57.

Regional Disparities

Neo-classical economists predict that, coupled with economic growth, the operation of the market, left to itself, tends to bring convergence of regional income. To be sure, China has been undergoing market-oriented reforms in the last two decades and its record of economic growth is as "miraculous" as those of the East Asian tigers. But China's experience of the last two decades shows that convergence is by no means automatic. In a recent book on regional disparities, Wang Shaoguang and Hu Angang (1997) reach the following three conclusions.

First, inter-provincial inequality has been widening. The Chinese economy converged briefly in the early years of reform, but the trend was soon reversed. Disparity in per capita GDP between China's coastal and interior provinces has been on the rise since 1983. What is worse, the divergent trend has accelerated since 1990 (World Bank, 1997). Figure 3.8 displays two sets of weighted coefficients of variation (CVw) of per capita GDP in constant prices, which are measures of relative inequality between provinces. The top curve shows a U-shaped time path, with inequality declining from 1978 to 1991 and then reversing course. The bottom curve differs from the top one in that Beijing, Tianjin and Shanghai are not included.[8] Excluding the three cities yields a noteworthy change in CVw:

The direction of change in CVw is different. Regional dispersion did decrease marginally in the initial years of reform, but the 12 years following 1983 saw a steady increase in relative dispersion. Consequently, CVw at the end of the period was 0.073 higher than that in 1978.

Second, regional gaps in China are unusually large. Figure 3.9 presents data on per capita GDP in China's 30 provinces in 1997. Apparently, the coastal provinces were better off than the central provinces, which, in turn, surpassed the western provinces. Except for Guangxi, all the coastal provinces had per capita GDP higher than the national average. Shanghai's was 4.5 times the average. At the other extreme, Guizhou's per capita GDP was equivalent to only 37 percent of the national average. In fact, aside from Heilongjiang, none of the central and western provinces had per capita GDP higher than the national average. Compared to 17 countries for which data are available, China's degree of inter-regional inequality appears to be the worst (Table 3.4).

Third, regional inequality is a multi-dimensional phenomenon. No matter which dimension we look at, there are notable regional variations. The rich and poor provinces do not differ merely in per capita GDP. Rather, regional inequality manifests itself in almost every aspect of economic and social life. Measured by human development indicators, for instance, the difference between China's most-developed and least-developed provinces is comparable to that between the Western industrial countries and the poorest countries in the world (UNDP, 1995:139–41).

General Polarization

From the above discussion, it is clear that recent reforms have widened the gaps between regions, between urban and rural populations, and between rich and poor households in both urban and rural China. These inequalities are overlapping and inter-related. Together, the growing inter-regional, inter-personal and rural-urban income differentials make China's overall income distribution much more unequal today than ever before in the history of the People's Republic (see Figure 3.10). In the early 1980s, China was an egalitarian society with income inequality well below the world average. By the mid-1990s, although the degree of income inequality in China was still lower than in most Latin American and Sub-Saharan African countries, "there is no room for complacency" (World Bank, 1997:2). China's income distribution has already exceeded the inequality found in most transition economies in Eastern Europe and many high-income countries in Western

Figure 3.9   Per Capita GDP as % of National Average, 1997

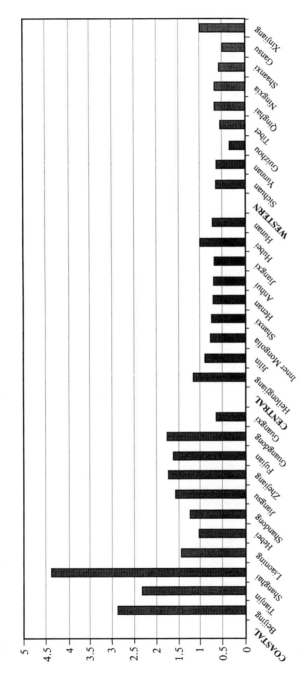

Source: Kang Xiaoguang (2000).

Table 3.4   International Comparison of Regional Disparities in Per Capita GDP or Per Capita Income

Country	Year	Max/Min	CV
China(a)	1978	14.27	0.73
China(b)	1978	3.87	0.34
China(a)	1994	13.96	0.87
China(b)	1994	4.13	0.39
Yugoslavia	1988	7.80	0.54
Greece	1988	1.69	0.10
Spain	1988	2.23	0.17
Germany	1988	1.93	0.13
France	1988	2.15	0.26
Canada	1988	2.30	0.28
Japan	1981	1.47	0.12
Italy	1988	2.34	0.26
Portugal	1988	1.66	0.23
Belgium	1988	1.61	0.15
United Kingdom	1988	1.63	0.15
Netherlands	1988	2.69	0.19
U.S.A.	1983	1.43	0.11
Australia	1978	1.13	0.05
South Korea	1985	1.53	0.15
India	1980	3.26	0.36
Indonesia(a)	1983	5.30	0.46
Indonesia(b)	1983	4.00	0.34

Source: For data on China, see *China Statistical Yearbook 1995* (Beijing: China Statistical Press, 1995), p. 38; *1995 Statistical Yearbooks of 30 Provinces and Autonomous Regions* (Beijing, China Statistical Press, 1995). For data on Yugoslavia, Italy, Greece, Portugal, Spain, Belgium, Germany, U.K., France and the Netherlands, see Daniel Ottolenghi and Alfred Steinherr, "Yugoslavia: Was it a Winner's Curse?" *Economies of Transition*, Vol. 1, No. 2 (1993), p. 229. For data on Canada, see Donald, J. Savie, *Regional Economic Development: Canada's Search for Solution*, 2nd edition (Toronto: University of Toronto Press, 1992), p. 191. For data on the U.S., see David M. Smith, *Geography, Inequality and Society* (Cambridge: Cambridge University Press, 1987), p. 41. For data on Japan, see Institute of Japan Studies, the Chinese Academy of Social Sciences, *Problems, Solutions, and Mechanisms: Experience and Lessons of Japan's Economic Development* (Beijing: Economics Science Press, 1994), p. 235. For data on Australia, see Benjamin Higgins, "Economic Development and Regional Disparities: A Comparative Study of Four Federations," in R. L. Matheas (ed.), *Regional Disparities and Economic Development* (Canberra: The Australian National University, 1981), pp. 69–70. For data on India, see K. R.G. Nair, "Inter-State Income Differentials in India, 1970–71 to 1979–80," in G.P. Mishra (ed.), *Regional Structure of Development and Growth in India* (New Delhi: Ashish Publishing House, 1985), p. 9. For data on Indonesia. see Haj Hill and Anna Weidemann, "Regional Development in Indonesia: Patterns and Issues," in Haj Hill (ed.), *Unity and Diversity: Regional Economic Development in Indonesia Since 1970* (Singapore: Oxford University Press, 1980), pp. 6–7. For data on South Korea, see Kyung-hwan Kim and Edwin S. Mills, "Urbanization and Regional Development in Korea," in Jene K. Kwon (ed.), *Korean Economic Development* (New York: Greenwood Press, 1990), p. 415.

Figure 3.10   Inequality in China

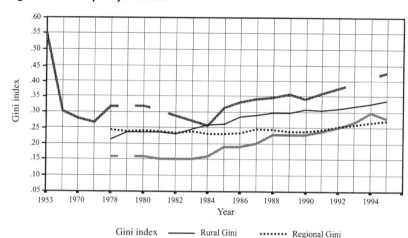

Source: Author's data bank.

Europe as well as in some of its large Asian neighbours, such as India, Pakistan and Indonesia, countries that had often been treated in the development literature as classic cases of large income inequality (World Bank, 1997:1–2, 7–8).

Income inequality has grown in many countries in the 1980s and 1990s but not in all countries. What really distinguishes China from all others, however, is the fact that in China, it has increased both to a greater extent and more rapidly than almost anywhere else. The World Bank reports that the increase in China's overall inequality was "by far the largest of all countries for which comparable data are available" (World Bank, 1997:7–8).

Such a steep rise in inequality in such a short period of time is highly unusual in both historical and comparative perspectives. Looking ahead, unless the trend of increasing polarization could be somehow halted or reversed, the glaring inequalities prevailing in Latin America and Sub-Saharan Africa are likely to emerge in China soon.

Growing inequality has given rise to a pervasive sense of economic insecurity in China, which in turn threatens political support for the ongoing market-oriented reforms. Recent surveys revealed that the urban residents who felt under great pressure in life had risen from 65.4 percent in 1995 to 83.5 percent in 1999 (Ru, 2000:77). It is against this background that China has joined the WTO.

Who Stands to Lose from the WTO Membership?[9]

A Win-Win Decision?

At a specially convened press conference on 10 January 2000, American President Clinton told the audience, "Bringing China into the WTO is a win-win decision." According to Clinton, what the U.S. got was a very good deal: American products and services would gain significant new access to virtually every sector of China's economy.[10] What did China get in return? The U.S. Secretary of Agriculture Dan Glickman was frank, "Absolutely nothing."[11] Clinton agreed, "China makes one-way concessions to open its markets to American goods, services, and farm products ... while the U.S. makes no new market access commitments at all" (Clinton, 2000). If what Clinton said was true, one may wonder whether China has gained anything at all from this WTO deal.

Indeed, the short-term benefits China would attain through WTO membership are very limited, whatever the long-term benefits may be. As Nicholas Lardy points out, for China, the single most important economic benefit associated with WTO membership is the permanent most-favoured-nation (MFN) trading status in the markets of WTO member countries. However, China has already received permanent MFN status from every country in the WTO except the U.S. The U.S. has provided MFN status for China on a yearly basis for more than 15 years. Although the U.S. Congress has consistently threatened to revoke China's MFN status, nobody believes that it would ever actually happen, because doing so would hurt the U.S. as much as it hurts China. Hence, as something already in hand, the value of this so-called "principal benefit of membership" should be heavily discounted (Lardy, 1999).

Another potential benefit for China is that, according to the WTO rules, the U.S. — the largest market for Chinese exports — would have to remove import quotas on such Chinese labour-intensive products as textiles, shoes and toys by certain dates. However, the U.S. has no intention of following the WTO schedule. Therefore, in the November bilateral negotiation, it forced China to accept a four-year protection period for the U.S. textile industry after the quotas are lifted in 2005. In addition, the U.S. is introducing a country-specific safeguard mechanism that addresses imports solely from China, rather than from other parts of the world. In case of an import surge that may threaten a particular American industry, the mechanism can be used to protect it. The country-specific safeguard applies to all industries and will remain in force for 12 years after China accedes to the WTO.

Moreover, the agreement provides strong protection against dumping. China agreed that for 15 years after its accession to the WTO, the U.S. might maintain its current antidumping policy (treating China as a non-market economy) in future anti-dumping cases. With all those protection measures in place, Clinton proudly told the audience at the press conference mentioned above, "In fact, we'll gain tough new safeguards against surges of imports, and maintain the strongest possible rules against dumping products that have hurt Americans in the past."[12] Since any surge of exports to the U.S. is unlikely before 2015, this benefit of increased exports of labour-intensive products would remain a potential one for quite a long time to come.

Whereas China gains no new access to the U.S. market, the U.S. and, for that matter, other countries, will secure market access to whole areas of the Chinese economy to which they were previously denied, as China has become a WTO member state.

Agriculture

Tariffs on agricultural products will decline sharply from an average of 31 percent to roughly 14 percent by January 2004. China will also create new tariff-rate quotas that allow American producers to export bulk commodities such as wheat, corn and rice. In the meantime, China promises to eliminate all export subsidies. To prevent the Chinese government from manipulating imports, the agreement stipulates that private companies rather than state enterprises will handle the importing of a substantial share of these goods.

Manufacturing

Chinese tariffs on imports of industrial goods will drop from an average of 24.6 percent in 1997 to 9.4 percent in 2005. Foreign companies will have the right to sell, distribute and market industrial goods, including steel and chemicals, without the intervention of government bodies. They do not have to go through Chinese middlemen as is now necessary. They also have the right to handle after-sales service, repairs and maintenance.

Auto Industry

In the auto sector, China will cut tariffs from the current 80–100 percent level to 25 percent by mid-2006, with the largest cuts in the first years after accession. Auto-parts tariffs will be cut to an average of 10 percent by mid-2006. Foreign auto companies will have full distribution and trading rights. The provision of credit to finance car purchases will also be permitted.

Finance

The U.S. banks will be able to lend to Chinese businesses in local currency two years after China joins the WTO, and to individual Chinese after five years. Foreign insurance companies can offer property and casualty insurance nationwide. In addition, foreign firms will be allowed a 33 percent stake in all securities fund management joint ventures, rising to 49 percent three years after China joins the WTO.

IT and Telecommunications Industries

China will participate in the Information Technology Agreement (ITA) and eliminate all tariffs on products such as computers, semi-conductors, telecommunications equipment and other high-technology products. Foreign telephone companies, at present restricted to equipment sales, will be able to own up to 49 percent of all telecommunications service ventures upon China's entry into the WTO and up to 50 percent two years later. Foreign firms will also be allowed to invest in Internet companies, including content providers, from which they were previously barred.

Movies

China will import 40 foreign films a year, double the current number, and 50 by the third year of the agreement, and foreign film and music companies can share in distribution revenues for 20 of the films.

Winners and Losers

Surely there are people in China who stand to gain from the country's WTO membership. Educated élites, for instance, will definitely be winners because their investment in education will have higher returns once production factors are valued in international rather than domestic markets. Moreover, producers of certain industrial goods (e.g., textiles, toys, garments, shoes, colour TVs, washing machines, electric fans, bicycles, portable stereos and computer parts, and the like) and agricultural goods (e.g., tea, fruits, vegetables, livestock and aquatic products) may gain because, with fewer trade barriers, those labour-intensive sectors may become more competitive in international markets.

In the long run, the Chinese people in general may also benefit from the WTO membership. For one thing, as consumers, they may have more and better choices of goods and services at lower prices. Moreover, trade liberalization may increase China's overall productivity, thus helping to improve the welfare of the nation as a whole. However, whether the general public can actually profit from the WTO membership is contingent on the equal distribution of gains and costs associated with greater openness. People are consumers and producers at once. For those who lose their jobs, more choices of goods and services at lower prices may make little sense. Similarly, a productivity-enhancing change may not benefit everyone if the potential gainers do not compensate the losers.

As Olson (1965) points out, the losses of the potential losers tend to be concentrated and transparent, while the gains of the potential gainers tend to be diffuse. Thus, we would expect that the losers of the WTO deal strongly resist openness, while the winners only half-heartedly defend it. From the political point-of-view, therefore, more attention should be paid to the losers than to the winners.

Who stands to lose after China has become a WTO member? Farmers and workers are most likely to suffer negative consequences from the deal, in the form of lost jobs and downward pressure on wages. The WTO membership requires China to dismantle its remaining import barriers. This will entail painful domestic restructuring and adjustment because these barriers have been used primarily to protect state-owned industries and farmers.

After joining the WTO, China will have to cut agricultural tariffs substantially. The overall average duty for agricultural products will fall from 22 percent to 17.5 percent. On American priority agricultural products, tariffs will drop from an average of 31 percent to 14 percent by January 2004, with even sharper drops for beef, poultry, pork, cheese, citrus and other fruits, vegetables, tree nuts, forest and fish products, and other commodities. In addition, WTO membership will oblige China to use a tariff-rate quota (TRQ) system and non-state trading for certain sensitive commodities, including wheat, corn, rice, cotton and soybean oil. Under this system, a specific quantity of imports will be allowed in at a low duty (on average, 1–3 percent) while imports above that level will face a higher duty. Moreover, a specific share of the TRQ will be reserved for importation through state trading enterprises and a specific share will be reserved for importation by non-state trading entities. If a TRQ share that was reserved to be imported by a state trader is not contracted for by October for any given year, it will be reallocated to non-state trading entities. The introduction of private trade is a way to ensure that the Chinese government does not impede quota-holders from utilizing their quotas and that imports occur.

With such dramatically expanded market access opportunities, foreign companies are expected to sell China large amounts of wheat, corn, rice, cotton, soybeans, wool, dairy products and other commodities. For example, China now imports roughly 2 million tonnes of wheat a year; the China–U.S. agreement immediately permits 7 million tonnes with almost no tariff. The China–U.S. agreement also promises to bind tariffs at a low rate for soybean (3 percent) and soybean meal (5 percent), and to eliminate quota limits on them. Moreover, under the agreement, China will establish a large, low-duty TRQ for cotton, with a substantial share reserved for private importers. All in all, the China–U.S. deal was so good that Scott Shearer, director of national relations for American Farmland Industries, called it "the largest market-access agreement in U.S. agricultural history."[13]

A good deal for American farmers means that China will see an upsurge of agricultural imports. In fiscal year 1999, American agricultural exports to China amounted to $1.1 billion. According to United States Department of Agriculture's (USDA's) "conservative" estimates, China's WTO accession would result in $1.6 billion annually in additional U.S. exports of grains, cotton, oilseeds and related products by 2005. Exports of other products will bring in additional $350–450 million annually. Altogether, a gain of $2 billion each year in expanded exports to China is expected.

Based on individual households, China's small-scale farmers can never compete with giant American producers. In the last two decades, prices of agricultural products, especially of grains, have been declining in international markets, whereas the situation in China has been just the opposite. Except in 1984 and 1989, such prices have always been moving upward. As a result, starting from late 1993, the prices of China's main agricultural crops (wheat, corn, rice and cotton) have exceeded those in international markets. Take corn as an example. In March 1999, it was priced at 1,440 *yuan* per tonne in the domestic market but only 720 *yuan* on the Chicago market. Even taking into consideration transportation costs, it was still much cheaper to buy from abroad (Wen, 2000). Not only are the prices of Chinese agricultural products generally higher, their quality is also generally inferior. What is more, all those products are already over-supplied in China. It is estimated that WTO membership would force China to reduce its corn production by 7.7 percent, wheat by 4.7 percent, soybean by 4.5 percent, cotton by 3.8 percent, oilseed by 3.6 percent, and sugar by 2.5 percent (Fan, 2000). China now is a net corn exporter, but inflow of cheaper American corn will soon make it a net corn importer. Cotton growers will suffer particularly badly. Currently, China is the world's largest producer and consumer of cotton, accounting for 20–25 percent of the world's total in both categories. Under the China–U.S. agreement, China will establish a large, low-duty TRQ for cotton with a substantial share reserved for private importers, which would lead to expanded U.S. cotton sales in China.

Large inflows from abroad could drive millions of Chinese farmers out of work. It is estimated that between 13 and 15 million growers of China's main agricultural crops will become unemployed between 2000 and 2010, among whom about 10 million will have to be transferred to non-agricultural sectors.[14]

When millions of farmers flow into cities looking for jobs, they have to compete with millions of SOE and collective workers whose jobs are also threatened by foreign rivals. Under the terms of the agreement between China and the U.S., not only will industrial tariffs be much lower, foreign manufacturers will also have the right to trade and distribute freely inside China — something China has severely restricted this far. With barriers to imports removed, foreign companies will be able to secure market access to those areas where Chinese producers are not competitive, including, among others, information industries, automobile, papermaking, steel, chemicals, petrochemicals, machine-making, and pharmaceuticals, tele-communications, and the like. In the last 20 years, foreign exports to China have grown from negligible levels to more than $150 billion each year, a large proportion of which consists of manufactured goods. These figures can grow substantially with the new access to the Chinese market that WTO membership creates.

Due to over-investment in the first half of the 1990s, almost every industry in China already has excess capacity. An indication of excessive production capacity is deflation. The prices of producer goods began to fall in 1996. The next year saw the decline of agricultural prices. What is worse, since October 1997, consumer prices have been falling for 30 months in succession. According to surveys conducted by the Ministry of Domestic Trade, 93.8 percent of commodities were already over-supplied in 1996. The ratio increased to 98.4 percent in 1997. After 1998, there has been no single commodity in the Chinese market that is not over-supplied. Zheng

Xilin, deputy director of the State Commission of Economy and Commerce, disclosed that in 1999, the use rate of production capacity for over half of industrial goods was less than 60 percent.[15]

Greater openness would exacerbate the problem of excess capacity. China has hesitated to dismantle its remaining import barriers because they could protect domestic firms, especially those state-owned and collective entities. Without Western-style safety nets, in the past, China, like many other Third World countries, has relied on public employment to reduce social risks. Today, these state-owned and collective entities still employ over two-thirds of all urban workers. Removing import barriers will force thousands of such firms out of existence and the remaining ones to downsize. It is estimated that redundant industrial employees alone amount to about 20 million. The overall redundant urban labour force is probably in the neighbourhood of 25–30 million. Restructuring may be necessary for China's long-term development and downsizing may be desirable from the perspective of efficiency, but if restructuring and downsizing are too rapid, it will result in massive urban unemployment. Only a fraction of these newest additions to the ranks of unemployment will find jobs in new, foreign-owned, labour-intensive manufacturing enterprises. Even those who survive the great shocks of bankruptcy and lay-offs are unlikely to enjoy rising real wages to go along with their rising productivity, for floods of imports will put more downward pressure on wages in general, and the wages of unskilled Chinese workers in particular.[16]

The impact of WTO membership may also have a regional dimension. In the last two decades, China's coastal provinces have performed extra-ordinarily well, leaving inland provinces far behind (Wang and Hu, 1999). External shocks associated with greater openness may cause some pain for coastal provinces, but they should be able to adapt to the new situation with relative ease. Inland provinces are much more vulnerable to international competition. Historically, wheat, corn, cotton and oil crops have been their staples, while coastal provinces tend to have a more diversified agricultural structure, producing, in addition to grains and cotton, tea, fruits, vegetables, livestock, aquatic products, and the like. As far as industrial structure is concerned, inland provinces tend to concentrate on resource extraction and heavy industries, while coastal provinces are good at producing consumer goods. With poorer natural endowment and more limited financial resources than their coastal counterparts, inland provinces would find it much harder to restructure their agriculture and industry, even if they were determined to do so. Thus, WTO membership would mean more opportunities for relatively affluent coastal provinces but fewer opportunities for struggling inland provinces.

In sum, the social consequences of WTO membership will be profound. As foreign imports begin to flood the Chinese market, millions of Chinese farmers and workers will be made redundant, thus deepening the urban-rural divide,[17] widening regional disparities, exacerbating tension between social groups, and thereby making the overall inequality even worse.[18]

Political Implications

The above discussion makes it clear that the potential losers in WTO membership are exactly the same groups that have borne the costs of recent reforms. They are farmers and workers, especially those living in inland provinces. What is the political significance of this finding? Anyone with some knowledge of China must also know that these people have been the very social foundation of the Chinese Communist regime. In the first decades of the People's Republic, farmers and workers benefited from redistribution of land and wealth and enjoyed high political, if not economic, status. Therefore, they supported the regime with no reservations. The early years of reform made their life less secure but, nevertheless, most of them experienced income increases. If there was discontent at all, it was targeted mostly at their immediate superiors, namely, village heads and factory managers. Entering the 1990s, as China's reform looked more and more like a zero-sum game, farmers and workers became more frustrated. In comparison with Mao's era, they found their political and social status declining; in contrast with their expectations of a comfortable life (*xiao-kang*), they have been disappointed by slow material improvement in recent years; witnessing the rise of "the new rich" in Chinese society, they consider the growing gap between the "haves" and the "have-nots" to be unjust and unacceptable. In a word, when farmers and workers make social comparisons, they feel deprived.

The uneven distribution of the gains and costs of recent reforms have given rise to distributional conflicts. Such conflicts take various forms, including revolts against illegal levies in the countryside, labour disputes in urban areas and crimes in society at large. Table 3.5 gives the information about the incidence of labour disputes. In the first half of 1994, the total number of labour disputes was barely 8,000. The same period of 1999, however, witnessed over 55,000 cases, almost seven times the 1994 number. Whereas most labour disputes involve only individual workers, they may

Table 3.5   Incidence of Labour Disputes

Period	Total number of labour disputes	Number of collective labour disputes	Total number of workers involved in labour disputes	Number of workers involved in collective disputes
Jan–Jun 1994	7,905			
Jan–Jun 1995	12,956		31,144	
Jan–Jun 1996	14,852	1,050	40,413	33,646
Jan–Jun 1997	26,600	1,821	97,006	56,425
Jan–Jun 1998	34,879	2,798	134,436	84,208
Jan–Jun 1999	55,244	3,955	230,243	144,273

Source: Ru Xin, *Shehui lanpishu*, various years.

also assume an organized form. As Table 3.5 shows, the incidence of collective labour disputes has also been on the rise, increasing from 1,050 cases in 1996 to 3,955 cases in 1996, quadrupling in the space of three years. These figures indicate that labour-management relations have deteriorated considerably in the last few years. When disputes cannot be mediated through existing institutional means, workers may resort to strikes. There are no time-series data on strikes available, but one thing is certain: Strikes have become a common form of distributional conflict and the incidence of strikes has been increasing. Some strikes involved as many as 10,000 workers.[19] The situation in the countryside is more or less the same.

Growing inequality may hurt the legitimacy of the Chinese government in two ways.[20] First, for a regime whose claim to legitimacy has long been based upon egalitarian principles, it can never justify an ever-growing inequality. Were one to single out one factor underlying the support for the Communist regime by farmers and workers, it would be their expectation of protection from insecurity, inequality and uncertainty by a strong redistributive state. Recent reforms might have been necessary for restructuring the economy, but from the perspective of farmers and workers, those reforms have eroded security, equality and certainty. The government may be able to persuade them that some people must get rich first so that everyone will eventually get rich. But, if it fails to distribute the gains from reforms more or less evenly and if the gap between those who flourish and those who stagnate becomes unacceptably large, then the moral foundations of the regime will be shaken.

Second, higher inequality may lead to slow economic growth. An ability to achieve high growth rates has been used to justify everything the government has done since the late 1970s. Prior to 1997, the Chinese government was able to deliver what it had promised, even though the gains of growth were not evenly distributed. Now the economy is slowing down and no one knows whether the economy can resume its growth potential any time soon. A number of recent cross-country empirical studies sound an alarm: They establish that countries with higher inequality tend to grow more slowly than others. For instance, Alesina and Rodrik (1994) found that inequality variables had significantly negative coefficients in growth regressions, when controlling for variables such as initial income, schooling and physical capital investment. China's own experience seems to confirm this observation. When China was a relatively egalitarian society, its reforms yielded high growth. When inequality reached a relatively high level in the mid-1990s, however, China's engine of growth seemed to lose steam.[21] Economic stagnation may undermine the legitimacy of a regime that gives first priority to growth.

If WTO membership were to further concentrate the benefits of greater openness and market transition in the hands of a few, and no adjustments through redistribution took place, people's patience with growing inequality would wear thin and their frustration would sooner or later reach a crisis point. Experience elsewhere suggests that no political regimes could maintain political stability under conditions of severe economic disparity. China's own history is also full of uprisings, rebellions and revolutions sparked by economic injustice. Social tension and instability are harmful to market-oriented reform and trade liberalization as well as economic growth.

Growing inequality is by no means an inevitable consequence of market-oriented reform or greater openness. There are open market economies with fairly even distribution of wealth and income. An important intervening variable here is the role of government. The government may exacerbate or alleviate inequality in a country. If the government does not pay any attention to the issue of distributive justice, it is not possible for inequality to diminish. However, a government that commits itself to distributive justice may not be able to reduce inequality, either, if its extractive capacity is weak. Only when the government's commitment and capacity to reduce inequality are both strong, is it likely that the distribution of the gains and costs of reform and openness will be fair.

In all of today's advanced industrial countries, the expansion of the role of the market and greater exposure to international trade have gone hand in hand with the strengthening of the institutions of social insurance. The governments in those countries seem to have responded to the fear of internal uncertainty and external risk by showing their commitment and capacity to ensure relatively equal distribution of gains and costs. In other countries (e.g., Latin American countries), market transition and greater openness are often not accompanied by mechanisms that can make domestic and international competition socially bearable. This is due to the lack of either the willingness or the capacity to tackle the issue of inequality, or both. As a result, liberalization is often short-lived.

Throughout the 1980s and much of the 1990s, the Chinese government set aside the socialist ideal of distributive justice. Deng Xiaoping seemed to believe that the prosperity would automatically "trickle down" as long as the economic boom continued. To foster faster growth, top Chinese leaders, therefore, were willing to tolerate growing inequality. In this sense, the increasing inequality in China was part of a deliberate scheme from the outset. By the late 1990s, it became increasingly clear that growth by itself could not address the issue of inequality. On the contrary, growing inequality might derail market reform and imperil future growth. This forced the Chinese government to change its policy orientation. Since 1997, the government has made efforts to ameliorate the polarizing tendencies in Chinese society.

With the commitment to distributive justice restored, what matters now is whether the Chinese government has the ability to deliver. Numerous studies show that the massive fiscal decentralization practised between 1978 and 1993 significantly weakened the central government's extractive capacities (Wang and Hu, 1993). Consequently, the ratio of central revenue to GDP has shrunk to a level far below those in most other countries. The severe fiscal strain deprived the central government of the ability to redistribute resources across the country, even if it had so desired. In 1994, the Chinese government introduced a new fiscal system that aimed at increasing its fiscal revenue. However, while the new system helped to stop the so-called "two ratios" (namely, the ratio of total government revenue to GDP and the ratio of central to total revenue) from declining further, it failed to strengthen the central extractive capacity (Wang, 1997). As Figure 3.11 shows, in the 21 years between 1978 and 1998, the ratio of total government revenue to GDP fell from almost 31 percent to around 12 percent, a drop of nearly 20 percent. The situation was particularly precarious for the central government, whose revenue accounted for only 7 percent of GDP in 1998. Even compared to low-income countries, the extractive capacity of the Chinese central government appears to be weak (Table 3.6). By the mid-1990s, over half of the central government expenditure was

Figure 3.11   Distributive Capacity of the Chinese Central Government

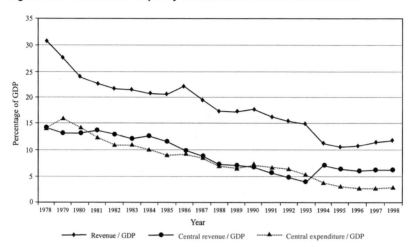

Source: State Statistical Bureau (1999). *Statistical Yearbook of China (1999)*. Beijing:
Statistical Press.

Table 3.6   Central Extractive Capacity in Comparative Perspective

Country/Area	Central government revenue as % of GDP		Central government expenditure as % of GDP	
	1980	1996	1980	1996
China	13.2	5.5	14.4	8.0
Low Income	12.9	14.4	14.8	17.4
Middle Income	N/A	17.9	N/A	19.9
High Income	22.7	28.7	26.2	32.1
East Asia & Pacific	N/A	11.0	N/A	11.6
World	22.2	26.6	25.4	29.8

Source: World Bank (1999). *1999 World Development Indicators*. Washington, D.C.:
World Bank.

financed by debts. With so little at its disposal, the Chinese central government can hardly play the role of redistributor, and is thus unable to tame
market forces and to make them socially bearable.

As China has joined the WTO, globalization may further undermine
the government's power to tax. Foreign investors are very adroit at playing
national governments against one another. In their view, low taxes are
synonymous with a good business climate. If the Chinese government were

persuaded into reducing taxes, its extractive capacity could be further crippled.

The Future

Recent reforms in China have produced both winners and losers. As inequality grows at a very fast pace, the distributive conflicts between the winners and losers have been intensified. It is against this background that China has joined the WTO. If the Chinese government sits by idly and remains indifferent, WTO membership will aggravate the distributive conflict. Such conflict is a threat to political support for the ongoing market-oriented reforms and greater openness. Unless an open market economy is accompanied by institutions that can mitigate the pains it may cause, it will not be able to deliver sustainable growth. When an open market economy becomes socially insufferable, even its own survival will be at risk. "Social insurance legitimizes a market economy because it renders it compatible with social stability and social cohesion." (Rodrik, 1999) Thus, dealing with pervasive economic insecurity should be a key component of the unfinished agenda of the Chinese reforms.

The Chinese government seems to have placed the task on its agenda, which is exemplified by a number of its recent decisions. In the last couple of years, the government has speeded up its efforts to establish social safety nets. In the second half of 1999, the government increased the income of the urban poor, especially of the unemployed and retired. A total of 54 billion *yuan* was allocated to about 84 million urban residents. This was the largest transfer scheme China had even seen.[22] In its coming Tenth Five-year Plan (2001–2005), the government makes the development of inland provinces its top priority, which is a crucial step to narrow the regional gaps. All these moves indicate that the Chinese government has been moving away from the reform strategy that is based on "the Washington Consensus," and is beginning to launch what Stiglitz (1998) calls "second generation reform." Since the willingness to provide social insurance is in place, now the key is whether the Chinese government is able to re-engineer its institutions of resource extraction, a prerequisite for the institutions of social insurance to function.

The Chinese government is aware of this need. Since 1993, it has tried to rationalize its fiscal system. But merely working on the fiscal system may not be able to fix its underlying defects. Cross-national evidence suggests strongly that societies with institutions of voice or participation are better at extracting the social resources necessary for providing social insurance (Rodrik, 1998). Indeed, when large segments of the population lack an effective mechanism of voice in matters that affect them, they would naturally resist any effort at state extraction. On the other hand, if most people do not feel alienated from the economic and social system and believe they have a stake in it, they can be induced to become more co-operative. Hence, the institutionalization of voice is probably the best way to alleviate economic insecurity and eventually produce more stable economic outcomes in China.

Notes

1. See articles and exchanges on such Chinese websites as www.chinabulletin. com, <202.99.23.237/cgi-bbs>, www.washeng.com.
2. Xinhua News Agency, 15 November 1999; *People's Daily*, 18 January 2000; *Economic Daily*, 21 January 2000.
3. OECD, Open Markets Matter: The Benefits of Trade and Investment Liberalisation, Paris, OECD, 1998; IMF, World Economic Outlook, Washington, D.C., May 1997; Anne O. Krueger, "Why Trade Liberalization is Good for Growth," *The Economic Journal*, Vol. 108 (September 1998):1513–22.
4. For instance, the small, highly open economies of central and northern Europe (e.g., Austria, the Netherlands, Norway) have some of the world's highest shares of government spending in GDP.
5. In Chile, for instance, the first priority of the incoming democratically elected government in 1990 was to restore benefits for low- and middle-income groups and to develop new social programmes targeted at high-risk groups, because the country had become increasingly open to trade under the Pinochet regime.
6. During this period, there were moments when the game looked like a zero-sum one. For instance, it was reported that in 1988, more than one-third of urban households experienced a decline in their real income. That was one of the reasons why millions of Chinese took to the streets in the early summer of 1989 (Wang, 1992).
7. Gini coefficient is a measure of relative inequality ranging from 0, absolute equality, to 1, absolute inequality.
8. Unlike most provinces, the three centrally-administered metropolises are much more urbanized and industrialized. As a result, they enjoy extraordinarily high levels of per capita GDP relative to the national average. For this reason, treating these metropolitan areas like other provinces may greatly bias our analysis of regional disparities.
9. Unless indicated otherwise, information about the gains and costs of China's WTO deal comes from www.whitehouse.gov.

10. Associated Press (AP), 10 January 2000.
11. Remarks by the U.S. Secretary of Agriculture Dan Glickman at 2000 Commodity Classic in Orlando, Florida, 6 March 2000, www.whitehouse. gov.
12. AP, 10 January 2000.
13. AP, 10 January 2000.
14. www.cei.gov.cn, 3 December 1999.
15. Chen Wenhong, "The Economic Implications of China's WTO Membership," http://www.future-china.org/csipf/activity/19991106/mt9911_03.htm.
16. Some in China hope that WTO membership would allow the country to export more labour-intensive goods so as to alleviate its employment pressure. A report by the Center of Development Research under the State Council, for instance, forecasts that once China joins the WTO, its textile industry would be able to create 5.4 million additional job opportunities. However, a detailed study done by the State Textile Bureau concludes that the benefits that WTO membership would bring to the Chinese textile industry have been exceedingly exaggerated, because about 80 percent of China's textile exports go to countries that impose no quota control. The WTO membership would not affect such exports one way or the other. It would affect only part of exports to the U.S. and European countries whose markets are protected by the WTO agreement on Textiles and Clothing before 2004. It is estimated that, before the agreement expires, China's exports of textile at best will increase by $200 million each year. Even after 2004, the U.S. has forced China to accept a country-specific textile safeguard that will remain in effect until 31 December 2008, four years after the WTO agreement on Textiles and Clothing expires. Thus, even though China's textile industry is competitive, it is unlikely that its exports of textiles will increase speedily in the next eight years.
17. Chinese economists predict that, before 2005, the incomes of rural residents will drop, while those of urban residents will increase, which will further widen the already existing urban-rural gaps.
18. In Brazil, after a quarter century of liberalization, the difference between rich and poor is wider than ever. Unemployment is over 9.5 percent, and workers' buying power is 27 percent of what it was in the 1980s. The situation in Mexico is more or less the same.
19. Ru Xing, et al. (eds.), *Shehui lanpishu: Zhongguo shehui xingshi fenxi yu yuce* (Social Bluebook: Analyses and Forecast of Social Situation in China) [Beijing: Shehui kexue wenxian chubanshe (Social Science Literature Press), various years].
20. Lipset (1981) points out: "Legitimacy involves the capacity of the system to engender and maintain the belief that the existing political institutions are the more appropriate ones for the society." (p. 64)
21. Why would that be the case? Because "the central processes that determine

resource allocation — through capital markets, through the political system and through social circumstances — are influenced by the distribution of wealth in important ways. More unequal societies tend to develop larger groups of people who are excluded from opportunities others enjoy — be they a better education, access to loans, or to insurance — and who therefore do not develop their full productive potential ... These incomplete realizations of economic potential...affect aggregate economic potential, and therefore aggregate output and its rate of growth" (Ferreira, 1999).

22. *Xinhua*, 5 March 2000.

References

Alesina, A. and D. Rodrik (1994), "Distributive Politics and Economic Growth," *The Quarterly Journal of Economics*,109:465–89; T. Persson and G. Tabellini (1994), "Is Inequality Harmful for Growth? Theory and Evidence," *American Economic Review*, 84(3):600–21.

Alesina, A. and R. Perotti (1996), "Income Distribution, Political Instability, and Investment," *European Economic Review*, 40(6):1203–28.

Bates, Robert and Da-Hsiang Donald Lien (1984), "A Note on Taxation, Development and Representative Government," *Politics and Society*, 14(1):53–70.

Cheibub, Jose Antonio (1998), "Political Regimes and the Extractive Capacity of Governments: Taxation in Democracies and Dictatorships," *World Politics*, 50:349–76.

Clinton, Bill (2000), "Expanding Trade, Projecting Values: Why I'll Fight to Make China's Trade Status Permanent," *The New Democrat, Welcome to Our World*, 1(12) (January/February).

Fan, Ping (2000), "Shichanghua guochengzhong di zhongguo nongcun he nongmin" (Chinese Countryside and Farmers in the course of Marketization). In Ru Xing et al. (eds.), *Shehui lanpishu: Zhongguo shehui xingshi fenxi yu yuce* (Social Bluebook: Analyses and Forecast of Social Situation in China). Beijing: Shehui kexue wenxian chubanshe (Social Science Literature Press), pp. 371–87.

Ferreira, Francisco H. G. (1999, June), "Inequality and Economic Performance: A Brief Overview to Theories of Growth and Distribution." Retrieved from the World Bank, Inequality, Poverty, and Social Economic Performance Website: http://www.worldbank.org/poverty/inequal/econ/index.htm.

For instance, the small, highly open economies of central and northern Europe (e.g., Austria, Netherlands, Norway) have some of the world's highest shares of government spending in GDP.

Haggard, Stephen (1990), *Pathways from the Periphery: The Politics of Growth in the Newly Industrialized Countries*. Ithaca: Cornell University Press.

Hirschman, Albert O. (1970), *Exit, Voice and Loyalty: Response to Decline in Firms, Organizations, and States*. Cambridge: Harvard University Press.

Hoffman, Philip T. and Kathryn Norberg (ed.) (1994), *Fiscal Crises, Liberty, and Representative Government, 1450–1789*. Stanford: Stanford University Press.

Hu, Angang (1999), "Kuaru xinshiji de zuida tiaozhan: woguo jinru gaoshiye jieduan" (The Biggest Challenge in the New Century: China Enters a Period of High Unemployment). Unpublished manuscript, the Chinese Academy of Science.

—— (2000), "High Unemployment in China: Estimates and Policies." Paper presented at International Conference on Centre-Periphery Relations in China, Hong Kong, 25–26 March.

Kang, Xiaoguang (2000), *Bixu liji caiqu cuoshi jiejue shouru fenpei bupingdeng chixu kuoda de wenti* (Immediate Actions Needed to Address the Problem of Rapidly Growing Inequality). Unpublished manuscript, the Chinese Academy of Science.

Katzenstein, Peter J. (1985), *Small States in World Markets: Industrial Policy in Europe*. Ithaca: Cornell University Press, 47–57.

Lardy, Nicholas R. (1999), "China's WTO Membership," Policy Brief, No. 47 (April), the Brookings Institution.

Levi, Margaret (1988), *Of Rule and Revenue*. Berkeley: University of California Press.

Lewis, W. Arthur (1979), "The Dual Economy Revised," *The Manchester School*, 37:212.

Lipset, Seymour Martin (1981), *Political Man: The Social Bases of Politics*. Baltimore: The Johns Hopkins University.

Olson, Mancur (1965), *The Logic of Collective Action: Public Goods and the Theory of Group*. Cambridge: Harvard University Press.

Rodriguez, Francisco and Dani Rodrik (1999), "Trade Policy and Economic Growth: A Skeptic's Guide to the Cross-National Evidence." Unpublished manuscript.

Rodrik, Dani (1998), "Where did All the Growth Go? External Shocks, Social Conflict and Growth Collapses." Unpublished manuscript, Kennedy School, Harvard University.

—— (1999), "Institutions for High-Quality Growth: What They Are and How to Acquire Them." Unpublished manuscript, Kennedy School, Harvard University.

—— (forthcoming), "Why do More Open Economies Have Bigger Governments?" *Journal of Political Economy*.

Ru, Xing et al. (eds.) (1998, 1999, 2000), *Shehui lanpishu: Zhongguo shehui xingshi fenxi yu yuce* (Social Bluebook: Analysis and Forecast of the Social Situation in China). Beijing: Shehui kexue wenxian chubanshe (Social Science Literature Press).

State Statistical Bureau (1998), *Annual of Prices and Family Incomes and Expenditures in Chinese Cities*. Beijing: China Statistical Publishers, p. 9.

Stiglitz, Joseph E. (1998), "Second-Generation Strategies for Reform for China." An address given at Beijing University, Beijing, China, 20 July.

UNDP (1995), *Human Development Report 1995*. New York: Oxford University Press.

Wang, Shaoguang (1992), "Deng Xiaoping's Reform and the Chinese Workers' Participation in the Protest Movement of 1989." In Paul Zarembka (ed.), *Research in Political Economy*. London: JAI Press Inc., Vol. 13 (1992), pp. 163–97.

—— (1997), "China's 1994 Fiscal Reform: An Initial Assessment," *Asian Survey*, XXXVII(9) (September), 801–17.

—— (1997), *Tiaozhan shichang shenhua* (Challenging the Market Myth). Hong Kong: Oxford University Press.

Wang, Shaoguang and Hu Angang (1997), *Zhongguo guojia nengli baogao* (A Study of State Capacity of China). Hong Kong: Oxford University Press.

—— (1999), *The Political Economy of Uneven Development: The Case of China*. Armonk, New York: M. E. Sharpe.

Wen, Tiejun (2000), "WTO yuanzhe dui woguo nongye ji qita fangmian de yingxiang" (The Impacts of WTO Membership on Our Agriculture). Unpublished manuscript, Ministry of Agriculture, 2000.

World Bank (1997), *Sharing Rising Incomes: Disparities in China*. Washington D.C.: World Bank.

Xu, Xinxin and Li Peilin (1999), "1998–1999 nian: Zhongguo jiuye shouru he xinxi chanye de fenxi he yuce" (Employment, Income, and IT Industry: Analyses and Forecasts, 1998–1999). In Ru Xing et al. (eds.), *Shehui lanpishu: Zhongguo shehui xingshi fenxi yu yuce* (Social Bluebook: Analysis and Forecast of Social Situation in China). Beijing: Shehui kexue wenxian chubanshe.

Yang, Yiyong (2000), "2000 nian Zhongguo jiuye xinshi jiqi zhengce xuanze" (Unemployment in 2000 and Policy Options). In Liu Guoguang et al. (eds.), *Jinji lanpishu 2000* (Economic Bluebook 2000). Beijing: Social Sciences Documentation Press, pp. 149–55.

Ying, Shihong et al. (1998), *Dangqian Zhongguo chengshi pingkou wenti* (Urban Poverty in China). Nanchang: Jiangxi People's Press.

4

Redefining Hong Kong's Strategy of Growth and Development

Yun-wing Sung

Introduction

Few people in Hong Kong took note of the devaluation of the Thai baht on 2 July 1997, one day after the reversion of Hong Kong to China. Hong Kong was then enjoying an unprecedented boom. During the fanfare of reversion, the stock market and the real estate market had risen to historic highs. Few could imagine that Hong Kong would soon get caught in the Asian financial crisis (AFC) and suffer the worst economic setback since the Korean War, when Hong Kong lost its entrepôt trade and hinterland as a result of the Communist victory in China and the onset of the Cold War in East Asia.

The severity of the crisis surpassed all forecasts. In March 1998, the Hong Kong government was still forecasting a 1998 growth of 3.5 percent when, in fact, the economy was experiencing negative growth. The 1998 growth rate was –5.1 percent, the worst on record. Since 1961, when official data on Hong Kong's gross domestic product (GDP) became available, the annual growth rate has never been negative until 1998.

Among the East Asian economies with sound economic fundamentals, namely, Taiwan, Singapore and Hong Kong, Hong Kong had the worst economic performance in 1998 (the growth rates of Taiwan and Singapore were 4.3 percent and 0.4 percent, respectively).

Hong Kong's poor performance during the crisis can easily be blamed on its fixed exchange rate system as it has to deflate its wage/price structure to regain competitiveness, which is much slower than depreciating its currency. The pros and cons of Hong Kong's Linked Exchange Rate system is a complicated subject that will be discussed later.

Besides the complications of exchange rate arrangements, the AFC revealed that there were serious limitations in the strategy of Hong Kong's economic growth, which was based on outward processing or relocating labour-intensive manufacturing processes to China, while Hong Kong itself concentrates on providing more skill-intensive services for processing operations in China. Hong Kong was transformed from a low-cost manufacturing centre into the service hub of an industrializing Guangdong in a decade. The process generated substantial incomes for Hong Kong, both from the profits of its investments in China and also from the growth of skill-intensive services. By the time of Hong Kong's reversion, the process of relocating labour intensive manufacturing to the mainland was near completion. The manufacturing labour force in Hong Kong fell from a record of 905,000 in 1984 to 288,887 by 1997. Most of the firms that could have benefited from relocation have already moved. Hong Kong has to look for new sources of growth.

Moreover, the prosperity generated by the relocation of manufacturing led to a real estate bubble which burst in late 1997 with the onset of the AFC, vastly exacerbating the economic crisis. The gigantic bubble can be attributed to a clause in the 1984 Sino-British Agreement over the future of Hong Kong that restricted the sale of new land up to 1997 to a limit of 50 hectares per year. This restriction was a move by Beijing to prevent a suspected conspiracy by the British Hong Kong Government to sell so much land before the reversion that the Hong Kong Special Administrative Region (HKSAR) would be deprived of a most valuable resource.

The restriction was intended to ensure a smooth transition in 1997. However, it turned out to be a very destabilizing factor in the transition. As a result of prosperity and restricted supply, the price of residential property rose sevenfold in 10 years from 1987 to 1997 (Liu, 1998:13). The bubble burst in late 1997 and many home-owners discovered that they were saddled with negative equity.

After the AFC and the real estate crash, policy-makers in Hong Kong realize that they must look for new sources of growth. As it is already a developed economy with a very high per capita income, Hong Kong must specialize in high value-added activities. The promising opportunities are going to be in finance, professional and business services, and innovation and technology. The reversion of Hong Kong to China and the then impending entry of China to the World Trade Organization (WTO) pose opportunities as well as challenges to Hong Kong.

The chapter is structured as follows. After this introductory section, section two discusses the limitations of Hong Kong's strategy of growth and development in the pre-reversion era. Section three discusses the strengthening of the Linked Exchange Rate system, to ward off financial crisis and also to facilitate long-term growth. Section four discusses the new sources of Hong Kong's growth. Section five examines the challenges and opportunities of "one country, two systems" for Hong Kong. Section six analyzes the impacts of China's entry to the WTO on Hong Kong. Section seven concludes.

Achievements and Limitations of Hong Kong's Growth before 1997

In the 18-year period from China's opening in 1979 to Hong Kong's reversion in 1997, the average annual growth rates of Hong Kong's GDP and per capita GDP were 6.2 percent and 4.6 percent, respectively. As the level of development of the Hong Kong economy was quite high in 1979, this is a respectable growth performance. However, the AFC dealt a severe blow to Hong Kong. Even with the 10.05 percent GDP growth in 2000, the real per capita GDP of Hong Kong at the end of 2000 would still be lower than that in 1997. If the economic recovery continues as expected, the 1997 level of real per capita GDP will not be surpassed until 2002.

During its export-oriented industrialization since the 1950s, Hong Kong has accumulated valuable know-how or human capital in the production, marketing and management of labour-intensive consumer products. Such human capital has increasing returns and led to the explosive growth of Hong Kong exports in the 1960s. However, by 1980, such human capital was becoming obsolete with rising wages in Hong Kong. Faced with rising wages, most manufacturing firms in Hong Kong could not relocate their labour-intensive processing activities to low-wage economies overseas because they were small and had limited resources. The opening of China was opportune for Hong Kong as China has the advantage of geographic and cultural proximity.

Achievements and Limitations of Outward Processing

The relocation of Hong Kong manufacturing led to the export-oriented industrialization of Guangdong. From 1978 to 1997, Guangdong's exports (in nominal U.S. dollars) grew at the average annual rate of 23 percent per year, and Guangdong's GDP grew at the average annual rate of 14 percent per year. Guangdong, which ranked seventh in its GDP among the provinces in 1978, rose to the top in 1989. Guangdong has been China's number one province in exports since 1986, in GDP since 1989, and in industrial output since 1995. Guangdong's exports were US$76 billion in 1997 (or 42 percent of China's total), on a par with Switzerland and surpassing Russia. If Guangdong were a nation, it would have been the world's 19th exporter in 1997. It is no exaggeration to say that Hong Kong investment has been the backbone of China's spectacular export drive.

By relocating the labour-intensive processing operations to China, Hong Kong can concentrate on the higher value-added services for processing operations in China, including product design, marketing or order taking from overseas importers, sourcing, quality control, trade financing and co-ordination of shipping. Hong Kong's "take" in outward processing is thus relatively high in comparison with China's.

The "take" of China in export processing is given by the rate of value-added in processed exports, or the rate of processing margin (the percentage by which the value of processed exports exceeds the value of imported inputs, using the former as the base). The rate of value-added for Hong Kong is revealed in the rate of re-export margin (the percentage by which the value of re-exports exceeds the value of imports for re-exports, using the latter as the base).

It is known that the "take" of China is less than that of Hong Kong. The rate of processing margin of China's processed exports (from processing operations or from foreign-invested enterprises) was 20 percent or less from 1990 to 1995, whereas the re-export margin earned by Hong Kong in the same period was around one-third (Sung, 2000: Table 5).

Outward processing is lucrative for Hong Kong partly because Hong Kong's skills in organizing production of labour-intensive consumer goods are valuable, and partly because the rigidity of the Chinese system engenders unnecessary dependence on Hong Kong services. For instance, China's processing operations are dependent on Hong Kong's trade financing because of the system of credit rationing in China, which favours state-owned enterprises. China depends on external investors to perform international marketing and order-taking from overseas importers because it is cumbersome for Chinese nationals to get passports to travel overseas. Processed exports depend on imported raw materials because it is difficult to depend on the quality and reliability of local suppliers. The rigidity of China's economic system hampers the development of forward and backward linkages to local enterprises.

Outward processing has generated tremendous wealth for Hong Kong. From 1993 to 1996, the income generated from Hong Kong's China-related entrepôt trade was 16 percent of Hong Kong's GDP (Sung and Wong, 2000: 225). However, the gain is once-for-all as it arose from the reallocation of resources from low-value manufacturing to higher value-added services. By 1997, manufacturing had shrunk to negligible proportions and the reallocation process was near completion. Only technological progress and innovation can generate continuous economic growth. Moreover, Hong Kong has more or less abandoned manufacturing to specialize in financial and business services. An economy narrowly based on financial services is highly vulnerable to financial disturbances, as evidenced by recent events.

Another weakness of outward processing is that, in the long run, China can acquire the know-how of marketing and organizing the production of labour-intensive consumer goods. Though the process of substituting local skills for those from Hong Kong has been slowed down by the rigidity of the Chinese economy, such substitution is gradually taking place. For instance, China's processing margin has increased from 20.8 percent in 1995 to 34.4 percent in 1998, reflecting the development of both forward and backward linkages.

An example of forward linkage is that China's exports are increasingly using local ports, including Shanghai and Yantian, instead of using Hong Kong's port. The proportion of China's exports re-exported through Hong Kong fell from a record of 50 percent in 1993 to 35 percent in 1999. The share of China's imports from third economies through Hong Kong also fell from 40 percent in 1997 to 31 percent in 1999.

It should be noted that Hong Kong's China-related trans-shipment and offshore trade are not included in re-exports. The decline in China's trade taking the form of re-exports through Hong Kong does not indicate the demise of Hong Kong's middleman role in China's trade. Trans-shipment is not regarded as part of Hong Kong's trade because it goes to the final destination on a through bill of lading, though the goods change vessels in Hong Kong (e.g., from river vessels to container ships). Offshore trade refers to trade that is handled by Hong Kong traders but does not touch Hong Kong at all in transportation.

Recently, there has been a substitution of trans-shipment and offshore trade for re-exports through Hong Kong because China has liberalized foreign investment in shipping and cargo forwarding (Sung, 1998: 90).Within China, it is now easier to arrange direct shipment not touching Hong Kong, or trans-shipment via Hong Kong. It should also be noted that the modernization of China's container ports, including those in Shanghai and in Yantian, has a lot to do with the investments of Hutchison-Whampoa, a Hong Kong company.

However, the declining share of China's trade taking the form of re-exports via Hong Kong does indicate that Hong Kong's role in China's trade has changed somewhat. When a Hong Kong-owned firm in China exports its goods through Yantian instead of Hong Kong, it is likely that the Hong Kong owner and Hutchison-Whampoa will earn higher profits, as the costs of the Yantian port are lower than those of Hong Kong, but it leads to unemployment of Hong Kong truck drivers and Hong Kong port workers. It should be noted that Hutchison-Whampoa is a very profitable global company and only a small share of its profits are earned in Hong Kong. The price of its shares rose to a new record in April 2000.

In a nutshell, in performing its role as the gateway to China, Hong Kong is substituting higher-skilled services (e.g., port management, cargo forwarding) for less-skilled ones (e.g., trucking).

From surveys conducted on Hong Kong's traders (Hong Kong Trade Development Council, 1998), the interviewees expect the bulk of the more skilled trade-supporting services will continue to be performed in Hong Kong. These services include regional headquarters, material sourcing, merchandising, marketing and promotion, market research, business negotiation, trade financing, insurance, freight forwarding and consolidation, product development, and arbitration. However, it is expected that the bulk of the less-skilled services and the production-related processes will be performed in China. These include manufacturing, packaging, quality control, warehousing and inventory control, and sample making or prototyping.

In the long run, more services in the production chain may devolve from Hong Kong to China. To maintain its role as the trading hub of China, Hong Kong has to upgrade its skills continuously as the lower level skills will devolve to China.

Diversification beyond Outward Processing

Outward processing is not a blind alley. The industrialization of Guangdong generates demand for industrial services, infrastructure and personal services as well. Hong Kong's direct investment in China has diversified from manufacturing to real estate, finance, infrastructure, hotels and other sectors as China opened more sectors for foreign investment. Hong Kong was by far the foremost investor in China, accounting for 55 percent of cumulative foreign direct investment (FDI) from 1979 to 1997.

Hong Kong's investment in China is huge. Largely as a result of the size of Hong Kong's investment in China, China has become the foremost recipient of FDI among developing economies since 1992, and Hong Kong has become the foremost source of FDI among developing economies since 1991. Since 1993, China has been the second largest recipient of FDI in the world after the U.S., and Hong Kong has been the world's fourth-largest source of FDI after the U.S., U.K. and Germany.

In 1995, Hong Kong's FDI in China was US$20 billion, or nearly three times the total inward FDI of US$7 billion in Mexico, which was the world's number two recipient of FDI among developing countries. Hong Kong's 1995 FDI in Guangdong alone amounted to US$8 billion, exceeding the total inward FDI in Mexico.

Though Hong Kong's investment in China is huge, the economic integration between the two is highly uneven due to the many differences in their political, legal and economic systems. The integration of export-oriented industries (outward processing) has developed extremely rapidly because their products are exported to the world market, and they are not hampered by China's foreign exchange controls. Foreign investment in industries selling to China's domestic market faces more problems due to China's foreign exchange controls.

Similarly, the integration of service industries is slow because most services cannot be exported and are sold in the domestic market. Moreover, high-end services such as financial services, telecommunications and the information industry are highly regulated, and China's regulatory regime is cumbersome and non-transparent. Despite the many barriers to integration, Hong Kong has been able to achieve a foothold in many service sectors as a result of the vast business network that grew from its pioneering investments in outward processing.

China's entry to the WTO will speed up the integration of services. However, there is a fear that Hong Kong's service providers will lose out to multinational service providers. Again, Hong Kong must upgrade its skills continuously to maintain its lead in the service sectors.

Through its huge investments that started with outward processing, Hong Kong has built a vast business network in East Asia, particularly in China. Companies such as the Hang Seng Bank, the Hongkong and Shanghai Banking Corporation (HSBC) and Hutchison-Whampoa have become truly global. These Hong Kong-based global corporations are valuable assets in Hong Kong's drive to become a world-class city comparable to New York and London.

Strengthening the Linked Exchange Rate System

As mentioned earlier, Hong Kong's poor performance during the AFC can partly be blamed on its fixed exchange rate system. Hong Kong has to deflate to regain competitiveness.

However, a floating exchange rate system has its drawbacks in a financial crisis. Depreciation in a financial crisis is dangerous as it can lead to loss of confidence and further depreciation, as evidenced by events in many East Asian economies. Unlike Taiwan and Singapore, which have some controls on capital flows, Hong Kong's economy is completely open. It is much more difficult to contain speculative attacks once the exchange rate is allowed to depreciate. Though depreciation has worked for Taiwan and Singapore, it might not work for Hong Kong. In a nutshell, the complete openness of Hong Kong's economy dictates its inflexible link with the U.S. dollar, which implies slower adjustment to regain competitiveness.

Costs and Benefits of the Linked Exchange Rate System

Another problem is that there had been defects in the institutional set up of Hong Kong's exchange rate system which were exploited by speculators in the AFC. The defects were remedied in September 1998 by the "seven technical measures" of the Hong Kong Monetary Authority (Yam, 1998).

In spite of this, however, there are still lingering doubts that it may not be strong enough for the next crisis. There are also people who believe a flexible exchange rate system might have served Hong Kong better simply because deflation is slower and much more painful than depreciation.

However, in a world of globalized financial markets, the exchange rate of a small economy can easily fluctuate widely unless there are some capital controls. Capital controls are completely alien to Hong Kong's tradition and philosophy. In any case, the Basic Law forbids such controls.

In terms of developmental strategy, Hong Kong's link with the U.S. dollar and complete freedom of capital movements give Hong Kong unique advantages over Shanghai. The link with the U.S. dollar lowers exchange risks and promotes international transactions. In such financial transactions, Hong Kong thus has a unique edge over other Chinese cities.

Though deflation to regain competitiveness is slow and painful, Hong Kong's labour and wage system has become more flexible as a result of the AFC. In a small economy such as Hong Kong, the prices of land and labour determine its competitiveness. The price of land is very flexible, and commercial rents in Hong Kong are now competitive. Wages (the price of labour) take time to adjust downwards, but Hong Kong's labour recruitment has become much more flexible due to the AFC. Even the civil service, a traditionally highly inflexible institution, has switched to hiring contract labour. Hong Kong is thus much better prepared to cope with the next financial crisis.

New Developments in Financial Infrastructure

It has often been pointed out that Hong Kong could develop into a truly first-rate international financial centre as China's rapid development would imply a huge demand for foreign funds (Liu, 1998:23). Many Chinese enterprises have been listed in the Hong Kong market and, in a couple of decades, Hong Kong could become the world's largest stock market.

Complete openness is a strength for an international financial centre, but it is also a liability in a financial crisis. Moreover, managing the Hong Kong currency will be increasingly difficult as it is used for the transaction of the shares of Chinese enterprises listed in Hong Kong. The volume of such transactions will be exceedingly large. In the long run, it is better to trade such stocks in U.S. dollars to insulate the local economy from the flow of funds involved in offshore financial activities.

The HSBC has agreed to assume the risk of clearing U.S. dollars in Hong Kong and a Real Time Gross Settlement (RTGS) clearing system in U.S. dollars was established in the third quarter of 2000. This will promote U.S. dollar-based financial transactions in Hong Kong and also enhance Hong Kong's status as an international financial centre. Presently, the bulk of syndicated loans and bonds in the Hong Kong market are denominated in foreign currencies (mostly U.S. dollars). A large number of mutual funds are quoted in U.S. dollars. However, stocks are quoted and traded in Hong Kong dollars, though more and more of them are likely to be quoted and traded in both U.S. and H.K. dollars in the future. In this context, the maintenance of the Linked Exchange Rate will strengthen Hong Kong's aspiration to become a world class financial centre.

A Second Board (Growth Enterprise Market, GEM) was established in Hong Kong in November 1999 to facilitate new companies to raise capital. Many new technology companies raised capital through the Board, including technology companies in China.

The New Sources of Hong Kong's Growth

Despite the severe impact of the AFC, Hong Kong's recovery is very strong. The year-on-year percentage change in real GDP in the four quarters of 1999 were –3.0, +1.1, +4.4 and +8.7. The recovery is partly driven by the deflation in Hong Kong's wage-price structure to more competitive levels, and Hong Kong also benefited from the recovery of other East Asian economies.

Hong Kong has also found new sources of growth. These include investments in Internet and Information Technology (IT) companies, strengthening of Hong Kong's position as a financial centre, and promotion of technology and human capital. The Hang Seng Index, driven by expectations and technology stocks, set a new record of 18,300 in late March 2000, surpassing the pre-crisis record of 16,800 in August 1997. While many of the new IT companies have yet to show profits, they have attracted so much investor interest that government officials have repeatedly given warnings of a technology stocks bubble.

The New Economy

Telecommunications have long been an important component of the Hong Kong economy, and Hong Kong has the world's highest per capita ownership of mobile phones and pagers. Since the government's launching of the Cyberport project in March 1999, Internet and IT companies have mushroomed in Hong Kong.

Technology stocks had been the craze in Hong Kong's capital market from mid-1999 to April 2000, when the fall of technology stocks in the U.S. and East Asia ended the craze. Technology stocks accounted for 90 percent of the new public offerings in the last quarter of 1999 and first quarter of 2000. The share of finance and real estate stocks in total market capitalization, which had been dominant in the Hong Kong stock market, declined sharply, and the share of telecommunications and technology stocks rose rapidly. A symbol of the change is that China Telecom surpassed HSBC as the company with the largest capitalization in February 2000. In the one-year period from the end of February 1999 (just before the announcement of the Cyberport project) to the end of February 2000, the Hang Seng Index rose by 80 percent. However, finance and properties stocks rose by only 17 percent and 41 percent, respectively, but the index for commerce and industry stocks, which reflected the movement of technology stocks, rose by 156 percent.

Besides the mushrooming of Internet and IT enterprises, the "old economy" has also embraced IT rapidly. Companies in the "old economy" of finance and real estate that have introduced e-commerce rose from 5 percent to 30 percent of the total in one year.

Some critics regard the craze in technology stocks as a mere bubble. However, besides being an active "new economy" capital market, Hong Kong has some strong advantages in nurturing the "new economy." While Hong Kong is not particularly strong in IT technical expertise, it has no lack of enterprising youths willing to risk their future in the "new economy." Hong Kong also has a vast regional business network encompassing China and East Asia and truly global companies which can back up new ventures through strategic alliances. Hong Kong businesses have a huge potential demand for e-commerce because they run large industrial networks in China, sourcing materials world-wide. Large-scale sourcing can readily support e-commerce and the emergence of logistics centres.

Hong Kong has the potential to be a centre of "new economy" activities, including e-commerce, IT services and financing of technology start-ups. Hong Kong can also attract the regional headquarters of multinationals specializing in IT.

Technology and Human Capital

As mentioned above, technical progress is the only long-run source of growth. During Hong Kong's growth through outward processing in the 1980s, Hong Kong did not invest much in technology. To rectify this neglect, the Hong Kong government appointed a Commission on Innovation and Technology in early 1998. In late 1998, the government announced that an Applied Science and Technology Research Institute would be established to engage in mid-stream research, to bridge the gap between basic research undertaken in the universities and the commercial applications of corporations. An innovation and technology fund of HK$5 billion would be set up. The idea is that Hong Kong can become a regional centre of innovation and technology, drawing on the mainland's research strengths and turning them into commercial applications.

The government's promotion of innovation and technology was first greeted with scepticism. However, the idea caught on fast with the success of technology stocks in the U.S. and in Hong Kong. As mentioned above, many "old economy" companies are adopting IT rapidly.

To become a world-class city, Hong Kong must draw on talents world-wide. Though Hong Kong has been quite open to skilled professionals everywhere, it was paradoxically closed to the mainland's skilled professionals, who are more likely to find Hong Kong an attractive place in which to live and work. In early 2000, the Hong Kong government allowed the importation of mainland talents in innovation and research from the mainland without quota. As the mainland has a vast pool of talents, they may be the key to Hong Kong's future growth.

Challenges and Opportunities of "One Country, Two Systems"

There had been doubts about the viability of "one country, two systems" because it was an untried formula. After nearly three years of experience, most observers agree that the formula has worked quite well, though the period is too short to quiet all sceptics. Most observers agree that China has exercised great restraint towards Hong Kong. In the 2000 rankings of the Heritage Foundation, Hong Kong retained its reputation as the freest economy in the world, despite the "right of abode" controversy and the 1998 government intervention in the stock market.

However, the formula of "one country, two systems" places limits on the possible forms of economic integration. For instance, it is virtually impossible for Hong Kong and the mainland to form a formal trade bloc on the model of the European Union (EU).

Though "old-style" integration based on discriminatory preferences on trade in goods is impractical, the reversion of Hong Kong presents opportunities of "new-style" integration through policy co-ordination. The reversion of Hong Kong, the AFC, and China's impending entry into the WTO have promoted such co-ordination.

"One Country, Two Systems": Limits on Economic Integration

Hong Kong's reversion does not change the framework of Hong Kong-mainland economic relations, which has long been laid down in the Sino-British Declaration of 1984 and in the Basic Law. For all practical purposes, Hong Kong is a separate economic entity. It is a separate customs territory with its own borders and immigration controls. It has a currency of its own which is linked to the U.S. dollar and it runs its own monetary and fiscal policies. It does not pay any tax to the central government.

Despite Hong Kong's reversion to China, there is very little hope that

Hong Kong and the mainland can form some kind of trade bloc such as a customs union or a common market. A customs union is out of the question and it requires that Hong Kong and the mainland levy the same external tariff, which is zero as Hong Kong is a free port. Both the 1984 Sino-British Declaration and the Basic Law have specified that Hong Kong would continue to be a free port. A common market is even more problematic as it requires free migration within the bloc and this runs against Hong Kong's very strict immigration controls against the mainland.

"One Country, Two Systems": Opportunities for Policy Co-ordination

Instead of old-style integration through discriminatory preferences, it is more fruitful to concentrate on the new-style integration through policy co-ordination. Such co-ordination would not contravene the obligations of Hong Kong to the WTO. It is also less likely to affect the international perception of Hong Kong as an autonomous entity. Moreover, such co-ordination would be consistent with the reputation of Hong Kong as a free economy open to the whole world.

Hong Kong's reversion to China in 1997, the AFC and China's entry into the WTO have promoted policy co-ordination between China and Hong Kong. Since 1997, policy co-ordination has moved forward in seven areas, namely, border area issues, regional infrastructure, tourism, technology policy, financial markets, co-ordination to stabilize the exchange rate and co-ordination on China's WTO entry.

Border Area Issues

Border area issues involve border checkpoints, environmental protection and co-ordination of cross-border infrastructure. These issues involve co-ordination with Guangdong, though cross-border infrastructure involves the State Council (the Ministry of Transport and the Planning Commission) as well.

A Hong Kong/Guangdong Co-operation Joint Conference was established in March 1998, headed by Hong Kong's Chief Secretary and Guangdong's Vice Governor. In September 1998, the Joint Conference reached agreements on environmental protection, on minor extensions of working hours of border checkpoints, and on measures to boost cross-border tourism.

To protect the environment, the two sides agreed to subject all large-scale public works in the border areas to environmental evaluation and mutual consultation. The two sides will undertake a joint study of air quality in the Pearl River Delta in 1999, as pollutants in the Delta have led to a substantial deterioration in air quality in Hong Kong.

Congestion of border checkpoints has long been a source of complaint. Passenger crossings often take an hour or more, and a large number of commuters suffer as a result. There have long been proposals to allow 24-hour operation of the major passenger checkpoints, but the agreement reached in late September 1998 after long negotiations is disappointing, as the opening hours of the four land crossings will be extended by only one to two hours. Even after the extension, no checkpoint will be open from 11.30 pm to 6.30 am.

It appears that the Hong Kong government has reservations about 24-hour operation of passenger checkpoints, as retail sales in Hong Kong have plummeted since the AFC, partly because Hong Kong shoppers have swarmed to Shenzhen, where prices of goods and services are much lower. Greater ease of passenger crossing is likely to depress retail sales further and aggravate unemployment in Hong Kong. It will also depress real estate prices in the northern New Territories.

Shenzhen has also proposed to construct a building at the Lok Ma Chau checkpoint, designed for joint inspection to save the trouble of two inspections. However, the Hong Kong government is less than enthusiastic. Checkpoint congestion is a barrier to trade in services. It is ironic that Hong Kong, which is long known as the bastion and champion of free trade, implicitly relies on a trade barrier to protect its employment and other vested interests. However, checkpoint congestion during the Easter vacation of 2000 was so serious that the public was outraged. The government appeared to be preparing for further measures to ease checkpoint congestion.

Hong Kong and Guangdong reached an agreement on five measures to boost cross-border tourism in the Joint Conference of September 1998. Besides facilitating mainlanders visiting Hong Kong, the measures also increased the attraction of Hong Kong to overseas visitors as they can visit more places in Guangdong without a visa. Moreover, Hong Kong tourist agencies can share in part of the tourist business involving overseas tourists visiting Guangdong and also Guangdong tourists visiting Hong Kong or elsewhere.

Regional Infrastructure

It has been alleged that there are too many seaports and airports in the Pearl River Delta, largely because a municipality can obtain a higher status through having an international seaport or airport. Beijing has not been able to rationalize the many airports and seaports proposed by the local governments of the Pearl River Delta (Sung, Liu, Wong and Lau, 1995: 193–98). Bureaucratic co-ordination has been neither effective nor efficient.

Market forces can help to rationalize regional infrastructure through competition. In particular, the participation of foreign capital in infrastructure development would imply more efficient resource use as foreign investors will help government officials to evaluate the cost-effectiveness of projects. Overdevelopment of local airports in the Delta has been attributed to the lack of participation of foreign capital (Sung, Liu, Wong and Lau, 1995:202).

Recently, China has allowed increasing participation of foreign capital in infrastructure projects, including seaports. Hutchison-Whampoa has invested in many ports in the Delta, including Yantian, Gaolan and other feeder ports (Cheng and Wong, 1997:61). Its investment has helped to rationalize the situation and Yantian has emerged as the main subsidiary port to Hong Kong in the region.

Due to the efforts of Hutchison-Whampoa, the design capacity of Yantian reached 1.7 million containers in 1999. However, Yantian needs time to grow and Hong Kong will remain the major hub for years to come, with Yantian serving as a subsidiary port (Cheng and Wong, 1997:62–68). Despite higher costs, the Hong Kong port is very efficient due to its very frequent shipping schedules. For instance, in 1999, Hong Kong had 450 weekly container services to 170 ports in 60 countries whereas Yantian had only 13 weekly services.

Though container throughput stagnated in Hong Kong in 1998 due to the AFC and Hong Kong lost its position as the world's busiest container port in 1998 to Singapore, Hong Kong controlled its costs and regained the number one position in 1999 with a container throughput of 16.2 million. While the share of China's cargo going through Hong Kong will diminish, the absolute volume of cargo handled by Hong Kong will continue to rise.

Tourism

Hong Kong's tourist industry has been severely hit by the AFC because the Hong Kong dollar did not depreciate. At the end of May 1998, the government announced a package of seven measures to stimulate the sagging economy. One of the measures involved a 30-percent increase in the quota allocated to mainlanders joining the Group Tour Scheme to visit Hong Kong (such tours were started in the early 1980s and the quota was instituted to avoid illegal immigration). Another measure was to simplify visa formalities for Taiwanese tourists who tour Hong Kong on their way to the mainland. Such measures brought an upturn. The agreement with Guangdong in September 1998 on promoting cross-border tourism mentioned above also helped. In 1999, total tourist arrivals grew by 11.5 percent, and the number of tourists from the mainland grew by 18.8 percent. Tourists from the mainland exceeded 3 million or around 29 percent of total tourist arrivals.

Hong Kong Disneyland, scheduled to open in 2005, is projected to attract 3.4 million overseas tourists per year. By 2020, the Park will reach full capacity, attracting 7.5 million overseas tourists per year. The bulk of the overseas tourists will be from the mainland and this will necessitate further co-ordination between Hong Kong and China.

Technology Policy

As mentioned above, the government's technology policy tries to synergize the mainland's strength in research and engineering with Hong Kong's expertise in marketing, finance and product design. Importation of talents from the mainland started in early 2000.

Upgrading Hong Kong's technology is perceived to be in the interest of Guangdong and the mainland as the labour-intensive processing industries in Guangdong need upgrading. In July 1999, China's State Council designated Shenzhen a pilot hi-tech development area to promote hi-tech jointly with Hong Kong. Beijing has already approved the setting up of around 50 hi-tech institutions in Shenzhen, where they can co-operate with Hong Kong businesses.

Financial Markets

In 1992, China approved the public listing of selective state enterprises in the Hong Kong stock market. Their shares are called H-shares. Listing in Hong Kong speeds up the mainland's enterprise reforms as listed firms have to follow international accounting standards. Just before the reversion in May 1997, H-shares comprised 24 companies with market capitalization of US$7 billion or 1 percent of Hong Kong's market. The number of

H-shares rose to 39 by October 1997 when the AFC hit Hong Kong. By April 2000, there were 45 H-shares. Growth since the AFC has been slow.

Besides H-shares, red chips (stocks of listed Hong Kong companies controlled by mainlanders) were also important. In May 1997, there were around 50 red chips with a market capitalization of US$49 billion (10 percent of Hong Kong's market). A China-Affiliated Corporations Index or Red Chips Index was introduced starting 16 June 1997 as such shares were very popular.

The AFC ended the red chips bubble. Abuses and mismanagement of China's companies epitomized by the 1998 closure of the Guangdong International Trade and Investment Corporation (GITIC), the second largest corporation owned by Guangdong, continued to dampen investor interest in H-shares and red chips. However, in early 2000, China's expected entry into the WTO revived some interest in red chips.

As mentioned above, as more Chinese enterprises seek listing in Hong Kong, Hong Kong could become the world's largest stock market. The establishment of a U.S. dollar clearing system in Hong Kong in the fall of 2000 would promote the listing of Chinese enterprises in Hong Kong.

Co-ordination to Stabilize the Exchange Rate

Unlike other East Asian economies, the mainland and Hong Kong have stood firm and they have maintained their exchange rates against the U.S. dollar during the AFC. Both governments have reiterated their determination to keep their exchange rates stable. Co-ordination in exchange rate policies between the mainland and Hong Kong have contributed to financial stability in East Asia (Sung, 1998:165–67). President Clinton has acknowledged the importance of the economic roles of the mainland and Hong Kong in the AFC in his visit to China and Hong Kong in late June and early July 1998.

Unlike Hong Kong, the mainland's long-run interest is best served by a flexible rather than a fixed exchange rate. Hong Kong benefits from a fixed exchange rate much more than the mainland because Hong Kong is a small economy where international transactions are relatively much more important. A fixed exchange rate system facilitates international transactions. While many small economies have pegged their currencies to those of their major economic partners, most large economies allow their exchange rates to float. For large economies, the burden of a fixed exchange rate system usually outweighs the gains. However, during the AFC, exchange rate stability served the interests of China as well as that of its neighbours. East Asian financial markets were very unstable in 1998, and devaluation of the *renminbi* would trigger another round of devaluation and financial turmoil in East Asia. China had relatively little to gain from devaluation as long as financial markets in East Asia were unstable.

As financial stability has returned to Asia, China can allow more flexibility in its exchange rate movements. After China's entry into the WTO, China's huge surplus in trade may shrink due to import liberalization. There are signs that China may allow more flexibility in its exchange rate to cope with WTO entry.

Co-ordination on China's WTO Entry

Hong Kong has long supported China's entry into the WTO. Hong Kong government officials and politicians have also lobbied the U.S. government and the U.S. Congress to grant Normal Trading Relations (NTR) status to China in early 2000.

In his Policy Address in October 1999, Tung Chee-hwa announced the setting up of an interdepartmental group chaired by the Financial Secretary to liaise with mainland authorities on matters related to China's WTO entry. Its purpose is to get acquainted with the arrangements for the opening up of the mainland market, and to enable Hong Kong businesses to capitalize on the emerging opportunities. Additionally, China's Ministry of Foreign Trade and Economic Co-operation (MOTECH) and Hong Kong's Trade and Industry Bureau have set up a joint committee since November 1999 to strengthen communication on economic and trade issues. Given Hong Kong's huge trade and investment links with the mainland, policy co-ordination in this area is long overdue.

The Dilemma of Immigration from the Mainland

Most Hong Kong residents have a large number of family members in the mainland. Their migration to Hong Kong is controlled by a quota of 150 per day or 54,750 per year. This quota is a very high barrier to economic integration. Spouses of Hong Kong residents often have to wait for ten or more years before they can migrate to Hong Kong.

Cross-border marriages have become increasingly popular since China's open policy. A 1999 Hong Kong government survey estimated that Hong Kong residents have 794,000 children in China (including 520,000 born outside wedlock), of whom around 267,600 (including 170,000 born outside wedlock) have the right of abode in Hong Kong, according to the Basic Law (i.e., at least one of their parents has to be a permanent resident at the time of the child's birth) (Census and Statistics Department, 1999).

Mechanical calculation indicates that, in five years, Hong Kong can absorb these 267,000 children who have the right of abode. However, their population will keep rising over time, partly because more children will be born to existing couples, and partly because there will be more cross-border marriages. Moreover, part of the quota has to be used for migration of spouses. The absorption of children who have the right of abode can take forever.

Presently, due to fears of population pressure, public opinion is in favour of strict controls on migration, not only for family reunion, but also for children who have the constitutional right of abode in Hong Kong. This mentality is best termed "Superfortress Hong Kong." However, the mentality and logic of "Superfortress Hong Kong" are inconsistent with Hong Kong's long term integration with the mainland. As a result of the high costs of living in Hong Kong, more and more Hong Kong residents have moved to Shenzhen to live and commute to Hong Kong to work. At the end of April 2000, the Hong Kong government estimated that there were 40,000 Hong Kong residents who had moved to Shenzhen (*Ming Pao*, 27 April 2000). A survey of the Hong Kong-China Relation Strategic Development Research Fund revealed that up to a million Hong Kong residents may consider relocating to Shenzhen in the next decade or two.

In the long run, it is inevitable that a large number of Hong Kong residents will relocate to Shenzhen and commute to Hong Kong to work. However, such a scenario is inconsistent with "Superfortress Hong Kong." On the one hand, planners envisage a million Hong Kong residents living in Shenzhen and commuting to Hong Kong to work every day. On the other hand, if these commuters fall in love with mainlanders and get married, their spouses and children have to wait forever to obtain permission to enter Hong Kong. Government officials cannot plan when and where or whom individuals will marry.

The profitability of Hong Kong Disneyland depends largely on the patronage of tourists from the mainland. Government projection indicates that more than 10 million tourists from the mainland will visit Hong Kong every year by 2020. If children who have the right of abode in Hong Kong still have to wait endlessly in the mainland for permission to migrate, many will enter Hong Kong through Disneyland tours and stay illegally.

It is clear that "Superfortress Hong Kong" does not make sense in the long run, and Hong Kong's present stringent controls on migration have to be relaxed. Paradoxically, the ultimate solution to population pressure in Hong Kong lies in deeper integration with the mainland. Hong Kong can encourage people to relocate to Shenzhen by expanding the capacity of border crossings to facilitate commuting. Hong Kong can also encourage retired people to relocate to the Zhujiang Delta by building housing estates there designed for retirees.

Impacts of China's Entry to WTO

It is widely recognized that entry into the WTO will pose adjustment problems for some of China's major economic sectors, especially agriculture and heavy industries (steel, chemicals and automobiles). As long as China can manage the transitional problems, the long-run benefits are large, as WTO entry will boost reform and opening in China. China is going through the most difficult phase of her reform process, namely, reform of state-owned enterprises (SOEs), banks and financial institutions. Entry into the WTO may well provide the decisive boost to China's reform and opening, assuming China can manage the pains of transition.

Neither Hong Kong nor Taiwan are heavily involved in China's disadvantaged sectors, namely, agriculture and heavy industries. Hong Kong and Taiwan are heavily involved in China's export-oriented light industries, which stands to benefit directly from WTO entry. Hong Kong, as the service hub of China, is also heavily involved in China's services sector. WTO entry will speed up the opening of China's services, providing tremendous opportunities for Hong Kong.

Impacts on Exports

Besides gaining NTR status from the U.S., China will also gain some protection against anti-dumping duties that are becoming increasingly prevalent. The WTO has clear procedures on anti-dumping duties. A country that intends to levy anti-dumping duties has to notify the affected country beforehand and can only impose such duties after a process of consultation and investigation that establishes injury for the industry concerned. As China was not a member of the WTO, some anti-dumping duties were levied on China even without prior notification. In early 1993, Mexico levied anti-dumping duties on China without notification. The average duty was a huge 300 percent, with the highest rate exceeding 1,000 percent! Mexico admitted that such a course of action would not have been taken if China were a member of the WTO.

China's textile and clothing exports will expand because the Multi-Fibre Arrangement (MFA) will be phased out in 2005. The greater part of Hong Kong's remaining textile and clothing industries will relocate to China. The gain to Hong Kong will be substantial as Hong Kong has expertise in marketing and organizing production in these industries.

China's entry to the WTO will reinforce the spectacular expansion of Chinese exports and boost the relocation of the labour-intensive industries of Hong Kong and Taiwan to the mainland. Such industrial relocation will again accelerate the structural transformation of Hong Kong into the service hub of China.

Impacts on Industries Selling to China's Domestic Market

While Hong Kong's outward processing industries will benefit from China's entry to the WTO, the impact on Hong Kong's manufacturing companies selling in China's domestic market is uncertain. These companies will face a more open market, but there will also be more competition.

Hong Kong has a strong reputation in the production of auto parts, especially micro-motors for automobiles. China's automobile industry is quite inefficient and needs restructuring. To capitalize on the opportunity, Hong Kong has to upgrade the quality of its products and forge strategic alliances with Chinese and foreign partners.

Impacts on Services Trade

China's entry to the WTO will expand both China's imports and exports. Imports will expand with import liberalization, and exports will expand as China will gain some recourse against protectionism. Given the efficiency of Hong Kong as a trading centre, the expansion of Chinese trade will imply a greater demand for Hong Kong services.

As Hong Kong has a strong comparative advantage in services, China's entry to the WTO will strengthen the position of Hong Kong as the service hub of China. Services require people-to-people contacts. Geographic and cultural proximity is thus very important assets in services trade. Hong Kong residents do not need a visa to visit China. Hong Kong already has a head start in the services sector in China built upon its pioneering investments in outward processing. Hong Kong banks, including the Hong Kong and Shanghai Bank, the Bank of China Group with its 13 sister banks, and the Bank of East Asia have long established branches in China. China's offshore markets in stocks, bonds, loans and foreign exchange are active in Hong Kong. Besides financial services, Hong Kong should be able to find opportunities in telecommunications, IT, e-commerce, advertising and freight forwarding.

However, Hong Kong service providers will face keen competition. China's high capital requirements for foreign banks and high sales requirement for foreign retail and wholesale businesses (annual sales over US$2 billion and US$2.5 billion, respectively) imply that smaller Hong Kong businesses cannot enter the China market on their own. However, with their knowledge and experience of the China market, Hong Kong firms can form alliances with foreign partners.

The Middleman Role of Hong Kong

The Hong Kong stock market has reacted very positively to China's entry to the WTO. However, there are observers who worry Hong Kong will lose its middleman role if China becomes more open because foreign businesses can deal directly with China.

There had been a popular belief, especially in the Cold War era, that Hong Kong's middleman role thrived on China's isolation. That view has been proven wrong as Hong Kong has benefited tremendously from China's initial opening. The more recent worry is that, with China's continual opening and reforms, the gap in skills and expertise between the mainland and Hong Kong is narrowing rapidly, and Hong Kong will soon lose its uniqueness.

Though the gap in economic development between the mainland and Hong Kong is certainly narrowing, it is not likely that Hong Kong will rapidly lose its comparative advantage as a service hub. There are significant economies of scale and economies of agglomeration in trading and service activities and it is very difficult for other cities such as Taipei, Singapore and Shanghai to compete with Hong Kong because Hong Kong is the established centre for China's trade and investment (Sung, 1991:28–42). For the same reason, other cities have found it very difficult to challenge the leading positions of New York and London in world finance.

China is entering the third decade of its reform era and many big multinationals have already entered the China market and are dealing directly with China. China's entry into the WTO will attract a wave of small-and-medium-sized enterprises (SMEs) into the China market. Most SMEs will not be big enough to enter the China market directly on their own, and they will seek help from Hong Kong firms and partners. In this age of electronics and the Internet, the average firm size in developed countries are getting smaller, and SMEs are proliferating. Moreover, even though big multi-nationals are dealing with China directly, they still source supporting services from Hong Kong.

Impacts on Taiwan-Mainland Trade via Hong Kong

Taiwan will be able to join the WTO after the entry of China. There is a popular belief that Taiwan would be obliged to establish direct links with the mainland and Hong Kong would suffer greatly as a result. The belief is too simplistic. Both the U.S. and Cuba have been WTO members for a long time and there are no direct air or shipping links between them.

Tensions have escalated due to the recent election of Chen Shui-bian. Before the election, the mainland was eager to establish "three links" (mail, travel and trade) but Taiwan wanted to go slow. After Chen's election, the reverse seems to be the case. The mainland is blacklisting prominent pro-Chen Taiwanese businessmen.

Under WTO rules, either Taiwan or the mainland can apply the "Exclusive Clause" (article 13 of the WTO Constitution) to prevent direct links. Application of the clause may be difficult as it needs to be supported by two-thirds of WTO members. Even without applying the clause, the mainland or Taiwan can still go slow on direct links. The establishment of shipping and air links requires bilateral negotiations which can get stuck for all kinds of reasons.

However, the entry of the mainland and Taiwan into the WTO may diffuse some of the tensions. The mainland's entry would strengthen reformers and pragmatists in Beijing. Taiwan's international status would be strengthened by WTO membership, Taiwan-mainland business relationships would come under the multilateral framework of the WTO and Taiwan would feel more secure. This increases the possibility of a compromise.

Though WTO membership for the mainland and Taiwan does not imply automatic establishment of shipping and air links, it does demand open and unrestricted market access to member economies. It implies Taiwan has to liberalize its control over imports of selected items from the mainland and also allow direct investment from mainland companies. This would, of course, increase trade and investment between Taiwan and the mainland, even in the absence of direct shipping and air links.

If a political compromise is reached, the prospect of Taiwan-mainland trade is potentially bright, as the two economies are complementary as well as dynamic. It should be noted that Taiwan could unilaterally relax some of its control without the co-operation of the mainland. For instance, Chen Shui-bian is likely to liberalize the restraints on investment in the mainland by Taiwan's major corporations. Such restraints were exercised through foreign exchange and other controls under Lee Teng-hui's policy of *jieji yongren* (restrain from rush and exercise patience).

The opening of direct trade between the two economies will affect Hong Kong's shipping. Presently, Taiwan-mainland trade via Hong Kong amounts to around one million containers or 6 percent of Hong Kong's container throughput. Even with direct links, part of Taiwan's trade with the mainland, especially the trade with Guangdong, will still go through Hong Kong. With direct links, Hong Kong may lose 4 percent of its container throughput, which is not a disaster.

However, the impact of direct air links on passenger traffic and tourism is likely to be more significant. The value of time for passengers is much higher than for freight and passengers are more likely to take the most direct route. Taiwan has long been the second largest source of tourists for Hong Kong. In 1999, Taiwanese visitors to Hong Kong totalled two million, or 19 percent of total tourist arrivals.

The negotiation of direct air or sea links is often very time-consuming in the best of circumstances. With political mistrust on both sides, the negotiations will probably be protracted. The impact of the opening of direct links will very likely be gradual.

Even in the very long run, an appreciable portion of Taiwan-mainland trade and investment may still go through Hong Kong, partly because Hong Kong is the foremost service hub of China, and partly because Guangdong will continue to be an important partner of Taiwan's trade and investment. For instance, though South Korea and China established direct commercial links in 1991, a substantial portion of China-South Korean trade and investment continues to go through Hong Kong.

Mainland-Taiwan reconciliation is in the fundamental interest of Hong Kong and the Asian region. Hong Kong would lose some trade and tourists, but war in the Taiwan Straits would be a disaster for Hong Kong. Even a cold war would be very unsettling for investors. Reconciliation would mean peace and prosperity for the region. Though Hong Kong's share of Mainland-Taiwan trade would diminish, the gains would be greater as the pie would grow faster.

Conclusion

Despite the severe impacts of the AFC, the Hong Kong economy is recovering strongly in 2000. The many defects exposed by the AFC have largely been remedied. Hong Kong's Linked Exchange Rate has been strengthened and Hong Kong's financial infrastructure will soon be enhanced with the capability of U.S. dollar clearing. Measures have been taken to strengthen Hong Kong's technical capacity and a nascent "new economy" is rapidly emerging.

However, while 2000 growth rates are satisfactory, the unemployment rate stayed at the high level of 5.5 percent in early 2000. Even as prosperity is returning, its fruits are distributed quite unequally. Hong Kong's march towards higher value-added services and a knowledge-based economy inevitably implies hardship for those who are less skilled. The problem of unemployment has been compounded by the rapid increase in population due to returning migrants and immigration from the mainland.

As mentioned above, the policy of "Superfortress Hong Kong" is not consistent with long-run integration with the mainland. Hong Kong has to make hard choices and gradually relax the very stringent controls on migration of mainlanders. There will be burdens on Hong Kong's social welfare and social services and also the pressures of unemployment. However, Hong Kong can relieve such pressures through reforms of social welfare and social services. For instance, Hong Kong can impose length of residency requirements on eligibility for social welfare and social services. It is preferable to reduce the economic incentives of migrating to Hong Kong and let eligible individuals choose where to locate their families because the present stringent controls on migration impose huge social and economic costs and disrupt family life. If commuting between Hong Kong and Shenzhen is convenient enough, many families may choose to live in the mainland as long as their right to enter Hong Kong is assured.

By itself, deep integration with the mainland will not correct the problems of maldistribution and unemployment in Hong Kong. However, the problems will be alleviated as the cost of living will be lower in the mainland. Deep integration will also lower the price of property in the New Territories, which will make living in Hong Kong more affordable.

Despite the many joint committees established after the reversion, the present co-ordination between Hong Kong and the mainland is quite ad hoc and reactive, lacking in overall vision and strategy. For instance, 24-hour operation of passenger checkpoints has been delayed repeatedly.

The Policy Address of our Chief Executive, Mr. Tung Chee-hwa, in October 1999 has sections on "Strengthening Ties with the Mainland" and "Joint Development of the Pearl River Delta Region," but there is no articulation of an overall vision of future integration. The articulation of such a vision is important because it would set the basis for a community-wide debate which would raise the awareness and far-reaching implications and potential of deep integration with the mainland.

References

Census and Statistics Department (1999), "Special Topics Report No. 22: Hong Kong Residents with Spouses/Children in the Mainland of China." Hong Kong.

Cheng, Leonard K. and Wong Yue-chim Richard (1997), *Port Facilities and Container Handling Services.* Hong Kong: City University of Hong Kong Press.

Hong Kong Trade Development Council (1998), "The Rise in Offshore Trade and Offshore Investment." Hong Kong.

Liu, Pak-wai (1998), *The Asian Financial Crisis and After: Problems and Challenges for the Hong Kong Economy,* Occasional Paper No. 89. Hong Kong: Hong Kong Institute of Asia-Pacific Studies, The Chinese University of Hong Kong.

Sung, Yun-wing (1991), *The China-Hong Kong Connection: The Key to China's Open-Door Policy.* Cambridge: Cambridge University Press.

——— (1998), *Hong Kong and South China: The Economic Synergy.* Hong Kong: City University of Hong Kong Press.

——— (2000), "Costs and Benefits of Export-Oriented Foreign Investment: The Case of China," *Asian Economic Journal,* 14(1):55–70.

Sung, Yun-wing, Liu Pak-wai, Wong Yue-chim Richard and Lau Pui-king (1995). *The Fifth Dragon: The Emergence of the Pearl River Delta.* Singapore: Addison Wesley.

Sung, Yun-wing and Wong Kar-yiu (2000), "Growth of Hong Kong before and after Its Reversion to China: The China Factor," *Pacific Economic Review,* 5(2):201–28.

Yam, Joseph (1998), "Review of Currency Board Arrangements in Hong Kong," *Hong Kong Monetary Authority,* 5 December. Hong Kong.

5

Hong Kong's Technology Roadmap

Charles K. Kao

Introduction

As an aspiring world city, the development and use of technology have always played an unsung but important role. As we enter the twenty-first century, Hong Kong stands as a thoroughly modern city with an infrastructure comparable to the best world cities. Its use of technology has enabled Hong Kong to march in tune with global progress. Its development of technology is not significant. There is a consensual opinion that Hong Kong must take bold and necessary steps to strengthen its technology development, or lose its healthy competitive position.

Why is the development of technology so important? Hitherto, Hong Kong has made good progress by being able to use technology advantageously. What has changed? Rapid advances coupled with a fast rate of maturation in key technologies are outstripping our ability to adopt the technologies before they become obsolete. Even if information technology is enabling information and knowledge to be readily accessed on a global basis, at an affordable cost, and key technologies are available from multiple sources as they approach a maturity state, we cannot act fast enough to stay competitive.

In this environment, unless we participate effectively in the technology development process, we will not have an opportunity to compete on an equal basis. The cognizance of the time-dependent progress of technologies is of paramount importance. We must participate in the course of technological progress before we can appreciate the evolving market and opportunities for future products and services. With a focused participation in up-stream, and in particular mid-stream research and development to match our advantages, the required foresight for the identification of opportunities will be gained.

This chapter provides an account of the three stages of technology development in Hong Kong: the pre-1983 period, the 1991 Technology Roadmap, and the year 2000 Technology Roadmap. The year 1983 was when the Sino-British agreement was reached for the return of Hong Kong to Chinese sovereignty, as a Special Administrative Region. Towards the beginning of 1990, the awareness of the importance of participating in technology development was heightened for the people of Hong Kong. A technology roadmap was produced and published as a book in 1991. It is interesting to note that the year 1991 roadmap, if implemented at that time, would have given Hong Kong a significantly advantageous technological position as it entered the twenty-first century. However, it is never too late to start, and in the year 2000 Hong Kong is in a better financial position, after nearly a decade of successful economic growth, to make the necessary investment for its entry as a technology participant a success.

Pre-1983 Days

Hong Kong was a trading port undertaking entrepôt business before the People's Republic of China was established in 1949. From that point till 1983, the border between Hong Kong and China was a line of practical separation. Hong Kong found its entrepôt role curtailed. Much of its trade and commerce had to be redirected. With the injection of capital from the people who migrated into Hong Kong from the mainland prior to the closing of the border, a number of manufacturing businesses began operation. The most dominant was the textile industry. Other industries, large and small, sprang into existence. Hong Kong became a manufacturing centre.

After the visit of President Nixon to China, the entrepôt role of Hong Kong for trade and commerce between China and the rest of the world slowly returned. Trade between Hong Kong and the mainland also increased. The availability of low-cost labour in the neighbouring area to Hong Kong stimulated investment, from Hong Kong into China, to establish manufacturing facilities. Gradually, the border was opening.

The Sino-British negotiation for the return of sovereignty to China came initially as a shock to the people of Hong Kong. The immediate aftermath was a loss of long-term confidence by the people of Hong Kong. The British government declared that it was not abandoning the people of Hong Kong and leaving them without any protection. It would negotiate with China a deal that would allow Hong Kong to operate without changing its then current status, for 50 years. In 1983, when the principle of "one country, two systems" with a basic law for Hong Kong (prepared with direct Hong Kong participation) was agreed, the fears of the people of Hong Kong were largely allayed. Nevertheless, many people migrated to other countries around the world, seeking the right of abode in the countries of their choice. For a while, the exodus seriously depleted talents available in Hong Kong.

The 1991 Technology Roadmap

After 1983 came the period when the Hong Kong government under British jurisdiction attempted to deliver Hong Kong as a jewel to China on 1 July 1997. The Tiananmen incident did shake the confidence of the people of Hong Kong and the British government introduced a scheme to allow some Hong Kong people to have British citizenship with the right of abode in the U.K., and started making efforts to substantially improve Hong Kong's infrastructure, so that Hong Kong would be a viable world city to compete with possibly even London and New York. These actions were taken as a means to shore up people's confidence, and as a way to maintain the prosperity of Hong Kong, an action welcomed by both Hong Kong and Britain, and even by China. Before the actual date for Hong Kong's return to China, with a number of years of stability and with increased opening of China, most people had by then made plans to stay in Hong Kong. During this period, real estate was booming. The industrial sector moved their production to the neighbouring regions in the Pearl River Delta. The neighbouring town, Shenzhen, became a satellite industrial town of Hong Kong. The size of the labour force employed by Hong Kong interests in the Delta a labour force which came from all parts of China increased over this period to several million. Hong Kong became a service centre providing both consumer and producer services.

The government continued to hold advisory committee meetings such as the Industrial Technology Development Council (ITDC), where government officials, industrialists and academics, in their personal capacity, gave advice to the government on industrial and technology issues. The sub-committees of ITDC covered all the important industrial sectors. Through these committees, consultants were invited to review the position of the industrial sectors and to provide strategic decisions. One sub-committee, named the Technology Review Board (TRB), undertook an overall review process. The 1991 Hong Kong Technology Roadmap (Kao and Young, 1991) was one of the products of this Board. A summary of the

Report is presented here together with a selected extract on Information Technology (IT).

Summary of the 1991 Roadmap Report

An in-depth investigation into four areas of technology with particular potential for Hong Kong was undertaken. These areas were:

Information technology
Biotechnology
Materials technology
Environmental technology

Since the nature of these technologies and Hong Kong's position in each were very different, the four Parts were handled separately and in formats appropriate to each. The common emphasis running through the presentation of all the technology areas was the use of specific illustrative examples to focus the analysis. For each technology area and with particular reference to the examples, the then current research and development (R&D) status in Hong Kong was given, together with an assessment of the additional R&D required to bring products to commercial viability. The comparative advantages of Hong Kong were emphasized, since these advantages provided the main justification for commercial development in the face of worldwide competition. This method of analysis permitted an in-depth discussion leading to firm conclusions, and avoided the pitfalls of vagueness and over-generalization that would be inevitable in any attempt at completeness. However, the materials technology section presented a more generic discussion, necessitated by the more fragmented nature of that sector in Hong Kong.

The strength of the economy of Hong Kong lay principally in the financial and trading sectors, while the sector characterized by advanced technological development and innovation had yet to emerge as a mainstream local industry. It was the goal of this study to provide illustrations of some promising processes and their necessary supporting structure that could assist the growth of this important industrial sector. The roadmap concept was adopted to allow the readers, as it were, to walk from the present situation to the target technological opportunities, with an awareness of the R&D investment issues involved. Through this study, the messages to the investment community and to the entrepreneurial indus-trialists were clear: namely, (1) opportunities were available for developing new technology-based industries in Hong Kong, and (2) the tertiary education sector was ready to deliver technical assistance in a variety of ways.

Using the metaphor of a roadmap, the study considered both the starting point (the present technological and infrastructural strengths and weaknesses of Hong Kong, as well as assessments of the global scene and market), the destination (represented by the potential business opportunities) and the road to get there including the toll costs (represented by R&D and other investments). It was up to entrepreneurs to make their own choices based on estimates of cost, risk and benefit. An illustrative technology roadmap in pictorial form is shown in Figure 5.1.

Analysis of the Impact of Information Technology

Information extracted from the 1991 Roadmap showed the impact of technology on the information industry in 1991.

Equipment-makers

Traditionally, equipment-makers in the telecommunications industry worked closely with the carrier network operators in anticipation of the service demands of the customers. They designed and manufactured customer premises, system and network equipment. Vast investments were made in technology R&D with the aim of extending the capabilities of the network for delivery of telephone-related services at better quality and lower cost. This healthy and productive marriage between the equipment-makers and the network operators greatly benefited the customers.

Recent developments in the provision of information services had been pushed by advances in technology and pulled by the rising importance of information flow for business and for entertainment. As a result, a broad range of new businesses were created. Private networks were built to compete with the public carriers. Cable TV (CATV) networks were constructed for the explicit purpose of distributing television programmes to customers through cables. With the extensive use of optical fibre cables in all the networks, the distinction between these networks was disappearing. New services could proliferate and could be introduced in any of these networks.

The equipment-makers faced a new competitive environment, with networks provided by a multiplicity of players in an increasingly deregulated environment. Technological advances increased design versatility and

Figure 5.1 Technology Roadmap in a Conceptual Context

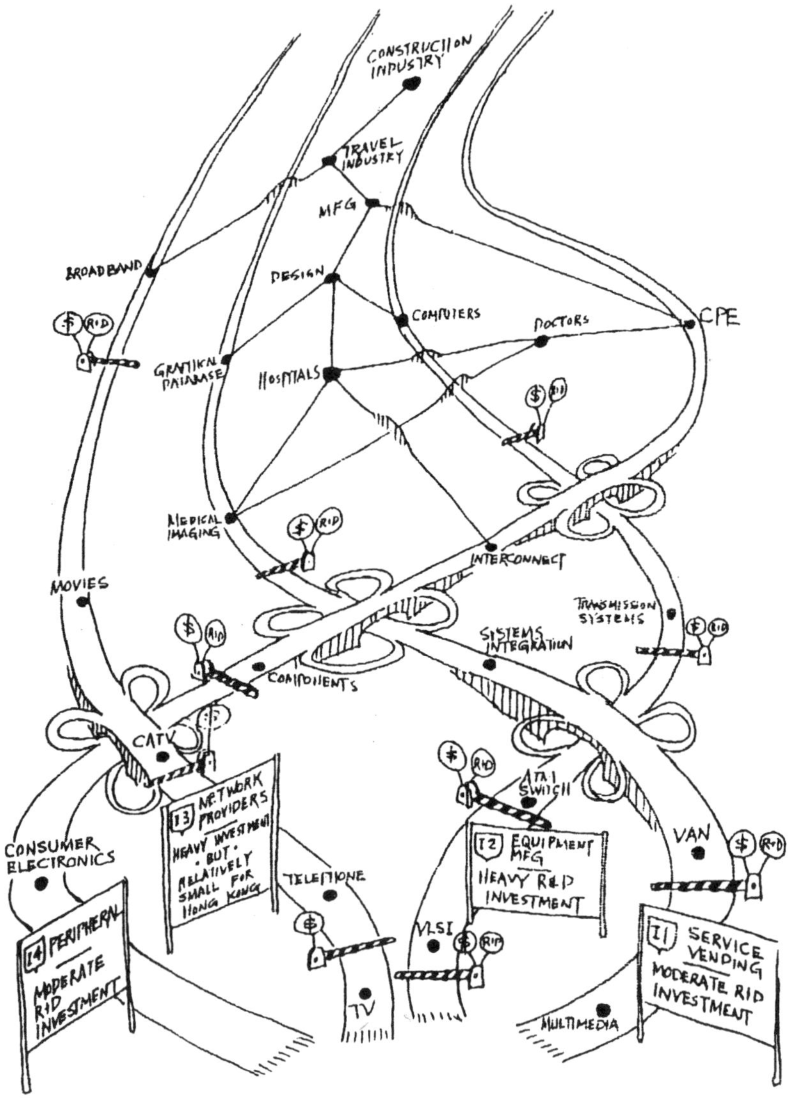

Source: Kao and Young (1991), p. 29.

adaptability to the extent that equipment interconnectivity was the key to success.

Network Operators

Common carriers operated in a regulated environment. They were obliged to connect all customers, however remote, to the telecommunications network. The customers could connect approved equipment such as telephones, computers and fax machines to the network. The calls were charged by the carrier operators according to time, distance and bandwidth at a rate approved by the regulatory commission. The approval was given based on justifiable capital and operation costs, and on an acceptable profit margin.

The common carrier operators strove to satisfy all customer demands at a low charge per call, with little or no waiting time, and with many convenient call features. This was achieved by working with the equipment-suppliers to improve call features and to reduce cost per call through technological improvements.

In most developed countries, the monopoly status of the common carriers was gradually eroded through deregulation. First, by-pass networks were permitted to either lease lines from the common carriers or to construct their own networks and connect selected customers, mainly corporate users, at a lower rate per call-minute along a given route. Second, alternative cellular radio networks offering switched connections for telephone and paging services were permitted to operate as independent competing entities. Third, value-added services were introduced as deregulated services on any network.

The role of the common carrier network operators was forcibly changed. They operated in a dual role, that of network providers and that of service providers offering certain network features and value-added services. They had to prepare for the gradual but inevitable deregulatory trend and for entry into the deregulated information service markets.

The legacy of a regulated operation and the incompleteness of deregulation in the foreseeable future would influence the strategy of the common carrier operators. They would continue to act mainly as the network provider, preferring centralized rather than distributed network control. They would shy away from service provision and yet would not like the service vendors to take the necessary control of some of the network functions. Meanwhile, the regulatory commissions continued to act with insufficient understanding of the complex effects of deregulation. This state of affairs could emasculate the network operators and would encourage the entry of agile and aggressive service vendors on alternative networks, possibly with different tariff arrangements.

Service Vendors

CATV was a new common carrier for entertainment on television. A cable television company installed the CATV distribution network and organized the reception and transmission of TV programmes to the subscribers. It differed from the telecommunications common carrier network operators in two distinct aspects. First, it sold a service, namely, provision of high quality TV programmes, to the customers at a charge. Second, it relied on TV broadcasters, super-stations and local studios for the TV programmes. These vendors of entertainment services resembled the telecommunications network providers only in that they constructed and maintained a relatively independent network specially constructed to reach the customers. In many ways, a CATV company was an entertainment services vendor with an integrated approach.

Given a city or a country criss-crossed with fibre networks for tele-communications and CATV, it was definitely possible for new service vendors to utilize the spare bandwidth capacity of these networks to provide new services. In fact, the value-added network services such as Merrill Lynch's stock market information service, legal document search service and journal article database service were examples of information services provided on existing telephone networks by service vendors as separate independent viable businesses. With the introduction of integrated services digital networks (ISDN) and the broadband networks, data and voice services would be joined by services involving video signals. Already the possibility of providing so-called multimedia services was arousing considerable interest. The combination of video film footage, still pictures, voice, music and text is a powerful combination of entertainment and information service in this information intensive age.

One such service, namely, the medical imaging service demonstrated how the network information handling capability could be utilized for a new form of socially important service. The implementation of such a new service on existing fibre networks would yield valuable experience in developing the necessary auxiliary interconnection hardware and software and the system integration know-how. It would demonstrate the viable business prospects of the medical imaging service.

Customers

Customers believed that very soon, a variety of services would be available catering to their every wish, whether for improved conveniences or for newly identified needs. The network providers and the service vendors were eager to satisfy this potentially huge market demand. However, we lacked the experience of integrating the right elements together to make new service introduction less of a financial risk. The early failures in the introduction of new services such as the picture phone by the common carriers, and the interactive TV by the cable TV operators, made network providers very nervous about introducing any new service. The service vendors were also cautious and would only venture forward one step at a time, deeply conscious of the difficulties faced in their early attempts.

A combined effort at tailoring a customer-defined service with full participation of the service vendor, network provider, equipment manufacturer and system integrator was the likely way to success. The market should be predefined and the investment and return should be predicted. A good candidate could be the medical imaging service. It was sufficiently similar to a telephone service in that all hardware and software could either be bought or readily adapted from existing products. Control and operation were sufficiently familiar for all concerned. The social and economic benefits could easily be identified. Improvements could benefit the speed and quality of service delivery. Some multimedia system approaches could be introduced. A graphic database, a distributed vector database and graphic computer-assisted design (CAD) tools would open up a path towards developing a host of multimedia services.

This combination of effort could occur in Hong Kong, especially if the rules for access to and interconnection of the communication networks could be resolved. In fact, there was no better place than Hong Kong, with all the right prerequisites already in place, for this development to occur. It could establish for Hong Kong several important new businesses in the information vending, network operation and system integration areas, besides strengthening its electronics hardware and software enterprises.

Broadband Technology Underpinning Information Technologies[1]

The development of a new medical imaging service as a precursor development led to the development of a host of broadband integrated services in Hong Kong. Medical image transfer had been identified as the candidate for initial application on the new broadband-integrated services digital networks (B-ISDN) because of the timeliness of its social and economic benefits and also because its implementation was regarded as a good representative of a wide range of broadband services. The experience from this application would lead to better understanding of many new issues such as equipment connectivity, network operation, multimedia integration, gateway connection between private and public broadband communication networks, and evolution of customer premises equipment.

The possibility of developing B-ISDN was strengthened by recent advances in fibre-optic transmission technology and high-speed, high-density integrated circuits. Research on concomitant broadband technologies in switching, image processing, traffic flow control, distributed database and services integration had also been making significant progress. Academic research on broadband communication networks had been intensive throughout the last decade, and the total R&D investment by manufacturers in the U.S., Japan and Europe came to billions of dollars. To launch a trial of broadband services, the fundamental enabling technologies already existed, and the local communication researchers plus their overseas contact network were able to point the way to the acquisition of state-of-the-art technology. Many hardware components were available on the market, including circuit switches, network operation equipment (OA&M), databases, remote electronics (RE), local area networks (LAN) and various interface modules. Research prototypes of some other components, such as the asynchronous transfer mode (ATM) packet switch, also existed. Customer premises equipment (CPE) suitable for certain broadband applications also existed, including workstations, displays, printers and image processing oriented super computers. The major effort needed in putting together a broadband trial would be in the area of software development, especially in call-processing software and application software.

Switching

A B-ISDN node equipped with switching capability would allow flexible connections among users. In some applications with very light traffic load, switching might possibly be performed through broadcasting over a LAN. But, in general, a switch would be needed.

There were two basic approaches in broadband switching: circuit switching and ATM packet switching. Circuit switching applied to fixed-rate communications and ensured a fixed switching delay. ATM packet switching, in principle, could apply to all types of communications. Since the B-ISDN was to provide services of a variety of bit rates, call-attempt rates and holding-time characteristics, no single switching technology could be optimal for all individual traffic types. In fact, for both the efficiency of switching and the smooth evolution of the telecommunications network, it was unlikely that all traffic types should be integrated at the switching level. Therefore, while ATM switching would be indispensable for many types of services, circuit switching would probably also remain in the network. In fact, the transport of voice data for plain old telephone service (POTS) was likely to stay with circuit switching for a long time, and even the transport of the control data for POTS could take years to become integrated into the packet traffic.

The huge bandwidth of single-mode fibres permitted independent services to be introduced along the same physical network as if they were using separate lines, with independent switching and control, greatly simplifying system management and switching. Different services probably should be categorized according to the mechanisms of management and switching in their implementation rather than the line of business in their applications. Ultimately, a multi-media application might have to invoke several different categories of services at the same time.

Customer Premise Equipment (CPE)

The variety of CPE items was quite application-dependent. Typically, workstations, databases, application processors, information generating/receiving devices, and remote control devices were involved.

Broadband applications in the medical industry were associated with medical imaging. This included high-resolution scan images and the dynamic display of three-dimensional images for modern reconstructive surgery. The bulk of the database capacity was needed for storing picture data. To process such medical images, massive processing power was needed. A super computer specially designed for this type of task was the Connection Machine with an accumulated power of two gigaflops (billion floating point operations per second) over its numerous parallel processors. The price ranges between US$1 and 2 million. For diagnostics, remote control of cameras was available, but remote control of scanning tools were still under development. At that time, computer-aided Tomography (CAT) scan and magnetic resonance imaging (MRI) scan stored the images on disks, which were manually transported onto workstations for processing.

Depending on the nature of the application and on the characteristics of the user, CPE could be connected to the public broadband network either directly or through the gateway of a private network. An institutional user with substantial internal traffic might want to have its own private LAN in order to achieve information privacy, a reduced tariff charge, and an insulation from possible interference from the public network. Also, a private network would be suitable for the initial field trial of new services. A private network with the digital standard 3 (DS3) bit rate of 44.7 Mb/s typically costs US$70,000. The DS3 rate is suitable for the transmission of full-motion video with the grade of resolution depending upon the degree of data compression. A DS3 interface for connecting to the versa module eurolard (VME) bus of, say, a SUN microsystem workstation, typically costs US$20,000.

Image Processing, Compression and Animation

Video communications were expected to generate the bulk of broadband traffic. There would be at least two kinds of video data. The first type involved visual images such as medical image transfer, high definition television (HDTV), picture phone and on-line movies. Another type was the visualization of numerical data in science, engineering, social statistics, the stock market and other professions. The application of video conferencing could conceivably include shared viewing of both kinds of video data.

The bit rate of the state-of-the-art switching technology was relatively limited in comparison to the transmission bandwidth over single-mode fibres. Image compression reduces the bandwidths needed for switching, as well as transmission. Currently, the most popular approach for the compression of both still and motion pictures is discrete cosine transform (DCT). Certain techniques in computer graphics were being applied to the processing of motion images, for example, the identification of separate entities within a picture.

Image processing, compression and animation research were actively pursued. Multimedia (vision plus other media) communications and data visualization were also becoming focuses of attention.

Advent of Year 2000

Analysis of the Impact of Other Technologies

From the extract from the 1991 Roadmap, we see how technology progress changes the structure and operation of the information industry. Similar analyses were given in 1991 for biotechnology, materials technology and environmental technologies. Readers may refer to the 1991 report for details. As we move past the year 2000, we can add the following new tasks as work to be done.

1. For IT, software, particularly open software technology and netware, is a good topic. We need to design and build system hardware and firmware that are adaptable to anticipated system and network changes either through rapid redesign or through software changes. The future demands will be wholly application driven which in turn are driven by changes in the mode of transactions and communication.

2. For biotechnology, Chinese medicine is a good choice. A lead compound that binds with bodily receptors is regarded in Western medicine as the molecular level facilitating an understanding of the potency of medicine. In Chinese medicine, the multi-element brew seeks to restore the equilibrium of the bodily functions. The first useful step in merging these two approaches is through the use of analytical techniques including the use of biotechnology. Chinese medicine, with thousands of years of empirical practice, has yielded proven medicine with curative effects. The new technology can be applied to set better quantitative limits to the usefulness of these proven medicines as a first step towards setting some quantitative limits for the active ingredients. The field has great potential but the road forward is far from clear. However, quantification can introduce greater confidence in people using this form of medicine, and thereby establish a much larger market.

3. For materials, key materials for surface finishing, packaging and environmental safety are important. The plastics industry in Hong Kong has already been developing plastic materials for a host of applications and has even entered the area of making injection molding machines and other tools. The extension of this work includes active materials for electro-conductance and luminescence. Recently, polymeric materials have been found to be a useful substrate for building nano devices with the unit active device reduced to a single atom.

4. For nano-technology, producing one or more devices or sub-systems involving the use of active elements of atomic dimensions might be a good start. A sensor could be a likely candidate.

5. Environmental technology has grown in importance and may now be

incorporated in every area of technology. Hence it is no longer mentioned separately.

An additional, and fundamental reason for choosing the above five areas is that all these areas are undergoing a significant technological stepwise transition caused by our ability to manipulate matter at the atomic level. While atomic size devices and applications are unlikely to appear within the next two decades, the limits of our current technology will gradually fall away. Our advanced instrumentation has allowed us to begin investigating atomic-scale actions, explicitly instead of implicitly. Our vision has been broadened. At this critical phase, we have a unique opportunity to enter the race on a level playing field.

The Need to Develop Technology

The remarkable growth of the economy of Hong Kong over the past decades was caused by a rapid increase in domestic production, and more importantly by a significant shift in economic activities. The shift was towards economic sectors with greater sophistication and higher added values. Container and air transport, financial services, electronics and computers, as well as fashion apparel and up-market toys gradually displaced plastic flowers, cheap radios and the lower end of the textile industry. While many factors contributed to these developments, public investment into the necessary infrastructure has been vital. Infrastructure is to be understood here in a broad sense, embracing not only physical structures such as roads, ports and industrial buildings but also education, communication capabilities, the banking and financial system, and indeed, the very framework of government, especially as it related to trade and industry. The community and, in particular, the government can be justifiably proud of the forward-looking strategic planning that was adopted in the past decades, without which we would not have the infrastructure so much taken for granted today.

The shift in the economy led to a marked improvement in the economic well-being of the average Hong Kong citizen. The opportunities for upward mobility contributed to social and political stability and helped shape the perception of Hong Kong as a vibrant metropolis, both in our own eyes and in those of the world. These remarks, nonetheless, were valid, oft repeated and well known. They emphasized the need for looking ahead and planning for future infrastructural needs.

In the decades ahead, Hong Kong, as an economic entity, will rely on a broad spectrum of activities; in addition to finance, tourism, management services for industries sited in the Pearl River Delta and entrepôt trade, industry will certainly continue to play a prominent role. Hong Kong's experience since the 1960s, like that of Japan and the other Asian NICs, confirms that a trend towards greater utilization of modern technology is inevitable in the industrial sector, as well as in the service sectors. The industrial and service sectors need not be sharply distinguished. Many of our industries in a sense provide services (e.g., the telecommunications industry) while the service sectors make use of many products produced by technological industries (e.g., the use of computers in banking). Technological innovations not only allow traditional needs to be fulfilled more efficiently, but also create novel needs. They represent novel and exciting business opportunities that are being created at an unprecedented rate. Future technology needs and opportunities must be anticipated, and the necessary technology infrastructure must be put in place. The need is urgent, since competitive neighbours, especially Taiwan, Korea and Singapore, are directing vast public resources to the development of a broad range of technologies. The threat to the continued competitiveness of Hong Kong has become evident, indeed alarming.

Technology Policy

In the light of these circumstances, a large measure of consensus is emerging within the community, that steps must be taken, as a matter of priority, to foster the development of technology in Hong Kong. There is, however, less agreement on what the most effective steps might be, or the extent to which government should be involved in "intervening" in the "natural" course of economic development, especially through the disbursement of public funds in building up a technology infrastructure. The failure to reach an agreement could be blamed on viewing technology as one undifferentiated type of activity. Government should invest public funds and adopt a forceful policy on infrastructure items in technologies.

This problem is exacerbated by the different images that the term "technology" conjures up. Some equate technology with such industries as aerospace, semiconductor chips and mainframe computers, areas in which Hong Kong obviously could not compete head-on. To others, the term could mean the adoption of technological products as tools in existing industries, which would not by themselves be labelled as technological enterprises; examples could include lasers for cloth-cutting in the garment industry, mainframe computers in banks and facsimile transmission or cellular telephones in business. One might then say that Hong Kong is in many respects already at the forefront of technology usage. Yet others see technology as enterprises heavily dependent on R&D, and thus argue for massive increases in R&D expenditure, in both the public and the private sectors.

The way out of this maze of contradictions is to attempt a much closer look at the technology landscape, in order to differentiate the various sectors in terms of their requirements and potentials, in relation to the particular circumstances of Hong Kong. By singling out individual items and business opportunities that appear promising, the necessary policy and investment questions could be brought from the abstract down to the particular, and be answered in some reasonable and objective fashion.

The Need for Selectivity

The necessary technology infrastructure involves the provision of: places for tertiary and postgraduate education, access to information resources, and measures to attract and retain skilled and experienced personnel. However, there is also the need to provide a comprehensive infrastructure for individual technology sectors. To cover all key technology bases would be prohibitively expensive, while to select any specific technology for preferential development would carry connotations of intervention. There is understandably a need for caution.

Actions Taken After the 1991 Roadmap Report

Looking at the various consultants' reports (Appendix), generated after 1991, for the various industrial sectors, the actions suggested by the 1991 Technology Roadmap were obviously not taken on board by the consultants. Many of the recommendations made by the consultants were to simply purchase the then latest equipment, replacing the less efficient older machines, thereby achieving cost reduction and quality improvement of the products for the competitive markets. Creative designs and good adaptation of machine functionality were accomplished through downstream research and development work undertaken locally.

In the meantime, the larger industrial companies made significant progress in building optimized operations, by spreading their manufacturing, design, transport, and distribution processes globally, to achieve high efficiency and the lowest costs. This approach enabled these companies to shorten the time interval between taking on an order and delivering the products. Despite the thin margin, they succeeded in delivering quality products, quickly and at highly competitive prices, from the factory to the store floor for immediate display. In addition, Hong Kong companies were able to be the suppliers of a vast array of products with an aggregated operational efficiency close to that of a single product company. This was no mean achievement.

At the same time, despite the 1991 Roadmap, which could have given Hong Kong an earlier start in increasing its value-added activities, being left to gather dust, the action taken during this time period did begin to make people aware of the importance of technology. Ten years later, a window of opportunity triggered by the economic downturn in Southeast Asia in 1998 revived the interest in technology. Within 15 months, an inflow of capital started. At this juncture, Hong Kong, with its experience of operating globally and at maximum efficiency, saw the opportunity to innovate with the use of technology. Hong Kong was preparing itself to deliver the best manufactured goods and services, and would do so at maximum value addition to any product or operation.

By 1991, Hong Kong was ready for moving to high-value addition, innovation and technology-driven producer activities. The delay was due principally to the pre-occupation of society with making money from real estate. On the other hand, the delay allowed Hong Kong to achieve a real growth in its economy. It was also fortunate that the 1998 financial crisis arrested the price increase spiral in Hong Kong and stopped the speculative pressure to squeeze more profit out of the real estate sector. The 40 percent fall in real estate value rescued Hong Kong from reaching an unsustainable cost base for development of any productive economic activities. It was also fortunate that the timing for entering technology and innovation-driven productivity was just right for Hong Kong. The opening of new markets in the IT service industry was extremely timely. Being a communications centre, Hong Kong had a state-of-the-art communication network strategically connected to the global network. The development of IT services would improve every endeavour in the commercial sector and the industrial sector. Within the past few years, Hong Kong has opened its broadband network facilities, and a large number of IT services, aimed at promoting and improving business efficiency and effectiveness. Hong Kong showed interest in tapping the maturing strength of the biotech-based industry, materials industry, etc. Its electronics based industry was ready to enter hi-tech operations. It was interesting to note that the plastics material industry had already entered hi-tech operations in 1996.

The Year 2000 Scenario

The New Role of R&D

The requirement for R&D in technology for a country, a region, or a corporation engaged in specific activities, obviously differs in the scale and the scope of the activities involved, as well as in the specific coverage. Hong Kong recognizes its need to engage in R&D in support of its delivery of services, especially in financial and producer services. The purpose of direct participation in selected R&D work is to provide a better recognition, and a sharper focus on Hong Kong's ability in using technology to improve its competitive edge in the global market.

It is the rapid advances in technology that have made the conduct of R&D imperative. Up-stream research pushes the frontiers of knowledge and opens new avenues for the discovery of techniques and materials that delimits our current knowledge and technical capacity. Mid-stream research looks at promising discoveries in more depth and directs them to useful purposes. Such research is conducted with special applications in mind and is directed towards achieving the breakthroughs necessary for significant improvement in techniques, materials, devices, sub-systems or systems. Down-stream research is directed towards incremental improvement in available tools needed for next generation products. Much of down-stream research is aimed at making products with improved specifications and at a lower cost. Development is the process of making a product to fit form, function and market requirements.

As technology advances accelerate, two issues become apparent. Transfer of technology becomes less practical, since within the finite time period it takes to do the transfer, one or more new technologies could make the technology under transfer obsolete. The fast maturing new technologies could open up new market sectors for a range of new products enabled by the emerging new technologies. These two facts make direct participation in research necessary. It is the participants who can sense the opportunities early and have the option of taking the necessary action towards the creation of new products for the new market.

Hence, with technology advancing rapidly, the playing field for a new entrant with a new product can be relatively level. In other words, adding innovation to the foresight gained through R&D, the entrant can create a level playing field with improved products for existing markets as well as for new markets. It does imply that catching up is no longer a viable means to compete.

The R&D process is a complicated one. Over time it becomes so embedded in the economic sector that, for technology intensive products, the cost of goods can include more than 10 percent in R&D costs. The overall R&D costs for an advanced country are around 2 percent of GDP. For Hong Kong, the current figure is around 0.6 percent of GDP, way behind the more industrialized economies. Partly, this low figure is due to the way R&D is defined over the service industry and partly, it is due to the low margin activities in which Hong Kong's industrial sector has so far been engaged. Having a low percentage does not mean that Hong Kong is non-competitive or that the overall margin is low for all its economic activities.

The role of R&D in Hong Kong will grow in importance as we need to embed both innovation and technology into every economic endeavour. What then, is the role of Hong Kong?

Situational Analysis

The Role of Hong Kong

As an aspiring world city, Hong Kong identifies its role as a provider of services. We shall define this role explicitly. Hong Kong's role is that of an "integrated services provider." Hong Kong delivers the services necessary to accomplish a task, be it a commercial deal, a massive construction project, a comprehensive supply base, a manufacturing complex, or a globally-distributed enterprise, at a speed and cost to match customer needs. It can even nurture and create attractive products to attract investment. Ultimately, it is customer satisfaction that guarantees Hong Kong's competitiveness and a growing role in the world community.

The Current Infrastructure

The physical transport systems of Hong Kong for both sea and air are amongst the largest and most efficient in the world. The information network has received a great deal of attention recently. Large investments have been made and are continuing. Not only are the networks representing state-of-the-art, they are also operating on an interconnected and deregulated manner. The introduction of new services should be readily implementable and effectively operable. International connections are being expanded due to the availability of cable and satellites from multiple sources. Internet fever has reached Hong Kong both in the stock market and in the companies providing Internet-based services. Reorganizations through mergers and acquisitions are occurring almost daily. Even though Singapore started Internet activities earlier, recent developments in Hong Kong are seen to be more dominant. With the imminent start of the electronic services delivery (ESD) service by the Hong Kong government, everyone's life will be affected.

The banking and financial sector is spurring the growth of electronic transactions and e-commerce. The popularity of Mondex and store value payment schemes is more widespread in Hong Kong than anywhere in the world. Convenience stores, university campuses and public transport are spearheading such usage. Internet stock market transactions and Internet-based stock information designed to help investors are rapidly growing in popularity. Customer membership is increasing.

The opening of the Growth Enterprise Market Board opened a new financial channel for new technology start-ups, and this, coupled with the increase in venture and incubation capital, means that new businesses are blossoming.

In the short period of around two years, the people of Hong Kong have been drawn into the exciting world of technology. Even the real estate companies are now channelling their vast capital investments into the areas of technology.

The recommendations of the Chief Executive's Commission on Innovation and Technology reinforced the message that the twenty-first century is the century of technology. The innovative use of technology will allow the economy of the world to develop on a sustainable growth basis, thereby preserving our habitat and our future.

Specifically, the establishment of a new Science Park and a research centre called the Applied Science and Technology Research Institute (ASTRI) is in progress. This injection of government support approved by the Legislators sends the right message. It has already attracted important hi-tech companies to Hong Kong and will transform the image of Hong Kong to that of a service provider with capabilities in R&D services. There are realistic hopes that large transnational corporations and world famous universities are considering establishing tech-labs in Hong Kong.

A tech-lab is a brand new concept currently under debate. The premise of needing a laboratory where technologies are tried out as an integral part of a product design, development and manufacturing activity, is a critical requirement. The tech-lab activities centre on new developing technologies at the mid-stream research stage and tailoring them to fit the envisaged requirements of a product. This means that new technologies are being tried out as the would-be product in a laboratory-like environment, when both the product and the technology can be modified to meet a yet-to-be-firmed-up goal. It is a laboratory for establishing the fastest route to using developing technologies in products. The word "lab" is chosen to connote that trial and error is the order of the day.

Human Resources

The work force in Hong Kong is already famous for being hardworking, highly flexible, tenacious and fast learning. The work force is also mobile and can readily be expanded. Besides, as part of the Chinese diaspora, Hong Kong attracts people from developed and developing regions. Recently immigration laws have been amended to open the way for Ph.D. level scientific and technological talents to come to Hong Kong from the mainland.

Within Hong Kong, the eight universities form the main source of production of trained personnel. Over 20,000 graduates are produced yearly in all disciplines.

Hong Kong has at least three universities designated as research universities and at least two other universities with strong research in some specific areas. Up-stream research is funded by the Research Grants Committee, while mid-stream research is funded through the University Grants Committee, the Industrial Support Fund and direct from industries. Occasionally, down-stream research is also conducted at the industrial centres run by universities, or directly supported by industry and business communities. Other research is conducted by industries at their incubation units or at their own research facilities both in Hong Kong and overseas.

With internal strength and the ability to attract talents from around the world, Hong Kong can and is building up the necessary human resources. The importance of having a strong and motivated pool of human resources, and having good linkages between the up-, mid- and down-stream R&D activities both internally and on a global basis, cannot be overemphasized.

Market Analysis

Hong Kong is strategically located at the centre of the world's major developing markets. With its well-established inter-linkages within this area and globally, Hong Kong should be in high demand as an integrated services provider. The developed world sees this market potential as future growth opportunity. The developing areas see the trading pattern as a way of sustaining the upward growth in their standard of living. Currently, the developing areas supply labour for human power intensive activities needed for the manufacture of low-cost products. As technology advances and technology utilization intensifies, the developing areas will rapidly become a vibrant market for all commodities as the wealth gap narrows. Within the twenty-first century, a civilized and comfortable living standard may be expected in most parts of the world. The delivery of appropriate services to enable this transition to be smooth and beneficial can well be one of the pre-occupations of Hong Kong.

During this period, the pattern of supply and demand will shift gradually but markedly. The Internet in its present form and in its next generation form can be likened to the building of superhighways started in the 1940s in Germany and the U.S. The information highway provided by the Internet will develop significant cultural and behavioural changes.

IT enables information to be gathered, processed and distributed in large quantities and almost instantaneously. These are the tools which we shall be using to transform the pattern of supply and demand in our lives. Already we are seeing the beginning of this IT revolution. The cost of information processing and transmission has now fallen to a level where almost everyone can afford to connect to the Internet. The value-addition offered by an IT-enabled service will govern the price tag of that service could charge. We shall be able to organize supply and demand in a revolutionary way to suit our new mode of living. Every individual demand is likely to be met. Whether this state of affairs is what we want, remains to be seen.

It is important to point out that we are at the beginning of a social paradigm shift. The availability of all information to an individual makes that person as powerful as a corporation or a sovereign state. In practice, we shall need an army of people to sieve through the massive amount of data and parcel it into digestible bites, or even better, to package it in just the way that answers our question. This will be the market of the future, where a new brand of shops will supply us with the right information and deliver the right physical goods to us to satisfy our needs. The process will be more efficient and will enable us to be more productive.

Of course, as an integrated services provider, Hong Kong would use all the IT tools to integrate its services so as to deliver the needed services fast and cost effectively. Hong Kong is a powerful engine and a vital cog in the global economic growth system.

The Information Technology of the Twenty-first Century

Comparing the Information Technology Scenarios, 1991 and 2000

Most of the discussions in the 1991 Technology Roadmap remain valid in 2000. Due to the fast advances in technology across a broad front around the world, we have made considerable progress in the reduction of costs for transmission, storage and processing of data. In addition, with the wireless technology almost made available anywhere, any time access to anyone possible. As a result, restructuring of the communications industry is now taking place. All knowledge-based enterprises are changing. Communications network companies that provide the basic network for transport, the media and entertainment companies that provide the software, and information service vendors that help to make pertinent and value-adding data available to businesses and individuals, are being regrouped, broadened or merged. The conduct of business will still follow well-tried principles, but all supply and demand organizations are being restructured. In this transitional stage, a small number of first movers will make it big. On a long-term basis, IT will sharpen competitiveness and should benefit customers. There will be more businesses addressing niche markets and there will be greater interdependence between large and small enterprises.

Equipment-makers

Past predictions did not anticipate the speed of development of a commercial Internet. All equipment-makers made the effort to make inter-connections of equipment a little easier but it is the IP network equipment that has made the biggest impact. CISCO is the leading company that introduced the servers to make connections to the Internet possible for a large number of users. They increased the speed of the server so that multimedia broadband traffic can be handled.

CISCO also adopted a way of introducing new products in phenomenally short periods of time. They shortened the product development time from years to months by buying the small companies that were making new products speculatively. This process exploited the determination of creative talents to get products to the market early. Of course, for every success, there are many failures along the way. Many small entrepreneurial companies fell by the wayside.

Network Operations

The role of the common carriers has been permanently changed. The monopolistic status of network operators could be seen as the cause of their slowness to change. Many Post Telephone Telegraph Corporations (PTTs) around the world have yet to make a move.

In the year 2000, the world's telephone network operators are just beginning to shift their business base. Their transformation is likely to be dramatic, as their whole enterprise must be fundamentally changed. Already we see the supermergers such as ATT with a cable TV giant, and Deutsches Bundes Post German PTT's (DBP) acquisition of the largest German cellular phone operator. They are examples of transformations. The success of DoCoMo was achieved when it was split from NTT and operated as a separate unit. This example shows another route to effecting change.

Customers and Service Vendors

The current service providers are tapping an unexpected source of money. The stock market in the U.S. evaluated of information services by counting the size of their customer base. If a service web-site has amassed a large number of customers who frequent the site, its valuation is given a high rating. The logic is as follows. If the site can offer, in the future, something that the customers would like to buy, then the customer base would allow big sales to be achieved. This anticipation of huge future proceeds is the basis for valuation. As a result, the present losses can be tolerated if the site has attracted and can retain a large customer base.

The first-in advantage created several successful portals, such as Amazon.com, Yahoo and e-Bay. They now have the task of investing the money they have made from the stock market and making good investments in associated businesses, or even in non-associated businesses, to build a solid future. This type of growth was not anticipated in the 1991 forecast.

The technological advances, in the meantime, lowered the cost of digital signal processing and transmission. The Internet became the most important means for delivering information services. The addition of photogenic components and sub-systems permitted further reductions in cost and improvements in performance. The hardware could be software-enabled so that reconfiguration could be achieved by a small change in the software. As a result, a huge market of new products for Internet applications was created.

Comparison with 1991

If we had followed the 1991 prediction and taken action to strengthen our network and our experience base, we might have had the chance of being among the first movers. As it turned out, we did miss the opportunity. Our recent spurt of activity, however, was in the right direction and should strengthen our operational base significantly in the use of IT and in our success in building an IT industry.

The Year 2000 Hong Kong's Technology Roadmap

We now discuss the Year 2000 Technology Roadmap for the year 2000 and beyond for four chosen areas of technology. They are information technology, biotechnology, materials and nano-technology.

These areas are chosen because they are the enabling technologies that push progress in technology as a whole, and can be applied to the making of many products. The up-stream, mid-stream and down-stream research will be embedded in all our activities. Participation in R&D, narrowly or broadly defined, will serve as our ears and eyes, to hear and see new requirements and opportunities. We should be ready to start action when needed. Since Hong Kong is a provider of integrated services, we need to strengthen and sharpen our services by making full use of technology. An innovative approach to the use of technology in all our endeavours is also a must.

A sample project in each technology area is given below:

Information Technology

Dense Wavelength Division Multiplexing (DWDM) systems adaptation to fit performance requirements of developing areas is a key direction to be followed. System design know-how, sub-system tailoring and key enabling component-making, should all be pursued. This project may attract partners from outside Hong Kong.

Biotechnology

During the past 10 years, biotech research in Hong Kong has accumulated a wide range of experience from participating in R&D and commercialization activities. Areas include: genomic sequencing, isolating active compounds for potential drug discovery, genetic modification of plants, artificial skin, replacement human parts, drug development, vaccine development, Chinese medicinal plant toxicity studies, bacterial removal of heavy metal contamination, growing plants from cells and growth hormone. Even with the choice of Chinese medicine as a targeted area for research in Hong Kong, biotechnology remains a peripheral activity.

Even though the Hong Kong Institute of Biotechnology (HKIB) has been chosen as the designated centre for the incubation of biotech start-ups, the growth of biotech is still largely dependent on private sector responses.

The roadmap for biotech is one of building a cluster of activities with synergy among them. The reason for the need to continue work in this area is clear. Biotech will permeate into many areas. Hong Kong needs to participate in this global effort, even if only as an intelligent participant. This activity would allow Hong Kong to have the basic skills and human resources to mount a major effort when required.

Materials

Polymeric material development has been in progress in Hong Kong for many years. Extrusion techniques and precision part forming have helped the toy and packaging industries. Recently added interests have been the use of polymers and organic compounds for flexible display panels and precision mechanical parts with a high degree of surface perfection and dimensional stability. Liquid crystal technology continues to progress for display and projection display purposes.

With the entry of the third generation cellular phones and a host of wireless devices such as personal communications services/personal digital assistants (PCS/PDA), low power light-emitting displays and liquid crystal displays (LCD) with broadband multimedia responses will be in great demand. Hong Kong should mount a concerted effort in making ready photonic connection devices as well as wireless devices and sub-systems. At the same time, portable devices and systems should have connections into both optical and/or electronic ports of the fixed network. The future trend of the fixed network will be to have optic to the desk for broadband signals carried by DWDM systems.

Nano-technology

Interest in Nano-technology is increasing at the universities. It is important for Hong Kong to have both up-stream basic research and down-stream applied research in this area.

Nano-technology will have an impact on every field from creating new materials, for example, to synthesizing materials with new properties not obtainable from natural materials, to assisting micro electromechanical systems (MEMS) such as micro motors in Nano-metre dimensions. Small electromechanical systems can be built as sensors that can be injected into blood veins or as guided probes with excavation capabilities. The range of uses is limitless.

A concerted effort is being mounted by the universities to establish an area of excellence in this area. It should be directed towards achieving a specific system for an application. It should use a Nano-tech modified material with novel characteristics. As an example, Lucent recently announced the deployment of a practical MEMS for switching DWDM light beams in their fibre sub-marine system.

Organizational Issues

The work on these four separate technologies, or even the work on one technology, is likely to be undertaken at a number of locations. These activities must be carried out using the team concept, namely, the personnel from the universities, industry and research centres must have close contact via telephone, video and data links, and physical visits. As suggested here, three of the four technology areas are being driven by a lead project. A lead project in biotech should be set up through a consultation process. It is hoped that people from universities, ASTRI and industry will work as a single team for each lead project. More lead projects should be developed.

Postscript

The year 2000–2010 roadmap suggests a way of looking at the impact of innovation and technology on the role of Hong Kong. Although the discussion emphasizes the importance of participation in R&D activities, it is apt to note that an integrated service provider must include in its arsenal the ability to find rapid solutions to any service problems. Hong Kong must have a complement of abilities from manufacturing to deal making.

It is not the intention of this essay to be the Technology Roadmap of Year 2000. It is the intention of the author to illustrate the approach to be taken for the preparation of a Year 2000 Technology Roadmap. A team of experts should undertake this task just as the Year 1991 Technology Roadmap was prepared. This chapter is called the Technology Roadmap of Hong Kong, intended as a historic sketch of the development of technology in Hong Kong and the forecasting process to the future.

Note

1. Extracted from Kao and Young (1991).

Reference

Kao, Charles K. and Kenneth Young (eds.) (1991), *Technology Road Maps for Hong Kong: An In-depth Study of Four Technology Areas*. Hong Kong: Office of Industrial and Business Development, The Chinese University of Hong Kong.

Appendix

Consultants' Reports Generated around 1991

1. Techno-economic and Market Research Study on Hong Kong's Plastics Industry 1990–1991 (Vols. I & II).
2. Techno-economic and Market Research Study on Hong Kong's Plastics Industry 1994–1995.
3. Final Report on Techno-economic and Market Research Study on the Textiles and Clothing Industry for Hong Kong Government Industry Department (February 1987).
4. Techno-economic and Market Research Study of Hong Kong's Textiles and Clothing Industry 1991–1992.
5. 1995 Techno-economic and Market Research Study on Hong Kong's Textiles and Clothing Industries (Vols. I & II).
6. Techno-economic and Market Research Study on Hong Kong's Metals and Light Engineering Industries 1992–1993.
7. 1996–1997 Techno-economic and Market Research Study on Hong Kong's Metals and Light Engineering Industries.
8. Techno-economic and Market Research Study on Hong Kong's Electronics Industry 1988–1989.
9. Report on Techno-economic and Market Research Study on Hong Kong's Electronics Industry 1993–1994 (Vols. I–III).

Source: Industry Department, HKSAR Government.

6

Business as Usual? Changing Business Networks in Pacific Asia in a Globalizing Era

Henry Wai-chung Yeung

Introduction

Researchers in organization studies often argue that there are distinctive ways of organizing businesses in different parts of the world. We often hear the phrase "business as usual" which refers to the phenomenon of relatively stable and enduring patterns of business practices in specific localities and societies. This stability in business patterns and organizations often persists in the face of rapid change external to the societies concerned. Together, these patterns of social and organizational structuring form different business systems. Whitley (1992:13) defines business systems as "distinctive configurations of hierarchy-market relations which become institutionalized as relatively successful ways of organizing economic activities in different institutional environments." To him, business systems are distinctive and enduring ways of structuring market economies that are wide-ranging and long-term in nature. Once established in particular institutional contexts, these business systems may develop considerable cohesion and become resistant to major changes. Even such powerful changes as internationalization and globalization are deemed to have only limited effects on the nature of business systems (Whitley, 1994, 1998, 1999). Business systems are difficult to reconfigure unless there are significant changes in the dominant institutions on which these business systems are built. This is particularly the case in the Asia-Pacific region where national business systems are socially and institutionally embedded. In the words of Backman (1999:365), "[o]ld habits are hard to break" in the context of the opaque and corrupt business systems in some Asian countries.

The analytical question I want to raise in this chapter is whether in Asian business systems there can really be "business as usual" in today's context of accelerated globalization. Globalization is defined in this chapter as a set of dialectical processes which simultaneously create an inter-dependent world economy and accentuate the importance of differences between societies and in space (Yeung, 1998a, 1998b). These processes include global flows of materials (e.g., people, goods) and intangibles (e. g., capital, technology, information and services). My argument here is that in assessing the impact of globalization tendencies, it is important to distinguish between business systems as enduring national structures, and firms in these systems as key actors of economic change. The lack of attention to business firms as agents of organizational and system change is a major lacuna in the business systems perspective.

In this chapter, I aim to show how globalization tendencies can transform the dynamics of Asian business systems and, subsequently, their nature and organization (Yeung, 2000a). I argue that the dialectical tendencies of globalization towards homogenization and differentiation have a differential impact on the configurations and dynamics of Asian business systems and their constituents. While Asian business systems tend to be relatively enduring over time because of their historical legacies and institutional embeddedness, major business firms emerging from these national business systems may be much more susceptible to changes brought about by globalization tendencies. This is because key actors in major Asian firms are increasingly participating and enrolled into global actor networks which in turn reshape the ways these actors conceive and operate their business firms/networks. Although business systems are much more structurally embedded in specific national social organizations and political-economic institutions, actors in business firms are significantly more mobile and receptive to change. It is possible that globalization has only limited effects on Asian business systems at the structural level and, yet, significant transformational impact on Asian business firms at the level of key actors. The dynamics of Asian business systems is explained by the nature and degree of enrolment of their actors into the global economy. Facilitated by globalization, this enrolment process enables actors to experience different organizational and business practices abroad. It also allows these actors to transform their own business firms and networks, subject to some binding effects of their domestic business systems. If these dynamic changes occur collectively among business firms in a clearly defined business system, fundamental institutional changes may be forthcoming and this may result in significant changes in the dominant forms and organization of the national business system itself.

This chapter is organized into three sections. The first section examines briefly the existing configurations of Asian business systems before they experienced the full impact of globalization tendencies as encapsulated in the recent Asian economic crisis. The next section draws upon actor network theory to describe the enrolment of Asian actors and élites into networks at different spatial scales and how these processes of enrolment are facilitated by globalization tendencies. I also discuss the impact of these actor networks on the dominant forms and organization of Asian business systems. The concluding section offers an agenda for future research on business networks in Asia.

Existing Configurations of Asian Business Systems

The nature of Asian business systems has already received significant attention in the literature (Whitley, 1992; also Redding, 1990; Hamilton, 1991; Gerlach, 1992; East Asia Analytical Unit, 1995; Weidenbaum and Hughes, 1996; Orrù et al., 1997; Chu and Wu, 1998; McNamara, 1999; Richter, 1999). Instead of reviewing comprehensively the entire configuration of Asian business systems, I focus here on several key characteristics: (1) formation of intra- and inter-firm business networks; (2) reliance on personal relationships; and (3) strong state-business relations (Yeung, 2000b). As will be argued in the next sub-section, these three dimensions of Asian business systems have been significantly reconfigured through the participation of key actors in globalization. In the first place, Whitley (1992:7) argues that "different kinds of business and market organization develop and dominate different market economies as a result of major variations in social institutions and constitute distinctive business systems." As such, the focus of the business system approach is not so much on culture *per se* (cf. Redding, 1990; Hefner, 1998; Douw et al., 1999), but rather on the institutional structures of particular business systems that are socially constructed over time and space. The social organization of business firms, as a result, is largely shaped by these institutional structures (Orrù et al., 1997).

For example, one of the most well-known characteristics of Chinese business systems is the important role and extensive influence of business networks or "bamboo networks" (Hamilton, 1991; Weidenbaum and Hughes, 1996; Yeung, 1998c). Personal relationships or *guanxi* are one of the most important mechanisms to implement co-operative strategies in Chinese business networks, although their importance obviously changes over time and differs according to geographical and sectoral (e.g., property) contexts (Guthrie, 1998; Tsang, 1998; Yeung and Olds, 2000). Chinese family firms in Hong Kong, for example, are the archetypal example of Chinese business systems. Their origins are complex, but can be broadly linked to cultural factors (Wong, 1988; Wang and Wong, 1997; Chiu, 1998) as well as colonial state practices. With hindsight, the latter factor is perhaps critical because the bias of the colonial government in Hong Kong against ethnic Chinese capital, particularly in the industrial sector, provided the institutional condition for the emergence of networks of small-and-medium family-controlled firms. These Chinese family firms could not rely upon state support and had to resort to family and business networks for capital, labour and other critical resources to support flexible production (Sit and Wong, 1989; Chiu et al., 1997; Eng, 1997; Enright et al., 1997; Yeung, 2000c). The reliance on personal relationships, however, is not restricted exclusively to the ethnic Chinese (e.g., Björkman and Kock, 1995; Windolf and Beyer, 1996; Lane and Bachmann, 1998; Olds and Yeung, 1999). Hodder (1996:52), for example, argues that "*guanxi* (or reciprocity) is not a 'thing,' or 'variable' or 'channel.' It does not characterize 'the Chinese,' nor is part of a cultural mantle by which individuals can be identified as Chinese" (Nathan, 1993; Dirlik, 1997; Ong and Nonini, 1997; Yao, 1997). Instead, co-operative relationships in Chinese business systems are largely embedded in personalized business networks, whereas their Western counterparts tend to enter into co-operative relationships based upon firm-specific business strategies. Inter-personal relationships continue to serve as the foundation of co-operative relationships in Chinese business networks (Yeung, 1997a, 1997b).

On the other hand, it is important to stress the role of the state and its apparatus in constructing industrial and business networks in Asia. This perspective originates from the developmental state literature which first made its impact on development studies during the early 1980s (Johnson, 1982, 1995; Deyo, 1987; Amsden, 1989; Wade, 1990). In much of this literature, the empirical focus is on how the state in Japan and several of the Asian newly industrialized economies (South Korea, Singapore and Taiwan) have actively and directly shaped national developmental trajectories through the establishment of economic planning agencies, the pursuit of strategic industrial policy and the promotion of "national champions." These national champions are private firms in highly promising industries and sectors. They are strongly encouraged by the state through loans, grants and subsidies, monopoly rights, tax holidays and import protection. The inevitable outcome of this strong involvement of the state in industrial development is the formation of strong state-business relations. In South Korea, the dominance of the *chaebol* in domestic business owes much to the support of its authoritarian regime (Kim, 1997; Lee, 1997; McNamara, 1999; Steers, 1999). Replicating the success of the *keiretsu* networks in Japan, the *chaebol* have developed a cosy relationship with the state and its ministries for mutual gains. Today, the top four largest *chaebol* (Daewoo, Hyundai, LG and Samsung) have made it to the top 100 transnational corporations from developing countries. They have become formidable competitors in the global economy (van Hoesel, 1999; Yeung, 1999a).

In Japan, the *keiretsu* is not as dominating in Japan's industrial organization as its counterpart from South Korea. Gerlach's (1992) excellent study of Japanese *keiretsu* has shown that much of their dynamics originate from their internal strength rather than from state support *per se*. Through cross-equity ownership of related firms, these complex networks of *keiretsu* linkages have enabled informal exchange of information on product and process innovations and facilitated the development of captive markets in Japan for mutual support. Their role in Japanese production networks abroad is much more varied because of geographical distance and host country preferences for local content and local linkages. In the electronics industry, for example, Aoyama (2000) shows that while the *keiretsu* has played a very important role in the formation of regional production networks, Japanese firms rely heavily on these *keiretsu* networks for access to the global market rather than for access to local suppliers. The agglomeration tendencies of Japanese electronics firms in major urban areas in Asia do not necessarily reflect the territorial development of locally embedded intra-firm networks and spatial clusters specific to product chains and/or technology. They may be more related to the level of urbanization and market development in individual Asian countries. These findings have major implications for understanding the changing role of firm networks in constituting different business systems in Asia (Tsui-Auch, 1999).

In Taiwan, the state-business relationship has evolved from family-centred industrial organization to one in which large firms have much better access to state resources and subsidies (see Mathews, 1997 and Mathews and Cho, 1998 for the case of the semi-conductor industry). Faced with the lack of competitiveness vis-à-vis large firms, small- and medium-sized Taiwanese firms have to leverage their strategic advantages of flexibility and adaptability through informal networks and subcontracting relationships. Some of these small firms have even brought their networks across national borders into China (Hsing, 1998) and Southeast Asia (T. J. Chen, 1998). A recent paper by Buck (2000) has specifically examined the growth, disintegration and decentralization of Taiwan's industrial networks in the context of the state-led land reform programme, redistributive agricultural policies and conservative financial policies since the mid-1960s. He argues that the rapid proliferation of small firm networks in Taiwan was driven by the contingent actions of rural household entrepreneurs which culminated in tremendous rural industrialization, a phenomenon we observe so well in Mainland China today (Lin, 1997; W. Chen, 1998). These industrial and business networks organized by small-and-medium firms were the unintended consequences of state policies rather than a creation by state-led development.

In Southeast Asia, the case of Singapore points to a radically different empirical situation in which the developmental state has actively developed the island economy into a major node in the global spaces of flows (Rodan, 1989; Perry et al., 1997; Low, 1998; Yeung and Olds, 1998). Instead of developing industrial networks constituted exclusively by local firms, the state favours the development and deepening of global-local linkages through which Singapore can gain from the influx of foreign high-technology investments and these global corporations can benefit from Singapore's evolving local supplier networks (see Brown, 1998; Perry and Tan, 1998 for a case study of Singapore's electronics industry). The state is also highly active in developing an "external wing" for the national economy through the regionalization of domestic firms (Yeung, 1998d, 1999b). This process of outward orientation of the national economy has again been spearheaded by statutory boards and government-linked companies. The unique configuration of state-business relationships in Singapore provides an institutional foundation for the emergence of a business system significantly different from the typical Chinese business system outlined earlier.

In other Southeast Asian countries, it appears that political-economic alliances based on patron-client relationships have taken precedence over state-driven industrial and business networks in these still developing economies. This preference for political connections is particularly important in the context of the state's ethnic-biased redistributive economic policies through which indigenous capitalists (known as *pribumi* in Indonesia and *bumiputra* in Malaysia) have been given special rights and privileges. A natural outcome is the rise of so-called *ersatz* capitalism in these Southeast Asian economies (Yoshihara, 1988; McVey, 1992; cf. Yeung, 1999c). In this case, Chinese business systems described above have embedded themselves in the political-economic alliances of the host Southeast Asian countries. Whereas some ethnic Chinese have consolidated and strengthened their intra-ethnic group networks to overcome hostile business and institutional constraints in the host countries, other more pragmatic ethnic Chinese have engaged in patron-client relationships with indigenous Southeast Asian capitalists. This process of "network juxtaposition" has resulted in a hybrid network structure in Southeast Asia comprising family networks and political-economic alliances. Still other ethnic Chinese have chosen an "exit strategy" by internationalizing their business operations into other parts of Asia and beyond. In their internationalization processes, these ethnic Chinese from Southeast Asia have once again leveraged on their transnational networks of personal and business relationships (Yeung, 1998e, 1999d; Yeung and Olds, 2000).

To sum up, Asian business systems are characterized by the formation of intra-firm networks through vertical and horizontal integration, and inter-firm networks through embeddedness in social and business relationships. While cultural affinity and historical legacies may partially explain some of these complex network relationships among social actors and business firms, national institutional structures are equally, if not more, important mechanisms for the (re)production of these business systems. In most Asian countries, these national institutional structures have been actively shaped by the developmental policies of nation states and, in some cases (e.g., Hong Kong), by their colonial predecessors. In a globalizing era in which the nation state has allegedly been made increasingly "powerless" (cf. Weiss, 1998; Glassman, 1999), one wonders whether globalization is fundamentally reshaping the institutional foundations of Asian business systems. This is the analytical question I want to consider in the following sub-section.

Changing Dynamics of Asian Business Systems

There are significant transformations in the institutional governance and organizational structures of the global economy today (Held et al., 1999; Olds et al., 1999; Mittelman, 2000; Yeung, 2000a). Even though they may not fundamentally reconfigure national business systems, globalization tendencies have at least made apparent multiple possibilities and opportunities through actors' enrolment and participation in globalization. This increasing awareness of globalization tendencies is particularly important for key actors and élites in Asian business systems who are being enrolled into global actor networks and thereby are connected to different business systems. While concurring with Whitley (1992, 1996, 1998) that some very demanding conditions must be met before significant transformations in business systems occur, I believe that there is no particular reason why we should not pay attention to emerging changes which may influence the dynamics of these business systems. From an evolutionary perspective, these emerging changes can lead to dynamic changes in the social organization and institutional structures of business systems if the "equilibrium" of existing parameters is disrupted by sudden and unexpected events. In the case of Asian business systems under globalization, certain emerging changes at the level of key actors may disrupt the "equilibrium" of these business systems. This disruption of the path-dependent nature of Asian business systems is particularly apparent during and after the recent 1997/1998 Asian economic crisis (Baer et al., 1999; Henderson, 1999). Before considering the impact of globalization on the dominant forms and organization of Asian business systems, I first examine the changing dynamics of Asian business systems by focusing on the enrolment of Asian actors into global actor networks.

How then are key actors from Asian business systems enrolled into and influenced by global networks elsewhere? These actors are defined as political, social or business élites who are capable of affecting institutional changes at the national level. There are at least four inter-related mechanisms through which this enrolment into global actor networks is made possible: (1) engaging with global managers and financiers in international business and finance; (2) participating in international media and research on business activities; (3) gathering knowledge and experience through international educational institutions; and (4) connecting with international organizations and multilateral institutions. While I do not intend to provide conclusive evidence for the exact impact of each of these mechanisms on Asian business systems, I aim to shed some light on the role of actors in the internal workings of these mechanisms. Where appropriate, I will cite relevant empirical studies to support my analysis.

First, the emergence of Asia as a major global economic powerhouse is linked to both the globalization of non-Asian firms into Asia and the globalization of Asian firms into non-Asian host countries. Though Whitley (1996, 1998) argues that the consequences of these globalization tendencies for national business systems and firms are limited, it is by no means clear that these limited effects of globalization do not represent a long-term process of changing dynamics of Asian business systems. In particular, the two-way globalization of firms between Asia and other regions implies that key actors in Asian business systems are compelled to learn new management and business practices from their competitors, suppliers, customers, and so on. At the same time, these same actors need to undo some of their previous learning and practices in order to compete effectively against foreign competitors in Asia as well as on their home turf. It is true that this process of business contacts between East and West occurred long before (e.g., during Meiji Japan in the mid-nineteenth century; see Westney, 1987; Hamilton, 1997). But the sheer scale, scope and speed of these contacts today make them highly influential in the changing dynamics of Asian business systems.

This process of organizational learning through international business and international finance occurs in several ways. For example, Asian actors may appoint non-Asian actors to manage their operations both in Asia and in host countries outside Asia. These global managers are often endowed with significant experience in managing transnational operations in national economies with distinctive business systems. Their involvement in Asian firms may reshape the norms and practices in these organizations (e.g., see Reich, 1991 for the case of Sony; Mair, 1994 for the case of Honda). Asian actors may also pick up organizational knowledge and practices in non-Asian host countries through transnational operations (e.g., see Mathews and Snow, 1998 for the case of Acer from Taiwan). This knowledge and these practices can originate from their intensive interaction with customers and suppliers in the host countries or from their previous employment in foreign firms. Actor networks are formed between Asian actors and their customers, suppliers and competitors on a global scale, facilitating inter-personal information and knowledge flows and organizational adaptation. By examining the international human resource management practices of Singaporean companies in China, Tsang (1999a, 1999b) recently found that expatriation has an important function for knowledge transfer and training.

On the other hand, actor networks in international finance represent one of the most influential mechanisms for effecting dynamic changes in Asian business systems. This is because for those Asian firms and/or countries in search of financial resources from outside their home countries and/or regions, it is important to secure the consent and recognition by global financiers for good governance and return on investments. These global financiers are leading bankers, fund managers and brokers. They are often based in major global cities which serve as their command centres of global investments (Sassen, 1991). The successful enrolment of Asian actors into these global financial actor networks is imperative in an era of more intensified competition, greater financial requirements for expansion and investments, and higher risks associated with excessive reliance on domestic finance. To ensure that global financial élites are comfortable with their financial positions and obligations, key actors in Asian firms/countries are required to follow certain accounting standards and business norms in global capital markets. This necessity for securing global finance provides a key force to effect dynamic changes in Asian business systems.

Second, this quest for global finance requires actors in Asian business systems to come to terms with actors in international media and research on business activities. This is because today's global financial system is increasingly characterized by a broader array of actors beyond just the bankers and financiers. As Thrift and Leyshon (1994:301) argue, "money, the international financial system, and international financial centers" have simply "'traditionalized' over the last 30 years or so … because of the breakdown of state authority and its replacement by *more diffuse* sources of governance" (my emphasis). Such detraditionalization is accentuated by the enormous task of understanding, managing and communicating about global economic change in a more reflexive manner. This is a style of understanding, managing and communicating that draws a broader array of actors into playing a significant (albeit variable) role in materially and discursively constructing the multiple economic systems that make up the global economy (Thrift, 1996; Hollingsworth, 1998). Actors in international media and research houses play an increasingly important role in producing reflexively texts and information about Asian business systems which can significantly hinder or facilitate Asian actors' access to global finance. For example, top international financial newspapers (e.g., *The Financial Times*), magazines (e.g., *Fortune*) and media (e.g., CNN and CNBC), credit-rating agencies (e.g., Standard and Poor's), stock-broking firms and other research houses (e.g., Morgan Stanley) regularly produce reports on Asian firms (and, sometimes, Asian economies). The "consumers" of these texts are key actors in the global financial industry and international business, including investment bankers, fund managers, brokers, and so on. The successful enticement of these global actors into favourable assessments of Asian firms requires these Asian actors to enrol themselves into global actor networks in international media and research activities (e.g., see Olds and Yeung, 1999 for the case of Cheung Kong Holdings and Hopewell

Holdings from Hong Kong). Not only are Asian firms participating in producing such texts (and counter-texts) through setting up their own credit-rating firms, stock-broking houses, and so on, some of them are also opening their doors to welcome global actors to "inspect" their operations. Such processes of enrolment and enticement have major implications for the changing norms and practices of these Asian firms and, perhaps eventually, their national business systems.

Third, an indisputable trend in today's Asian business systems is that most key actors in these systems have spent some time during their educational life in institutions located in North America, Western Europe and Australia. Most significantly, the globalization of business knowledge is linked to the emergence and, perhaps, domination of top business schools located in North America and Western Europe (Thrift, 1998; 1999). Key actors in Asian family businesses now face the challenge of professionalizing their management and business practices. Other actors in Asia's non-family businesses are also active in organizational re-engineering and management restructuring to prepare for global competition. This process of professionalizing Asian capitalism(s) is driven both by internal and external factors. Internally, more patriarchs in Asian family firms have allowed their heir-apparent to be educated in top business schools abroad. Exposed to professional management training in these business schools, the eventual return of these successors to Asian family businesses contributes to the changing dynamics of Asian business systems in two ways. On the one hand, personal contacts and relationships developed by these successors abroad potentially widen the social and geographic scope of "Asian" business networks when external non-Asian members are "brought" or socialized into "Asian" business networks. Key Asian actors thus not only are enrolled into global financial actor networks with their friends and acquaintances from business schools, but also sometimes actively entice these actors into their own networks in Asia. This process of enrolment and enticement implies that the concept of exclusive Asian business networks should be broadened to include non-family and non-Asian members (e.g., see Mitchell, 1995 and Olds, 1998 for the case of Li Ka-shing's investments in Vancouver).

On the other hand, the return of a professionally trained family heir represents an important step towards the professionalization of Asian business. When the heir eventually takes over the family business, he/she tends to adopt a much more open view towards the involvement of professionals in the management of the family firm (e.g., see Fung, 1997;

Magretta, 1998 for the case of Li & Fung from Hong Kong). This is certainly not the same phenomenon as predicted in the existing literature on Asian family firms when paternalism, nepotism, personalism and fragmentation are widely believed to be the key characteristics of their organizational rigidities (e.g., Redding, 1990; Chen, 1995; Fukuyama, 1995; cf. Yeung, 1999e).

Fourth, Asian élites are now more connected with international organizations and multilateral institutions than ever. These powerful supra-national economic organizations and financial institutions include the IMF, World Bank, OECD, APEC, UNCTAD, and so on. These are institutions that engage in private and public debate over economic reform at a national and sectoral level and occasionally participate in the development of specific economic restructuring programmes in the Asia-Pacific region. Representatives of multilateral institutions implement diffuse forms of governance that have significant effects in shaping the business practices of Asian firms, in particular through recommendations (and implementation pressure) on the systemic reform of nationally-regulated financial systems (including banking and stock markets). Multilateral institutions, such as the IMF, are able to reshape Asian business networks in a thorough and yet diffuse manner by encouraging and/or requiring the restructuring of the institutions and power structures in Asia which large Asian businesses (especially the conglomerates) engage with in reciprocal relations of interdependence. By entraining other actors (the nation state) and the necessary codes, procedural frameworks, regulations, material incentives, and so on, that are required to effect the activation of power, multilateral institutions directly and indirectly transform the nature and operation of Asian business systems.

These dynamic changes to Asian business systems brought about by international organizations, however, cannot be effective without the consent and involvement of Asian élites. Here, the issue of power relations becomes paramount because any significant changes to the existing configurations of Asian business systems imply a concomitant demise of certain interest groups (e.g., cronies and rent seekers) and the emergence of other groups (e.g., supporters of democracy and transparency). Why then would key actors in Asia participate and enrol into these actor networks of multilateral institutions? Some Asian actors are clearly opportunists who participate in these global actor networks in order to ride on the same "wave" and secure their own legitimacy in business and politics. Other Asian actors find the path-dependent nature of Asian business systems virtually impossible to transform without significant external pressures. Enrolling into global actor networks helps these Asian actors to advance their ideas of reforming and transforming domestic business systems (see below). The last group of Asian actors enrolls into networks of international organizations to promote global understandings and interaction. It is unlikely that this would lead to the demise of national business systems in favour of a new cross-national economic co-ordination system. What is clear, however, is that this process of enrolling Asian actors into the global networks of international organizations and multilateral institutions has a potential long-term impact on the dominant forms and organizations of Asian business systems.

Impact of Globalization on the Dominant Forms and Organization of Asian Business Systems

As outlined earlier, the market organization of most Asian economies is dominated by strong state-business relations explained by the historical legacies and institutional structures of Asian economies (Whitley, 1992, 1999). The dialectical tendencies of globalization, however, seriously disturb this relatively stable configuration of "institutional equilibrium" in many Asian economies. On the one hand, the enrolment of key Asian élites into global actor networks has enabled them to construct certain political discourses to legitimize their reform agendas. Privatization and deregulation are some of the reform efforts institutionalized by Asian political élites to embrace the benefits of participating in globalization. These efforts are likely to generate a long-term impact on the dominant forms and organization of Asian business systems. For example, the recent 1997/1998 Asian economic crisis has provided such a context for change and reforming Asian business systems (Henderson, 1999). There are, of course, different interpretations of the origins of the Asian economic crisis (see, for example, Rhodes and Higgott, 2000). My concern here is with the role of Asian actors in the midst of this crisis and their discursive practices in dismantling or strengthening the prevailing structures of Asian business systems. In effect, some powerful domestic élites within Asia have been quick to jump on the globalization bandwagon to pursue their own hidden agendas of implementing structural reforms and building institutional capacities, which otherwise could not be pursued without an "externally-imposed" necessity to do so. As a consequence, the (contested) discourse of globalization "itself has become a political force, helping to create the institutional realities it purportedly merely describes" (Piven, 1995:8).

The cases of South Korea and Singapore show how a careful deconstruction of an Asian identity enables political élites in the former to shape the restructuring initiatives and those in the latter to distinguish their city-state from other ailing Southeast Asian economies to minimize the "contagion effect" of the Asian economic crisis. In South Korea, the IMF rescue package represents three agendas at work — a conventional IMF agenda, a U.S. trade- and investment-opening agenda and a Korean-imposed institutional reform agenda (Mathews, 1998; Wade and Veneroso, 1998). The first two agendas are clearly interrelated and not widely accepted by the Koreans. Bello (1998:425) thus notes that "the Fund is very unpopular [in South Korea], not only because it is seen as administering the wrong medicine, but because it is viewed as a surrogate for the U.S.A., imposing a programme of deregulation and liberalization in trade, investment and finance that Washington had been pushing on the country — with little success — before the outbreak of the financial crisis." In fact, as the U.S. Deputy Treasury Secretary Lawrence Summers said, "The IMF has done more to promote America's trade and investment agenda in Korea than 30 years of bilateral trade talks" (quoted in Hale, 1998:12). The third agenda, however, has been so rigorously pursued by the political élites in South Korea that "by the middle of 1998 [South Korea] was rebuilding a new version of a 'Korean model' — turning the crisis to its own advantage by reforming the political-economic structures, which were in fact long overdue for reform but which could not be tampered with in the absence of a major crisis" (Mathews, 1998:748).

What exactly did the Korean élites make of the heavy-handed IMF intervention in December 1997 which was certainly not the first time that Korea had fallen into the IMF's grasp (previous occasions were in 1971 and 1980–1983)? The "old" Korean model of rapid economic development was based on high foreign debt for expanding industrial capacity and large *chaebol* for steering the national economy. The role of state agencies in directing development was also very important (Amsden, 1989; Wade, 1990; Kim, 1997; Lee, 1997; Chang, 1998; cf. Thornton, 1998). Such a model sustained South Korea's high growth rates during the 1980s. By the 1990s, the model was sustained by taking on risks on a larger scale and by depending on continuously favourable global economic conditions. Just before the crisis, the model was becoming so powerful that it threatened to become a political force beyond the control of existing state agencies and newly created democratic institutions. It could only be "stopped" by a major crisis (Mathews, 1998). The unravelling of the Korean model in late 1997, therefore, witnessed the Korean élites, led by the Kim Dae-Jung administration, taking the extraordinary opportunity created by IMF intervention to transform the Korean model from a developmental system to a "more mature" business system. According to Mathews (1998), these Korean élites from the various government ministries indeed instigated structural reforms into the IMF agreement rather than being forced to concede to such reforms in the case of Indonesia. These reforms covered matters such as (1) greater transparency in corporate governance and structure; (2) reducing the levels of mutual debt repayment guarantees; (3) opening the way to corporate bankruptcy procedures; and (4) reform of the financial sector, including the separation of the Bank of Korea from the Ministry of Finance.

Similarly in Singapore, the political élites tried to deconstruct the Asian "miracle" by distancing themselves from other Asian economies in which strong state intervention was believed to have been turned into massive corruption and cronyism. They were also quick to point out that because of the PAP government's good governance, Singapore was less troubled by the economic downturn (Yeung, 2000d, 2000e). In a talk to the U.S. Council on Foreign Relations in October 1998, Senior Minister Lee Kuan Yew said that the afflicted Asian economies had opened up their capital accounts too fast and too soon. To him, "the liberalisation of capital accounts should have been calibrated to match the level of sophistication in their banking supervision systems and banking laws" (quoted in *The Straits Times*, 22 October 1998). In fact, the Asian economic crisis not only did not affect Singapore too seriously in material terms, but also offered further discursive legitimacy to the state to re-regulate the domestic economy. By naturalizing the processes of economic globalization and its negative impact on those economies with weak and "corrupted" states, the political élites in Singapore were able to rally support from both labour and capital. In other words, by positioning the Asian economic crisis at regional and global scales, these political élites legitimized the strengthened role of the PAP-led state in domestic governance. For example, Lee Yock Suan, then Minister for Trade and Industry, noted that:

> ... the problems in the [Southeast Asian] region will not be solved by turning away from globalization ... In this increasingly borderless world of trade and commerce, countries which try to hide behind national barriers will find themselves progressively marginalised ... Globalization is an *inevitable* process. Those who embrace it can harness its benefits. However, appropriate domestic policy measures and frameworks to strengthen the regulatory regime and financial institutions must be put in place first. In addition, parallel

measures need to be taken to improve the competitiveness of domestic enterprises as well as develop the skills of the workforce. (30 July 1998; my emphasis)

The Minister argued that for Singapore and its enterprises to compete effectively in the global economy, the state needed to implement appropriate policies without having to shut these local enterprises out from external competition or to rely on subsidies from the government. The political legitimacy of a strong state in domestic governance was apparently secured through a discursive construction of an inevitable external world of globalization in which Singapore either survives with good state governance or falls through a free-for-all neo-liberal approach to economic governance (e.g., during the recent wage-cutting drive to lower business costs in Singapore). The state subscribed to IMF-style neo-liberalism and attempted to liberalize the Singapore economy to "embrace" globalization and to attract global capital. Singapore has since moved swiftly to liberalize its financial sector to become more competitive in the regional and global financial markets. The Singapore government has recently announced the most comprehensive liberalization programme ever for the banking sector. The objectives of the liberalization programme are: (1) to encourage banks in Singapore to be efficient and innovative; (2) to nurture robust local banks which can stand up to leading international banks; and (3) to encourage strong foreign banks to take a stake in Singapore's financial system (*The Straits Times*, 17 May 1999:38). Deputy Prime Minister (DPM) Lee Hsien Loong (also chairman of the central bank, Monetary Authority of Singapore) noted that "the banking environment is being transformed, in the region and globally. Existing franchises and market shares are being challenged. Competition, not protection, is the only way to develop strong local banks which measure up against the best international players."

In fact, this financial liberalization programme had already begun in 1990 when the Monetary Authority of Singapore (MAS) raised foreign shareholdings of Singapore banks from 20 percent to 40 percent. Foreign banks could compete freely with local banks in wholesale domestic banking, offshore banking, and treasury and capital market activities. They accounted for more than one-third of resident deposits, 45 percent of loans to resident borrowers and about 90 percent of business with non-residents (*The Straits Times*, 17 May 1999:38). On 17 May 1999, the Singapore government announced that by 2001, six Qualifying Full Bank (QFB) licences will be issued to foreign banks which will be allowed to set up additional branches and off-premise automated teller machines and share an ATM network among themselves — practices previously disallowed (*The Straits Times*, 18 May 1999:51). The MAS will also increase the number of restricted banks from 13 to 18 by 2001 to cater to offshore banks, and give offshore banks greater flexibility in Singapore dollar wholesale business.

This recent liberalization of Singapore's banking sector has significant impacts on local banks, which will have their interest margins squeezed with stiffer competition from 22 full-licence, 13 restricted and 98 offshore foreign banks in Singapore. These local banks have been well protected by the MAS for a long period, no new licences for full and restricted banks having been granted since 1970 and 1983, respectively. DPM Lee again noted that:

> Government protection and strict MAS supervision have enabled local banks to grow into sound, well-capitalised institutions ... The present situation is not sustainable. Even if the Government does not liberalise the banking industry, local banks will be unable to maintain the status quo. Globalization and electronic delivery channels have altered fundamentally the competitive landscape. Further rapid developments in Internet banking will enable foreign banks to reach out extensively to domestic consumers, reducing and eventually neutralising the advantages of an extensive branch network and Government protection. (*The Straits Times*, 18 May 1999:48)

The likely impact of this banking liberalization programme on local banks is to foster mergers and acquisitions to consolidate and to achieve economies of scale for continuing expansion and growth. In fact, the Singapore government has already taken the lead on 24 July 1998 by merging the state-owned Post Office of Singapore Bank (POSB) and the Development Bank of Singapore (DBS), a government-linked bank. After the merger, DBS will be able to tap into deposit-rich POSB to become a huge and possibly dominant force in the regional banking industry (*The Straits Times*, 25 July 1998). DBS was already a net lender in the interbank market even before the proposed merger. The former chairman and CEO, Mr. Ngiam Tong Dow, declared that "our aim is to become a regional bank with a global reach" (*The Straits Times*, 20 April 1998). DBS was on the prowl for more acquisitions in the Asia-Pacific region. Since the beginning of the Asian economic crisis, DBS has acquired an 85 percent interest in an Indonesian bank, increased its stake to 50.3 percent in Thai Danu Bank and taken a 60 percent stake in Philippines' Bank of Southeast Asia and another 65 percent stake in Hong Kong's Kwong On Bank (*The Straits Times*, 17

December 1998). Together these acquisitions cost DBS more than S$330 million. After the proposed merger, DBS is expected to have total deposits of S$59.3 billion, shareholders' funds of S$9.4 billion and total assets of S$93.4 billion, enabling it to extend its global reach into the region and beyond. Referring to HSBC Holdings, the London-based global player in the banking industry, a financial analyst said that the proposed merger basically is "the [Singapore] Government's way of forcing the pace on the private sector to re-capitalise and fulfil its wish for a HSBC here [in Singapore]" (*The Straits Times*, 25 July 1998).

What then will be the likely impact of this banking liberalization on Singapore's three Chinese-controlled local banks (i.e., OUB, OCBC and UOB)? DPM Lee expected that "[t]here is room for consolidation, but we hope that there will be at least two Singapore institutions ... If we succeed in building up two such strong local banks, our financial system will have two pillars of strength and stability" (*The Straits Times*, 17 May 1999:38; 18 May 1999:49). Clearly, the Singapore government highly values the synergy among these three local banks and favours their consolidation into one single banking group. The challenge ahead for these three banks controlled by three different families (OUB by the Lien family, OCBC by the Lee family and UOB by the Wee family) is how to face strong competitive pressures in the domestic market. Some of them have responded by chartering new strategic visions for the new millennium (OUB2000 Programme and OCBC's Roadmap 3.0). Others have expanded aggressively abroad by opening new branches (UOB in China) and/or through acquisition. To meet these challenges of liberalization, local Chinese banks in Singapore cannot avoid globalization and open competition, rather they must embrace and participate in globalization to explore new avenues for change and expansion.

Nevertheless, some Asian élites have been consciously withdrawing from global actor networks and retreating back to nationalism as a political weapon to contest globalization tendencies. This inward-looking political discourse tended to focus on the politics of differences. In Malaysia, for example, Prime Minister Mahathir discursively constructed globalization in a polar opposite direction. He put much more emphasis on the perils of globalization. In his speech at the APEC Business Summit on 15 November 1998, Mahathir noted that "Globalization too is good but it can be abused, abused in such a way that instead of worldwide prosperity, there will be worldwide poverty or extreme disparities between rich and poor, international and civil disorders, revolts, rebellion and all kinds of crisis."

To him, globalization can be a conspiracy — a strategic tool deployed by the West to re-colonize their former colonies. The prime suspect is global currency trading and its speculative practices. This "re-colonization" does not necessarily take a physical form because "[c]olonial control of land by military strength can no longer be accepted by societies worldwide. But physical colonialism like this is no longer necessary. Control through currency trading has similar effects" (*The Straits Times*, 20 June 1998). In his usual characteristic politicization of public speeches, he warned Malaysians to guard against a new era of colonialism:

> All Malaysians should work together to defend the sovereignty of our nation. What we are doing is actually defending our independence, no less than that. Do remember, those who created the economic turmoil that we are facing are just like the colonisers, who once colonised us. (*The Straits Times*, 20 June 1998)

It appeared that within Asia itself, there is a great deal of bitterness, even anger, at what is being seen as the attempt by the West to absolve itself of any responsibility for the crisis. Although pronouncements by Malaysia's Prime Minister Mahathir are often extreme, there are many in Asia who share at least some of his views. There is, as Higgott (1998, 1999) has pointed out, an emerging "politics of resentment" within some Asian countries. Commenting on this kind of globalization discourse, UN Secretary General Kofi Annan warned of a backlash from developing countries (including Southeast Asia), fearing that globalization is a tool of the industrialized North to "re-colonize" the weaker, but booming, South. He said that "throughout the developing world, the awakening to globalization's down side has been one of resistance and resignation, a feeling that globalization is a false god foisted on weaker states by the capitalist centres of the West" (*The Straits Times*, 19 September 1998). He observed three main reactions to this growing "globalization backlash": nationalism, a move towards "illiberal solutions" with recourse to strong leaders, and politics of populism. These political discourses of "resentment" have the effect of reinforcing or, worse, deepening existing path-dependency in certain Asian business systems (Yeung, 2000e). In Malaysia, the imposition of capital control since 1 September 1998 has given domestic banks some breathing space to recapitalize their reserves. But the same measure has also backfired because foreign capital hesitates to invest in Malaysia's financial sector. The recent financial sector restructuring exercise initiated by the central bank, Bank Negara, will witness decline in the market share and influence of banks owned by ethnic Chinese. The central bank issued a directive on 29 July 1999 to consolidate Malaysia's 21 commercial banks, 25 finance companies and 12 merchant banks into six major banking groups (*The Straits Times*, 31 July 1999). Through this restructuring exercise, banks controlled by ethnic Chinese businessmen, mostly family-owned business, will be losing their favour with Bank Negara and be forced to be absorbed into other banking groups. As Bank Negara governor Ali A. H. Sulaiman said, "there was no place for family-run banks to survive in the long run in the face of globalization" (*The Straits Times*, 12 August 1999). Indeed, the exercise will see eight Chinese-controlled banks merged into two banking groups led by Public Bank (controlled by Teh Hong Piow) and Southern Bank (controlled by Khoo Kay Peng). The crisis has led to the collapse of certain political-economic alliances between ethnic Chinese rent-seekers and their political patrons in Malaysia. As a defining attribute of Malaysia's business system, Chinese capital was, and still is, subservient to Malay bumiputra hegemony. Gomez (1999:192–93) observed in his highly detailed analysis of political patronage among nearly 40 Malaysian Chinese-controlled companies listed in the Kuala Lumpur Stock Exchange that:

> Politicians abuse their hegemony to distribute to party members state-controlled concessions in the form of licenses, contracts, subsidiaries and privatized projects. Funds to acquire these concessions are secured through favorable loans from banks and other financial institutions owned or controlled by the government. Distribution of such concessions to party members helps leaders secure or promote their positions … Political patronage, sophisticated but unproductive corporate manoeuvres, and the rise in market value of quoted stock have contributed to the emergence of a politically well-connected "new rich," most of whom are Malays.

Conclusion

This chapter has shown that in an era of accelerated globalization, "business as usual" is no longer a valid way to understand the changing dynamics of Asian business systems. While I concur that the enduring properties of different social systems of production and national institutional structures continue to reinforce differences in national business systems (Hollingsworth, 1998; Whitley, 1998, 1999), globalization tendencies have a significant impact on the dynamics of these business systems. This impact is particularly effective at the level of key actors and élites in these business systems because of their enrolment and enticement into various forms of actor networks at different spatial scales. Through their connections with actors in international business, finance, media, research, education and multilateral institutions, Asian actors and élites are increasingly capable of effecting changes in existing norms, conventions and practices of Asian business systems. In other words, globalization tendencies provide the key mechanism through which the dynamics of Asian business systems can be unleashed and their existing configurations reshaped and transformed. These tendencies also alter drastically the institutional contexts in which the stability and endurance of Asian business systems is maintained.

Though the transformations of Asian business systems under globalization are path-dependent, the specific directions and modes of transformation depend critically upon the dialectics of globalization tendencies, and the nature and spatial scales of Asian actors being enrolled into actor networks elsewhere. I have argued in this chapter that globalization tendencies are not merely homogenizing national differences in social organization and institutional structures, but they also simultaneously accentuate material and discursive differences, a consequence of their highly uneven nature and impact (Yeung, 2000a). Most debates in globalization studies are clearly misconceived because of their focus on the dichotomous choice between homogenization or differentiation. To understand the changing dynamics of Asian business systems in a globalizing era, it becomes imperative for us to transcend this dichotomous view of globalization by examining how the dialectical tendencies of globalization can be deployed by Asian actors and élites, who are enrolled into actor networks at different spatial scales, to effect changes in the norms, conventions and practices of their embedded business systems.

In particular, I have considered how the enrolment of Asian élites into global actor networks has facilitated the transition of Asian business systems towards network-based governance structures at the firm level and reduced state-business relationships at the structural level. The key processes associated with these transformations in Asian business systems are the professionalization of management, privatization and deregulation, financial liberalization and institutional reforms (Henderson, 1999). These processes cannot be effectively realized without the material and discursive constructions of globalization tendencies by key Asian actors and élites. Their impact on the dominant forms and organizations of Asian business systems should also be seen as highly uneven both geographically between countries (e.g., in Southeast Asia) and structurally between different sectors of national economies (e.g., financial vs. manufacturing industries).

What then are the future evolutionary trajectories of business networks in Pacific Asia? Not long ago, in the late 1980s and the early 1990s, *keiretsu* networks were praised as the most important competitive advantage for Japanese firms to establish themselves successfully in North America and Western Europe (Reich, 1991; Gerlach, 1992; Tyson, 1993). Just a couple of years later, popular academic writing again praised the role of "bamboo networks" in propelling Asian prosperity (Weidenbaum and Hughes, 1996). The only difference is that this time ethnic Chinese outside Mainland China were put in the limelight. Strangely enough, all these praises vaporized as soon as the 1997/1998 Asian economic crisis broke out. Instead, we heard "networks" being condemned unreservedly as the main culprit or the fundamental cause of the crisis. While this chapter hopes to shed some light on the nature and dynamics of business networks in Asia (Yeung, 2000f), the future of these networks in the post-crisis era remains highly uncertain. Two pressing issues are critical to our understanding of the future role and functions of networks in post-crisis Asia: (1) network instability and (2) methodological challenges.

First, whilst most researchers would acknowledge the usefulness of networks, few would recognize that enrolment in networks is accompanied by obligations which, in the worst situation, can produce a "lock-in" effect. The concept of networks implies some kind of leveraging upon group synergy beyond the capabilities of individual members. When a crisis (internal or external) sets in, this "lock-in" effect tends to produce an effect through which all members of the network suffer from the misdeed of other member(s) if it is an internally-driven crisis, or from the extra burden of an externally-driven shock. The inherent instability of networks may, therefore, hamper the performance of individual firms and actors. This theoretical point is best observed in the case of some Chinese business networks in Southeast Asia which were under siege in the recent Asian economic crisis (Yeung, 1999c, 2000e). These effects are real and tend to be more applicable to externally-driven networks in Asia or, in the words of Dicken and Hassler (2000), "fragile networks." Dicken and Hassler (2000) make some speculations on the possible future shape of production networks in Indonesia's clothing industry and question the long term viability of that industry. To them, these "fragile networks" are highly vulnerable to the threat of relocation because buyers and agents from outside Indonesia may easily skip Indonesia in favour of other Asian and even non-Asian locations for cost-effective manufacturing of apparel products. Edgington and Hayter (2000) also conclude that the expansion and deepening of Japanese production networks and their spatial divisions of labour depend on the full recovery of Asia from its worst-ever economic and, in some countries, political crisis.

Second, how to study networks remains a fundamental methodological impasse in economic geography, organization studies and economic sociology. Although existing studies have adopted a wide range of methodologies from case studies to large-scale surveys and historical research, there is still no clear consensus on how best to map out and disentangle networks and their constitutive relationships. Murdoch's (1997: 332) recent suggestion does not help much either:

> Network analysis is quite simple: it means following networks all the way along their length; there is no need to step outside the networks for all the qualities of spatial construction and configuration of interest will be found therein.

There is a danger that paying excessive attention to actors in networks will descend into a mechanistic framework that atomizes agents and focuses solely on the links between them, without a sense of the social processes that constitute these relationships. Perhaps some methodological middle ground needs to be reached so that studying networks means more than tracing networks all the way along their length (as exemplified in most global commodity chains and actor networks studies). It also requires us to think more deeply about the structural properties of these network relationships and their constitution in society and space. Only through these kinds of empirically-grounded analyses, are we able to understand not only why networks are enduring features in Asia, but also what constitutes their dynamics after the recent Asian economic crisis.

References

Amsden, Alice (1989), *Asia's Next Giant: South Korea and Late Industrialization*. New York: Oxford University Press.

Aoyama, Yuko (2000), "Networks, Keiretsu and Locations of the Japanese Electronics Industry in Asia," *Environment and Planning A*, 32(2):223–44.

Backman, Michael (1999), *Asian Eclipse: Exposing the Dark Side of Business in Asia*. Singapore: John Wiley.

Baer, Werner, William R. Miles and Allen B. Moran (1999), "The End of the Asian Myth: Why were the Experts Fooled?" *World Development*, 27(10):1735–47.

Bello, Walder (1998), "East Asia: On the Eve of the Great Transformation?" *Review of International Political Economy*, 5(3):424–44.

Björkman, Ingmar and Soren Kock (1995), "Social Relationships and Business Networks: The Case of Western Companies in China," *International Business Review*, 4(4):519–35.

Brown, Ross (1998), "Electronics Foreign Direct Investment in Singapore: A Study of Local Linkages in 'Winchester City'," *European Business Review*, 98(4): 196–210.

Buck, Daniel (2000), "Growth, Disintegration, and Decentralization: The Construction of Taiwan's Industrial Networks," *Environment and Planning A*, 32(2):245–62.

Chang, Ha-Joon (1998), "Korea: The Misunderstood Crisis," *World Development*, 26(8): 1555–61.

Chen, Min (1995), *Asian Management Systems: Chinese, Japanese and Korean Styles of Business*. London: Routledge.

Chen, Tain-Jy (ed.) (1998), *Taiwanese Firms in Southeast Asia: Networking Across Borders*. Cheltenham: Edward Elgar.

Chen, Weixing (1998), "The Political Economy of Rural Industrialization in China: Village Conglomerates in Shandong Province," *Modern China*, 24(1):73–96.

Chiu, Catherine C. H. (1998), *Small Family Business in Hong Kong: Accumulation and Accomodation*. Hong Kong: The Chinese University Press.

Chiu, Stephen W. K., Ho Kong-chong and Lui Tai-lok (1997), *City-States in the Global Economy: Industrial Restructuring in Hong Kong and Singapore*. Boulder: Westview Press.

Chu, Yen-Peng and Wu Rong-I (eds.) (1998), *Business, Markets and Government in the Asia-Pacific*. London: Routledge

Collinge, Chris (1999), "Self-organization of Society by Scale: A Spatial Reworking of Regulation Theory," *Environment and Planning D: Society and Space*, 17 (5):557–74.

Deyo, Frederic C. (ed.) (1987), *The Political Economy of the New Asian Industrialism*. Ithaca: Cornell University Press.

Dicken, Peter and Markus Hassler (2000), "Organizing the Indonesian Clothing Industry in the Global Economy: The Role of Business Networks," *Environment and Planning A*, 32(2):263–80.

Dirlik, Arif (1997), "Critical Reflections on 'Chinese Capitalism' as Paradigm," *Identities*, 3(3):303–30.

Douw, Leo M., Cen Huang and Michael R. Godley (eds.) (1999), *Qiaoxiang Ties: Interdisciplinary Approaches to "Cultural Capitalism" in South China*. London: Kegan Paul.

East Asia Analytical Unit (1995), *Overseas Chinese Business Networks in Asia*. Parkes: Department of Foreign Affairs and Trade, Australia.

Edgington, David W. and Roger Hayter (2000), "Foreign Direct Investment and the Flying Geese Model: Japanese Electronics Firms in the Asia Pacific," *Environment and Planning A*, 32(2):281–304.

Eng, Irene (1997), "Flexible Production in Late Industrialization: The Case of Hong Kong," *Economic Geography*, 73(1):26–43.

Enright, Michael J., Edith E. Scott and David Dodwell (1997), *The Hong Kong Advantage*. Hong Kong: Oxford University Press.

Fukuyama, Francis (1995), *Trust: The Social Virtues and the Creation of Prosperity*. London: Hamish Hamilton.

Fung, Victor (1997), "Evolution in the Management of Family Enterprises in Asia." In Gungwu Wang and Siu-lun Wong (eds.), *Dynamic Hong Kong: Business and Culture*. Hong Kong: Hong Kong University Press, pp. 216–29.

Gerlach, Michael L. (1992), *Alliance Capitalism: The Social Organization of Japanese Business*. Berkeley: University of California Press.

Glassman, Jim (1999), "State Power beyond the 'Territorial Trap': The Internationalization of the State," *Political Geography*, 18(6):669–96.

Gomez, Edmund Terence (1999), *Chinese Business in Malaysia: Accumulation, Accommodation and Ascendance*. Surrey: Curzon.

Guthrie, Douglas (1998), "The Declining Significance of *Guanxi* in China's Economic Transition," *The China Quarterly*, 154:254–82.

Hale, David D. (1998), "The IMF, Now More Than Ever: The Case for Financial Peacekeeping," *Foreign Affairs*, 77(6):7–13.

Hamilton, Gary G. (ed.) (1991), *Business Networks and Economic Development in East and South East Asia*. Hong Kong: Centre of Asian Studies, The University of Hong Kong.

Hamilton, Gary G. (1997), "Hong Kong and the Rise of Capitalism in Asia." In Gungwu Wang and Siu-lun Wong (eds.), *Dynamic Hong Kong: Business and Culture*. Hong Kong: Hong Kong University Press, pp. 118–48.

Hefner, Robert W. (ed.) (1998), *Market Cultures: Society and Values in the New Asian Capitalisms*. Singapore: Institute of Southeast Asian Studies.

Held, David, Anthony McGrew, David Goldblatt and Jonathan Perraton (1999), *Global Transformations: Politics, Economics and Culture*. Cambridge: Polity.

Henderson, Jeffrey (1999), "Uneven Crises: Institutional Foundations of East Asian Economic Turmoil," *Economy and Society*, 28(3):327–68.

Higgott, Richard (1998), "The Asian Economic Crisis: A Study in the Politics of Resentment," *New Political Economy*, 3(3):333–55.

——— (1999), "The Political Economy of Globalization in East Asia: The Salience of 'Region Building'." In Kris Olds, Peter Dicken, Philip Kelly, Lily Kong and Henry Wai-chung Yeung (eds.), *Globalization and the Asia Pacific: Contested Territories*. London: Routledge, pp. 91–106.

Hodder, Rupert (1996), *Merchant Princes of the East: Cultural Delusions, Economic Success and the Overseas Chinese in Southeast Asia*. Chichester: John Wiley.

Hollingsworth, J. Rogers (1998), "New Perspectives on the Spatial Dimensions of Economic Coordination: Tensions between Globalization and Social Systems of Production," *Review of International Political Economy*, 5(3):482–507.

Hsing, You-tien (1998), *Making Capitalism in China: The Taiwan Connection*. New York: Oxford University Press.

Jessop, Bob (1999), "Some Critical Reflections on Globalization and Its Illogic(s)." In Kris Olds, Peter Dicken, Philip Kelly, Lily Kong and Henry Wai-chung Yeung (eds.), *Globalization and the Asia Pacific: Contested Territories*. London: Routledge, pp. 19–38.

Johnson, Chalmers (1982), *MITI and the Japanese Economic Miracle*. Stanford: Stanford University Press.

—— (1995), *Japan: Who Governs? The Rise of the Developmental State*. New York: W. W. Norton.

Kelly, Philip F. (1999), "The Geographies and Politics of Globalization," *Progress in Human Geography*, 23(3):379–400.

Kim, Eun Mee (1997), *Big Business, Strong State: Collusion and Conflict in Korean Development*. Albany: SUNY Press.

Lane, Christel and Reinhard Bachmann (eds.) (1998), *Trust Within and Between Organizations: Conceptual Issues and Empirical Applications*. Oxford: Oxford University Press.

Lee, Yeon-ho (1997), *The State, Society and Big Business in South Korea*. London: Routledge.

Lin, George C. S. (1997), *Red Capitalism in South China: Growth and Development of the Pearl River Delta*. Vancouver: University of British Columbia Press.

Low, Linda (1998), *The Political Economy of a City-State: Government-Made Singapore*. Singapore: Oxford University Press.

Magretta, Joan (1998), "Fast, Global, and Entrepreneurial: Supply Chain Management, Hong Kong Style: An Interview with Victor Fung," *Harvard Business Review*, 76(5):103–14.

Mair, Andrew (1994), *Honda's Global Local Corporation*. New York: St. Martin's Press.

Mathews, John A. (1997), "A Silicon Valley of the East: Creating Taiwan's Semiconductor Industry," *California Management Review*, 39(4):26–54.

—— (1998), "Fashioning a New Korean Model out of the Crisis: The Rebuilding of Institutional Capabilities," *Cambridge Journal of Economics*, 22(6):747–59.

Mathews, John A. and D. S. Cho (1998), *Tiger Chips: The Creation of a Semiconductor Industry in East Asia, 1975–2000*. Cambridge: Cambridge University Press.

Mathews, John A. and Charles C. Snow (1998), "A Conversation with the Acer Groups' Stan Shih on Global Strategy and Management," *Organizational Dynamics*, 27(1):65–74.

McNamara, Dennis L. (ed.) (1999), *Corporatism and Korean Capitalism*. London: Routledge.

McVey, Ruth (ed.) (1992), *Southeast Asian Capitalists*. Ithaca: Cornell University Southeast Asia Program.

Mitchell, Katharyne (1995), "Flexible Circulation in the Pacific Rim: Capitalism in Cultural Context," *Economic Geography*, 71(4):364–82.

Mittelman, James H. (2000), *The Globalization Syndrome: Transformation and Resistance*. Princeton: Princeton University Press.

Murdoch, Jonathan (1997), "Towards a Geography of Heterogeneous Associations," *Progress in Human Geography*, 21(3):321–37.

Nathan, Andrew (1993), "Is Chinese Culture Distinctive?" *Journal of Asian Studies*, 52(4):923–36.

Olds, Kris (1998), "Globalization and Urban Change: Tales from Vancouver via Hong Kong," *Urban Geography*, 19(4):360–85.

Olds, Kris, Peter Dicken, Philip Kelly, Lily Kong and Henry Wai-chung Yeung (eds.) (1999), *Globalization and the Asia-Pacific: Contested Territories*. London: Routledge.

Olds, Kris and Henry Wai-chung Yeung (1999), "(Re)shaping 'Chinese' Business Networks in a Globalising Era," *Environment and Planning D: Society and Space*, 17(5):535–55.

Ong, Aihwa and Donald Nonini (eds.) (1997), *Crossing the Edges of Empires: Culture, Capitalism, and Identity*. London: Routledge.

Orrù, Marco, Nicole Biggart and Gary G. Hamilton (1997), *The Economic Organization of East Asian Capitalism*. London: Sage.

Perry, Martin, Lily Kong and Brenda Yeoh (1997), *Singapore: A Developmental City State*. Chichester: John Wiley.

Perry, Martin and Tan Boon Hui (1998), "Global Manufacturing and Local Linkage in Singapore," *Environment and Planning A*, 30(9):1603–24.

Piven, Frances Fox (1995), "Is It Global Economics or Neo-laissez-faire?" *New Left Review*, 213:107–14.

Redding, S. Gordon (1990), *The Spirit of Chinese Capitalism*. Berlin: De Gruyter.

Reich, Robert B. (1991), *The Work of Nations: Preparing Ourselves for 21st-Century Capitalism*. London: Simon and Schuster.

Rhodes, Martin and Richard Higgott (2000), "Introduction: Asian Crises and the Myth of Capitalist 'Convergence'," *The Pacific Review*, 13(1):1–29.

Richter, Frank-Jurgen (1999), *Strategic Networks: The Art of Japanese Interfirm Cooperation*. New York: International Business Press.

Rodan, Garry (1989), *The Political Economy of Singapore's Industralization: National State and International Capital*. London: Macmillan.

Sassen, Saskia (1991), *The Global City: New York, London, Tokyo*. Princeton: Princeton University Press.

Sit, Victor F. S. and Wong Siu-lun (1989), *Small and Medium Industries in an*

Export-Oriented Economy: The Case of Hong Kong. Hong Kong: Centre of Asian Studies, The University of Hong Kong.

Steers, Richard M. (1999), *Made in Korea: Chung Ju Yung and the Rise of Hyundai*. London: Routledge.

The Straits Times, Singapore, various issues.

Thornton, William H. (1998), "Korean and East Asian Exceptionalism," *Theory, Culture and Society*, 15(2):137–54.

Thrift, Nigel (1996), *Spatial Formations*. London: Sage.

—— (1998), "The Rise of Soft Capitalism." In Andrew Herod, Gearoid O Tuathail and Susan M. Roberts (eds.), *An Unruly World: Globalization, Governance and Geography*. London: Routledge, pp. 25–71.

—— (1999), "The Globalization of Business Knowledge." In Kris Olds, Peter Dicken, Philip Kelly, Lily Kong and Henry Wai-chung Yeung (eds.), *Globalization and the Asia Pacific: Contested Territories*. London: Routledge, pp. 57–71.

Thrift, Nigel and Andrew Leyshon (1994), "A Phantom State? The Detraditionalisation of Money, the International Financial System and International Financial Centres," *Political Geography*, 13:299–327.

Tsang, Eric W. K. (1998), "Can *Guanxi* be a Source of Sustained Competitive Advantage for Doing Business in China?" *Academy of Management Executives*, 12(2):64–73.

—— (1999a), "Internationalization as a Learning Process: Singapore MNCs in China," *Academy of Management Executives*, 13(1):91–101.

—— (1999b), "The Knowledge Transfer and Learning Aspects of International HRM: An Empirical Study of Singapore MNCs," *International Business Review*, 8(5/6):591–609.

Tsui-Auch, Lai Si (1999), "Regional Production Relationship and Developmental Impacts: A Comparative Study of Three Regional Networks," *International Journal of Urban and Regional Research*, 23(2):345–60.

Tyson, Laura D'Andrea (1993), *Who's Bashing Whom? Trade Conflicts in High-Technology Industries*. Washington, D.C.: Institute for International Economics.

van Hoesel, Roger (1999), *New Multinational Enterprises from Korea and Taiwan*. London: Routledge.

Wade, Robert (1990), *Governing the Market: Economic Theory and the Role of Government in East Asian Industrialization*. Princeton: Princeton University Press.

Wade, Robert and Frank Veneroso (1998), "The Asian Crisis: The High Debt Model versus the Wall Street-Treasury-IMF Complex," *New Left Review*, 228:3–23.

Wang, Gungwu and Wong Siu-lun (eds.) (1997), *Dynamic Hong Kong: Business and Culture*. Hong Kong: Hong Kong University Press.

Weidenbaum, Murray and Samuel Hughes (1996), *The Bamboo Network: How*

Expatriate Chinese Entrepreneurs Are Creating a New Economic Superpower in Asia. New York: The Free Press.

Weiss, Linda (1998), *The Myth of the Powerless State.* Ithaca: Cornell University Press.

Westney, D. Eleanor (1987), *Imitation and Innovation: The Transfer of Western Organizational Patterns to Meiji Japan.* Cambridge: Harvard University Press.

Whitley, Richard (1992), *Business Systems in East Asia: Firms, Markets and Societies.* London: Sage.

—— (1994), "The Internationalization of Firms and Markets: Its Significance and Institutional Structuring," *Organization,* 1(1):101–24.

—— (1996), "Business Systems and Global Commodity Chains: Competing or Complementary Forms of Economic Organization?" *Competition and Change,* 1(4):411–25.

—— (1998), "Internationalization and Varieties of Capitalism: The Limited Effects of Cross-national Coordination of Economic Activities on the Nature of Business Systems," *Review of International Political Economy,* 5(3):445–81.

—— (1999), *Divergent Capitalisms: The Social Structuring and Change of Business Systems.* New York: Oxford University Press.

Windolf, Paul and Jurgen Beyer (1996), "Co-operative Capitalism: Corporate Networks in Germany and Britain," *British Journal of Sociology,* 47(2):205–31.

Wong, Siu-lun (1988), *Emigrant Entrepreneurs: Shanghai Industrialists in Hong Kong.* Hong Kong: Oxford University Press.

Yao, Souchou (1997), "The Romance of Asian Capitalism: Geography, Desire and Chinese Business." In Mark T. Berger and Douglas A. Borer (eds.), *The Rise of Asia: Critical Visions of the Pacific Century.* London: Routledge, pp. 221–40.

Yeung, Henry Wai-chung (1997a), "Business Networks and Transnational Corporations: A Study of Hong Kong Firms in the ASEAN Region," *Economic Geography,* 73(1):1–25.

—— (1997b), "Cooperative Strategies and Chinese Business Networks: A Study of Hong Kong Transnational Corporations in the ASEAN Region." In Paul W. Beamish and J. Peter Killing (eds.), *Cooperative Strategies: Asia-Pacific Perspectives.* San Francisco: The New Lexington Press, pp. 22–56.

—— (1998a), "Capital, State and Space: Contesting the Borderless World," *Transactions of the Institute of British Geographers,* 23(3):291–309.

—— (1998b), "The Social-spatial Constitution of Business Organizations: A Geographical Perspective," *Organization,* 5(1):101–28.

—— (1998c), *Transnational Corporations and Business Networks.* London: Routledge.

—— (1998d), "The Political Economy of Transnational Corporations: A Study of the Regionalisation of Singaporean Firms," *Political Geography*, 17(4):389–416.

—— (1998e), "Transnational Economic Synergy and Business Networks: The Case of Two-way Investment between Malaysia and Singapore," *Regional Studies*, 32(8):687–706.

—— (ed.) (1999a), *The Globalization of Business Firms from Emerging Economies*, two volumes. Cheltenham: Edward Elgar.

—— (1999b), "Regulating Investment Abroad? The Political Economy of the Regionalisation of Singaporean Firms," *Antipode*, 31(3):245–73.

—— (1999c), "Under Siege? Economic Globalization and Chinese Business in Southeast Asia," *Economy and Society*, 28(1):1–29.

—— (1999d), "The Internationalization of Ethnic Chinese Business Firms from Southeast Asia: Strategies, Processes and Competitive Advantage," *International Journal of Urban and Regional Research*, 23(1):103–27.

—— (1999e), "Limits to the Growth of Family-owned Business? The Case of Chinese Transnational Corporations from Hong Kong," *Family Business Review*, 12.

—— (2000a), "The Dynamics of Asian Business Systems in a Globalising Era," *Review of International Political Economy*, 7(3).

—— (2000b), "A Crisis of Industrial and Business Networks in Asia? Asian Networks in Crisis?" *Environment and Planning A*, 32(2):191–200.

—— (2000c), "Neoliberalism, Laissez-faire Capitalism and Economic Crisis: The Political Economy of Deindustrialisation in Hong Kong," *Competition and Change*, 4:121–69.

—— (2000d), "State Intervention and Neoliberalism in the Globalising World Economy: Lessons from Singapore's Regionalisation Programme," *The Pacific Review*, 13(1):133–62.

—— (2000e), "Economic Globalization, Crisis, and the Emergence of Chinese Business Communities in Southeast Asia," *International Sociology*, 15(2):269–90.

Yeung, Henry Wai-chung (ed.) (2000f), "Theme Issue on Industrial and Business Networks in Asia," *Environment and Planning A*, 32(2):191–304.

Yeung, Henry Wai-chung and Kris Olds (1998), "Singapore's Global Reach: Situating the City-state in the Global Economy," *International Journal of Urban Sciences*, 2(1):24–47.

—— (eds.) (2000), *The Globalization of Chinese Business Firms*. London: Macmillan.

Yoshihara, Kunio (1988), *The Rise of Ersatz Capitalism in South East Asia*. Singapore: Oxford University Press.

7

Political Freedom and Development in Asia: Prospects for Democratization

Jose V. Abueva

Introduction

This is an exploration of the relationship in the Asian region between political freedom and democracy on the one hand and economic freedom and development on the other. The wider context is political freedom in the world as shown in the Freedom House report: *Freedom in the World: The Annual Survey of Political Rights and Civil Liberties 1998–1999*, and human development in the world as depicted in *The 1999 Human Development Report* by the United Nations Development Programme (UNDP).

On the eve of the new millennium, Freedom House reported:

> 88 of the world's 191 countries (46 percent) were rated as Free, meaning that they maintain a high degree of political and economic freedom and respect basic civil liberties. This was the largest number of Free countries on record... Another 53 countries (28 percent of the world total) were rated as Partly Free, enjoying more limited political rights and civil liberties, often in the context of corruption, weak rule of law, ethnic strife, or civil war.... Finally, 50 countries (26 percent of the world total) that deny their citizens' basic [political] rights and civil liberties were rated Not Free (Karatnycky, 1999).

The Freedom House survey reported "that at the end of 1988 there were 117 electoral democracies, representing over 61 percent of the world's countries and nearly 55 percent of its population." Out of the 117 electoral democracies, 88 were rated Free (over 75 percent) and the remaining 29 (about 25 percent) were rated Partly Free. I shall deal with the various types of democracy below.

In terms of the global population of 5.9 billion people living in 191 sovereign states, 2.35 billion people (40 percent) in 88 states are rated Free; 1.57 billion (26.5 percent) in 53 states are rated Partly Free, and 1.98 billion

(33.5 percent) in 50 states are rated Not Free. This is the highest proportion of the world's population living in freedom in the history of the Freedom House survey since the 1970s.

The continued expansion of freedom in the world would validate the claim that we are witnessing, if not also participating in, a "global democratic revolution" that began in the 1970s and has deepened since the collapse of the Soviet Union in 1989. The dimensions of this phenomenon are indicated in Table 7.1.

Table 7.1 The Global Trend in Freedom

	Free	Partly Free	Not Free
1988–1989	61	39	68
1993–1994	72	63	55
1998–1999	88	53	50

Tracking Democracy over Time

	Number of (electoral) democracies
1988–1989	69
1993–1994	108
1998–1999	117

Comparative Political Freedom and Human Development in Asia

Turning to Asia, Freedom House indicates that "19 of the region's 38 countries are Free (50 percent), 9 are Partly Free (24 percent) and 10 are Not Free (26 percent)." It adds: "Despite the looming presence of Communist China and the rhetoric of 'Asian values,' 24 (63 percent) of the region's polities are electoral democracies." I shall deal below with the debate on democracy and its variants in different parts of the world.

My own selection for this chapter includes 23 Asian countries. These are rated by Freedom House on the basis of the degree of their political freedom — and ranked by me according to their individual ratings on political rights and on civil liberties by Freedom House — as shown in Table 7.2.

By Freedom House's own concept, all the eight countries that are rated as Free (35 percent) plus the seven that are rated as Partly Free (30 percent), or a combined total of 65 percent, appear to be electoral democracies. On the other hand, the eight countries rated as Not Free (35 percent) are not electoral democracies. According to my understanding of the concept of

Table 7.2   **Political Freedom in 23 Asian Countries: Political Rights and Civil Liberties, 1998–1999**

Free (8)	Partly Free (7)	Not Free (8)
1st Japan	5th Bangladesh	9th Brunei
2nd Taiwan (ROC)	6th Sri Lanka	9th Cambodia
2nd South Korea (ROK)	6th Nepal	10th China (PRC)
3rd Philippines	6th Pakistan	10th Laos
3rd Thailand	7th Singapore	10th Bhutan
4th Papua New Guinea	7th Malaysia	11th Vietnam
4th Mongolia	8th Indonesia	11th North Korea
4th India		11th Myanmar

"electoral democracies," it refers to those countries that regularly hold reasonably free and fair elections to choose their highest national leaders. But Freedom House specifies that Malaysia does not qualify as an electoral democracy, because the "governing United Malays National Organization enjoys huge and unfair advantages in national elections." Likewise, Freedom House does not regard Singapore as an electoral democracy because the People's Action Party has enjoyed similar advantages vis-à-vis the opposition parties.

Ranked according to their scores in the *UNDP Human Development Index* (HDI), the same Asian countries appear below in relation to each other and in their global ranking by the UNDP among 174 countries. The *1999 Human Development Report* of the UNDP classifies these countries into three categories: High Human Development, Medium Human Development and Low Human Development. Japan is designated as "1st Japan/HDI 4th" because among the 23 Asian countries I have included in this chapter, Japan has the highest score in the HDI in Asia and ranks 4th in the world (Table 7.3).

The HDI is a good general measure or indicator of the extent to which the people in various countries are enjoying or not the benefits of a healthy and longer life, education and livelihood, regardless of their degree of political freedom or their political system, or culture (see supporting tables and graphs at the end of this chapter).

Correlation between Political Freedom and Human Development

Individual countries can be compared in terms of their political freedom as

Table 7.3   Human Development in Asia and in the World, 1999

High HD (4)	Medium HD (13)	Low HD (4)
1st Japan/HDI 4th	5th Malaysia/HDI 56th	18th Laos/HDI 140th
2nd Singapore/HDI 22nd	6th Thailand/HDI 67th	19th Nepal/HDI 144th
3rd Brunei/HDI 25th	7th Philippines/HDI 77th	20th Bhutan/HDI 145th
4th S. Korea/HDI 30th	8th Sri Lanka/HDI 90th	21st Bangladesh/HDI 150th
	9th PR China/HDI 98th	
	10th Indonesia/HDI 105th	
	11th Vietnam/HDI 110th	
	12th Mongolia/HDI 119th	
	13th Myanmar/HDI 128th	
	14th Papua New Guinea/ HDI 129th	
	15th India/HDI 132nd	
	16th Cambodia/HDI 137th	
	17th Pakistan/HDI 138th	

measured by Freedom House and their human development as indicated by the HDI prepared by the UNDP. By combining these two indicators, one can see that Japan, a parliamentary democracy and constitutional monarchy, is Free, supposedly the freest in Asia. At the same time, she has a very high score in HDI, in fact the highest in Asia and the fourth highest among 174 countries. South Korea, a presidential-parliamentary democracy, rates second in political freedom in Asia, along with Taiwan (ROC). In HDI, South Korea scores 4th in Asia and High and 30th in the world. Taiwan, a presidential-parliamentary democracy, is Free; although she is not included in the UNDP listing because she is not a member of the United Nations, she also ranks high in HDI.

One can say that in Japan, South Korea and Taiwan, political freedom and human development and economic freedom are positively correlated. Such a correlation has long been visibly demonstrated in the industrialized democracies of the West (Western Europe, North America) and more recently in Israel, Australia and New Zealand. They all score high in both political and economic freedom and in development, which are factors that tend to support and sustain each other. Their broad middle class, marked by high incomes, education and productivity and a sense of autonomy, and a free press, make possible the vibrant civil society needed in participatory democracies.

Among the 23 Asian countries in this study, the positive correlation between political freedom and human development in Japan, South Korea and Taiwan is exceptional. On the whole, the statistical analysis of the Asian countries shows the absence of a strong linear relationship between political freedom and human development (Figure 7.1). It shows that three countries (Partly Free Singapore and Malaysia and Not Free Brunei) show good performance with respect to human development. Countries that do not

Figure 7.1   The Relationship between Political Freedom and Human Development

perform that well with respect to human development include the Free Philippines, Partly Free Bangladesh, Sri Lanka, Nepal and Pakistan, as well as Not Free countries.

Unlike Japan, South Korea and Taiwan, Singapore, a tightly managed, dominant party regime rated as Partly Free, ranks High in HDI, 2nd only to Japan in Asia and 22nd in the world. Economic freedom and effective governance in Singapore make her a leader in economic development in Southeast Asia.

Moreover, tiny Brunei — with a population of 300,000 and a traditional, autocratic monarchy rated as Not Free — ranks High in HDI, third in Asia and 30th in the world because the oil-rich sultanate makes possible a high level of social services, a modern infrastructure and high per capita GDP. Likewise, Malaysia, a parliamentary polity with a constitutional monarchy and dominant party, is rated as Partly Free, but she scores a high Medium in HDI, 5th in Asia and a high Medium and 56th in the world.

In the case of Singapore, Brunei and Malaysia, citizens enjoy high per capita income, a high level of education and longevity while their political freedom is constrained. High human development co-exists with lack of political freedom.

Among our 23 Asian countries, there are 5 others that rank Free or high in political freedom, along with Japan, Taiwan and South Korea. These are the Philippines and Thailand, which rank third in Asia, and Papua New Guinea, Mongolia and India, which rank fourth. They all rank Medium in Human Development. In HDI Thailand, a parliamentary democracy and constitutional monarchy "influenced by the military," is 6th in Asia and 67th in the world. In HDI the Philippines, a presidential-legislative democracy, is 7th in Asia and 77th in the world.

With their HDI scores also in the low Medium category are the Free countries of Mongolia, Papua New Guinea and India. Mongolia, a presidential-parliamentary democracy, is 12th in Asia and 119th in the world in HDI. Papua New Guinea, a parliamentary democracy, is 14th in Asia and 129th in the world in HDI. India, a parliamentary democracy, is 15th in Asia and 132nd in the world in HDI. Recognized as the world's largest democracy and a developing country, India is also the world's second most populous nation (988.7 million). Its ability to uphold political freedom amid formidable socio-economic problems has been remarkable.

While being rated Free or High in political freedom, the Philippines and Thailand are far exceeded in human development by Partly Free Singapore and Malaysia and Not Free Brunei. It must be considered, however, that the populations of the Philippines (75.3 million) and Thailand (61 million) are much larger than Singapore's (3.9 million) and Brunei's (300,000). Even much lower in HDI than Singapore, Brunei and Malaysia are the three democracies of Mongolia, Papua New Guinea and India.

Sri Lanka — a presidential-parliamentary democracy plagued "by insurgency," and rated as Partly Free — scores higher in human development than the Free or democratic countries of Papua New Guinea, Mongolia and India. Also scoring higher in human development than these three democracies — ranking 11th in human development among our 23 Asian countries — is Vietnam, a Communist one-party polity. Rated as Not Free, Vietnam ranks 11th or is among the lowest of our 23 Asian countries in terms of political freedom, along with North Korea and Myanmar.

The People's Republic of China (PRC) — a Communist one-party polity rated as Not Free — allows relatively little political freedom to its one billion two hundred million citizens. However, it has instituted basic economic reforms that allow them economic freedom. Consequently, China has become a dynamic economic power as well as a formidable military power in Asia. In fact, the PRC also ranks 9th in human development among our 23 Asian countries. It ranks higher in HDI than the democracies of Mongolia, Papua New Guinea and India; the Partly Free countries of Indonesia, Bangladesh, Nepal and Pakistan; and all the other Not Free countries of Vietnam, Cambodia, Laos, Bhutan, North Korea and Myanmar.

Clearly, in Asia democracy or High political freedom (Japan, Taiwan and South Korea) can correlate positively with High human development. Democracy or High political freedom (the Philippines and Thailand, and to a lesser degree Mongolia, Papua New Guinea and India) can also correlate with Medium human development. The most notable exceptions are Singapore and Brunei, which are High in human development but only Partly Free or Not Free in political freedom, respectively.

Also notably exceptional are China and Vietnam among the Not Free countries that score well in Medium human development (China ranking 9th in Asia and Vietnam, 11th). To reiterate and emphasize, in human development, the two Communist countries surpass the democracies of Mongolia, Papua New Guinea and India, and the Partly Free countries of Bangladesh, Nepal, Pakistan and Indonesia. In human development, Myanmar (Burma), rated the lowest among the Not Free countries, also exceeds the democracies of Papua New Guinea and India, the Partly Free countries of Bangladesh, Nepal and Pakistan, and the other Not Free countries of Cambodia, Laos and Bhutan.

Degrees of Political Freedom and Variants of Democracy

Thus far, we have used the concept of "political freedom" as the degree to which the people in a country can and do actually exercise and enjoy their political rights and civil liberties. Freedom House elaborates on this concept, which it used in judging and classifying the world's polities as Free, Partly Free, or Not Free, and which I have borrowed for my comparison and assessment of Asian polities.

> Political rights enable people to participate freely in the political process, which is the system by which the polity chooses authoritative policy makers and attempts to make binding decisions affecting national, regional, or local community. In a free society, this represents the right of all adults to vote and compete for public office, and for elected representatives to have a decisive vote on public policies. Civil liberties include freedoms to develop views, institutions, and personal autonomy apart from the State (Freedom House, 1999).

Political freedom is a *sine qua non* of the kind of political system called "democracy" as distinguished from authoritarian or dictatorial rule and totalitarianism. Democracy may be defined in its minimal or procedural meaning which is useful in comparing the world's political systems. We have already used the concept of "electoral democracy" in the sense of a political system in which "all elected national authority must be the product of free and fair electoral processes" (Karatnycky, 1999).

Synonymous with "electoral democracy" is the concept of "procedural democracy," according to which "a political system is democratic to the degree that its most powerful decision-makers (president or prime minister and legislature)" (Abueva, 1997:2) are "selected through fair, honest and periodic elections in which candidates freely compete for votes and in which virtually all adult population is eligible to vote" (Huntington, 1991:7). We may add the criterion that "there is possibility of alternation in power of the contending groups" (Mainwaring and Shugart, 1997: 297–98). In addition to, or transcending, "electoral democracy," "substantive democracy" or "optimal democracy" puts the political system "to the test of policy performance — the capacity of its institutions and leaders to deliver what is promised and expected" in the constitution and by the nation's leaders (Abueva, 1997:2).

Democracy as an ideal or model political system originated in the West. Over a long period, it was established and developed as a set of political institutions and practices in response to the culture, challenges and circumstances of each country. When Western democracy was transplanted into non-Western countries and former colonies with very different cultures and histories, the import necessarily had to undergo adaptation and change in its new and different milieu. Following World War II, leaders in many newly independent states soon gave up or drastically modified the imported institutions of Western democracy in favour of varying forms of authoritarian or consensual rule more conducive to their own cultures and predilections.

As variants of Western democracy or even authoritarian regimes in some developing countries succeeded in unifying their countries and achieving political stability, and a substantial measure of social and economic development, their political leaders have questioned the judgment of their political systems as undemocratic by Western leaders and scholars. In Asia as elsewhere, some political leaders and scholars have challenged the right of non-Western countries to determine the kind of democratic political system best suited to their own values, traditions and cultures. Admittedly, democracy has gained such a nearly universal legitimacy and appeal that most countries, including the most authoritarian ones, affirm their adherence to human rights and democracy in their constitutions and ideologies.

In practice, some governments have made an implicit trade off in the observance of human rights that are supposed to be indivisible. They would seem to justify their neglect or suppression of political rights and civil liberties embodied in the Universal Declaration of Human Rights in terms of their progress in promoting the International Covenant on Social, Economic and Cultural Rights. To ward off external pressure on their countries to observe human rights, ASEAN Foreign Ministers in 1993 "emphasized that the protection and promotion of human rights in the international community should take cognizance of the principles of respect for national sovereignty, territorial integrity and non-interference in the internal affairs of states" (Muyot, 2000:98).

The Singaporean political scientist and diplomat, Chan Heng Chee, is perhaps the most articulate advocate of non-Western variants of the Western model of democracy. She poses the following questions: (1) "Must all democracies be liberal democracies? (2) Is it possible to have democracies that are not liberal? (3) Must all democracies look like versions of Anglo-American democracy, or will they become Asian democracies and African democracies?" (Chan, 1993:7). In effect, Chan answers her own questions: "No" to the first; "Yes" to the second; "No" to the third. She avers that democracies in Asia are sufficiently different from Western liberal democracies and significant in their own right. The former should, therefore, be regarded, in her view, as a different variant to be recognized and accepted as "Asian democracies."

Concluding her brief review of Asian political systems, Chan extrapolates the following characteristics as common to "Asian democracies:"

1. A communitarian sense which teaches that the individual is important as part of a group or society, rather than the notion that the individual is the centerpiece of democracy and society.
2. Across the board, there is greater acceptance of and respect for authority and hierarchy whether it is in India, China, or Japan and the countries of Southeast Asia. Adversarial opposition against the state and people in positions of power are not absent but certainly not a normal reflex.
3. The dominant party which can remain in power for two to three decades. (Examples of this are the Liberal Democratic Party in Japan, the United Malays Nationalist Organization in Malaysia, the People's Action Party in Singapore, the Golkar in Indonesia, the Congress Party in India.)
4. Nearly all Asian countries have a centralized bureaucracy and a strong state which is also an interventionist state with a large state sector (Chan, 1993:21–24).

Finally, Chan avers that democracy should be regarded more as a means rather than an end. The "end goal should be a good society which incorporates a good government"; "then democracy is but one virtue in the basket [of virtues] to be weighed" (Chan, 1993:26).

Liberal Democracy, Illiberal Democracy and Authoritarianism

In response to critics of the imposition of Western liberal democracy as a universal standard applicable to all countries, it can be said that the concept of "electoral democracy" or "procedural democracy" is a minimal, operational standard that is already widely accepted and applied at least formally. With the constant diffusion, learning and adaptation of political thought around the world, democratic norms and modes of governance are no longer simply Western but increasingly a part of the universal heritage of humankind. Asian, African and Latin American peoples have established and developed their own kinds of democracy that would pass the test of "electoral" or "procedural" democracy as a common if less than universal, minimum standard of good governance.

The 88 countries rated Free by Freedom House include several that are non-Western and developing countries. Representing 46 percent of the world's 191 countries, they would conform to the standard of "liberal democracy." The 53 countries rated Partly Free (23 percent of the world total) may be regarded as "illiberal democracies." But the 50 remaining countries rated Not Free (26 percent of the world total) may not be called democracies without making meaningless the political genus we recognize and call "democracy." Looking at our sample of 23 Asian political systems, we can apply the same rule of classification without disrespect or any feeling of superiority, especially as we know only too well the shortcomings and even perversions that mark our own polities and countries.

In comparing Asian countries with other countries, Chan Heng Chee may be over-generalizing in saying, "Across the board, there is greater acceptance of and respect for authority and hierarchy whether it is in India, China, or Japan and the countries of Southeast Asia." She does not support this assertion or hypothesis with empirical evidence. If she considers China and Vietnam as democracies, being "Asian democracies" according to her own definition, this would be stretching the meaning of "democracy" in its minimal or procedural sense, as generally understood. To reiterate, this is a political system marked by regular, free and fair elections for the selection of the major political decision-makers by most adult citizens who enjoy political rights and civil liberties.

As scholars, we are engaged in the quest for truth according to our best lights. Those who prefer democracy — and the freedom and human rights that go with it — to other political systems, would also regard democracy as both a means and an end of society. For without freedom and human rights, the human community is greatly diminished. To say this is not to overlook or minimize the difficult choices that the leaders and people of particular countries have had to make in building their societies, economies and political institutions, nor is it to deny every people's right to self-determination. President Jiang Zemin is right in saying: "Every country has the right to choose the social system, ideology, economic system and path of development that suits its national conditions" (Isaacson, 1999:4).

Political and Economic Change and Continuity in Asia

In the past 70 years, Asian countries have undergone political change ranging from peaceful to violent evolutionary change. With the exceptions of Japan, China and Thailand, the Asian countries in our survey achieved independent statehood after World War II from European, Japanese, or American colonial rule. Most nationalist leaders in the independence struggle vowed to install a democratic polity upon attaining independence but few post-independence democratic regimes developed and sustained their nascent and fragile democratic institutions.

Some who had more success would also suffer reverses and still have to build viable and sustainable democracies. From the start, the founding leaders in certain countries, such as the PRC and the Democratic Republic of Vietnam, opted to establish authoritarian regimes that would enable them to direct and control their political and economic development.

I can only illustrate the phenomena of political and economic change and continuity with regard to some of the Asian countries. In going over my review, it would be helpful to bear in mind Chan Heng Chee's characterization of the common features of Asian political systems and my comments on it.

China went through dynastic, imperial rule, Western and Japanese encroachments on its sovereignty and territories, nascent national unification under Sun Yat Sen and Chiang Kai Shek, and a successful Communist revolution in 1949 that drove the KMT forces under Chiang to Taiwan. Mao unified China as the world's largest Communist state but plunged her into economic disaster through his economic experiments and a cultural revolution.

After Mao's death in 1976, Deng Xiaoping's ascendancy and economic reforms enabled China finally to achieve its economic great leap forward into self-sustaining economic growth at the highest levels in the world. Deng's successors have continued with the economic reforms and instituted some political reforms under the "one country, two systems" paradigm, exemplified lately by Hong Kong's becoming a Special Administrative Region.

Pro-democracy dissidents were crushed at Tiananmen Square in Beijing in 1989, but the underground democracy movement is alive. The democratic opening in Hong Kong and the dramatic example of democracy on Taiwan demonstrate the advantages of matching economic freedom with political freedom. Competitive local elections and governance show contrasts with authoritarian national governance. With external moral support and pressure, the home-grown democracy movement awaits the crucial support of a faction of the national leadership to gain momentum for political liberalization.

On the eve of independence from Great Britain, India was convulsed in the bloody partition that gave birth to Muslim Pakistan, geographically divided into West and East Pakistan. In turn, East Pakistan seceded to become Bangladesh. India opted to remain a secular, democratic state, the largest and one of the poorest nations to become and remain a democracy. Unlike India, Pakistan and then also Bangladesh alternated between military rule and democracy; to date Pakistan has lapsed into military rule and Bangladesh is an electoral democracy. India has made remarkable progress in its industrialization and has joined the club of nations with nuclear military capability. Enmity and armed rivalry between India and Pakistan has continued over Kashmir, and Pakistan's production of nuclear missiles has heightened tension between them.

In area and population, Sri Lanka is miniscule compared to India, Pakistan and Bangladesh. But in the decades since its independence, Sri Lanka achieved impressive social and economic development compared to its three neighbours in the region. Its progress has continued but is burdened by the unceasing and economically ruinous civil war between the ruling Singhalese majority and the ethnic Tamil Sri Lankans. Sri Lanka's HDI is tenth among our sample countries, ahead of China, India, Pakistan, Indonesia and Vietnam.

After achieving economic status as newly industrializing countries (NICs) under military rule, South Korea and Taiwan achieved political liberalization that culminated in their transformation in the 1980s to new democracies in Asia. With their open economies and political freedom, the two countries and Japan continue to lead in economic development in Asia. The robust and open economies of China, Hong Kong, Taiwan and Singapore enabled them to withstand the economic turmoil that engulfed East and Southeast Asia from July 1997.

In the 1980s, it was the astounding economic development and high growth rates of Japan, South Korea, Taiwan, Hong Kong and Singapore that economic observers called the East Asian "economic miracle." This was followed by Malaysia, Thailand and Indonesia. On this account, economic forecasters were then predicting that the next century would be "the Asian Century." Then came the economic crisis and currency turmoil that began in Thailand and engulfed most of Asia. China, Taiwan and Hong Kong were best able to cope with the challenge. Malaysia, South Korea and Thailand rebounded by 1999. Indonesia was plunged into economic as well as political crises. The Philippines coped with the crisis until 1998 when it was confronted with more political and economic problems.

North Korea, the most orthodox Communist regime in Asia, is rated last with Myanmar among the eight Not Free countries. It has serious economic problems, including threats of famine, and has only about a third of South Korea's GDP per capita. Divided Korea, like divided Germany, has shown how two political and economic systems, one capitalist and free, the other authoritarian with a centrally controlled economy, can have very different outcomes for their peoples. After 50 years of political tension and insecurity in the Korean peninsula, the recent historic meeting of the leaders of North Korea and South Korea augurs well for eventual unification of the estranged peoples and the long-term development and democratization of North Korea.

Indonesia waged a successful war of independence with the Netherlands and was governed by Sukarno as a quasi parliamentary democracy for almost 20 years. His coalition rule did not develop the economy. His dalliance with the Communists ended in 1965 in political chaos, massive violence against the ethnic Chinese, and a military takeover under Suharto. Military hegemony under Suharto gradually led to rapid economic growth and then later on to growing demands for political liberalization amid corruption and the abuse of power by the military.

Economic freedom and development that made Indonesia an NIC also led students and civilians to demand democratization. Their agitation forced Suharto to resign after over 30 years as President, in favour of Vice-President Habibie. The groundswell for democratization led to the defeat of Habibie by Wahid in the 1999 elections. In East Timor, a war between the forces of independence and the Indonesian military and militias ended in independence for East Timor, which Indonesia had annexed in 1965. The consolidation of the fledgling democracy proceeds as Muslims and Christians clash in some parts of the archipelago, and Aceh and Irian Jaya struggle for secession and independence.

The Philippines established the first democratic republic in Southeast Asia during the Filipino Revolution of 1896, only to be colonized by the U.S. Filipinos enjoyed increasing political autonomy and self-rule in their "colonial democracy," and regained their independence from the U.S. in 1946 after the Japanese occupation. As a young democracy in Asia then, the Philippines was second only to Japan in socio-economic development from the late 1940s to the early 1950s. But high population growth rates, protectionist economic policies, populist and corrupt politics and government — amid chronic social injustice, agrarian problems, and Communist and Muslim insurgencies — have combined to slow down socio-economic development since then.

In 1972, Marcos imposed a rapacious authoritarian rule that lasted over 13 years, until early 1986. His overthrow in the peaceful EDSA revolution in 1986 marked the restoration of democracy but with a politicized military that tried seven times to topple the government of Corazon Aquino. The consolidation of democracy under Aquino, Ramos and Estrada has been complicated by a population of 75 million, and by chronic problems of poverty, injustice and unemployment that force tens of thousands of Filipinos to seek work overseas.

The peace agreement in 1996 between the government and the Moro National Liberation Front was based on a firmer recognition of the right of the Moros, as Muslim Filipinos, to greater regional autonomy and development. However, war is raging in Mindanao between the government and its armed forces and the Moro Islamic Liberation Front that seeks independence and the establishment of a Bangsa Moro Islamic State. Meanwhile, the otherwise weakened Communist New People's Army is taking advantage of the turmoil in the south. These are lingering signs of the weakness of Filipino democracy and development.

Emerging from British colonial rule after World War II, Malaya and Singapore would become parliamentary democracies even as they were threatened by Communist insurgency. In 1963, Malaysia was formed with the addition of Sabah and Sarawak. The federal system assimilated the traditional sultanate into the modern polity. The predominant Malays assumed greater constitutional political power vis-à-vis the ethnic Chinese citizens who dominate the economy, in order to tilt the ethnic balance in favour of the bumiputras. In Malaysia, as in Singapore, the dominant party has continuously controlled and exercised power, and opposition forces have had no realistic chance of coming into power. Apparently, sustained economic prosperity and political stability have given legitimacy to the monopolistic ruling party and the political system. But Mahathir's persecution of his former deputy has fanned the opposition's demands for democracy.

As leader of the People's Action Party, Lee Kuan Yew led the development of Singapore with singular political and economic skills and transparent honesty, making it an NIC by the 1970s. Singaporeans experienced prosperity, social development, and political order and stability. Similarly, Malaysia, beginning with Tungku Abdul Rahman, was governed by a succession of leaders, and finally Mahathir, who propelled her to considerable industrialization, economic prosperity and political stability. Compared to the Filipinos, Singaporean and Malaysian leaders have managed to rule continuously under their ruling parties for over 30 years to date. It is this one-party hegemony and other political constraints that have made Freedom House rate Singapore and Malaysia as Partly Free in 1998–1999. They are also referred to, arguably, as "illiberal democracies."

Since 1932, Thailand has seen an alternation of military rule and parliamentary democracy, and since the 1940s steady social and economic development. It has had the great advantage of the unifying and humanizing leadership of a beloved monarch in King Bhumibol Adulyadev in the past 30 years. Moreover, Thailand's agricultural development and increasing industrialization have produced for its people enough food at affordable prices and ample employment which allow per capita incomes higher than that of most of our 23 Asian countries. Its strategic location astride east-west travel routes, its interesting, exotic culture and moderate cost make Thailand a favourite tourist destination, and as a result its foreign exchange earnings are also much higher than those of most other Asian countries.

Vietnam was finally united as a Communist state in 1975, following some 30 years of anti-colonial liberation wars. With its human and material resources expended, Vietnam had to rebuild and develop and eventually compete as well with its neighbours in a globalizing environment. With such debilitating wars as background and a population now of 78 million, it is no small feat that Vietnam has been able to feed her people and achieved Medium Human Development. Leaders of the Communist Party, the heroes and heirs of the national revolution and anti-colonial wars, have the legitimacy to govern the country and they are introducing economic reforms to achieve faster economic development.

Prospects for Liberalization and Democratization in Asia

The examples of South Korea, Taiwan, Thailand, and lately Indonesia suggest the various ways in which authoritarian regimes that achieve appreciable prosperity and social development in a free and competitive economy can create conditions that trigger the people's demands for political liberalization and democratization. In these countries, students and intellectuals joined opposition leaders to persuade some leaders in factions of the ruling party to make the decisive shift away from authoritarianism. Economic freedom and prosperity led to demands for political freedom.

In general, factors in the society, culture and the nation's historical experience create conditions that influence the kinds of political systems that emerge in a particular country. But it is the national leaders' perceptions and interpretations of those conditions, and their vision of the country's future that determine their actual priorities, choices and actions as leaders.

In the course of time, leaders have to decide what to do as they confront the needs and challenges of national unification and survival, especially under threats from external and internal enemies and hazards, of political order and stability, of economic development and equitable redistribution of wealth, of political participation, direction and control, of power sharing and empowerment of various groups and sectors in society, and so on. Leaders have to calculate and balance these various goals and processes and their consequences for their own power and longevity in power, and for the greater good of the people and community.

Chan has explained some of the values, attitudes and behaviour that influence Asian leaders in their preferences concerning leadership, citizenship, governance and political systems. Evidently, there are also other sets of orientations that have led to alternative choices and actions by leaders.

It is suggested that political liberalization and democratization are more likely to happen in the kinds of political systems rated as Partly Free than those rated as Not Free. But those already rated Free have a great deal more to accomplish to improve the standards, structures and processes of governance. Electoral democracies may not long endure if they cannot remove or reduce their more glaring imperfections, such as corruption, weak enforcement of laws, cronyism or political favouritism, bureaucratic waste and inefficiency, a partial judiciary, and many more.

Ultimately, electoral or procedural democracies will be judged by their ability to deliver the substance of policies and programmes, to fulfil political promises. The ability of the Partly Free or even some Not Free polities to deliver social services, economic prosperity, security and public safety, political order and stability, and good infrastructure can mark them as legitimate and desirable to their citizens and leaders at some stages of the country's development. This is largely the reason for their sustainability and longevity.

As our "cases" have shown, the emergence and broadening of the middle class, and the political awareness and activism of civil society and its organizations can spark political change in conjunction with sympathetic members of the leadership groups. Dynamic and transforming leaders can make the crucial difference in the equation of political change More-over, nations are less and less isolated from the rest of the world. It is commonplace to recognize that globalization links up various markets or economies, different political systems, and different cultures through telecommunications, travel and computers. All these are assisting the impact of the global democratic revolution on countries that are Free, Partly Free, or Not Free. Various governments, international organizations, international non-governmental organizations and universities are also assisting.

Statistical Appendix

The SAS System
Correlation Analysis
2 'VAR' Variables POLFREE HDI
Simple Statistics

Variable	N	Mean	Std Dev	Med
POLFREE	23	6.478261	3.231515	6.000000
HDI	21	96.904762	46.481077	110.000000

Simple Statistics

Variable	Minimum	Maximum
POLFREE	1.000000	11.000000
HDI	4.000000	150.000000

Spearman Correlation Coefficients/ Prob > IRI under Ho: Rho=0/
Number of Observations

	POLFREE	HDI
POLFREE	1.000000 0.0 23	0.30657 0.1765 21
HDI	0.30657 0.1765 21	1.000000 0.0 21

The SAS System
Kendall Tau b Correlation Coefficients/ Prob > IRI under Ho: Rho=0/
Number of Observations

	POLFREE	HDI
POLFREE	1.000000 0.0 23	0.24641 0.1283 21
HDI	0.24641 0.1283 21	1.000000 0.0 21

For the statistical analysis, I wish to thank Dean Ana Maria L. Tabunda, Ph.D., of the Statistical Center, University of the Philippines. She computed the Spearman correlation coefficient and the Kendall tau b correlation coefficient, which are the appropriate coefficients when the data are ordinal. The estimated Spearman correlation coefficient between the variables Political Freedom and Human Development is 0.307. The estimated Kendall tau b correlation coefficient is 0.246. Both estimates indicate that the correlation between the two variables is not significantly different from 0 even at 0.10 levels of significance.

References

Abueva, Jose V. (1997), "Philippine Democratization and the Consolidation of Democracy since the 1986 EDSA Revolution: An Overview of the Main Issues, Trends and Prospects." In F. B. Miranda (ed.), *Democratization: Philippine Perspectives*. Diliman, Quezon City: University of the Philippines Press, pp. 1–82.

Chan, Heng Chee (1993), "Democracy: Evolution and Implementation, An Asian Perspective." In R. Bartley, Chan Heng Chee, S. P. Huntington (eds.), *Democracy and Capitalism: Asian and American Perspectives*. Singapore: Institute of Southeast Asian Studies, pp. 1–26.

Freedom House (1999), *Freedom in the World: The Annual Survey of Political Rights and Civil Liberties*. Washington, D.C.

Huntington, Samuel P. (1991), *The Third Wave: Democratization in the Late Twentieth Century*. Norman: University of Oklahoma Press.

Isaacson, Walter (11 October 1999), "Our Newstour to China," *Time*.

Karatnycky, Adrian (1999), "The Comparative Survey of Freedom 1989–1999, A Good Year for Freedom." In Freedom House, *Freedom in the World: Annual Survey of Political Rights and Civil Liberties*.

Mainwaring, Scott, Guillermo O'Donnell and J. Samuel Valenzuela (eds.) (1997), *Issues in Democratic Consolidation: The New South American Democracies in Perspective*. Notre Dame, Indiana: University of Notre Dame Press, pp. 297–98.

Muyot, Albert (2000), "ASEAN Human Rights Policy." In A. Muyot (ed.), *Social Justice and Human Rights in the Philippines*. Diliman, Quezon City: University of the Philippines Press.

UNDP (1999), *1999 Human Development Report*. New York.

8

Hong Kong's Partial Democracy under Stress

Siu-kai Lau

In the second half of the 1980s, when the Basic Law — the mini-constitution of the Hong Kong Special Administrative Region (HKSAR) — was drafted, a partially democratic political system was deemed by Beijing to be the most appropriate political framework to allow Hong Kong to maintain its stability and prosperity after the end of colonial rule, and simultaneously to partially satisfy Hongkongers' aspirations for democratic governance. At the centre of Hong Kong's partial democracy is an executive-led political system featuring a strong executive with exclusive control of the policy and legislative initiative. The political system can be described as partially democratic because, whilst Hongkongers are denied the right to elect their Chief Executive, they are to a certain extent granted the power to choose their legislators. The *raison d'être* of the legislature (the Legislative Council or Legco) is to prevent the abuse of power by the executive. The Legco is given the power to veto the bills from the executive, though other than that

Some of the data used in this chapter was collected by a research project entitled "Social Issues and Social Problems in the Early Years of The Hong Kong Special Administrative Region: Indicators of Social Development 1999." The project was generously funded by the Research Grants Council of the Universities Grants Committee (Project Number: POLYU5185/98H). The project was a joint enterprise of the Hong Kong Institute of Asia-Pacific Studies (HKIAPS) at The Chinese University of Hong Kong, the Centre of Asian Studies at The University of Hong Kong, and the Department of Applied Social Studies at the Hong Kong Polytechnic University. I am grateful to Ms. Wan Po-san, Research Officer of HKIAPS, for rendering assistance to the project in many ways. Special thanks are due to my two dedicated research assistants, Mr. Yiu Chuen-lai and Mr. Yip Tin-sang, for their help in administering the questionnaire, data analysis and information collection.

the constitutional powers at the disposal of the legislature are minimal (Lau, 1995, 2000a).

To make sure that the legislature poses no serious difficulties for the executive in the early years of the HKSAR, the composition of the legislature in the first ten years of post-1997 Hong Kong is such that not more than half of the 60-strong legislature is made up of members directly elected by Hongkongers. That is to say, the Chief Executive of the HKSAR, who is elected by an élitist electoral committee and unconditionally backed by Beijing, will receive ardent support from a legislature the majority of whose members are elected by voters coming from élite circles. It was anticipated that the executive-legislative relationship would be harmonious at least in the early years of the HKSAR if not afterwards.[1] Accordingly, Beijing saw the relationship between the executive and the legislature as basically complementary rather than conflictive (Xiao, 1990:254–56; Wang, 1997: 226–28). The possibility of executive-legislative gridlock or stalemate was so much discounted that the Basic Law virtually has no provision for handling it were it to come about.

On the surface at least, the executive-led political system of the HKSAR seems to have operated in accordance with design since the retrocession of the territory to China in 1997. Close to 100 percent of the bills introduced into the Legco by the executive have been dutifully passed by the legislators, though quite a number of them by a narrow margin. Almost all of the significant motions or bills tabled by the legislators themselves have been defeated in the chamber, relieving the Chief Executive — Tung Chee-hwa — of the burden of exercising his power of veto. It appears then that the Panglossian view of the executive-legislative relationship of the HKSAR held by Beijing is justified. Nevertheless, closer scrutiny will discover stresses and strains in the superficially tranquil political scene. They will become more and more serious in the near future, *ceteris paribus*. Instead of a co-operative executive-legislative relationship, the possibility of executive-legislative gridlock is looming large, threatening on the one hand to weaken the quality of governance in Hong Kong and on the other hand to aggravate political alienation and political mistrust in society.

That the executive-led system designed by Beijing should encounter stresses and strains much earlier than originally expected can be explained by the uncongenial political environment in which the system is implanted. Beijing's political fears and prejudices also play a part, as do Tung Chee-hwa's political personality and governing strategy. Both Beijing and Tung have also underestimated the conflict between the executive and the legislature inherent in the political system. Finally, the stresses and strains in Hong Kong's partial democracy are vastly magnified by the economic dislocations wrought by the Asian financial turmoil and its clumsy handling by the Tung administration.

In the final analysis, the executive-led political system as envisaged in the Basic Law is by and large a constitutional phenomenon reflecting the intentions of Beijing. To what extent a constitutional phenomenon materializes into a real political phenomenon depends on a host of factors beyond the control or even the comprehension of the constitution-makers. History is littered with cases where constitutional intentions are distorted beyond recognition by unforeseen circumstances and developments.[2] Hong Kong's experience, therefore, should not be seen as unique or idiosyncratic.

In the following discussion, I shall concentrate on the tight relationship between the executive and the legislature, which epitomizes the stresses and strains in Hong Kong's partial democracy. Findings about Hong Kong's public opinion come from a territory-wide survey conducted in the summer of 1999.[3]

Inherent Contradictions in Hong Kong's Partial Democracy

Ian Scott, a longtime observer of Hong Kong's political scene, sees the institutional components of Hong Kong's post-1997 political system as disarticulated, meaning that the relationships between the executive, the legislature and the bureaucracy are uncoordinated, poorly developed, fractious and sometimes dysfunctional. "In Hong Kong, with a system which is neither parliamentary fish nor presidential fowl, the executive, the bureaucracy and the legislature (which is divided within itself) each pursue their own agendas, punctuated by occasional skirmishes on the boundaries of their domains and by subterranean campaigns to extend their jurisdictions" (Scott, 2000:29).

While there is a kernel of truth in Scott's observation, his portrayal of the irregularities in the operation of Hong Kong's partial democracy is exaggerated. The fact that up to now the Tung administration is still capable of dominating the political scene despite all the challenges has not been given due recognition in his analysis.

Hong Kong's executive-led political system resembles a presidential system in many aspects except for the fact that the Chief Executive is not popularly elected.[4] Moreover, inasmuch as Hong Kong is not a sovereign nation, the central government in Beijing reserves the power to appoint or not appoint the winner in the electoral contest for the post of the Chief Executive. Compared with many presidents, however, the Chief Executive of the HKSAR has many more constitutional powers at his/her disposal. Just as in presidential systems elsewhere, the executive-led system of Hong Kong features a division of power between the executive and the legislature. In contrast with parliamentary systems, which distinguish themselves by power sharing between the executive and the legislature, there is a perennial possibility of executive-legislative confrontation and paralysis of government stemming from the failure of the executive to obtain stable and reliable majority support in the legislature.[5] "By and large, presidentialism has performed poorly. With the sole exception of the United States, all other presidential systems have been fragile — they have regularly succumbed to coups and breakdowns" (Sartori, 1997:86). U.S. exceptionalism lies ironically in the fact that party discipline is weak, if not non-existent, and the president, therefore, has ample opportunities to engage in horse-trading with individual members in Congress (Riggs, 1988). But even in the case of the U.S., to maintain strong and effective governance is difficult. In light of the nature of presidential systems, even under ideal circumstances, a certain number of inter-institutional conflicts in the political system of the HKSAR are inevitable and hence should be considered as healthy, indicating that the mechanism of "checks and balances" is at work. This is particularly true in the case of the conflicts between the executive and the legislature notwithstanding the subsidiary role of the latter in the governance of Hong Kong.

The power relationship between the executive and the legislature in Hong Kong's partial democracy is grossly asymmetrical. The government, headed by the Chief Executive of the HKSAR, is given a higher political status as well as the exclusive power to make policies and to initiate legislation. The Chief Executive is not only the head of the government, but he/she is also the head of the HKSAR and shall represent the Region. As head of the HKSAR, the Chief Executive enjoys a constitutional status much higher than that of the legislature whose members individually represent functional or geographical interests. The executive's exclusive power in policy-making and legislation, safeguarded in the Basic Law primarily by means of Article 74, in effect scuttles the ability of the legislature to propose private members' bills with meaningful policy implications. According to that article, "[m]embers of the Legislative Council of the Hong Kong Special Administrative Region may introduce bills in accordance with the provisions of this Law and legal procedures. Bills which do not relate to public expenditure or political structure or the operation of the government may be introduced individually or jointly by members of the Council. The written consent of the Chief Executive shall be required before bills relating to government policies are introduced."

Even if a private member's bill does on a rare occasion get tabled before the legislature, it has to undergo a very tough process for its passage. Unlike the passage of a government bill, which requires a simple majority of the legislators present, the passage of a private member's bill entails the division of the legislature into two sections: legislators returned by functional constituencies and those returned by geographical constituencies. Its passage is contingent upon majority support in each of the two sections. This mechanism makes it much easier for the government's supporters in the legislature to vote down those private members' bills opposed by the executive. In addition, the Chief Executive has the power to veto the private members' bills passed by the legislature, and such a veto can only be overridden by a two-thirds majority of the legislature.

Notwithstanding the asymmetrical power relationship between the executive and the legislature, the latter is still granted a critical negative power to veto the bills or budgets introduced by the government. As long as the legislators are united against the government, the veto power at the disposal of the legislature is a formidable weapon against the Chief Executive. Even though the legislature is deprived of the legislative or policy initiative by the Basic Law, the effective exercise of its power of veto would still allow it to wrest concessions from the government or to bring about an executive-legislative stalemate if the differences between the two institutions cannot be reconciled.

As the institutional mandate of the legislature is to check and balance the government, a legislator true to his/her role has perforce to score points from administrative failures in order to maintain support from his/her voters. A degree of tension between the executive and the legislators is unavoidable. Even pro-government legislators have to be wary about being seen as too pro-government. The division between a strong executive and a weak legislature in Hong Kong's partial democracy and their conflicting institutional imperatives constitute an inherent source of contradiction. As long as executive-legislative conflict remains within tolerable limits, it can be seen as politically salutary, just as executive-legislative tussles are not foreign to nations with a presidential system.

To make sure that the power of veto in the hands of the legislature is not used to bring about an executive-legislative stalemate or, even worse, to compel the executive to do the bidding of the legislature, the electoral system for the legislature is crafted with the explicit intention of fragmenting it and stuffing it with administration sympathizers (Lau, 1999a). Since the legislators directly elected by Hongkongers are most likely to be at loggerheads with a Chief Executive elected by Hong Kong's élites, their number will be limited to less than half of the membership of the legislature. Half of the legislators are returned by functional constituencies representing preponderantly business and professional interests. The rest of the legislators are elected by an Élitist Election Committee whose members' socio-economic backgrounds are similar to those voters in the electoral college who elect the Chief Executive.

The labyrinthine manner whereby the legislature is elected makes it impossible for any political party, or any organized political force for that matter, to control the legislature. Popular political parties face insuperable obstacles in developing themselves into powerful political forces since the popularly elected seats in the legislature constitute only a minority in the body. Furthermore, the proportional representation method used in the direct election of legislators inhibits the development of strong popular parties. Functionally elected legislators owe their allegiance to sectional interests and conduct themselves mostly as individuals and hence largely beyond the control of party discipline. The few legislators elected by the Election Committee are the products of factional infighting in the tiny electoral body. Naturally, they do not form a cohesive force on their own. Consequently, Legco is a highly fragmented and fissiparous political body.

There is a general feeling among political scientists that a fragmented legislature makes it difficult for a president to govern with effectiveness as he cannot bank on solid majority support there. Instead, the president has to do a lot of "horse-trading" with the legislators, sometimes on an individual basis, in order to form *ad hoc* majorities for the passage of his bills. And the plight of the president will be even worse if the proportional representation method is used to elect legislators.[6] Fortunately, for Hong Kong's Chief Executive, a majority of the legislators (most of those who are functionally elected or elected by the Election Committee) share with him similar political perspectives and policy orientations. Most important, many of them would refrain from opposing him for fear of offending Beijing. Even though this is not the same as having a solid bloc of majority support for the Chief Executive in the legislature, executive-legislative gridlock under normal circumstances is not likely. Still, there is no institutional guarantee of amicable executive-legislative interaction.

Together, the asymmetrical division of power between the executive and the legislature on the one hand, and the electoral system for the legislature on the other, are the institutional arrangements designed to minimize the possibility of executive-legislative gridlock or stalemate in Hong Kong's partial democracy. Strictly from the institutional point of view, the contrasting institutional logic of the executive and legislature will, just as in other presidential systems, still give rise to conflict between the two components of the political system. Nevertheless, such conflict should be limited and politically salutary.

The Strained Executive-Legislative Relationship

As mentioned above, since the establishment of the HKSAR, the administration under the leadership of Tung Chee-hwa has been able thus far to get almost all its bills passed in the legislature and to quash all attempts by the legislators to challenge the authority and prerogative of the executive. The only politically embarrassing incident, which hurt Tung largely in a symbolic way, was the failure of the vote of thanks for the second policy speech of the Chief Executive to pass the legislature on 4 November 1998.[7]

The scoreboard of the administration is particularly impressive when one takes into account the fact that even when an action taken by the legislators is widely popular in society, the administration is still capable of defeating the legislature, at the price of denting the prestige of those legislators who are the administration's sympathizers. A notable case in point took place in early 1999. When Secretary of Justice Elsie Leung Oi-sie appeared before a Legco panel to spell out her controversial decision to name Sally Aw Sian — the proprietor of the *Hong Kong Standard* — as a co-conspirator in a circulation fraud case involving the newspaper, but not to charge her. There was outrage both in the legislature and in society following the disclosure that Sally Aw Sian was not prosecuted partly because it might have put her newspaper group out of business (*SCMP*, 5 February 1999:1). A motion of no confidence in the Secretary of Justice was moved by legal representative Margaret Ng Ngoi-yee. Public opinion polls showed that Hongkongers were mostly behind this motion. In the end, however, the Secretary of Justice survived the vote of no confidence (*SCMP*, 12 March 1999:1). In the eyes of Tung, the vote of no confidence represented a sinister attempt by opposition legislators to challenge or even to usurp his prerogative under the Basic Law to appoint principal officials.

Tung was doubly upset by this legislative *demarche* as Elsie Leung was the only principal official in his administration who was handpicked by him, whereas all the others were carryovers from the colonial government. Tung therefore pulled out all the stops to crush the legislature. It was reported that, in view of the fact that even some Tung supporters in the legislature were against Elsie Leung, Tung even went so far as to ask property developers and other business leaders to help influence Legco's vote of confidence in the Secretary of Justice. He solicited the help of the backers of the Liberal Party — one of the major parties in the Legco — to pressurize the Party's legislators to support the Secretary for Justice.

Beneath the political feats achieved by the Tung administration are discernible signs of tension between the executive and the legislature, leaving both sides discontented and frustrated. It is noteworthy that many of the administration's important bills were passed in the legislature by only a narrow margin.[8] Heavy and time-consuming lobbying is frequently needed in order to form the *ad hoc* majorities to pass the administration's bills. Generally speaking, the relationship between Tung and the legislature is cool and is suffused with mutual distrust. At one point, Tung was forced to admit the poor state of the executive-legislative relationship and he called for the two institutions to seek a relationship based on mutual trust, mutual respect and mutual co-operation.[9] Tung's attitude towards the legislators is one of condescending neglect tinged, nevertheless, by fear and contempt. Right from the very beginning, Tung has made it clear that he would prefer to have as little to do with the legislature as is politically feasible. He refused to report back to the legislature after his periodic reporting duties to Beijing. He only agreed to attend three question-and-answer sessions in the legislature every year. His meetings with the political parties in the legislature are limited in number, though he meets more often with the pro-government parties and legislators (*MPDN*, 23 July 1998, A10). Moreover, Tung and his political advisers and senior officials rarely attend the monthly lunch meetings between members of the Executive Council and the legislature (*STD*, 26 July 1999:A13). Overall, the channels of communication between the legislature and the executive are sparse and ineffective.[10]

Opposition legislators are particularly offended by Tung's unfriendly stance towards the legislature. His relationship with the major opposition party — the Democratic Party headed by Martin Lee — has been deteriorating unabated. Personal animosity characterizes the relationship between Martin Lee and Tung Chee-hwa. A core member of the party — Lee Wing-tat — went as far as advocating a line of confrontation with

Tung for the purpose of exposing the undemocratic nature of his government (*HKEJ*, 9 January 1999:4). In an open letter to members of the party, Lee even explicitly named the Chinese Communist Party and Tung Chee-hwa as the Party's enemies (*HKEJ*, 20 September 1999:6). It should be noted that even Lee himself is seen as politically too moderate by the more radical Young Turks in his Party. In another incident, Christine Loh, chairman of the Citizens Party and a popular legislator, announced in a high-profile manner her decision not to seek re-election to the Legco in September 2000, the reason being her frustration with a government which refused to share power with the legislature (*SCMP*, 12 April 2000:1). As things stand, the differences between Tung and the opposition legislators in the legislature are beyond reconciliation. Conflicts between the two sides have grown increasingly emotional, personal and frequent.[11]

The relationship between Tung and some of his sympathizers in the legislature has also become increasingly strained. The two most important pro-Tung parties — the pro-business Liberal Party and the mass-oriented Democratic Alliance for the Betterment of Hong Kong (DAB) — are increasingly disappointed by the political price they have to pay for supporting some of the unpopular or controversial policies of the government and the meagre influence on government policies they have received in return. Tsang Yok-sing, the chairman of the DAB, even vented his discontent with the Tung administration in the open. He criticized the government for complacently taking for granted support from the DAB and admitted that both he himself and his party have incurred substantial losses in political prestige as a result of supporting some controversial government policies. In the eyes of Tsang, given the political sacrifices the party has made, it is still not receiving sufficient and well-deserved political respect and power from Tung. Tsang even threatened to oppose some unpopular government measures in the future (*MPDN*, 3 January 2000:A1; 6 January 2000:A9; 9 January 2000:A4). The trade unionists in the DAB, who constitute a critical force within the party, are conspicuously vociferous in denouncing the Tung administration for not looking after the interests of labour, and occasionally they refused to toe the party line.[12] This means that the relationship between the DAB and the government is far from stable and cordial.[13] Frustrations within the Liberal Party as a result of the absence of an equal exchange relationship with the Tung administration have been openly vented every now and then. Dissident voices within the party even questioned the wisdom of getting too close to the government while becoming too distant from the people.[14]

Another sign of the strained executive-legislative relationship is the deteriorating relationship between senior government officials and the legislators. Under the executive-led system of Hong Kong, senior officials are career civil servants rather than politically appointed ministers. Career civil servants rarely see themselves as politicians and are normally deficient in political astuteness and dexterity. Until the eve of the end of colonial rule, civil servants ran Hong Kong unencumbered by other political actors. They saw themselves as the trustees of Hong Kong's interests and as "above politics." They developed such high self-esteem and such a sense of self-importance that they have difficulty treating the legislators as equals since the emergence of a legislature with its independent power base. Politicians and political parties are denigrated as petty politicians catering to personal and sectional interests. Therefore, officials find the job of intensively lobbying the legislators to support governmental bills unpalatable. At the same time, their effectiveness as lobbyists is vitiated by their bureaucratic rigidity and by their inability to enter into horse-trading with the legislators. As a result, the morale of the senior officials is worsening and there is a tendency for them to leave the government and take up careers in the semi-public or private sectors. Legislators, on the other hand, find the senior officials uncooperative and unresponsive. There is a tendency for legislators, especially those in the political opposition, to vent their frustration with the government on the senior officials whenever the latter are found to have committed administrative misconduct whether serious or minor.[15] While legislative hostility towards officials is ubiquitous and is for all eyes to see, the officials' resentment towards the legislators is normally submerged.[16]

Yet another indication of the increasingly strained executive-legislative relationship is the simmering resentment of the legislators, including the pro-government ones, at the straitjacket placed on their legislative initiative by Article 74 of the Basic Law. Since the establishment of the HKSAR, the legislators have already made several attempts to enlarge their power to initiate legislation under that article. Once their legislative initiative is expanded, the legislators will be in a better position to meet the demands of their constituents and be in a stronger bargaining position vis-à-vis the government. Conversely, the Tung administration has tried equally hard to see to it that the Legco fails in its attempt to "usurp" the power that should rightfully belong to the executive. If the plot of the legislators is successful, the government fears that instead of an executive-led system, Hong Kong's political system will be transmogrified into a legislature-led system. In the eyes of both the executive and the legislature, huge stakes are involved and the room for compromise is extremely limited. Incessant executive-legislative skirmishes over Article 74 portend trouble for the relationship between the two institutions in the future because they show that there is no consensus between them on the basic rules of the political game.

The majority view in the Legco is that it is the President of the Legco alone who should have the power to determine whether a private member's bill has breached Article 74 and hence cannot be introduced. In fact, this view has been written into the Rules of Procedure of the Legislative Council.[17] However, the government insists that in line with the spirit of an executive-led system, that power should belong exclusively to the Chief Executive for he/she is in the best position to know whether a private member's bill is related to public expenditure or political structure or the operation of the government. Moreover, even if Article 74 makes it clear that "the written consent of the Chief Executive shall be required before [private member's] bills relating to government policies are introduced," there is no institutional guarantee that the Legco will dutifully abide by the stipulation. Instead, whether a private member's bill is introduced into the Legco hangs upon the relationship between the President of the Legco and the government.[18]

Furthermore, the legislators are of the view that their proposed amendments to the government's bills should not be governed by Article 74. That is to say, even if the proposed amendments touch upon public expenditure or political structure or the operation of the government, no written consent of the Chief Executive is required. Just the opposite view is held by the government, which is fearful that its policies and hence its legislative initiative will be dangerously undermined if the legislators can freely amend the government bills.[19]

So far the Tung administration has adopted three tactics to cope with the challenges from the legislature. First, the government will apply pressure on the President of the Legco to prohibit those "illegal" private members' bills from being introduced.[20] Second, if the government fails to prevent the "illegal" bills or amendments from being introduced, it will mobilize the pro-government legislators to vote them down.[21] If these two tactics do not work, the government's last resort is to pre-empt the legislators' offensive by making private members' bills or amendments into bills or amendments introduced by the government itself. This is meant to avert confrontation with the legislature. At the same time, it will relieve the Chief Executive of the predicament of whether or not to veto a private member's bill or amendment in case it gets passed in the legislature. To veto, it would further damage the government's relationship with the legislature. If the veto is overridden by a two-thirds majority in the legislature, the Chief Executive has to sign the bill or amendment into law or else dissolve the legislature. Since the Chief Executive has the power to dissolve the legislature only once during his term of office, if the re-elected legislature continues to support that bill or amendment, the Chief Executive has perforce to accept it. Nevertheless, thenceforward the threat of dissolution will no longer be available as a weapon for the Chief Executive to subdue the recalcitrant legislators. On the other hand, if the Chief Executive signs the bill or amendment into law without resistance, then a precedent will be set that the legislators' power to initiate legislation has been tacitly, albeit reluctantly, accepted by the Chief Executive. The setting of that precedent will set the stage for further erosion of the legislative initiative of the government. However, simply taking over the private members' bills from the legislators and turning them into government bills is bound to create ill-feeling towards the government in the legislature. In addition, legislators who are willing to allow the government to take over their private members' bills are likely to be scorned by their colleagues.[22]

As things stand now, it appears that Article 74 will persist as a stumbling block in any attempt to improve the executive-legislative relationship. It will continue to strain the relationship between the two institutions. At one point, a maverick legislator — Leung Yiu-chung — moved an ill-timed motion to amend Article 74 and the voting mechanism for private members' bills and amendments. While it is not surprising that the motion suffered a dismal defeat in the Legco, the debate swirling around the motion still gives a good idea of the resentment which exists towards the Basic Law-imposed constraints on the legislative initiative of the Legco (*MPDN*, 20 January 2000:A12). In fact, the second ranking member in the Legco, Leong Che-hung (medical functional constituency) — Chairman of the House Committee — has already issued a previous warning on future excecutive-legislative relationship. He warned that if the differences between the government and the legislature on Article 74 were not settled, there would be no way for the two to be on better terms. And Leong is not known for political radicalism (*HKEJ*, 24 July 1999:5).

In view of all these strains and stresses in the relationship between the government and the legislature, questions will be raised as to the ability of the government to sustain its achievement of having most of its bills sail through the legislature.

Non-Institutional Sources of Executive-Legislative Conflict

Apparently, the stresses and strains in the executive-legislative relationship since Hong Kong's return to China spring from the inherent contradictions in the Special Administrative Region's partial democracy. However, the intensity of the strains between the two institutions which we have witnessed indicates that more is at work than the competing institutional logic of the executive and the legislature. There are a number of non-institutional factors that are conducive to the strained executive-legislature relationship.

In the first place, the executive and the legislature have different bases of social support. Even though the executive, by virtue of the mode of election of the Chief Executive, is based on élite support and a majority of the legislators also find their support base in narrow élite circles, about one-third of the legislators still owe their political career to popular support. It is undeniable that the directly-elected legislators can claim a broader political mandate and can thus exercise a quantity of political influence disproportionate to their number in the Legco. It therefore comes as no surprise that a minority group of legislators are inclined to play havoc with the executive by advocating populism and practising adversarial politics.

Since the early 1980s, Hong Kong has suffered from an unrelenting trend towards widening social inequality and weakening of the social fabric (Lau, 1997). The economic recession resulting from the Asian financial turmoil in late 1997 has exacerbated the conflict between the rich and the poor. Intensified conflict in society inevitably is translated into sharpened conflict between the populist legislators and a government that is widely seen to represent primarily the interests of the wealthy.[23] While the grassroots-oriented legislators want to use the legislature to serve the interests of their constituents, they find their efforts obstructed by the Tung administration. Accumulating political frustration among the opposition legislators is bound to strain executive-legislative relationship.

Tung Chee-hwa owed his electoral victory in the Chief Executive contest largely to Beijing's support. According to the Basic Law, since he is appointed by the central government to the post, the Chief Executive has to be accountable to it, in addition to his accountability to the HKSAR. Inevitably, Tung is widely regarded by Hongkongers as pro-Beijing.[24] Conversely, inasmuch as all legislators are locally elected and do not owe allegiance to Beijing, legislators without exception depend on Hongkongers for their offices. The different relationships with Beijing on the part of the

Tung administration and the legislators mean two things. First, in view of the pervasive, though diminishing popular mistrust of Beijing in Hong Kong, any conflict between Beijing and Hongkongers can easily become executive-legislative conflict. The legislators will appropriate for themselves the exclusive right to be the guardian of Hong Kong's interests. Fortunately for Tung, Beijing has so far conducted itself very prudently in Hong Kong affairs and thus has avoided any uncalled-for clash with the Hongkongers. Second, Tung's dual loyalties to Beijing and to Hong Kong to a certain extent constrain his room for manoeuvre in handling his relationship with the legislature. As many of the opposition legislators are defined by Beijing as adversaries, it would be politically imprudent and even risky for Tung to develop cordial relationships with them.

What is worse is that Tung's political mentality, his governing strategy and his definition of an executive-led government are not conducive to smooth executive-legislative encounters. Tung's abhorrence of politics and his political conservatism have led him to adopt a negative stance towards a (partially) democratic legislature that constantly questions his political legitimacy, impudently or subtly. Tung's governing strategy revolves upon reliance on the career civil servants and a few close political advisers as his governing partners. Unfortunately for Tung, the mistrust between his officials and advisers, the low political prestige of his advisers, and the political ineptness of both officials and advisers have resulted in a disunited leadership core, its detachment from the governed and its declining popularity (Lau, 1999b, 2000b). At the centre of Tung's governing strategy is a deliberate effort to seek political legitimacy based on performance, especially performance in the economic realm. In the first few months of the HKSAR, this strategy appeared to be rather promising (Lau, 1998). The economic recession and rising unemployment following upon the Asian financial turmoil, however, have paralyzed Tung's efforts to legitimate his new regime. The result: growing public disenchantment with his government and declining public support for it.[25] Tung's definition of an executive-led government is so narrow and stringent that any form of power-sharing with the legislators — even the pro-government ones — is totally ruled out. Paralleling an exclusionary attitude towards the legislature is an obsessive pre-occupation with executive privileges.

An exclusionary but unpopular regime is vulnerable to attack by a legislature which simultaneously boasts of a higher degree of political legitimacy and feels slighted by the government. The occurrence of a series of events since 1997 has exposed the incompetence of the government and undermined the prestige of the civil servants.[26] They include the clumsy handling of the avian flu, the unprofessional management of the currency crisis and the confusion connected with the opening of the new airport. The erosion of public respect for the civil service is particularly damaging, for the new administration under Tung owed a large part of its popularity to public support for the civil service (Lau, 1999c). These mishaps naturally become the issues exploited by the legislature to take on the executive with the intention of wresting concessions from it. Legislators who need to perform in order to keep their constituents' support are bound to resent a government that is determined to deny them the policy influence they covet and believe that they deserve. There is a discernible trend of radicalization of the legislators, including the government-supporters. This trend is further reinforced by the tendency of all the political parties in the legislature to become more politically radical as a result of the increase in "class conflict" in society and the widened confidence gap between the government and the Hongkongers (Lau and Kuan, forthcoming).

The Absence of Arbiters

In Hong Kong's partial democracy, the extreme asymmetrical distribution of power between the executive and the legislature does not provide sufficient incentives for either side to enter into compromise with the other side. Executive-legislative differences are difficult to bridge because of a significant feature in Hong Kong's political scene: the absence of arbiters respected by both sides and having the power to compel both sides to settle their differences.

The monopolization of the legislative initiative by the executive has produced a situation of excessive jealousy of its powers and privileges on the part of the government, making it over-sensitive and over-reactive to possible encroachment by the legislature upon its bailiwick. Conversely, the inability of the legislators to participate in the policy-making process has aggravated their opposition towards the government. By means of public hearings and committee investigations, the legislature frequently resorts to its institutional powers to embarrass and pressurize the government.[27] It can even be said that as the Basic Law does not prescribe a particular degree and a format of power sharing between the executive and the legislature, there is an inherent tendency for the latter to resort to confrontational tactics against the former. Such tactics are probably the only realistic means at the legislators' disposal to force concessions from the government and to be accountable to their constituents. Occasionally, these confrontation tactics are used irresponsibly and unwisely, but unless the political conditions change, it can be predicted that such tactics will be pursued even more aggressively in the future. The Basic Law does not allow the legislature to overthrow the government and the power of the Chief Executive to dissolve the legislature is more a threat than an effective device to bring about a submissive legislature. The mini-constitution of Hong Kong thus does not provide the necessary constitutional mechanisms to break the executive-legislative gridlock.

Presumably the central government in Beijing, because of its higher constitutional status, can serve as a useful arbiter, but in reality it is in no position to do so. Beijing is too biased against the legislature to command respect and compliance from that body. Besides, the opposition legislators owe part of their popularity to their anti-Beijing stance, and they would, therefore, be unwilling to do Beijing's bidding. Moreover, Beijing is wary about being seen to meddle in Hong Kong's affairs, hence any explicit attempt at arbitration is to be avoided. The most Beijing can do, and in fact is doing, is to show displeasure with the opposition legislators in the hope of deterring them from confronting the Chief Executive.[28] Such tactics, however, are not only far from effective, but might even have worsened the situation and indirectly enabled the opposition legislators to appeal to public sympathy as political victims.

As far as the Basic Law is concerned, presumably the judiciary, like the judiciaries in presidential systems elsewhere, should play the indispensable role of arbitrating disputes between the executive and the legislature. The fact that Hong Kong is endowed with a Court of Final Appeal despite its non-sovereign status should allow the judiciary to play the significant role of the arbiter. Nevertheless, primarily out of mistrust of the judiciary on the part of the Tung administration, the tendency of the executive is to prevent the judiciary from meddling in the affairs between the executive and the legislature. Executive mistrust of the judiciary can be easily explained. For one thing, despite Hong Kong's return to China, the judiciary of the HKSAR is still very much dominated by judges trained in Western jurisprudence and immersed in liberal thinking. In fact, many of the judges are expatriates rather than local Chinese. The government is thus not sure that its views and interests will be given sympathetic attention by in-court trials.

Most important, the controversy over the right of abode, which led eventually to the government seeking an interpretation of the Basic Law from the Standing Committee of the National People's Congress in Beijing and the *de facto* overturning of the ruling of the Court of Final Appeal, has weakened the authority of the court and soured the relationship between the executive and the judiciary.[29] The Chief Justice of Hong Kong — Mr. Justice Andrew Li Kwok-nang — in a keynote speech at the opening of the new legal year in 2000, said, "When the courts come under unwarranted attack, it is the constitutional responsibility of the Government, that is, the executive authorities, to explain and defend the fundamental principle of judicial independence, whether or not the decision is in its favour." This remark was widely interpreted in Hong Kong as a subtle expression of the grudge against the government harboured by the judges (*SCMP*, 18 January 2000:1). On the other hand, even though the legislature is very much in favour of having the judiciary to mediate between itself and the government, the body is not united enough to take the government to court.

Another possible arbiter is public opinion. However, even though the highly developed and commercially oriented mass media in Hong Kong provide ample outlets for the expression of public opinion, public opinion as a political force is weak. In spite of the fact that the brand of negative journalism that pervades the media does produce tremendous pressure on both the government officials and the legislators, the electoral system in Hong Kong does not allow the voters to choose the Chief Executive and the majority of the legislators. From a structural point of view, the Basic Law has divided Hong Kong into two separate political arenas: the élite political arena and the mass political arena. The élite in the élite political arena are in control of Hong Kong's political powers and they do not owe their offices to popular support.

Moreover, public mistrust of both the legislators and the government has been on the rise before (Lau, 1996) and since 1997.[30] In fact, the entire political class in Hong Kong enjoys only low public trust.[31] Hongkongers are increasingly alienated from politics[32] and a politically estranged public is not in a position to mediate between the government and the legislature and to compel both sides to settle their differences. However, the detachment of the public from politics does not deter the executive and the legislature from trying to mobilize public opinion against each other. Examples abound of the legislature posing as the spokesman for the general public. The government, despite its aversion to mass mobilization, has occasionally succeeded in mobilizing public opinion pressure against the legislature.[33] Nevertheless, these offensives taken by both sides prove in the end to be more damaging to their relationship.

Conclusion

Events since the return of Hong Kong to China demonstrate clearly that the partial democracy, with an executive-led political system at its centre, is very difficult to operate smoothly. This partial democracy attempts to preserve the autonomy and dominance of the élite but at the same time to meet partially the democratic aspirations of the ordinary people. In the end, the political system contains inherent contradictions, which have been exacerbated by the economic and political conditions in post-1997 Hong Kong. As the partial democracy continues to democratize, notably in the enlargement of the proportion of directly elected members in the legislature, more stresses and strains between the executive and the legislature can be anticipated. Meanwhile, under circumstances of economic recession and escalating public expectations, the Tung administration has to scale down its social commitments, but at the same time increase government revenue by raising more taxes. The difficulty of effective governance is daunting. A deteriorating executive-legislative relationship will further complicate the problems confronting the HKSAR government.[34]

The original expectation of Beijing that the partial democracy of Hong Kong could operate efficiently in accordance with the design of the Basic Law has obviously not been fulfilled. In fact, experience in the last two-and-a-half years shows that much common sense, goodwill, trust and self-restraint from all sides are needed to obtain effective governance from the executive-led political system. Unfortunately for Hong Kong, none of these is so far in sufficient supply.

Notes

1. In Beijing's original reckoning, even though the Chief Executive would be widely seen as pro-Beijing and be held in suspicion by Hongkongers, the legislators — who owed their office to the local voters — would refrain from confronting the executive for fear of instigating Beijing's involvement in local affairs. Beijing, therefore, expected the Legco to act with restraint and prudence vis-à-vis the government.

2. The Founding Fathers of the United States, for example, had in mind a political system dominated by a powerful Congress where political parties had no constructive role to play. The subsequent rise of a powerful presidency and the dominance of American politics by two national parties are alien to the political thinking of the drafters of the American constitution (Hofstadter, 1969). A more recent example can be found in Russia, where a supposedly all-powerful

President Yeltsin in reality encountered tremendous difficulties in exercising effective governance. A noted political scientist even describes the super-presidential regime of Yeltsin since December 1993 as "impotently omnipotent" (Shevtsova, 2000).

3. The sample used in the questionnaire survey was drawn by means of a multi-stage design. The target population of the survey was the Chinese inhabitants of Hong Kong aged 18 or over. Since the full list of such adults was impossible to obtain, the list of permanent and residential areas prepared and kept by the Census and Statistics Department's computerized Sub-frame of Living Quarters was used as the sampling frame. With the assistance of the Department, a replicated and systematic random sample of 8,000 addresses was selected from the sampling frame. The sample was then divided into four sub-samples, each with 2,000 addresses. Four different questionnaires were used in the survey, one for each sub-sample.

   Data used in this chapter were collected by Questionnaire C. After the exclusion of vacant, demolished, and unidentifiable addresses, addresses without Chinese residents and addresses eventually unused, the actual sub-sample size for Questionnaire C was reduced to 1,689.

   The next stage of sampling involved the selection of households and eligible respondents by the interviewers. Interviewers were required to call at each address in the sub-sample and list all the households residing there. If there were two or more households, only one would be selected according to the random selection table pre-attached to each address assignment sheet. For each selected household, the interviewer was required to list all persons aged 18 or over and arrange them in order according to sex and age. The respondent was then selected from the list by means of a random selection grid (a modified Kish grid) pre-attached to each address assignment sheet.

   Face-to-face interviews with structured questionnaires were carried out by interviewers who were recruited from local tertiary institutions and were required to attend a half-day briefing session. Fieldwork was conducted mostly from the end of May to July 1999. All completed questionnaires were subsequently checked by follow-up phone calls to the respondents concerned as a means of data quality control. Additional data control checks were also made to improve data quality.

   At the end of the survey, 839 interviews had been successfully completed, yielding a response rate of 49.7 percent.

4. According to Giovanni Sartori, "a political system is presidential if, and only if, the head of state (president) (i) results from popular election, (ii) during his or her pre-established tenure cannot be discharged by a parliamentary vote, and (iii) heads or otherwise directs the governments that he or she appoints" (1997:84).

5. A voluminous literature on the flaws and fragility of the presidential system

has built up in recent years (Rose and Suleiman, 1980; Linz, 1990; Lijphart, 1992; Shugart and Carey, 1992; Valenzuela, 1993; Linz and Valenzuela, 1994; Mainwaring and Shugart, 1997; Mettenheim, 1997).

6. The case of Brazil, featuring a presidential system, a proportional representation formula for the election of legislators and multipartism in the legislature, is particularly revealing (Mainwaring, 1993; Sartori, 1997:176–78).

7. As the vote of thanks is a motion tabled by an individual member of Legco, its passage requires concurrent majorities in two voting divisions: (1) a division made up of functionally elected members, and (2) a division made up of directly elected members and members returned by the Election Committee. It failed to pass in division (2). Ironically, the rule of concurrent majorities was originally designed to scuttle private members' bills unfavourable to the executive, but in this incident it was adroitly used by the legislators to upstage Tung Chee-hwa (*MPDN*, 5 November 1998:A6).

8. For example, the passage of the vote of thanks motion for the third policy address of Tung Chee-hwa hinged on one single vote in the division of directly-elected and Election Committee-elected members of the Legco.

9. Tung made the comments after meeting 11 legislators with no political party affiliations (*SCMP*, 1 August 1998:1).

10. Before 1997, the Executive Council — a body made up of the colonial governor's advisers and senior officials — played an active role as a liaison between the government and the legislators. Since 1997, Tung's Executive Councillors have been on poor terms with the legislators. Feelings of mutual contempt have been haunting their relationship. There are very limited contacts between them.

11. During a question-and-answer in the Legco on 13 January 2000, the affable Tung Chee-hwa lost his temper when Martin Lee accused him of asking Beijing officials in Hong Kong to put pressure on legislators during key votes in the legislature. He castigated Lee for speaking irresponsibly (*SCMP*, 14 January 2000:1).

12. A telling example is the refusal of the trade unionists among DAB's legislators to support the government's decision to scrap the two municipal councils (*MPDN*, 3 December 1999:A2). Another example is that the trade unionists did not follow the party line to support the government's move to reduce the salaries of the newly recruited civil servants in the Finance Committee of the Legco (*SCMP*, 19 February 2000:6). Yet another example is the trade unionists' support for the Mass Transit Railway Corporation privatization bill in return for an amendment to the bill proposed by the government. The bill was opposed by the DAB (*SCMP*, 24 February 2000:1).

13. In an era of increasing market dominance and rising social inequality, the alliance between governing parties and pro-government parties will unavoidably become more fragile. See Burgess (1999).

14. See the open letter to the Liberal Party written by Ada Wong, a longtime party member (*HKEJ*, 19 March 1999:25).
15. On a number of occasions, the second most powerful person in the Tung administration — Chief Secretary for Administration Anson Chan Fang On-sang — was severely criticized by the Legco. An investigation by a special committee of the Legco on the chaos produced by the opening of the new airport was adamant that Anson Chan had to shoulder "special personal responsibility" for the matter (*SCMP*, 28 January 1999:1). Then, just less than a year later, the legislators expressed "dismay" at Anson Chan for failing to provide enough information to the Executive Council (the cabinet of advisers to the colonial governor) when it made its 1992 decision to allow the construction of a huge power station (*SCMP*, 9 December 1999:1).
16. The open and virulent attack on the legislators by a retired senior official — Kwong Hon-sang — reflects vividly the repulsion for the Legco deep in the hearts of his former colleagues in the administration. Kwong equated the criticisms of civil servants by the legislators with the political invective commonly found in the Great Proletarian Cultural Revolution in China between the late 1960s and mid-1970s (*HKEJ*, 28 July 1999:8).
17. See Section 31 of the Rules of Procedure of the Legislative Council of the HKSAR. It states: "A motion or amendment, the object or effect of which may, *in the opinion of the President or Chairman*, be to dispose of or charge any part of the revenue or other public moneys of Hong Kong shall be proposed only by — (a) the Chief Executive; or (b) a designated public officer; or (c) a Member, if the Chief Executive consents in writing to the proposal." (italics mine)
18. Up to now, the President of the Legco — Rita Fan Hsu Lai-tai — is on friendly terms with the government. No executive-legislative conflict on whether a private member's bill is related to government policies has flared up so far. Rita Fan was elected by the Election Committee.
19. The divergent views of the government and the legislature can be found in various newspapers (*TKP*, 5 July 1998:9; HKET, 8 July 1998:18; 10 July 1998: 14; 23 September 1998:23; *AD*, 23 September 1998:A13).
20. For example, the government actively persuaded Rita Fan not to allow legislator Leung Yiu-chung to amend a government bill relating to public holidays in 1998 (*HKEJ*, 30 July 1998:8). In another case, Rita Fan refused to allow legislator Lee Cheuk-yan to introduce two private member's bills relating to the right of collective bargaining by trade unions and discrimination against trade union members by employers, the reason being that they entailed public expenditure (*HKEJ*, 20 July 1999:5). In yet another case, Rita Fan forbade legislator Cheng Kar-foo to table a private member's bill having to do with the benefits of employees on the ground that it contravened governmental policies (*MPDN*, 18 July 1999:10). Leung, Lee and Cheng are all directly elected legislators.

21. On 9 September 1998, thanks to support from the functionally-elected legislators and the special voting mechanism for private members' bills and amendments to government bills, the bill introduced by Leung Yiu-chung (see fn. 28) was defeated (*HKEJ*, 10 September 1998:7). Another proposed amendment by the legislators relating to the charges of the cross-harbour tunnel in Hunghom was defeated in the Legco after strenuous lobbying efforts by the government, including Tung Chee-hwa himself (*HKET*, 9 July 1999:A3).

22. When the government realized that the two amendments to the government's bill on the electoral arrangements for the Legco election in 2000, proposed by Eric Li Ka-cheung (accountancy functional constituency) and Leong Che-hung (medical functional constituency), were likely to be passed by the legislature, it simply turned their amendments into government amendments (*SCMP*, 16 July 1999:6; *HKEJ*, 24 July 1999:5; and *MPDN*, 14 July 1999:A6).

23. In the survey, 46 percent of the respondents were of the view that the government principally took care of the interests of the wealthy. Only 15.5 percent believed it principally took care of the interests of the general public.

24. The proportion of respondents in the survey who believed that the government primarily took care of the interests of Hongkongers and those who thought it catered mostly to the interests of Beijing are about the same (29.6 percent and 29 percent, respectively).

25. In my survey, the performance of the government was rated as good by only 10.7 percent of the respondents. Conversely, 28.4 percent were dissatisfied. Moreover, the government's ability to govern was widely questioned. Less than one-third (28.3 percent) of the respondents expressed confidence in its governing ability. Public perception of poor performance by the government has not surprisingly eroded public trust in the government. Less than half (44.8 percent) of the respondents trusted the government. This figure is a low one in the history of Hong Kong.

26. While most of the respondents (57.6 percent) still preferred to have Hong Kong run by the civil servants, their confidence in them has fallen. Only 30 percent of the respondents had confidence in the civil servants, whereas 21.5 percent had no confidence. Hongkongers have notably low regard for senior officials, only 17.2 percent seeing great abilities in them. Declining confidence in senior officials has in turn led Hongkongers to question the time-honoured security of tenure they have. In fact, an overwhelming majority of respondents (82.3 percent) agreed with the suggestion that senior officials should not be given the "iron rice-bowl" (permanent employment).

27. Institutional struggles between the executive and the legislature are common-place in political systems where power is divided between them. See, for example, Ginsberg and Shefter (1999).

28. One way to do so is to bar some of the opposition legislators from travelling to the mainland.

29. The incident took place in 1999. In January 1999, the Court of Final Appeal laid down a ruling in a case concerning the eligibility of some "illegal" immigrants from Mainland China to become permanent residents of Hong Kong. The HKSAR government was the loser in this court case and it feared a large-scale influx of mainlanders into Hong Kong as a result of the court ruling. The government's attitude towards the court ruling was also widely shared by the general public, who were prejudiced against their compatriots from the mainland. Eventually, the government requested the Standing Committee of the National People's Congress to interpret relevant articles in the Basic Law. In June 1999, the Standing Committee came up with an interpretation, which is binding upon the court, in favour of the government. In the process, the prestige of the judiciary in Hong Kong and abroad has been very much damaged.
30. In my 1999 survey, only 30.9 percent of respondents said that they trusted the Legco.
31. In the 1999 survey, only 20.7 percent and 20.1 percent, respectively, of the respondents reported that these were trustworthy political leaders and political groups whom they could trust. Hongkongers are also cynical about political parties. More than half (51.9 percent) of the respondents agreed with the comment that Hong Kong's political parties were only interested in votes and paid no attention to the views of the people.
32. There are strong feelings of political inefficacy in Hong Kong. More than half of the respondents (61.5 percent) in my survey found politics and government complicated and difficult to understand. Hongkongers also feel that they have been neglected by the politicians. Only 14.1 percent of the respondents thought that the politicians were concerned about their problems.
33. The government succeeded in putting the opposition legislators on the defensive in the case of loans for first-time home-buyers (*MPDN*, 20 July 1998:A6), the tax-rebate incident (*MPDN*, 23 March 1999:A2), the right of abode issue, the controversy involving the cutbacks in social security and the debate on the abolition of the two municipal councils.
34. On 16 February 2000, the Legco, by an overwhelming majority, passed a motion tabled by the Democratic Party to oppose any government attempt to introduce sales tax into Hong Kong. This is an ominous development as far as effective governance by the Tung administration is concerned (*SCMP*, 17 February 2000: 1).

Periodicals

AD (Apple Daily)
HKEJ (Hong Kong Economic Journal)
HKET (Hong Kong Economic Times)
MPDN (Ming Pao Daily News)

STD (*Sing Tao Daily*)
SCMP (*South China Morning Post*)
TKP (*Ta Kung Pao*)

References

Burgess, K. (1999), "Loyalty Dilemmas and Market Reform: Party-Union Alliances under Stress in Mexico, Spain, and Venezuela," *World Politics*, 52:105–34.

Ginsberg, B. and M. Shefter (1999), *Politics by Other Means: Politicians, Prosecutors, and the Press from Watergate to Whitewater*. New York: W.W. Norton.

Hofstadter, R. (1969), *The Idea of a Party System: The Rise of Legitimate Opposition in the United States, 1780–1840*. Berkeley: University of California Press.

Lau, Siu-kai (1995), "Hong Kong's Path of Democratization," *Swiss Asian Studies*, 49:71–90.

—— (1996), "Democratization and Decline of Trust in Public Institutions in Hong Kong," *Democratization*, 3:158–80.

—— (1997), "The Fraying of the Socioeconomic Fabric of Hong Kong," *The Pacific Review*, 10:426–41.

—— (1998), "The Eclipse of Politics in the Hong Kong Special Administrative Region," *Asian Affairs*, 25:38–46.

—— (1999a), "The Making of the Electoral System." In Kuan Hsin-chi, Lau Siu-kai, Louie Kin-sheun and Timothy Ka-ying Wong (eds.), *Power Transfer and Electoral Politics: The First Legislative Election in the Hong Kong Special Administrative Region*. Hong Kong: The Chinese University Press, pp. 3–35.

—— (1999b), "From Élite Unity to Disunity: Political Élite in Post-1997 Hong Kong." In Wang Gungwu and J. Wong (eds.), *Hong Kong in China: The Challenges of Transition*. Singapore: Times Academic Press, pp. 47–74.

—— (1999c), "The Rise and Decline of Political Support for the Hong Kong Special Administrative Region Government," *Government and Opposition*, 34:352–71.

—— (2000a), "The Hong Kong Policy of the People's Republic of China 1947–1997," *Journal of Contemporary China*, 9:77–93.

—— (2000b), "Government and Political Change in the Hong Kong Special Administrative Region." In J. C. Hsiung (ed.), *Hong Kong: The Super Paradox*. New York: St. Martin's Press.

Lau, Siu-kai and Kuan Hsin-chi (forthcoming), "Partial Democratization, 'Foundation Moment,' and Political Parties in Hong Kong," *The China Quarterly*.

Lijphart, A. (ed.) (1992), *Parliamentary versus Presidential Government*. Oxford: Oxford University Press.

Linz, J. J. (1990), "The Perils of Presidentialism," *Journal of Democracy*, 1:51–69.

Linz, J. J. and A. Valenzuela (eds.) (1994), *The Failure of Presidential Democracy*. Baltimore: The Johns Hopkins University Press.

Mainwaring, S. (1993), "Presidentialism, Multipartism, and Democracy: The Difficult Combination," *Comparative Political Studies*, 26:198–228.

Mainwaring, S. and M. S. Shugart (eds.) (1997), *Presidentialism and Democracy in Latin America*. Cambridge: Cambridge University Press.

Mettenheim, K. von (ed.) (1997), *Presidential Institutions and Democratic Politics: Comparing Regional and National Contexts*. Baltimore: The Johns Hopkins University Press.

Riggs, F. W. (1988), "The Survival of Presidentialism in America: Para-Constitutional Practices," *International Political Science Review*, 9:247–78.

Rose, R. and E. N. Suleiman (eds.) (1980), *Presidents and Prime Ministers*. Washington, D.C.: American Enterprise Institute for Public Policy Research.

Sartori, G. (1997), *Comparative Constitutional Engineering: An Inquiry into Structures, Incentives and Outcomes*. Washington Square: New York University Press.

Scott, I. (2000), "The Disarticulation of Hong Kong's Post-Handover Political System," *The China Journal*, 43:29–53.

Shevtsova, L. (2000), "The Problem of Executive Power in Russia," *Journal of Democracy*, 11:32–39.

Shugart, M. S. and J. M. Carey (1992), *Presidents and Assemblies: Constitutional Design and Electoral Dynamics*. Cambridge: Cambridge University Press.

Valenzuela, A. (1993), "Latin America: Presidentialism in Crisis," *Journal of Democracy*, 4:3–16.

Wang, Shuwen (comp.) (1997), *Xianggang Tebiexingzhengqu Jibenfa daolun* (Introduction to the Basic Law of the Hong Kong Special Administrative Region). Beijing: Zhonggong zhongyang dangxiao chubanshe.

Xiao, Weiyun (comp.) (1990), *Yiguo Liangzhi yu Xianggang jiben falü zhidu* (One Country, Two Systems and the Basic Legal System of Hong Kong). Beijing: Beijing daxue chubanshe.

9

Ageing Population and Gender Issues

Fanny M. Cheung

Growth of the Ageing Population

Declines in mortality at younger ages, medical advances and better health care have resulted in longer life expectancy in both the developing and the developed world. At the same time, birth control has reduced the size of the younger population. These achievements in the twentieth century have changed the world's demographic structure. These demographic changes also pose one of the key challenges in social policies and human services in the twenty-first century.

Statistics compiled by the United Nations (UN) show that in 1999, 10 percent of the world's population was aged 60 years and older. By 2050, the percentage will rise to 22 percent (UNPD, 1999). In Asia, the corresponding proportion of the population aged 60 and over was 9 percent in 1999 and will reach 24 percent in 2050. In China, the proportion was 10 percent in 1999 and will reach 30 percent in 2050. In Hong Kong, the proportion of elderly is even higher: 14 percent in 1999 and an estimated 40 percent in 2050, the highest in Asia. Table 9.1 presents the proportions of ageing population in the Asia-Pacific region.

It may be argued that the UN projection of the proportion of the elderly population for Hong Kong has not taken into account the selective migration of younger immigrants from China. There are, however, no official statistics currently available in Hong Kong on the shift in the population make-up.

The increased life expectancy enjoyed by the world population also means that the life span beyond age 60 is much longer than demographers have previously envisaged. Most census statistics categorize the elderly population in one age group: that of age 60/65 and over. A large proportion of the population remains economically active beyond age 60. A large proportion of the population also lives beyond age 80. In many Asian

Table 9.1   Proportion of Ageing Population in Asia, 1999 and 2050

Country/Area	% total population aged 60 and over in 1999	% total population aged 60 and over in 2050	% ageing population aged 80 and over in 1999	% ageing population aged 80 and over in 2050
Asia	9	24	9	18
China	10	30	10	23
Hong Kong SAR	14	40	14	31
Japan	23	38	16	31
Macau	9	35	14	32
S. Korea	10	30	8	24
Brunei Darussalam	5	24	9	23
Cambodia	5	14	7	11
Indonesia	7	22	7	15
Malaysia	6	21	9	18
Philippines	6	20	9	14
Singapore	10	31	13	36
Thailand	8	30	10	21
Vietnam	7	23	10	17

Source: UN Population Division (1999).

countries, the statutory retirement age is 60 or 55. In 1999, the life expectancy at age 60 is another 16 years for Asian males and 19 years for Asian females, which is also the same for Chinese males and females. In Hong Kong, males may expect to live another 20 years and females another 24 years at age 60. These demographic changes mean that the undifferentiated grouping in census statistics limits the usefulness of these figures. The activity level, care demands and health needs of people in their 60s, 70s, 80s and beyond are varied.

According to UNESC, the elderly population could be further differentiated into the modest old (age 60 to 79) and the oldest old (80 and over) (UNESC, 2000). In 1999, 9 percent of the elderly population (over age 60) in Asia was aged 80 and over; in 2050, this proportion is expected to rise to 18 percent. In China, the corresponding proportions are 9 percent in 1999 and 23 percent in 2050; in Hong Kong, they are 14 percent in 1999 and estimated to be 31 percent in 2050 (Table 9.1).

Potential support for the elderly population comes from the economically active population. The potential support ratio is calculated on the basis of the proportion of the population aged between 15 and 64 to that aged 65 and over. With the decreasing fertility in Asia, this ratio will decrease from 11 in 1999 to 4 in 2050. In China, the ratio will drop from 10 to 3; in Hong Kong, the ratio will drop from 7 to 2. This means that by 2050, there will be only two younger persons potentially supporting one elderly person in Hong Kong.

Gender Composition of the Ageing Population

Sex-disaggregated data will highlight the differential implications of ageing for men and women. Except for countries in which women suffer from severe forms of discrimination, women worldwide have a higher life expectancy than men. This means that women will form the majority of the elderly population, especially in the oldest old age group. The female to male ratio of the world population in year 2000 was 1.1 for the 60–69 age group, 1.3 for the 70–79 age group, 1.8 for the 80–89 age group, 2.9 for the 90–99 age group and 4.0 for the centenarians (UNESC, 2000). In Asia, women constituted 53 percent of the population aged 60 and above, and 62 percent of the population aged 80 and above in 1999. In China, 52 percent of the population aged 60 and 65 percent of the population aged 80 were women; in Hong Kong, the corresponding figures are 51 percent and 63 percent, respectively (Table 9.2).

Table 9.2   Proportion of Women in the Ageing Population in Asia, 1999

Country/Area	Women as % of population aged 60 and over	Women as % of population aged 80 and over
Asia	53	62
China	52	65
Hong Kong SAR	51	63
Japan	56	67
Macau	56	67
S. Korea	59	74
Brunei Darussalam	50	53
Cambodia	64	59
Indonesia	54	58
Malaysia	53	56
Philippines	53	58
Singapore	53	62
Thailand	55	63
Vietnam	59	72

Source: UN Population Division (1999).

Among the elderly population, fewer women are economically active or are financially supported by their spouse. UN statistics show that in 1995, for the world population aged 60 and over, only 16 percent of the women, compared to 42 percent of the men, were still active in the labour force. For the same age groups in Asia, 19 percent of the older women as compared to 51 percent of the older men were economically active (Table 9.3).

Table 9.3 Labour Force Participation of Men and Women in the Ageing Population in Asia, 1995

Country/Area	% men aged 60 and over in labour force	% women aged 60 and over in labour force
Asia	51	19
China	42	14
Hong Kong SAR	—	—
Japan	49	21
Macau	—	—
S. Korea	46	25
Brunei Darussalam	50	0
Cambodia	51	38
Indonesia	62	32
Malaysia	47	21
Philippines	67	35
Singapore	27	7
Thailand	50	27
Vietnam	53	32

Source: UN Population Division (1999).

There are also large gender differences in the marital status of the elderly population. Among the world population aged 60 and over, 79 percent of the men and only 43 percent of the women were married. For Asia, 78 percent of the men and 44 percent of the women aged 60 and over were married. In China, the corresponding figures were 73 percent for males and 48 percent for females; those for Hong Kong were 82 percent and 50 percent, respectively (Table 9.4). These percentages would be further decreased for the age group of 80 and over.

Gender Dimensions in Quality of Ageing

Longevity does not directly imply higher status for women. Life expectancy has to be considered in conjunction with the quality of life. Quality of life

Table 9.4   Proportion of Married Men and Women in the Ageing Population in Asia, 1999

Country/Area	% currently married men aged 60 and over	% currently married women aged 60 and over
Asia	78	44
China	73	48
Hong Kong SAR	82	50
Japan	86	51
Macau	—	—
S. Korea	87	37
Brunei Darussalam	83	50
Cambodia	—	—
Indonesia	84	36
Malaysia	84	44
Philippines	81	49
Singapore	83	45
Thailand	80	47
Vietnam	84	45

Source: UN Population Division (1999).

of the elderly women may be examined in terms of economic security, housing and family, and health. These demographic patterns of ageing show that the elderly women are likely to be widowed or single, and would be economically dependent.

Women's lifetime overall labour force participation rate worldwide is lower than that of men, especially after marriage. A high proportion of women leave the paid labour force after marriage and childbirth; more of them are employed on a part-time basis; they predominate in the informal sector. For women who remain in the labour force, they face an earlier statutory retirement age than men do in many countries. As a result, their lifetime earnings are substantially lower than those of men. They do not receive the benefits of pension schemes or provident funds, which are tied to paid employment. In Hong Kong, for example, the Mandatory Provident Fund (MPF) System which commenced operation in December 2000 will only benefit the retired population, but not persons who have not engaged in paid employment. Women who are full-time homemakers or women who are not working in the formal sector will be left out of the retirement scheme. With an overall labour force participation rate of 48 percent among women in Hong Kong (Census and Statistics Department, 1996), the proportion of elderly women facing financial hardship will be substantial.

At present, elderly people constitute almost 60 percent of all recipients of the social security assistance scheme from the government. Women are the majority of recipients in this category. The difference in the gender ratio of welfare recipients increases with advancing age, with women constituting 70 percent of those recipients aged 80 or above (Social Welfare Department, 1997). The rising proportion of elderly women who have to rely on social security assistance is a trend that needs to be monitored.

In many traditional societies, women have limited access to rights of inheritance or property ownership. Thus, they need to depend on the family or the state for financial support and living arrangements. In Asia and the developing countries where family values are strong and government funding is limited, elderly support and services are still largely dependent on the family. Even in developed countries, devolutionists are challenging the rapid growth of entitlement benefits for older people and are curtailing the delivery of long-term health and human services (Estes and Linkins, 1997). Reduced government spending is shifting care back to the family. Only a small proportion of the elderly population live in institutions. In China, multi-generation households are the major living arrangements for the elderly (Yi and George, 2000). Unlike old people in more developed Western countries, the proportion of Chinese old people living alone is much lower: 8.0 percent and 10.2 percent for the modest old men and women, and 13.2 percent and 15.2 percent for the oldest old men and women. The limited facilities available for institutional care also account for the extremely low proportion of institutionalized elderly (less than 2 percent for the extremely old men and 1.1 percent for women). For Chinese elderly women, their lower social and economic status is one of the explanations cited for their even more limited access to long-term care facilities.

Asian family values have been revered as a celebrated cause for ensuring family care. However, co-residency of family members *per se* does not indicate the types of support or care received by the elderly person. There is little research or data on the types of physical, emotional and economic care transferred between family members (Velkoff, 2000). There is often an assumption that living with family members will serve the needs of the elderly persons. Little is known about the preferences of the elderly people in terms of their living arrangements, the mutual benefits to both generations and the extent of elderly abuse in these co-residency situations. Violence against elderly women is a topic that is receiving increasing attention in the field of domestic violence.

Quality of life of the elderly people is closely related to their health.

The health status of the elderly population is an area that lacks reliable and internationally comparable data (UNESC, 2000). The conventional categorization of old age means that persons over age 65 are excluded in many large-scale studies on physical and mental health. Even when epidemiological studies are available, the rates of various health problems for elderly men and women need to be viewed in context, given the multiplicity of pathological conditions in old age and the gender differential life expectancies. Health in old age is also linked to lifelong health. In countries where women are being discriminated against, older women's health status may be traced to the disadvantages they confront from early life, including inadequate nutrition and education, poorer maternity protection and less access to health care than their male counterparts.

It has been shown that marital status is an important determinant of health for elderly persons. Married people's longevity may result from pre-selection, protection, or greater financial security (UNESC, 2000). Unmarried older women are more likely to live in poverty, and are more vulnerable to risks, especially in countries where there is an inadequate formal support system. On the other hand, it has been shown in a longitudinal study on ageing in Beijing that intergenerational social support is related to the psychological well-being of older Chinese parents (Chen and Silverstein, 2000). Intergenerational exchanges of social support include providing instrumental support to children, not just receiving support from children. These exchanges of social support and satisfaction with children have positive effects on the morale of the older parents.

A Life-Cycle Approach to Gender and Ageing

Gender issues in lifelong health show that the physical, mental and social status of men and women in old age is rooted in the gender context throughout their lives. Starting from the prenatal period, childhood, puberty, adulthood, and through later life, females and males are exposed to different experiences in life according to their gender. Access to social resources and vulnerability to risks is influenced by cultural factors such as low valuation of girls and women as compared to that of boys and men.

Discrimination against women and discrimination against the elderly are a double jeopardy to elderly women. The growth of the ageing population and, in particular, the increase in the number of widows and older single women is one of the new challenges affecting the full implementation of the Beijing Declaration and Platform for Action, which was adopted by over 180 governments worldwide in 1995 to advance the status of women (Commission on the Status of Women, 2000). In the five-year review of the 1995 Beijing Conference on Women, women and ageing are highlighted as a cross-cutting issue for the original 12 critical areas of concern in the Platform for Action, including poverty, economy, health, violence against women, environment and institutional mechanisms for the advancement of women. These critical areas of concern are inter-related and have impacts on the rights and status of women in old age.

The gender dimension of ageing is not only restricted to the elderly population, but has differential implications on the life cycle of women and men. Programmes for the elderly may create, maintain or reinforce those gender roles and relations that are detrimental to the well-being and status of women. For example, family care for the dependent elderly person affects women and men differently. Especially in Asia, women are the predominant providers of informal care. The economic contributions of these caregivers are unrecognized, unrewarded and neglected by society, perpetuating the life cycle of disadvantage to women. With the increasing labour force participation of women on the other hand, there are conflicting demands and stresses placed on women at mid-life. Many middle-aged women bear the triple burden of childcare, elderly care and personal careers. The bulk of domestic and emotional labour still falls on the shoulders of women, irrespective of their employment status. Instead of re-examining whether the traditional form of sexual division of domestic labour is still appropriate in the new millennium, women are thrust into a no-win situation. Career-oriented women bear the guilt and blame for neglecting their family, even though their employment contributes to the economy of the family and society. Women who try to balance employment with family responsibilities face the risk of discrimination at work and the stress of role overload. Women who stay at home to take care of the family put themselves in an economically dependent situation and face financial risks in old age.

The Role of the Family

Stereotypical gender roles tie women to family responsibilities. Despite changes in objective conditions, there are still cultural lags in the social norms that focus on women's roles in the context of the family (Cheung et al., 1997). In Asian societies in particular, the family is often the centre of women's lives. The major roles of women are still the wife and mother taking care of family members. Increasingly, women's roles as daughters and daughters-in-law also demand that they become caretakers of elderly family members. Women's activities are affected by their family life cycles. It has been well accepted that women's labour force participation rates correspond to their family life cycle.

The dichotomy of public and private spheres associates men's work with the paid employment sector and women's work with the family and informal sector. Men are considered the primary breadwinners and women's income is regarded as secondary. On the other hand, women's work, that is, domestic labour, is also considered secondary and less valuable. Whether women are engaged in paid employment or not, the major responsibilities in household labour still fall on women's shoulders. Women spend longer working hours on household chores and emotional labour (Equal Opportunities Commission, 1997). These jobs are not remunerated and their economic contributions are ignored. Work in the private sphere is not valued in monetary terms. Under the present economic system, the social status of female homemakers is devalued in society.

Although more women have entered the public sphere, their traditional identity with the private sphere still prevails. Within the family, the stereotyped concept of womanhood is even more embedded. The family socializes its members according to prescribed cultural expectations that perpetuate male dominance and control (Cheung et al., 1999). With a patriarchal family ideology committed to a gender-hierarchy, the status of women is undermined. The preference for sons is prevalent across Asian societies. Daughters have less access to family resources. The manifestation of patriarchy varies in different cultural contexts. Patriarchy takes on more subtle forms in more urban and economically developed societies, where social expectations and attitudes restrict women's choices. It interacts with other social dynamics such as class and caste to impose harsher control on women.

Traditionally, patriarchy was justified as a form of protection for women. The man as head of the household is responsible for taking care of his wife, children and other dependent members of the family. With industrialization and urbanization, fundamental changes in the family structure have evolved throughout the Asian countries. Many women have joined the public sphere. Stability of the family unit can no longer be assumed. Divorce rates and the number of single parent households have increased, although at a lower rate than in Western countries. Domestic violence has begun to surface as a public issue (Cheung et al., 1999). Women are increasingly turning to the state for some of the traditional protective functions of the family — childcare, care for the elderly, protection against wife abuse and social security.

On the other hand, global economic restructuring has overtaken the state's gradual uptake of these protective functions. One of the effects of globalization is the privatization of public services, and the shift of responsibilities from public support back to the family. Feminization of employment in Asia under trade liberalization has not led to economic prosperity for women. Instead, the concentration of women at the margins of the labour market has led to the deterioration of the status of women workers (Ghosh, 1998). Feminization of poverty has become an issue of concern to working-class women.

Gender- and Class-disaggregated Data

The issues of gender disparity become more pronounced when class analysis is incorporated. Chow (1996) pointed out that an "inclusive feminist vantage point sees gender not through one lens but through a multiplicity of lenses that form a prism for analyzing the social construction of race, class, and gender" (p. xix). For professional women, the gender impact may not be as apparent as for working-class women.

The life-cycle pattern of labour force participation of working-class women with little education differs from that of professional women. Labour force participation, in turn, affects the economic security of these women in old age. With increased educational attainment among women in Hong Kong in the last quarter of the twentieth century, their labour force participation rate has shown a corresponding increase. The expansion in educational opportunities for women has resulted in a change in the pattern of labour force participation among women in general. With delayed marriage and childbirth, women stay in the work force longer. In 1996, women's overall labour force participation peaked in the 25–29 age group, and began to decline after 30. The M-curve in women's overall labour force participation through the life cycle that was found in the 1981 was no longer apparent.

However, disaggregation of the labour force participation rate of married women by education levels shows that the M-curve was still evident among women with primary or lower secondary level education. For these women, between 72 and 79 percent of the 20–24 age group were employed in the labour force. The rate declined to about 40 percent in the early 30s age group. This period coincides with the child-bearing and child-rearing family life cycle of these women. The rate increased to over 50 percent again after age 40 (Mak and Chung, 1997).

On the other hand, the pattern of labour force participation among university-educated women was much less affected by their family life cycle. Education helps to overcome the gender barrier on labour force decisions (Mak and Chung, 1997). These women were more likely to remain in the workforce even after childbirth. The availability of relatively low-cost domestic helpers has enabled most female university graduates to continue with their paid employment throughout most of their working life. Over 90 percent of these women were engaged in paid employment in their 20s; about 80 percent continued on in their 30s; over 65 percent remained economically active until retirement.

These differential work patterns among women from different classes are tied to their economic independence within the family as well as in old age. With most professional women remaining active in the labour force throughout their working life, their lifelong savings and retirement benefits would be more comparable to those of men. Working-class women who break off their labour force participation to take up unpaid family responsibilities face the double jeopardy of economic dependence when they are young and financial insecurity when they get old. The apparent achievements of professional women in Hong Kong often mask the inequality faced by working-class women. Many men and women alike do not recognize the real problems faced by women from different classes and backgrounds.

Implications for Policy and Research

The effects of gender are pervasive across the life cycle. Gender is structurally linked to different domains of discrimination in all cultures. However, the gender perspective is not mainstreamed in policy and research, either out of ignorance or out of a simplistic construction of gender equality. "Gender blindness" ignores the realities of gender as a key determinant of social inequalities throughout the life cycle. As a consequence, data are not disaggregated by gender and policies do not consider the possibility of gender differences. Gender "neutrality" may be a deliberate attempt to assume the guise of gender equality. In fact, it results in gender bias by neglecting the specific characteristics, needs, and circumstances of women and men arising from their experiences in the broader gender context. Gender "neutrality" is based on the premise of equal treatment of women and men, without recognizing that they have different life experiences. It fails to recognize that equal treatment may not produce equitable results.

Gender Analysis

Gender-based analysis aims at examining the differences in the lives of women and men and the diversity among women themselves, and identifying those differences that lead to social and economic inequity for women. Through the collection and utilization of sex-disaggregated data, the underlying causes of these inequities can be understood. Gender analysis will assess the differential impact of policies on women and men, and on different groups of women. Alternative policies can be designed with different strategies to achieve equitable outcomes for these women and men (SOM Ad Hoc Task Force, 1999).

The rapid growth of the ageing population in the twenty-first century is a major concern in human service planning. International experts in population and development have recognized the fundamental relationships between population, gender and development. A comprehensive policy on ageing requires the compilation of sex-disaggregated and class-disaggregated data, the use of gender analyses, and a life-cycle approach to gender analysis to provide a gender perspective in policy formulation and programme implementation. Given the predominance of women in the ageing population, gender-sensitive policies and programmes are needed to address the specific concerns of elderly women. In Asian societies, ageing issues are generating an active debate about gender, the family, the organization of the workplace and the policy approaches to address these challenges (Boling, 1998).

Policies on ageing depend on adequate research and data collection. Current census reports have lagged behind the demographic changes in the ageing population. The older age groups are undifferentiated after age 65 in most census data. Research studies usually restrict their target respondents to those under the age of 65. Given the fact that people over 65 will constitute close to one-quarter of the population in Asia by 2050, and over one-third of the population in Hong Kong by that time, more refined age grouping with sex-disaggregated data will provide a more useful database for policy-makers and researchers. Use of sex-disaggregated and class-disaggregated data in research will lead to very different conclusions in policies, especially when there are substantial sex differences (Cheung, 1999).

Gender analyses on ageing issues will identify the potential contributions and specific needs of elderly women and men in terms of economic security, living arrangements, health and well being, as well as active participation in the community. Gender analyses can also be used to evaluate the differential impact of policies and programmes on women and men. For example, retirement income policies for the elderly population should be designed not only to encourage greater financial self-reliance for retired people, but also to ensure gender equity in the provision of retirement protection. Such policies need to recognize that women are the majority of the elderly population, and to take account of women's needs in retirement. Women are less able to save for old age than men, because they are less likely to participate in the paid labour force, they earn less than men, they interrupt their employment history to care of children, and are more likely to engage in part-time work. Women who are homemakers have to rely on their husbands' retirement benefit scheme as a joint scheme. However, with increasing divorce rates, many marriages do not last long enough for women to receive these benefits. By identifying these differential experiences between women and men, different options for retirement income schemes should be considered. To address the needs of women, the scheme should provide them with retirement income regardless of their earning history, and should recognize their unpaid work as homemakers and family carers that has prevented them from accumulating savings (Ministry of Women's Affairs, 1996).

A life-cycle approach to gender analyses will provide a comprehensive perspective for inter-related policies on human services in relation to ageing. The needs and contributions of elderly women and men have to be linked to those in different stages of the life cycle. To facilitate this comprehensive approach, gender mainstreaming is necessary. Gender mainstreaming would incorporate gender perspectives into all levels of policies and resource allocation (SOM Ad Hoc Task Force, 1999). By mainstreaming gender analysis in all public policies, more integrative policies can be adopted. For example, the benefits of inter-generational exchanges in family care are not restricted to care of the elderly, but can be considered in conjunction with childcare options for the younger couples. What is the potential source of contributions from the active elderly people, and what are the level and types of care needed by the frail elderly with disabilities? What tangible support and incentives could be given to foster family care and exchanges to make it sustainable and equitable to women and men? How could the division of domestic labour evolve towards a more equitable basis in the long run? These interlocking questions have to be examined in a fundamental gender framework that cuts across "the goals, structures, priorities, policies, decisions, processes, practices, activities, and resource allocation as well as participation at all levels" (SOM Ad Hoc Task Force, 1999).

Policies for the Ageing Population in Hong Kong

In view of the growing ageing population, governments are beginning to address the needs of the elderly population in more focused policies. In Hong Kong, an Elderly Commission was set up in 1998 to advise the government on the formulation of a comprehensive policy for the elderly, to coordinate the planning and development, and to monitor the implementation of programmes and services for the elderly. Ensuring financial security for the elderly is considered fundamental to achieving the policy objective of caring for the elderly (Health and Welfare Bureau, 1999). However, without mainstreaming a gender perspective, the major initiative in this area was to set up the Mandatory Provident Fund System that, as pointed out earlier, will not provide dignified financial security to half of the female population. No alternative scheme is planned for ensuring the financial security of women who contribute to the economy in the informal sector or as homemakers. The Comprehensive Social Security Assistance Scheme that provides welfare assistance to the needy on application is not an equitable option. It does not achieve the goal of self-reliance for elderly women. The fiscal sustainability of welfare spending for a large proportion of the elderly population is a related area of concern.

On the area of family care, providing the necessary community care and support services is an important policy that will facilitate the family to take up the care-giving role. The initiatives of the Elderly Commission in this area are in the right direction. In addition to providing more day-care and home services to the elderly in need, the government is also reviewing the mode of provision of home-help services and the introduction of day-respite services as forms of support to families caring for their elderly members. On the other hand, initiatives to encourage the elderly to lead an active life have remained in the traditional models of social welfare that engage the elderly persons in social and recreational activities or in voluntary social services. The vast potential of the human talents from different groups of the elderly population could be looked upon as resources for both the family and the community. For example, the possible contributions of active elderly parents to childcare within the family as well as in the community could be explored, organized and promoted.

Gender Mainstreaming

With a few exceptions, a gender framework is currently absent from most Asian governments. In 1999, Asia-Pacific Economic Cooperation (APEC) initiated a Framework for the Integration of Women in APEC (SOM Ad Hoc Task Force, 1999). The Framework guides APEC to integrate women in the mainstream of APEC processes and activities. It is a response to the APEC leaders' recognition that "gender is a cross-cutting theme in APEC" (p. 3). The three major elements of the Framework are gender analysis, collection and use of sex-disaggregated data, and involvement of women in APEC.

The Hong Kong government announced in May 2000 that it would be setting up a Women's Commission to co-ordinate women's services and policies affecting women in Hong Kong. The Women's Commission should become the focal point in mainstreaming gender perspectives at all levels of government. By taking the lead in the collection and utilization of sex-disaggregated data, and by building capacity for gender analysis in the government, the Women's Commission can achieve the goal of incorporating the principles and methodology of gender analysis as an on-going part of policy decisions.

Conclusion

With changes in the levels of educational attainment and labour force participation of women in the past 30 years, the demography of our future ageing population will be different from that of the present population. Long-term planning for our future ageing population needs to take into account not only the current needs and potentials of elderly women and men, but also the situation of different cohorts of the population who will become the elderly women and men of the future. A life-cycle approach to gender analysis will provide a comprehensive perspective to gender-sensitive planning for the ageing population. Mainstreaming gender will ensure that women and men will have equitable access to, and benefits from, society's resources.

There was an awakening to the gender perspective in the social sciences at the end of the twentieth century (Cheung, 1999). The gender decon-struction of social research and policies has increased the sensitivity of social scientists to the differential interpretation of data and outcome. With rapid changes in gender roles and relations in the last century, the cultural lag in gender attitudes and beliefs has to catch up with the social reality.

The challenge of human service planning for the ageing population has highlighted the importance of mainstreaming gender from a life-cycle perspective in research, policy and planning in the new millennium.

References

Boling, P. (1998), "Family Policy in Japan," *Journal of Social Policy*, 27:173–90.

Census and Statistics Department (1996), *Hong Kong Annual Digest of Statistics*. Hong Kong: Government printers.

Chen, X. and M. Silverstein (2000), "Intergenerational Social Support and the Psychological Well-being of Older Parents in China," *Research on Aging*, 22: 43–65.

Cheung, F. M. (1999), "The Gender Dimension in the Social Sciences." In Ali Kazancigil and David Makinson (eds.), *World Social Science Report 1999*. Paris: UNESCO/Elsevier, pp. 220–25.

Cheung, F. M., A. De Dios, M. Karlekar and J. Vichit-Vadakan (1999), "Introduction: Violence against Women as a Global Concern." In F. M. Cheung, A. De Dios, M. Karlekar, J. Vichit-Vadakan and L. R. Quisumbing (eds.), *Breaking the Silence: Violence Against Women in Asia*. Hong Kong: Equal Opportunities Commission, pp. 2–12.

Cheung, F. M., B. L. L. Lai, K. C. Au and S. S. Y. Ngai (1997), "Gender Role Identity, Stereotypes, and Attitudes in Hong Kong." In F. M. Cheung (ed.), *Engendering Hong Kong Society: A Gender Perspective of Women's Status*. Hong Kong: The Chinese University Press, pp. 201–35.

Chow, E. N. L. (1996), "Introduction: Transforming Knowledgment: Race, Class, and Gender." In E. N. L. Chow, D. Wilkinson and M. B. Zinn (eds.), *Race, Class, and Gender: Common Bonds, Different Voices*. Thousand Oaks: Sage, pp. xix–xxvi.

Commission on the Status of Women (2000), "Further Actions and Initiatives to Implement the Beijing Declaration and Platform for Action." Paper submitted by the Chairperson of the Preparatory Committee for item 2 of the provisional agenda of the meeting of the Commission on the Status of Women acting as the preparatory committee for the special session of the General Assembly entitled "Gender Equality, Development and Peace for the Twenty-first Century." New York, 3–17 March 2000.

Equal Opportunities Commission (EOC) (1997), *A Baseline Survey of Equal Opportunities on the Basis of Gender in Hong Kong 1996–1997*. Hong Kong: EOC, Research Report No. 1.

Estes, C. L. and K. W. Linkins (1997), "Devolution and Aging Policy: Racing to the Bottom in Long-term Care," *International Journal of Health Services*, 27: 427–42.

Ghosh, J. (1998), "Gender, Trade and the WTO: Issues and Evidence from

Developing Asia." In V. Wee (ed.), *Trade Liberalisation: Challenges and Opportunities for Women in Southeast Asia*. New York: UNIFEM and ENGENDER.

Health and Welfare Bureau (1999), *1999 Policy Objectives: Care for the Elderly*. Hong Kong: Hong Kong government.

Mak, G. C. L. and Y. P. Chung (1997), "Education and Labour Force Participation of Women in Hong Kong." In F. M. Cheung (ed.), *Engendering Hong Kong Society: A Gender Perspective of Women's Status*. Hong Kong: The Chinese University Press, pp. 13–39.

Ministry of Women's Affairs (1996), *The Full Picture: Guidelines for Gender Analysis*. Wellington: Ministry of Women's Affairs.

Social Welfare Department (SWD) (1997), *Studies of PA/CSSA Recipients, 1993–1996*. Hong Kong: SWD.

SOM Ad Hoc Task Force on the Integration of Women in APEC (1999), *Framework for the Integration of Women in APEC*. Singapore: Asia-Pacific Economic Cooperation Secretariat.

United Nations Economic and Social Council (UNESC) (2000), "Concise Report on World Population Monitoring, 2000: Population, Gender and Development." Report of the Secretary-General to the 33rd Session of the Commission on Population and Development, 27–31 March 2000.

United Nations Population Division (UNPD) (1999), *Population Ageing 1999*. New York: UN publications.

Velkoff, V. (2000), "Future Research Directions." Paper prepared for item 7 of the provisional agenda of the UN Population Division's Technical Meeting on Population Ageing and Living Arrangements of Older Persons: Critical Issues and Policy Responses, New York, 8–10 February 2000.

Yi, Z. and L. George (2000), "Extremely Rapid Ageing and the Living Arrangements of Older Persons: The Case of China." Paper prepared for item 3 of the provisional agenda of the UN Population Division's Technical Meeting on Population Ageing and Living Arrangements of Older Persons: Critical Issues and Policy Responses, New York, 8–10 February 2000.

10

Civil Society and Democratization in Asia: Prospects and Challenges in the New Millennium

Emma Porio

Introduction

Political events in Asia during the last 15 years have shown that civil society is crucial in understanding the changes in economy and polity. These events have given rise to several interpretations of the concept and role of civil society and the democratization of political life. In turn, civil society movements (CSMs) have utilized different political and cultural schemes to advance their claims for democratic space and a share of societal resources. Emerging from the various nation-states in the region, these cultural schemes are shaped by their different political-economic contexts and levels of integration to the global systems of capital and information and communication technology.

Major social and economic transformations during the past decade have led to the decline of authoritarian governments and the resurgence of democratic institutions and systems of governance in Eastern Europe, Latin America and Asia. Throughout the Asia-Pacific region, the respective roles of the state, market system and civil society are being re-examined (ESCAP, 1998). In the forefront of this re-examination are developmental non-governmental organizations (NGOs) and community-based organizations (CBOs), which are challenging the traditional ways that the state and the market have allocated societal resources. Several political and economic developments have led to this re-evaluation, such as the deterioration and collapse of socialist regimes in Eastern Europe, the increasing integration of centralized economies like China and Vietnam to open capitalist economies, the fiscal crisis and the effects of structural adjustment. The breaking down of the Berlin Wall in 1989 symbolically ended Cold War politics among the superpowers. This also heralded the search for an alternative development paradigm (Porio, 1997). Assertions regarding the relationship between democracy and economic development became fashionable. Civil society, then, became an exciting prospect for this agenda.

The resurgence of democratic regimes has been mostly ushered in by the emergence of vibrant civil society groups and movements. This is clearly demonstrated in the statistics provided by Freedom House in New York. Their data show that the number of free or liberal democratic states has risen from 42 in 1972 to 56 in 1985 to 76 in 1995 — or from 29 percent in 1972 to 33.5 percent in 1985 to 39.8 percent in 1995 (cited in Bello, 2000; see also Chapter 7 by Jose Abueva). The third wave of democratization as described by Huntington (1991), then, seems to have been nurtured by civil society.

The twin phenomena of civil society and increasing democratization have captured the imagination of intellectuals, activists, political leaders and development assistance agencies, and generated many conferences, meetings and publications. They have also fuelled the advocacy of political and economic reforms. More importantly, they have spawned an alternative model of development assistance: the channelling of official development assistance and delivery of social services through NGOs, CBOs and private foundations. Civil society groups have become alternative service delivery routes for assistance or entry points for political intervention because of the failure of existing state agencies and institutions (Baron, 1999). Global statistics on foreign assistance attest to the centrality of NGOs in social development. In 1975, the proportion of total aid from OECD countries delivered through NGOs was less than 1 percent. In 1993, this had increased to about 5 percent, excluding similar aid from UN agencies and multilateral institutions (Riddell and Robinson, 1995; Silliman and Garner Noble, 1998). Largely, this is due to the perception that NGOs have more accountable and transparent structures and processes than state bureaucracies.

Objectives and Structure of This Chapter

This chapter examines the conceptual foundations of civil society and its role in shaping socio-political life in the past decade as well as their prospects and challenges for the next millennium. It argues that civil society is a key mediating force in changing state-society dynamics which, in turn, is also being reconfigured by the globalization of social life and the rise of identity and resource claims by various groups. Furthermore, state-civil society engagements have been influenced by communication technologies, facilitating the efficient movement of information, capital and human resources across groups and national boundaries. Finally, the growth of civil society must always be seen within the context of the Asian states trying to balance their functions of promoting political legitimacy and economic development.

The chapter is divided into four parts. The first part outlines the aims of the chapter while the second part reviews the conceptual foundations and interpretations of the term civil society. The third part explores the different roles that civil society has played in the democratization of socio-political life in some parts of the region. The final part concludes that civil society is a major factor in reconfiguring the global-local nexus of state-market-civil society relations which, in turn, define the challenges of civil society in the new millennium. The coverage of this chapter is mostly limited to Southeast Asia.

The Conceptual Bases of Civil Society

Civil society has a long intellectual and political history (Seligman, 1992). Several authors (e.g., Gellner, 1991; Kumar, 1993; Rodan, 1996; Yamamoto, 1996; He, 1997; Laothamatas, 1997, to name a few) have extensively discussed the issues regarding the emergence and role of civil society in several historical and political contexts. To provide a conceptual frame for this chapter, I will just briefly cite a few key interpretations of civil society.

Concept of Civil Society

Caroll (2000) defines civil society as "people coming together around a common concern, a concern which is linked to the values of the wider society, and insisting that the major institutions — the state, political parties and business take these values into consideration." Diamond (1994) gives a more extensive definition:

> Civil society is ... the realm of organized social life that is voluntary, self-generating, (largely) self-supporting, autonomous from the state, and bound by a legal order or set of shared rules. It is distinct from "society" in general in that it involves citizens acting collectively in a public sphere to express their interests, passions, and ideas, exchange information, achieve mutual goals, make demands on the state, and hold state officials accountable. Civil society is an intermediary entity, standing between the private sphere and the state. (p. 5)

According to Diamond (1994), civil society is alive and well when citizens participate in church groups, professional associations, women's groups, trade unions, human rights groups, and civic associations in order to press for state and economic reforms. It encompasses a vast array of formal and informal organizations engaged in a wide range of activities to achieve economic, cultural, educational and developmental goals. Pluralism and diversity characterize the groups comprising civil society. It is not synonymous with society and beyond being "voluntary, self-generating, autonomous and rule-abiding." The organizations of civil society are distinct from other social groups in several respects. They are concerned with public rather than private ends and relates to the state not to gain formal power but rather "to seek from the state concessions, benefits, policy changes, relief, redress, or accountability" (Diamond, 1994:7). In short, civil society is the politically active sector of society. Autonomous both from the state and from political parties, civil society encompasses masses of citizens engaged in public protest, social movements and NGOs acting in the public sphere. Civil society excludes the household, profit-making enterprises, political parties and groups striving to gain control of the state through armed rebellion (Silliman and Garner Noble, 1998).

Civil society is the realm of collective, public action between the private sphere and the state, which Serrano (1994) calls the "politically active popular sector" of society. Meanwhile, Kumar (1993:383) understands civil society as the space between the family and the state, or between the individual and the state; it is also the space in the non-state institutions which organize and educate citizens for political participation. Antonio Gramsci (1971) views civil society as one of the key elements comprising his three-part framework of the state, economy and civil society. It is the primary locus for creating ideology, a key element in building consensus and legitimizing power. Thus, hegemony of a particular group, whether cultural or social, is built on consent rather than coercion. Habermas (1989) conceptualizes it as "the realm which constitutes the intersection between state and society." Huang (1993), deriving inspiration from Habermas, conceptualizes it as the third sphere. He is also sceptical of the development of societal organizations in societies long dominated by party-state politics.

Civil society, in general, is the political space between the state and society. In particular, it is the space occupied and created by the non-profit sector between the state and the market. Often, the non-profit sector is dominated by NGOs in alliance with grassroots organizations or CBOs. Social movements constitute an important subset of civil society. Rocamora (1998) also added that the growth of civil societies has to be understood at

Figure 10.1 Schematic Representation of the Relationship of State, Civil Society and the Market in a Social Formation or Society

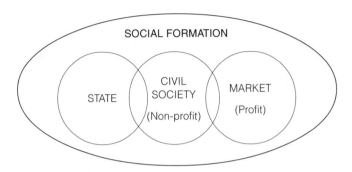

four inter-related levels: state, political society, civil society and international actors. They also argue that democratic movements have to be always calibrated within post-Cold War politics. Figure 10.1 provides a better appreciation of the relationship among these entities.

According to Rodan (1996:21), civil society is just one form of political space where opposition parties can articulate and negotiate their interests. Currently, the space of civil society enjoys wide support both in the North and South and from the élite to marginalized groups. Indeed, the discourse of civil society is quite seductive! But there is a need to demystify this situation and be more realistic about the power and potential of civil society in democratizing state and political power.

Because of their visibility and popularity, NGOs are almost taken by most people as the equivalent of civil society. But civil society is best conceptualized as a political space created by NGOs, CBOs, professional groups and other voluntary associations allied with broad-based movements (e.g., women's, indigenous people's, environmental movements). The composition of civil society is quite dependent on the political and economic context of the society and nation-state. In the same manner, so are the relationships, strategies, and skills of CSOs and networks in their engagements with the state.

The Empowered Civil Society

The previous section described the characteristics and organizational bases of civil society. But when does civil society become mobilized and visible to take on larger political issues? Or what are the conditions that push CSOs to take issues into a broader public arena and organize street protests, demonstrations and other mobilization activities challenging state action/ inaction? This section will attempt to describe the conditions, the evolving strategies and impacts of CSOs on the state, society and within civil society groups, and their capacity to create and consolidate the democratic process.

Several conditions transform CSOs into broad movements to challenge the state on its decisions and actions. Civil society groups go beyond their organizational concerns to work towards broader networks and coalitions when the following conditions are present. There is freedom to organize and exchange information and a shared perception that the traditional institutions of society like the state can no longer be relied upon to protect the rights of the citizen. Being able to obtain the wide support of the media and other institutions like the churches, CSOs generate widespread indignation against those who violate the basic rights of the citizen, giving rise to a broad-based social movement.

Historical evidence in the region has shown that vibrancy of civil society is generated by economic growth and the expansion of the middle class, as in the case of East Asian economies and some countries in Southeast Asia like Thailand. Civil society has also been critical in restoring democracy in formerly authoritarian regimes like the Philippines and Indonesia.

The attraction of civil society movements lies in their promise of social inclusion among marginalized groups in political and economic systems traditionally dominated by a few number of élites (Silliman and Garner Noble, 1998:10). More significantly, the tactics and strategies of civil society anchored on peaceful (i.e., reformist) mechanisms appeal to a broad spectrum of society. In this manner, then, CSOs/CSMs provide greater attraction and support compared to progressive groups aligned with the Left. The popularity of civil society-based movements in contemporary politics accounts to a certain extent for the decline of Left-inspired movements.

Civil Society: Asian or Western?

Several writers (e.g., Muzaffar, 1996; Serrano, 1994) have argued that civil society is rooted in western rational tradition and political culture anchored on the notion of state and citizenship. Serrano (1994), however, also argues that the values and practices associated with communal institutions in Asia find resonance in civil society:

> Voluntary action is deeply rooted in Asian communities. It is directed toward common concerns that cannot be adequately addressed by individual families and extended kinship support systems: production, exchange, rituals from birth to death, and collective security, all of which maintain community consensus and cohesion. The most common form of organization is the self-help and mutual-exchange group. In Indonesia, the *gotong royong* or mutual help is equivalent to *bayanihan* in the Philippines. Funeral associations, of which there are thousands in Thailand, are also mutual-benefit associations. (p. 272)

The tradition of voluntary associations in Asia has been rooted in the need to fulfil basic social security needs that are beyond the capacity of individual, family or clan. Thus, the priority of civil society organizations is to secure the autonomy of people's organizations so that their basic needs can be addressed. But this situation also reflects the relative inability of the central or local state to respond to the needs of its citizenry.

Contemporary CSMs have their bases in voluntary associations, groups and networks at the community level. But they have succeeded in connecting their local struggles for social security to the need for reforms in the larger political and economic structures. They have realized that broader structural changes are necessary in addressing the welfare needs of the people, especially the marginalized and disadvantaged groups. The traditional and cultural bases of CSMs have been largely transformed by the growing realization among civil society groups that the structural distribution of societal resources and the quality of life of individuals and communities are largely mediated by broader state policies and programmes. This can be seen in their evolving strategies that seem to indicate the increasing political sophistication of CSOs.

The argument that civil society is an alien concept in Asia is quite interesting because Serrano's earlier characterization of voluntary associations strongly resembles the associational life described by de Tocqueville in America a hundred years ago. Serrano's point, however, heightens an important principle: In understanding state-civil society dynamics, one must always recognize the different social, political, economic and cultural contexts that shape the character of civil society and the movements associated with it.

Another issue popularly articulated before the Asian financial crisis was that Asian values are not quite compatible with the western-based notions of liberal democracy. Alagappa (1995) noted that élites in a number of countries in the region — China, Vietnam, Myanmar, Indonesia, Singapore, Malaysia, Brunei and Laos — support economic development but reject democracy. Several Asian leaders, notably Singapore's Senior Minister Lee Kuan Yew, have argued that many of the institutions and practices associated with western democratic states cannot be applied to Asia at this point in time (Muzzafar, 1996).

Thus, acceptance or at least tolerance of voluntary associations and institutions that attempt to affect policies and programmes of the state is not high. Some political leaders have attempted to justify authoritarian regimes by asserting that democratic institutions, like civil society, are not compatible with Asian cultures and values. But Korea's President Kim Dae Jung has rejected this idea and argued that democracy has a place in Asian tradition. Moreover, Serrano and Muzaffar stress that many of these democratic values have been articulated by various religions and cultures found in Asia. But Alagappa notes that this retreat for cover under Asian values is really a resistance to the "reactionary imperialism" of the West in Asia.

Prior to the Asian financial crisis, Fukuyama (1995), deriving inspiration from the experiences of Singapore and Malaysia among others, asserted that the only competitor to liberal democracy is Asian paternalistic authoritarianism. However, the downfall of Suharto in Indonesia at the hands of civil society may have eroded the strength of this argument. Meanwhile, Gellner (1991:507) underscores the difficulty of generating a civil society capable of supporting a liberal democracy in communist and Muslim societies. Indonesians, however, in the wake of protests during the Asian financial crisis, argue that in traditional Muslim societies, there is no clear separation between the state and civil society. Indonesian NGO leaders maintain that the civil society, *masyarakat madani*, is part of the Indonesian Muslim tradition.

However, declining political legitimacy has forced some regimes in the region to accommodate the increasing tide of CSMs. The states' accommodation to civil society is strongly linked to their need for political legitimacy. Moreover, the commitment of these states to economic growth and modernization has pushed them to give their reluctant support to the ideas and practices of civil society groups. In China, for instance, the development of professional associations and other civil society groups, especially in urban areas, is seen as part of a modernizing society. In the same manner, the efforts of NGOs to strengthen the rule of law are seen as part of the restructuring of institutions in support of China's increasing integration to the capitalist system.

In Myanmar, meanwhile, the State Law and Order Council (SLORC) is an attempt by the military junta to gain political legitimacy. Thus, the opposition under Aung San Suu Kyi is tolerated to a certain extent while the state attempts to liberalize the economy and find a more formal political role for the military. In Indonesia, citizens endured the state's intolerance for civil society groups because of its promise of political stability and economic development. In the late 1990s, however, professional associations, intellectuals, human rights associations, Islamic organizations, Christian minorities and segments of the armed forces, began challenging top-level corruption and excesses of power. These civil society groups have become a major voice for economic and political reforms.

The expansion and growth of Asian economies have created discernible changes in the lifestyle of the population of these economies. In China, for example, higher disposable income and greater access to outside information have allowed an expanding middle class more educational, training and travel opportunities. In the same manner, the number of voluntary associations with professional, charitable, relief and educational goals has increased. Although subject to government regulation, these associations are allowed to define their own agendas. Progress in economic and political reforms has expanded the space for civil society groups in socio-political life. Thus, economic development and the expansion of a middle class facilitate the rise of CSOs and democratization.

In Korea, the NGOs were crucial to the political mobilization in the late 1980s (Silliman and Garner Noble, 1998:9). In 1986, Vietnam adopted *doi moi* or political and economic renovation; critics, however, have noted that economic benefits are not equally shared. Challenges such as these have pushed Vietnam to explore alternative models of governance.

Civil Society, Democracy and the State

The aim of civil society is not to transform the state but to democratize society (Atienza, 1994). In contemporary politics, the most visible, articulate and influential among the CSOs are the NGOs. They are the agents for consolidating and maintaining democracy rather than initiating it. The associational life of civil society serves as a training ground for democracy as participation in it sharpens political skills and increases the efficacy of citizens. Voluntary associations develop democratic attitudes and values and they also form and preserve civic culture that supports democracy. Participation in associational life increases tolerance and willingness to compromise and appreciation for the rights and obligations of a democratic citizen (Diamond, 1994, cited by Silliman and Garner Noble, 1998). This can be seen in the political and advocacy activities of NGOs to facilitate political participation and redress the inequalities of society. Furthermore, NGO networks, coalitions and groups constituting civil society institutionalize the values and ethos of civil culture necessary for a stable democracy (Dawisha and Parrot, 1994:125). Deriving inspiration from Huntington (1984), Diamond further argues that the functions of civil society include providing a countercheck to potential excesses of a democratic state and democratizing authoritarian states.

Silliman and Garner Noble (1998:18–19) credit civil society with the following achievements: (1) creating a vibrant public discourse; (2) redefining the content of politics; and (3) increasing institutionalization of democratic processes. Although the authors are describing civil society in the Philippines, I would argue that these achievements are applicable, albeit in varying degrees, to civil society in other countries in the region.

Civil society has redefined and broadened the content of politics. To a large extent, it has been responsible for the inclusion of issues previously viewed as not amenable to political action such as domestic violence, the rights of indigenous peoples to ancestral lands, community rights to natural resources. It has also exerted pressure for the institution of democratic processes like free elections and the promotion of human rights.

In the era of worldwide pressure for democratization, state leaders have allowed political space for civil society. A classic example is documented by the excellent study of He (1997) on the democratic implications of civil society in China. Describing the existence of semi-civil society or quasi-civil society in China, he asserts that these groups serve dual functions, namely: (1) as a channel for state control; and (2) as a new tool or source of legitimation. His dual-function thesis provides us with an excellent guide in understanding the place of civil society in countries like China, Vietnam and Cambodia. The presence of NGO leaders in the political administration of Wahid has strengthened the emerging civilian character of the Indonesian state. In the process, it has aided the Indonesian state in constructing its political legitimacy. In Vietnam, there is a different pattern of state-civil society relationship in the South as compared to the North; the South seems to provide a more supportive context in the development of CSOs. The presence of NGOs and their increasing role in the delivery of social services have been, to a certain extent, calibrated to increase the legitimacy of the central state based in Hanoi.

The socio-political activities of CSOs during the past two decades have contributed to their growing capacity to engage the state. Over time, CSOs and networks have grown in terms of skills, specialization and their capacities to assist marginalized groups. Niyom (1997), in observing the growth of NGOs, focuses on urban poor alleviation in Bangkok and notes the growing specialization and interdependence of these organizations. This allows them a greater sphere of influence over their partner-CBOs, as well as lesser dependence on state-funded programmes. But while the NGO community shares the core values of autonomy, pluralism, diversity, closeness to the grassroots, a bottom-up perspective and volunteerism, there is a healthy disagreement over strategy and the precise role of citizen organizations. This is especially true in societies with vibrant CSMs, as in the Philippines and Thailand.

Some authors, like Karaos (1994) and Atienza (1994), have argued that power in civil society has a moral force. Other authors (e.g., Bullard, 2000) have also asserted that this space is not benign or neutral because it is the arena where conflicting class interests are contested. Short of direct domination and coercion, the state and the market must gain the consent of civil society for their legitimacy. Whoever captures civil society captures all!

Some authors (e.g., Diamond, 1994; Coronel Ferrer, 1997) are unabashedly euphoric about the role of civil society in the restoration of democratic processes and institutions. Others like Rodan (1996), however, take a more balanced view. Reminiscent of the Gramscian tradition, these authors assert that civil society always has to be viewed within the struggle for power between state and societal institutions and stakeholders.

Contemporary analysts of civil society have derived their inspiration primarily from the political theories of Locke and de Tocqueville or from Hegel, Marx and Gramsci. Those who are inspired by the first group of theorists, (e.g., Diamond, 1994) celebrate the democratic role of CSOs/CSMs and credit these groups with consolidating and stabilizing democratic processes and institutions. Their ideas are strongly articulated in the developmental policies and programmes promoted by UN agencies, bilateral and multilateral institutions in third world and non-Western countries. But those who are inspired by the latter group of critical theorists are not as impressed with the contingent gains of CSOs/CSMs.

Civil Society, Democratization and the Middle Class

The emergence of civil society has been strongly associated with the expansion of the middle class in Latin America (O'Donnell et al., 1988) and other parts of the globe (e.g., Laothamatas, 1997). As argued earlier, the prominence of civil society discourse in contemporary politics is a function of modernization and economic growth, the expansion of the middle class, and the state's accommodation of the new forces as a way of strengthening its legitimacy. The emergence of new classes redefines the issues and the character of the opposition. A new economic system, meanwhile, gives rise to new sources of wealth and class interest gives rise to new fractures in new socio-political issues. Compared to the 1970s, when state opposition came mostly from peasants, workers and student movements, civil society has transformed political opposition in the 1980s and 1990s to include segments of the upper, middle and working classes (Hewison and Rodan, 1996).

The rise of the middle class has been a crucial factor in broad-based mobilizations that have often centred on demands on the state to institute economic and political reforms. Maisrikrod (1997), in examining political movements in Thailand, argues that the middle class was crucial in installing a democratic regime rather than in consolidating it. He further argues that democratic stability is always a compromise between the state and the capitalist class, on the one hand, and the inclusion of the middle class in the political process, on the other. This is understandable considering the constitution of civil society in Thailand — a loose coalition of intellectuals, professionals, NGOs, CBOs, workers and peasant organizations. In Taiwan, as well as in other parts of Asia, the middle, business and working classes have been credited with the increasing democratization of state politics.

Exploring the relationship between industrialization and the growth of middle classes in East and Southeast Asia, Rodan (1996:xi) argues that efforts "to establish greater space for political parties, and civil societies that feed into these organizations, are only part of the attempts to extend avenues for contesting state power." He questions the assertion of some writers that the expansion of civil society is closely linked with the advance of liberal democracy. The rise of civil society, then, is a particular form of accommodation by the state to contending social forces. Thus, it is an effort by political regimes to reconstitute and consolidate state power for greater legitimacy from the standpoint of its constituency and the international political order.

State-Civil Society Relations: Engagements and Evolving Strategies

The skills and strategies utilized by CSOs in relating to the state are in part dependent on the stage of social mobilization and political transitions. In the Philippines, Wui and Lopez (1997:1) observe the marked shift among civil society groups — from that of opposition and confrontation during the Marcos regime to that of negotiating and creating alternatives during the Aquino and Ramos administrations. Likewise, in Indonesia, during the struggle against the authoritarian regime of Suharto, there was a relative unity among CSOs and networks vis-à-vis the state. In these political shifts (from Suharto to Habibie and then to the Wahid administration), civil society groups were divided in their strategies of confrontation and negotiation. Thus, in different stages of the democratic transition, CSOs assume different roles and utilize different strategies in their relationship to the state.

The rise of civil society in Asia and its political impact are relative to their location in the configuration of political and economic power within a particular nation-state. This was clearly illustrated in the fight against the Marcos dictatorship and the ascendance of civil society in the Philippines' 1986 EDSA People Power Revolution. The Left, a key force in the political opposition against the Marcos regime, lost its traditional sphere of influence because it refused to participate in the 1987 snap elections called by Marcos and in the call-for-people support by the Church during the critical days of the EDSA Revolution. The same pattern can be seen in the subsequent role of civil society and other opposition groups in the Aquino and Ramos administrations.

The contentious strategies for engaging the state have often caused fragmentation among CSOs and networks. For example, debates over the role of NGOs in political elections have occupied the energies of CSOs, often distracting them from the more fundamental needs of their clientele groups. In the same manner, their lack of consensus regarding leadership and tactics have created political cleavages within the CSOs (Serrano, 1994).

The character of civil society's engagement with the state and the market has to be viewed historically according to the phase of the democratic movement. Nothing illustrates this better than the recruitment of NGO leaders to government positions. When NGOs are recruited to the business of policy-making and programme implementation, their strategies that worked so well during the phase of critical engagement with the state are rendered ineffective during this phase of strategic collaboration. The particular relationship of civil society groups and their leaders was clearly seen during the Aquino administration in the Philippines and recently in the Wahid administration in Indonesia. The overwhelming unity of civil society groups is quite impressive against a common enemy like an oppressive state (e.g., against the Marcos dictatorship or the authoritarian regime of Suharto). But once this common enemy is dislodged, the fragility of their alliances is unmasked.

Understanding the dynamics of civil society involves two essential elements: (1) the plurality of groups that makes up civil society with their class dimensions; and (2) fractions of the élite/dominant groups and their tendency to appropriate certain groups in civil society to gain legitimacy and suppress those who will challenge them. Recognizing these elements allows us to see more clearly the limits and potentials of CSOs' pluralism and heterogeneity. While diversity is a great strength among CSOs and networks, it is also their main weakness. Often, this creates divisions within civil society, which make them susceptible to the political manoeuvres of the dominant groups. This becomes more meaningful in the context of neo-liberal globalization that produces both gainers and losers, depending on the structural location of stakeholders. It is during these crucial times that class interests, which tend to be masked by civil society, come to the surface and increase the potential for divisiveness.

The Asian financial crisis has set the stage for the intensification of the above conditions and the political fragmentation among CSOs. The previous years of sustained economic growth led to the growth of the middle class and the democratization process, and facilitated the forging of collaborative partnerships and linkages between CSOs and the state in implementing developmental programmes. The crisis, however, brought back the confrontational strategies of CSOs in the earlier period. Capital flight, closing of factories and retrenchment of workers brought protests and strikes back into the forefront of state-civil society relations. This calls attention to the danger of being mesmerized by the contingent successes of CSOs and CSMs.

Globalization, State and Civil Society

State-civil society relations are being redefined by the globalization of economy, social movements and information technology. Both at national and local levels, the impacts of these broad forces are also being reconfigured by socio-political movements advocating greater political space as well as a larger share of societal resources. More than ever, the non-profit sector, or civil society, is faced with a formidable task, that of mediating between the state and the market, whose political and economic agendas often run counter to the values of equity and justice.

The social effects of globalization have intensified civil society engagement with the state. The growing economic integration and interdependence among nation-states threaten political and cultural sovereignty. In addition, information technology allows data and capital to move around the globe at the speed of light. Initial research findings show that the newfound freedom and efficiency gained from these technological changes seem to exacerbate existing structural inequalities.

Another factor that has shaped civil society engagements is the globalization of social movements (e.g., environment and the rights of children, women and indigenous people). Partly, these have been brought about by the development agenda of UN agencies and other multilateral institutions like the World Bank, which have spawned the development of global social movements (GSMs). These bodies have accorded NGOs political recognition and have broadly supported their activities. Aided by the techno-economic revolution and by these multilateral institutions, GSMs have transnationalized civil society engagements. While this new trend provides support and strength to local and national mobilizations, it has also generated conflicts and tensions from within and without. Civil society groups also create a new kind of élitism and exclusion among themselves vis-à-vis the state.

For example, the efforts towards economic integration in the region through the WTO and AFTA provisions have spawned a great deal of criticism from civil society, as witnessed in the Seattle (Fall 1999) and the Bangkok (February 2000) meetings. These political mobilizations have further complicated the deleterious effects of the Asian financial crisis.

Given these prevailing conditions, the demand for state reforms, participation of civil society and good governance has become part of the political idiom that informs much of the identity and resource claims in the post-modern age.

Civil Society in the New Millennium: Tensions and Challenges

Carroll (2000) enumerates the challenges and tensions of civil society, which emanate from its diversity and pluralism and from its engagement with the state and the market. These tensions revolve around the following issues: (1) the building of consensus on values among civil society groups with their pluralism and internal heterogeneity (i.e., no monopoly of "correct" values); (2) the interfacing or critical engagement with the global economy, the political society, the state; and (3) creating social institutions aimed at enlarging the space for public articulation and debate of issues and values. Other major challenges of civil society include poverty and inequity, good governance, globalization, and strengthening NGO/social development practitioner roles and capabilities (Racelis, 2000).

In responding to the above challenges, CSOs have to reconcile with forces that can aid or complicate their strategies for political and economic reforms such as social/political security issues, decentralization of state powers and the digital revolution in information technology. At the heart of the challenge is the question of how to reconcile the values associated with civil society (e.g., justice, compassion, economic freedom) with the values that inform the market and state bureaucracy (rationality, efficiency, profit). Economic and technological forces behind globalization seem to further widen the political and economic gap between those who are positively integrated to the global system and those who are not.

Civil society engagements with the state in the new millennium are, therefore, fraught with tensions and challenges generated by the globalization of capital and information technology, the devolution of state powers to local systems of governance, and the rise of identity/resource claims laced with fundamentalist and nationalist discourses.

References

Alagappa, Muthiah (1995), "The Asian Spectrum," *Journal of Democracy*, 6(1): 29–43.

Atienza, Jun (1994), "An Alternative Framework for Social Change," *Intersec*, 8 (4–5):4–6 (cited in her References).

Baron, Barnett (1999), "Some Reflections on NGOs and Civil Society." Presented at the Yonsei University — Asia Foundation Roundtable on NGOs, Korea.

Bello, Walden (2000), "Washington and the Demise of the 'Third Wave' of Democratization," *Focus on the Philippines*, Issue No. 5, Series 2000.

Bullard, Nicola (2000), "It's Time for 'Uncivil' Society to Act," *Focus on Trade*, No. 47.

Carroll, John J. (2000), "Civil Society: What is it?" Presented at the 15th Anniversary Lecture Series of the Institute on Church and Social Issues, Loyola Heights, Quezon City.

Coronel Ferrer, Miriam (1997), "Civil Society Making Civil Society." In Miriam Coronel Ferrer (ed.), *Civil Society Making Civil Society*. Quezon City: Third World Studies Center.

Dawisha, Karen and Bruce Parrot (1994), *Russia and the New States of Eurasia: The Politics of Upheaval*. New York: Cambridge University Press.

Diamond, Larry (1994), "Rethinking Civil Society: Toward Democratic Consolidation," *Journal of Democracy*, 5(3):4–17.

ESCAP (1998), "Regional Prospects for Social Development: An Overview." Part One of *Asia and the Pacific into the 21st Century: Prospects for Social Development*, Theme Study of the 54th Session of ESCAP, 20–28 April 1998.

Fukuyama, Francis (1995), "The Primacy of Culture," *Journal of Democracy*, 6 (1):7–14.

Gellner, Ernest (1991), "Civil Society in Historical Context." *International Social Science Journal*, 43(3):495–510.

Gramsci, Antonio (1971), *Selections from the Prison Notebooks*. London: New Left Books.

Habermas, Jurgen (1989), *The Structural Transformation of the Public Sphere: An Inquiry into a Category of Bourgeois Society*. Translated by Thomas Burger and Frederick Lawrence. Polity Press.

He, Baogang (1997), *Democratic Implications of Civil Society in China*. London: Macmillan Press.

Hewison, Kevin and Gary Rodan (1996), "The Ebb and Flow of Civil Society and the Decline of the Left in Southeast Asia." In Gary Rodan (ed.), *Political Oppositions in Industrializing Asia*. London: Routledge, pp. 40–71.

Huang, Philip C. (1993), "'Public Sphere'/'Public Sphere' in China?" *Modern China*, 19(2):216–40 (cited in his References).

Huntington, Samuel (1984), "Will No More Countries Become Democratic?" *Political Science Quarterly*, 99(2):199–200.

—— (1991), *The Third Wave: Democratization in the Late Twentieth Century*. Norman: University of Oklahoma Press.

Karaos, Anna Marie (1994), "Power and Revolution: Revolutionizing Our Concepts of Power," *Intersec*, 8(4–5):10–11 (cited in her References).

Kumar, Krishan (1993), "Civil Society: An Inquiry into the Usefulness of an Historical Term," *British Journal of Sociology*, 44(3):375–95.

Laothamatas, Anek (1997), "Development and Democratization: A Theoretical Introduction with Reference to the Southeast Asian and East Asian Cases." In Anek Laothamatas (ed.), *Democratization in Southeast and East Asia*. New York: St. Martin's Press.

Maisrikrod, Surin (1997), "The Making of Thai Democracy: A Study of Political Alliances Among the State, the Capitalists, and the Middle Class." In Anek Laothamatas (ed.), *Democratization in Southeast and East Asia*. New York: St. Martin's Press.

Muzaffar, Chandra (1996), "Democracy, the West and Asia." In Brid Brennan, Erik Hiejmans and Pietje Vervest (eds.), *ASEM Trading New Silk Routes. Beyond Geo-Politics and Geo-Economics: Towards a New Relationship between Asia and Europe*. Amsterdam: Transnational Institute (TNI) and Focus on the Global South, pp. 93–95.

Niyom, Prapapat (1997), "Critical Partnerships in Governance and Poverty Alleviation." In Emma Porio (ed.), *Urban Governance and Poverty Alleviation in Southeast Asia: Trends and Prospects*. Philippines: Global Urban Research Initiative (GURI) in Southeast Asia; the Department of Sociology and Anthropology, Ateneo de Manila University, and the Center for Social Policy and Public Affairs, Ateneo de Manila University.

O'Donell, Guillermo, Philippe C. Schmitter and Laurence Whitehead (eds.) (1988), *Transitions from Authoritarian Rule: Comparative Perspectives*. Baltimore and London: The Johns Hopkins University Press.

Porio, Emma (1997), "Urban Governance and Poverty Alleviation in Southeast Asia." In Emma Porio (ed.), *Urban Governance and Poverty Alleviation in Southeast Asia*, pp. 1–39.

Racelis, Mary (2000), "The Challenges that Philippine Civil Society Faces in Today's Milieu." Presented at the 15th Anniversary Lecture Series of the Institute on Church and Social Issues, Loyola Heights, Quezon City.

Riddell, Roger C. and Mark Robinson with John de Coninck, Ann Muir and Sarah White (1995), *Non-government Organizations and Rural Poverty Alleviation*. New York: Oxford University Press.

Rocamora, Joel (1998), "Liberation, Democratization and Transitions to Statehood In the Third World." In May Jayyusi (ed.), *Liberation, Democratization and Transitions to Statehood in the Third World*. Ramallah, Palestine: Nadia, pp. 17–24.

Rodan, Gary (1996), "Theorising Political Opposition in East and Southeast Asia." In Gary Rodan (ed.), *Political Oppositions in Industrializing Asia*. London: Routledge, pp. 1–39.

Seligman, Adam B. (1992), *The Idea of Civil Society*. New York: Free Press.

Serrano, Isagani R. (1994), "Civil Society in the Asia-Pacific Region." In Miguel Darcy de Oliveira and Rajesh Tandon (eds.), *Citizens Strengthening Civil Society*, World Assembly Edition. Washington, D.C.: McNaughton and Gunn, Inc., pp. 271–317.

Silliman, G. Sidney and Lela Garner Noble (1998), "Introduction." In G. Sidney Silliman and Lela Garner Noble (eds.), *Organizing for Democracy: NGOs, Civil Society, and the Philippine State*. Quezon City: Ateneo de Manila University Press, pp. 18–19.

Yamamoto, Tadashi (1996), "Integrative Report." In Tadashi Yamamoto (ed.), *Emerging Civil Society in the Asia Pacific Community: Nongovernmental Underpinnings of the Emerging Asia Pacific Community*. Tokyo: Institute of

Southeast Asian Studies and Japan Center for International Exchange, pp. 1–40.

Wui, Marlon A. and Glenda S. Lopez (1997), "State-Civil Society Relations in Policy-Making." In Marlon A. Wui and Glenda S. Lopez (eds.), *State-Civil Society Relations in Policy-Making*. Quezon City: Third World Studies Center, pp. 1–20.

11

Democratization and the National Identity Question in East Asia

Baogang He

Democratization and the national identity question haunt East Asia. Will Aceh achieve its independence from Indonesia as Indonesia takes the road towards deepening democratization? Will Taiwan become a "Republic of Taiwan" if China embarks upon rapid democratization? Will China undergo a process of disintegration if it progresses towards democratization? These are challenging questions for East Asia in the twenty-first century.

Intellectually, the complex relationship between democratization and the national identity question poses a difficult question and a general puzzle. It is a difficult question because there are various variables involved, and various forms of democratization and of the national identity question. It is a puzzle because it is apparent that democratization has been variously associated with peaceful separation, unification, disintegration and war. It is also a puzzle because there are two opposing views on the roles democratization plays in addressing the identity question. On one side, there is the view that the identity problem is exacerbated by democratization. Huntington (1996:6), for example, points out that "the initiation of elections forces political leaders to compete for votes. In many situations, the easiest way to win votes is to appeal to tribal, ethnic, and religious constituencies. Democratization thus promotes communalism and ethnic conflict." On the other side, there is the view that democratization can assist in managing the national identity issue. This can be exemplified by Stepan's (1997:50–51) suggestion that democratic accommodation could help ease ethnic tensions in Sri Lanka.

Can we find some general rules or regulations concerning the relationship between democratization and the identity question? Can democratization lead to a solution to the identity question? This chapter attempts to address these questions through an enquiry into the effect of democratization on the identity question in East Asia.

The analytical framework of the chapter takes democratization as an independent variable, and the national identity question as a dependent variable. This contrasts with Rustow's analytical framework which regards the national identity question as an independent variable and democratization as a dependent variable. Elsewhere He (2001) has argued against Rustow's framework, in favour of a reversal of his analytical order.

The definition of democratization includes multi-variables, including: initiating democratization (this crucial moment leads to a crisis and presents an opportunity to settle the national identity question); establishing the rule of elections (this leads to changes in the sources of legitimacy); protecting and guaranteeing civic and political liberties (this favours the development of the assertive media and the participation of people and civil society, and contributes to their role in settling and managing the identity issue); and finally, competing political power between parties (this raises the question of the role of opposition parties in settling the national identity question). Following Rustow's definition, the national identity problem refers to the phenomenon in which sections of national populations do not identify with the nation-states in which they live, and endeavour to create their own political identity through the reconstruction of cultural and ethnic identities. It also refers to a unification process in which two separate states or political entities want to merge on the basis of shared cultural identity or history. The identity question incorporates the problem of control over territories and resources, and the issue of redrawing the national boundary. According to the above definitions, it is evident that I am engaging in a multi-variant analysis of the effects of multi-democratization factors on two forms resolution of the national identity question: unification and secession.

It should be acknowledged that there are many other factors and conditions, besides democratization, which interact and thus play a significant part in determining the outcome of conflict over the identity issue. Nevertheless, because this chapter focuses principally on the part played by democratization in settling the national identity question, it adopts an abstraction and isolation approach. The abstraction and isolation approach involves isolating democratization factors from background variables such as the economic climate, the history of colonial rule, ethnicity, nationalism, the business sector and personal factors. The approach leaves aside the question of the interaction between democratization variables and other variables. It is noted, however, that background variables offer alternative explanations. For example, the Islamic Conference did not favour secession and, as a mediator, the former President Soeharto did not support the independence of Mindanao in the Philippines. These two factors played a part in the peaceful settlement of the Mindanao question during the process of democratization in the Philippines. I am aware of alternative explanations, but given the limits of the scope of the chapter, focuses on the theme of democratization effects.

The chapter selects four cases: the Philippines, Indonesia, Taiwan and Mainland China. The selection was made because national identity questions are salient in these cases and they present a variety of solutions and stories. The chapter also uses these cases to generate knowledge of a generalized rule about the democratization effects and the national identity question. The data on the new UN states since 1974 (see Appendix) are adopted to identify and support the argument of a general trend.

The chapter comprises six sections. Section One engages in a general discussion of the effects of democratization on the identity question. Section Two identifies the asymmetric effect of democratization on secession and unification. Sections Three to Six discuss how democratization has impacted on and will impact on the settlement of the identity question in the Philippines, Indonesia, Taiwan and Mainland China.

The Effects of Democratization on the Identity Question

I begin the discussion on the effects of democratization by comparing the different attitudes adopted by democratic and authoritarian regimes towards the national identity question. While both democratic and authoritarian regimes are faced with some form of the national identity question, wide differences are detectable between how they each approach the problem.

Undemocratic countries seem to have been less willing to allow secession than democratic ones. For instance, secession has been suppressed in the authoritarian states of Indonesia, China, Zaire, Iran and Iraq. Many democratic states such as the U.S., the U.K., Canada and France did not tolerate secession. Nevertheless, since 1974, 20 states have been granted independence, albeit reluctantly, by democratic parent states under international and domestic pressures (see Appendix).

Although secessionist movements have occurred under authoritarian regimes, they are unlikely to succeed under conditions of harsh suppression. By contrast, democratization processes make independence or secession movements much more likely to succeed. This is evident from the fact that out of 47 new member states recognized by the UN between 1974 and 1997, 26 were newly seceding states whose independent status was related to the democratization of parent states. This means that, in recent years, 57 percent of new states have been formed during the democratization of their parent states (See Appendix). In particular, democratization has facilitated successful secession in the former Soviet Union, Pakistan,[1] Ethiopia, Yugoslavia and Indonesia. It is important to note that all successful secessions, without exception, occur in the period immediately prior to or following the initiation of democratization, usually within the first three years. Once democratization is consolidated, however, it becomes more difficult for secession movements to succeed.

The factors of crisis-opportunity, the changing source of legitimacy, the role of opposition parties, the expansion of political freedom and the assertive media, the growth of civil society and change in power relations explain the correlation between successful secession and democratization.

Crisis-opportunity

The initiation of democratization always creates unstable political situations and political crises, which provide fertile conditions in which the secessionists' cause can flourish. In the case of the Soviet Union, in the early 1990s, democratization weakened the power of the state, empowered secessionists and the opposition to challenge the state on issues of national identity, and served the interests of suppressed ethnic minorities.

Moreover, political processes such as periodic elections offer political opportunities to address the identity question. In Quebec, for example, when the separatist Parti Quebecois returned to power in the province's general election in December 1998, it put the referendum on separation on the agenda again (Stewart, 1998:9).

The Changing Source of Legitimacy

Under democratic systems, leaders tend not to rely on issues of national identity and nationalism as the sole source of legitimacy, because legitimacy is already conferred through general elections. By contrast, authoritarian leaders, such as Marcos in the Philippines and Jiang Zemin in China, depend heavily on using nationalism and the national identity question as a source for their claim to legitimacy. It is argued that the Burmese military provoked rebellion and kept secession alive in order to have an excuse to continue its rule and thereby resist democracy. Moreover, democracy allows the voice of secessionists to be heard, while dictatorship does not. Indeed, authoritarian regimes benefit from the existence of identity problems, and so tend to perpetuate them. In contrast, democracies endeavour to settle the issue through peaceful and usually, but not necessarily, democratic means. In other words, authoritarian regimes rely substantially on the identity issue for their survival, while leaders of democratizing states are more likely to possess the motivation to settle the issue peacefully in order to ensure they gain electoral support and so enhance their political powers. In other words, once democracy is introduced, political leaders realizing they owe their legitimacy to democratization, will tend more towards compromise in settling the national identity question. For example, Habibie was motivated to offer autonomy concessions because the conflict surrounding East Timor was a major political burden for him.

One may point to an exception. Democratizing Russia, for example, used military force against Chechnya in 1999–2000. However, because the acting President Vladimir Putin did not enjoy legitimacy gained by a general election, he sought other means to legitimize his leadership. He chose a tough campaign against secessionism in Chechnya in order to win votes in the presidential election in March 2000.

The Role of Opposition Parties

Opposition groups often campaign on the national identity issue and rally support over secession problems. In democratizing states, the fact that oppositions intend to compete for political power often offers a critical solution to the difficult identity question. For example, Boris Yeltsin supported the demands for independence by the Baltic States in 1990–1991 and, in Ethiopia, the civil war continued until the leading opposition alliance, the Ethiopian People's Revolutionary Democratic Front (EPRDF), offered a cease-fire in July 1990. Prolonged civil war between Eritrea and the Ethiopian state played an important role in the process of settling the independence question, however, democratic mechanisms and rotating political powers also contributed to this process. In July 1991, the EPRDF leader, Meles Zenawi, who was elected president by the National Assembly, agreed that a referendum on the question of Eritrean independence should be held. A month after the referendum was held in April 1993, Ethiopia recognized Eritrea as a fully independent state (Derbyshire and Derbyshire, 1996:364).

The process of democratization has also involved the expansion of political freedom and the assertive media which enable people to express their views on the identity question (this will be discussed in the sections on Taiwan and Indonesia). It has also been accompanied by the growth of civil society which has had increasing influence in defining and settling the identity question. This general discussion of the effects of democratization will be further elaborated and clarified in the case studies examined below. In short, democratization provides an opportunity whereby the national identity question can be settled. Democratization creates and facilitates the conditions under which the national identity question can be managed; and provides democratic procedures to handle the national identity question in a peaceful manner.

An Asymmetric Effect

Democratization and the identity question have been associated with peaceful separation, peaceful autonomy, and peaceful unification, as well as conflicts or wars. This can be clearly demonstrated by Table 11.1 below.

While democratization does not determine peaceful separation, unification or independence, it does play various roles. Firstly, I examine the case of peaceful separation. Historically, Norway's secession from Sweden in 1905 was related to the democratic factor. A referendum was adopted, and democratization in Sweden empowered the Social Democratic Party which was opposed to the use of force in opposition to Norway's secession.[2]

Contemporarily, democratization facilitated the splitting of Czechoslovakia. Through democratization, Slovak nationalism thrived and

Table 11.1   Patterns of Linkage between Democratization and the Settlement of the Identity Question

Case examples	Patterns
Norway/Sweden, Slovak/Czech	Peaceful separation through democratization
Basque/Spain, Mindanao/Philippines, Albanian minority/Macedonia, Gagauz/Moldova	Autonomy offered to settle the identity question and unity maintained
Two Germanys	Unification associated with democratization
Sri Lanka and Yugoslavia	An inappropriate democratization programme exacerbated the identity question

elected Slovakians dominated parliament. Furthermore, the key element of democratization, which is compromise, facilitated political negotiation over the identity question. Moreover, it was parliamentary approval, without referenda, that decided the fate of Czechoslovakia. This decision can still be seen as "semi-democratic" for it was made by elected representatives. It could be argued that a combination of democratization effects and élite political manoeuvring led to a peaceful separation.

Germany presents a case of unification associated with democratization. Although the 1972 agreement affirmed the "inviolability" of the existing border, thereby ruling out the possibility of German reunification,[3] anti-regime demonstrations erupted in East Berlin in 1989, and subsequently democratization brought down the Communist state, facilitating the reunification of the two Germanys.

On 9 November 1989, the East German authorities abolished restrictions on foreign travel for GDR citizens. On 18 March 1990, the Grand Coalition led by Lothar de Maiziere was formed in GDR elections. On 12 April 1990, coalition partners (CDU, DSU, Democratic Awakening, Liberals, German Forum Party, Alliance of Free Democrats, FDP and SPD) agreed to accede the GDR to the Federal Republic under the terms of article 23 of the Basic Law. The Coalition saw its role as furthering "the process of German unification with parliamentary participation" (Glaessner, 1992:93). On 17 June 1990, in its fifteenth session, the *Volkskammer*, nominally the GDR parliament, promulgated guidelines for a new constitution which would annul the legal regulations of the GDR, committing individual citizens and state institutions to socialism, the socialist rule of law and democratic centralism. In order to smooth the way for the economic, social and currency union, the basic foundations of these constitutional guidelines stipulated that the sovereign rights of the GDR could be transferred to joint German institutions and institutions of the Federal Republic (Glaessner, 1992:95).

German reunification progressed rapidly and in two stages. The first stage was the signing, on 18 May 1990, of the State Treaty on Currency, Economic and Social Union. Due to the dismal economic climate in the GDR in the early 1990s, GDR politicians embarked upon a *de facto* renunciation of sovereignty by ceding responsibility for financial policy to the Federal Republic, abolishing the GDR currency and introducing the West German mark. As Walter Romberg, GDR Finance Minister, said, "the surrender of sovereignty over currency implied the loss of a major part of economic sovereignty and consequently of political sovereignty" (Glaessner, 1992:96). On 1 July 1990, a currency union made the Deutschemark legal tender in both East and West Germany. The introduction of the West German mark thus became the emblem of the unification process.

The second stage was the move towards the Unification Treaty. Although the State Treaty brought about the *de facto* annulment of GDR sovereignty, the state continued to exist in international law. In order to prevent the planned accession of the GDR to the Federal Republic amounting to an annexation, a second state treaty was required to enshrine the basis for a regulated accession — hence the Unification Treaty, which was signed on 31 August 1990 (Glaessner, 1992:99). On 23 September of the same year, 440 deputies in the *Bundestag* (47 against, 3 abstentions) and 299 deputies in the *Volkskammer* (80 against, 1 abstention) voted in favour of the Unification Treaty (Glaessner, 1992:100). On 3 October, a political union was formed which was followed by constitutional change that involved the government institutions of the FRG (West Germany) taking over the government of the GDR (East Germany) (Dunbar and Bresser, 1997:440–70).

Many factors such as the history of World War II, the rise of German nationalism, the revolution of 1989, the common culture of Germany, and the skill and role of individual leaders played important parts in achieving German unification. However, democratization also played a role, albeit a minor one, in promoting the unification of the two Germanys. The role of democratization can be summarized as follows. The emergent civil society and citizens' movements, such as New Forum, which protested against the communist system, were a driving force for democratization. Elections offered opportunities to change government in a peaceful manner and, in particular, to enable the coalition government coming to power to implement unification policies through the legislature. Democratization in the Soviet Union also played a crucial role. As Mikhail Gorbachev, in his congratulatory letter to Federal President Richard von Weizsacker, said, "Unification would not have been possible without the radical democratic reforms in our countries" (Glaessner, 1992:175).

President von Weizsacker remarked, "Our unity was not forced upon anyone but agreed peacefully" (Glaessner, 1992:236). Unification of the two Germanys was achieved through democratic means: Elections in both Germanys can be seen as quasi-referenda confirming unification by the people's consent. The unification process was initiated by elected representatives and endorsed by parliamentary votes in both parliaments. Nevertheless, as Habermas (1996:12) points out, a substantial degree of popular sovereignty on the matter was lacking. Moreover, unification was proposed on an equal basis, but ultimately East Germany joined West Germany on unequal terms.

The above cases illustrate the complex effect of democratization on the identity question. Democratization can be related to both peaceful separation and unification. Behind this basic fact, is there any general trend? Below is an argument about the asymmetric effect of democratization on the identity question.

Since 1974, around 100 states have democratized. Among them, 47 democratizing states have confronted the identity question. A majority of these 47 democratizing states face challenges from secession or independence, only around seven states face reunification questions.

If democratization is regarded as an independent variable, and the national identity question as a dependent variable, the impact of democratization on secession and unification is asymmetric. Democratization, other things being equal, plays a big role in facilitating independence or secession. In the context of a global trend towards independence or secession and a marginalization of reunification, democratization plays only a minor role in contributing to reunification, as in the case of Germany or, indeed, has little to do with reunification, as in other cases.[4] In other words, democratization is associated with far more political "divorces" than "marriages." Statistically, among the 47 new member states in the UN since 1974, the independence of 26 has been closely associated with the democratization of their "parent states." By comparison, among seven of the states which have successfully achieved reunification since 1974, only the unification of the two Germanys and the two Yemens was related to democratization. The reunification of Vietnam, Germany, Yemen and China-Hong Kong have nothing to do with democratization.[5] China's reunification with Hong Kong was the result of diplomatic negotiation, while the reunification of Vietnam was achieved through wars that followed the surrender, on 30 April 1975, of the southern government. In the case of Taiwan, democratization has resulted in a virtual abandonment of the project of reunification with China and in a *de facto* independence. Of note also is the fact that while the democratization of Moldova supported its independence from the former Soviet Union, it did not enable its reunification with Romania. In such a context, it is quite understandable that a democratic theory of secession predominates over political theories of secession while there is little development of democratic unification theory.

How can the asymmetric effect be explained? A tentative answer is offered here. Inherent in the idea of democracy is the greater likelihood that democracy can facilitate independence or secession rather than unification. This is because the notion of democracy presupposes the political autonomy of one people, rather than the reunification of peoples. Such a presupposition uses the logic of democratization in practice; that is, people will tend to use democracy to support their independence rather than unification because democratization creates favourable conditions for the construction of new national identities. Democratization programmes have empowered ethno-nationalism and contributed greatly to the cause of independence and/or secession. On the other hand, it is much more difficult to bring different peoples together into a nation through democratization than it is to establish an independent state. Of importance is the distribution of state powers among different nationalities. In a divided nation, it is more difficult for those nationality groupings who already have state power to yield or share power with others through democracy than it is for those who have not yet tasted state power, as in the case of secession movements, and who are fighting for power through democracy. Political élites have the incentive to establish their own state rather than be incorporated into a larger political unit. Above all, democratization provides them with such an opportunity.

It can be argued further that democratization itself does not decide the direction of unification or independence. As we have seen, democratization is associated with forces of unification in South Korea and independence forces in Taiwan. This illustrates the fact that we cannot make the general claim that democratization inevitably gives rise to independence movements or unification. The question of whether democratization strengthens independence forces in Taiwan or unification forces in South Korea is influenced by other background conditions and factors. A history of Japanese colonial rule and the KMT's suppression of the Taiwanese has strengthened anti-Chinese feeling and pro-independence movements in Taiwan. By contrast, the history of Japanese military rule in Korea promotes a pan-Korean nationalism across borders. In Korea, ethnicity is almost homogenous, thus constituting a basis for unification; while the composition of ethnicity is complex in Taiwan, thus producing both unification and independence forces. While under the mainland's blockade policy, Taiwan is isolated in international relations and is consequently forced to fight for independence and international recognition. South Korea has a UN seat, and thus has no motivation to demand independence. More important is the actual nature of the national identity question. In other words, who will take over whom? South Korea is much more likely to take over North Korea than Taiwan is to take over China. If this issue is combined with economic factors, then it is evident that people in affluent South Korea are more likely to support unification than their counterparts in Taiwan. This was demonstrated in East Germany where people were willing to support unification due to their poor economic conditions and West Germany was willing to offer help because it was in a position to assume control of East Germany. By contrast, Taiwan is economically better off than China, and its people are less keen to support unification than its West German counterpart. It is unlikely that Taiwan will take over China. All the above factors interact and, when the democratization factor comes into play, the result is that democratization has pushed Taiwan towards independence through empowering a growing native nationalism which defies the Chinese unification policy, while it has pushed South Korea towards unification.

The Mindanao Problem and Inclusive Democratization in the Philippines

In the Philippines, the process of democratization was confronted by the Mindanao problem, which concerns the struggle by the Moro secessionist movement, in the Southern Philippines, to achieve independence. Under Spanish colonial rule, Mindanao's population lived on the coast and in the interior. The Maguindanaons, the Marrannaos and Irannun converted to Islam. The Spaniards had only established and occupied some forts in Mindanao, but most of the population remained in an empire led by the Maguindanaons, who comprised many tribes. After World War II, a systematic policy of migration towards Mindanao was implemented by the Philippines government in order to distribute land to peasants in the over-populated areas of the islands of Luzon and the Visayas. These migrants began to exert pressure on the political and administrative organization of Mindanao and, as a result, the Lumad and the Muslims began to feel their living space and cultural identity were under threat. Thus, a conflict over land ensued and gradually escalated as land became more scarce. In 1968, Governor Udtong Metalam of Cotabato called for a Mindanao Independence Movement to realize Moro aspirations by establishing an Islamic State in Mindanao. In 1969, Nuruladji Misuari organized the Moro National Liberation Front (MNLF), which gave voice to demands for secession.[6]

In 1976, the Tripoli Agreement was reached between the MNLF and the Philippines delegation. Thirteen of the twenty-one provinces of the Southern Philippines were granted autonomy, with a legislative assembly, an executive council and Islamic law courts. Given the prevailing distribution of the ethnic population (4 million Muslims and 6.5 million Christians in 13 provinces), President Marcos called a referendum to decide whether the inhabitants of the region could have extended powers, under MNLF rule, or autonomy under the firm control of Manila. When Marcos won the referendum, Misuari called for a last-minute boycott and the MNLF denounced the referendum (Heraclides, 1991:172–73). Subsequently, in 1986, Marcos declared martial law in an attempt to suppress the southern secessionist movement.

Marcos' authoritarian regime was eventually overthrown by the "People Power Revolt" of 22–25 February 1986, and the re-democratization programme under Cory Aquino restored a presidential-style government which survived several military coups. The Aquino government considered granting autonomy as a possible solution to the Mindanao problem and regional autonomy was recognized in the 1987 Constitution.

When elected president in May 1992, Fidel Ramos began to accelerate the peace settlement as there was a great deal of international pressure and economic imperatives to develop Mindanao. Indeed, these were major factors leading to the peace settlement, although the process of democratization also made a significant contribution. For one thing, under a democratic system, the leadership was keen to see an end to the conflict. Second, Ramos felt he would have a better chance of extending his presidential term if a peace settlement was reached, as an extension of his presidency was likely to be seen as necessary for the successful implementation of the settlement. Third, peaceful resolution of the conflict was helped by the referenda, held in Mindanao in 1991, through which nine provinces chose not to join the autonomous region, and four voted to join. This strengthened and legitimized the unity of the Philippines state. Fourth, democratic rule or compromise was at work. With the backing of Ramos' ruling Lakas-NUCD Party, Misuari became the governor of the existing autonomous region and it was agreed he would control a proposed Southern Philippines Council for Peace and Development. All these initiatives provided legitimacy for the political unit of the Philippines. As Manuel Yan, head of the government's negotiating panel, pointed out, "Misuari, by running as governor, now recognizes the constitution. His men who've registered as voters have sworn on the constitution" (Tiglao, 1996b:24). This was seen as a win-win situation. Moreover, rebels who had been elected were forced to renounce violence in favour of more peaceful solutions. In other words, they were seduced into peace through electorate politics, self-rule and federalism. On 27 January 1997, the Philippine army and guerrillas of the Moro Islamic Liberation Front signed an interim cease-fire agreement (which had, it was claimed, halted fighting in which 33 guerillas and 4 soldiers had reportedly been killed) (FEER, 1997a). By April 1997, after over 20 years of fighting, it was reported that Mindanao was experiencing an economic recovery as investment in the region increased dramatically following the signing of the peace deal. Indeed, the government announced plans to further develop infrastructure in Mindanao to encourage greater economic development (*Asian Business*, 1997:50–54).

Nevertheless, people on the street have been misled into believing that the MNLF has now been given authority by the government over all the 14 provinces, with the result that some Filipinos believe the government has given away too much. In particular, Misuari can impose his will on the 14 provinces, even those predominantly Christian, through his control of the peace council (Tiglao 1996a). (It is not clear whether this is fact or the opinion of the misled people on the street.) What is worse, the Bangsamoro People's Consultative Assembly, which has attracted an estimated 200,000 supporters, passed a declaration that only an independent Islamic state can bring peace, not the September pact between Misuari and Ramos. For radical Muslim separatists, "the Koran is our Law, not the constitution" (Tiglao 1996b). These views have led to more conflict and on 16 June 1997, clashes began after rebels belonging to the Moro Islamic Liberation Front seized a government oil exploration site in the town of Sultan-sa-barongis. On 3 July 1997, rebel violence flared again when over 30 people died and 10,000 villagers fled their homes during week-long fighting between soldiers and separatist rebels in the southern Maguindanao (FEER, 1997b).

Two points should be made clear about the above events. First, it can be argued that the scale of conflict was reduced because of referenda, the peace accord and the granting of autonomy. The fact that small-scale conflicts continue to erupt does not discount the effectiveness of democratic processes in managing the identity issue. Second, it should be pointed out that the continuation of small conflicts is largely due to radicals in the MNLF insisting on the establishment of a Muslim state, which has precluded any possibility for negotiation on the issue of national identities.

The East Timor Question and Democratization in Indonesia

To settle the East Timor question, a democratic federal system should be adopted. Those against federalism argue that if the East Timorese are given more rights and autonomy, other provinces will follow suit and, as a result, central power will be weakened. But if the East Timor question is to be remedied, the province must be granted autonomy. It is important to differentiate East Timor from Aceh as they represent two entirely different cases. East Timor would have more autonomy than Aceh, which in turn has more autonomy than many other Indonesian provinces. If a complex federal system is developed in order to meet the different aspirations of the Indonesian regions and provinces, then such a system would be able to maintain the unity of the country and reduce the potential for conflict within Indonesia. Moreover, if federalism and autonomy do not work, the independence of East Timor becomes an option. Of course, the state of Indonesia is not naturally predisposed towards recognizing the rights of those who seek to undermine its territorial and national sovereignty. It was economic crisis that led to Indonesian democratization; and it is democratization that has impacted on the way in which the East Timor question was settled.

There are enormous difficulties with adopting systematic democratic management of the East Timor question. First, the business sector seems to support pro-integration and resists the democratic approach because there are economic investments from Jakarta and economic and strategic interests for Jakarta in East Timor. Second, the militia, supported by the army, has resisted democratic management of the East Timor issue.

Despite such difficulties and resistance, the effects of democratization on the resolution of the East Timor question are obvious and complex. The first and most obvious point to note is that different politicians tend to adopt different strategies to deal with the national identity question. If we compare the differing approaches of Presidents Soeharto and Habibie, we can see that the authoritative figure of Soeharto opted to ruthlessly suppress any secessionist movement in East Timor, while Habibie refrained from sending troops to East Timor to crush the independence movement. This, it can be argued, is due to his urge to create and maintain a democratic image and thus lead Indonesia into a new "democratic" order. Or perhaps he does not have the capacity to control the army. Either way, democratization plays its role: "seducing" leaders to follow democratic rules in the former situation, and weakening the power of central leaders in the latter situation.

Habibie offered East Timor comprehensive autonomy, which can be seen as another version of the Hong Kong model: foreign affairs, defence and international relations would continue to be controlled by Jakarta, while other areas and issues, such as the economy, culture and politics, would be the province of the East Timorese. Compared to the Soeharto era, the offer of autonomy to East Timor is a considerable advance.

Habibie has motivated to offer such concessions because the conflict surrounding East Timor was a major burden for him. Yet, although such an autonomy proposal went some way to resolving the East Timor problem, it did not go far enough. Just as the Kosovo Liberation Army demanded an independent state immediately, so some East Timorese wanted independence. When Habibie offered autonomy, dialogue and negotiation, the East Timorese felt that it was too little, too late. If the autonomy proposal had been offered by Soeharto, they would probably have been happy to accept it, but then their sights were set higher — full independence.

The second point to note is the impact democratization has on the media. As part of the democratization process, Indonesian people enjoy a degree of press freedom and freedom of association that was unknown during the Soeharto era, when all newspapers were under strict government control. Today, although the government still controls the major newspapers, it does not do so to the same degree, and people have greater opportunity to express their opinions. When the media were under the strict control of Soeharto, the question of East Timor was not a major issue because most Indonesian students believed East Timor to be a legitimate part of Indonesia. There had been little information available in the public domain about what had happened in East Timor. When controls upon the media became more relaxed, the truth began to emerge and this led people to start thinking about the issue. Some radical students were particularly sympathetic to the East Timorese situation and even the hard line views of the military were gradually changing. The same is true in Aceh. There have been media reports of the army's massacre of the secessionist movement in this province. When these reports spread, people began to think more about the secessionist movement, and have become more sympathetic towards its cause.

A further dimension of the democratization process is the activation of civil society and the growth of non-governmental organizations (NGOs). Numerous NGOs have been emerging, both in Indonesia, and internationally in Southeast Asia, which offer support to the East Timorese secessionist movement. Under Soeharto's authoritarian regime, the East Timorese gained very little international support. Today, however, international NGOs support the secessionist movement materially, spiritually and culturally.

Democratization has also changed power relationships. The army is no longer the decisive political player, but merely one of a number of major players. It was unlikely that the army would use the issue of the independence of East Timor as an excuse to reverse the democratic process and the democratic approach to the East Timor question. More importantly, regions are gaining more and more power. These changes in power relations may facilitate the acceptance of the federal system in Indonesia despite the fact that the centre resists it.

The Impact of Democratization on the Identity Question in Taiwan

The effects of democratization on Taiwan's national identity question are various and complex. People have different notions of "positive" or "negative" effects depending on their political positions. One may argue that the democratization of Taiwan has facilitated unification and made exchanges across the Taiwan Strait possible. The business sector has made use of the opportunity provided by democratization to transfer its surplus capital and technology to Mainland China, despite restrictions imposed by Taiwan's government. Such increasing exchanges and economic inter-dependence could facilitate unification. Nevertheless, the democratization of Taiwan has strengthened independence forces more than unification forces. Democratization, combined with factors such as a growing native nationalism in Taiwan; a history of Japanese colonial rule and the KMTs suppression of the Taiwanese; the isolation of Taiwan in international relations; and the mainland's blockade policy, has contributed to the independence movement.

The effect of democratization on the independence movement can be analyzed through the themes of protection of political and civil liberties, political competition among parties, and political elections and their impact on the strategies of political parties towards Taiwan's national identity question.

Taiwan's democratization has made it possible to discuss and construct Taiwan's national identity, and has provided protection for political and civil liberties, and permitted the relaxation of political controls on the mass media and individual expression. Under Chiang's regime, those who openly discussed the independence of Taiwan were heavily punished. Today, people can openly speak about independence without fear. Furthermore, since democratization, opposition parties have been allowed to exist and expand.

Democratization has redistributed political power and resources between mainlanders and Taiwanese in favour of the latter. The influence and power of pro-unification groups have decreased while pro-independence forces have increasingly gained influence and power. The mainlander-KMT élite cannot impose their vision of unification on the remaining segments of Taiwan's relevant political strata (Tien, 1994:89). The legislative and political changes in Taiwan in 1991, the Democratic Progress Party (DPP)'s influential seats in the National Assembly, and its successful demand for transparency in policies which concern the mainland have made any secret deal with Beijing out of the question. It was rumoured that secret negotiations across the Taiwan Strait were undertaken under Chiang Ching-kuo's instructions. After Chiang's death, in January 1988, Beijing hoped that Lee Teng-hui would continue the process and sent a five-man group for a secret visit to negotiate for reunification. This did not eventuate because of dramatic political changes in Taiwan (L. Sheng, 1998:69).

Under democratic conditions, political parties have used the national identity issue to shore up political power. To pre-empt the DPP's ability to exploit sub-ethnic cleavages and the identity issue, President Lee introduced the Taiwanization of the KMT. This has changed the image of the Party from an externally imposed mainlander institution to a Taiwanese-controlled party. The Taiwanese component of the party has risen steadily from 15 percent in 1976 to 35 percent in 1988, and to 54 percent in 1993. At the same time, the Central Standing Committee's Taiwanese membership rose from 19 percent in 1976 to over 60 percent in 1993 (Tien 1997:145). The KMT is now portraying itself with an indigenous image. Its anti-communist identity has faded into history. The indigenous wing of the KMT is also seeking the recognition of Taiwan as a sovereign entity separate from China. It is using the unification process to create conditions for greater autonomy, or eventual *de jure* independence (Johnston, 1993:15). Taiwanese KMT élites and some second-generation mainlanders do not share the vision of unification with Mainland China. As a result, Taiwan has decided to abandon the idea of conquering the mainland; its idea of nationalism has much less to do with unification than with independence. In the July 1997 fourth round of Constitutional revision, the KMT and DPP worked together to "freeze" the Taiwan provincial government which was seen as symbolic of Taiwan's subordination to China. In other words, the Governor of Taiwan province no longer needed to be elected and the governorship became symbolic without any substantial power.

The electoral results between 1995 and 1998 in Taiwan revealed opposition to both unification and independence. The majority of voters did not take an extreme position, but favoured the middle ground, namely, maintaining the status quo. Arguably, this result is due to a lack of consensus on basic security questions regarding the threat from China, and to the growth of the middle class and its calculation of strategies and choices. In the 1995 parliamentary election, Zhang Shijie, who urged voters to "use 'one country, two systems' to save Taiwan," received only 855 votes. The other candidates of the pro-China Labour Party received only 498 and 510 votes, respectively (Jacobs, 1997:25). The New Party, a pro-unification party, failed to gain even one post in the 1997 November election for city mayors and county magistrates. In the 1996 presidential election, the pro-independence DPP won only 21.3 percent of the vote, and the newly formed Taiwan Independence Party failed to win a single post. As the editor of *The Free China Journal* (1997:6) puts it, "the fact that it only garnered 0.19 percent of the total vote is an unmistakable indication that its secessionist campaign platform has little appeal to Taiwan's increasingly sophisticated voters."

Moreover, the outcomes of the elections have had an impact on the strategies of the DPP with regard to the independence question. Since electoral support for the DPP decreased partially due to its independence position in 1996, a major faction of the DPP has become pragmatic. It has adjusted its radical independence policy and moved towards the middle ground. During the campaign period for city mayors and county magistrates in November 1997, the DPP reoriented its objective. Stepping back slightly from the independence platform, the party channelled its campaign energies towards social welfare issues in Taiwan (Moon and Robinson, 1997:8). Hsu Hsin-liang, the DPP's chairperson, and his Formosa Faction also advocated negotiations with Mainland China on trade, postal and transportation ties, the so-called "three direct links." The strategy paid off at the polls because the DPP won an unprecedented victory by taking 12 out of the 23 county magistrate and city mayor posts, while the KMT only gained 8. Significantly, at the DPP's symposium, in 1998, a pragmatic and progressive consensus was reached. Despite the division within the DDP,[7] it was agreed that Taiwan should be viewed as enjoying independent sovereignty, and that cross-strait talks should resume first with discussions on economic ties, civilian exchanges and technical issues, and then eventually proceed to government-to-government negotiations (Engbarth, 1998; V. Sheng, 1998b:7). The DPP is becoming much more pragmatic than it was with regard to the independence issue. Some members even suggest that Taiwan should not waste taxpayers' money by maintaining diplomatic relations with a few small countries. The Formosa Faction also urged a bold step to fully open trade relations with Mainland China on the western side of the Taiwan Strait.

The DPP took 70 seats in the December 1998 Legislature election, which was seen as a defeat for the Party (Lu, 1998:2), while the KMT secured 123 of the 225 seats in the new Legislature, representing a solid majority. Moreover, the former Justice Minister, Ma Ying-jeou of the KMT, unseated the Democratic Progressive Party's Chen Shui-bian to become the new mayor of Taipei in the December 1998 election. Many members of the DPP have speculated that advocacy of independence could be frightening away any voters who prefer either the status quo in Taiwan's relations with China or Chinese unification (Lu, 1999:2). It should be noted that Chen Shui-bian, in his election campaign, insisted that "the biggest threat to Taiwan's security lies in its national identity," and that "if Taiwan cannot free itself from the myth that it is part of China, it will have no future" (V. Sheng, 1998a). In early 1999, many members of the DPP proposed that phrases such as "establishment of a Republic of Taiwan" and "determined by referendum" should be revised, but this was rejected (Lu, 1999:2). In the March 2000 presidential election, Chen Shui-bian softened his independence stance, urging three direct links with Mainland China, and promised that he would seek independence if he were elected to be president. This platform helped him to win the presidential election in 2000.

Chinese Democratization and the Taiwan Issue

The asymmetric effect identified earlier can help us to understand why China does not favour democratization, it sees democratization as detrimental to unification. Current Chinese leaders reject the democratic line of thinking. Qian Qichen, for example, said that it is a serious problem for a group of people to attempt to change the status of Taiwan through a referendum in Taiwan (*People's Daily*, overseas edition, 29 January 1999, p. 1). Tang Shubei, the vice-president of the Association for Relations Across the Taiwan Strait, also asserted that democracy is not an essential question and that democratic reform should not constitute an obstacle to negotiations on the reunification question. He stressed that Taiwan should not impose democracy on China, nor should China impose socialism on Taiwan (*People's Daily*, overseas edition, 28 January 1999, p. 5).

For the Chinese leadership, the idea of pan-Chinese nationalism is a guiding principle in dealing with the Taiwan Strait relationship. It is unlikely that the current Chinese leaders will accept the idea of democratic federalism. What if China embarks upon democratization? Will unification be achieved, or will Taiwan gain its independence in the process of Chinese democratization? Now let us hypothesize on the likely impact of Chinese democratization on the Taiwan issue.

The democratization of China would create political systems and institutions compatible with those in Taiwan, and thereby facilitate unification. It is likely that the democratization of China would help China improve its international reputation and its relations with the U.S.[8] It is also likely that the democratization of China would both intensify pro-unification pressure on Taiwan, as it would reduce the differences between political institutions (Tien, 1994:192–95)[9] and increase confidence in a peaceful solution among the Taiwanese. A democratic China, with decentralized powers and perhaps a confederation, would foster trust between China and Taiwan. Moreover, elected leaders in Mainland China would push unification further if they had an electoral mandate.

The democratization of China, however, would not guarantee successful unification with Taiwan. It might also facilitate the independence of Taiwan. Democratization cuts two ways when dealing with the national identity question: It can either facilitate independence or strengthen the unity of states. Spain, the Philippines, South Africa, St. Kitts and Nevis, Papua New Guinea, Nigeria and Turkey, have all been democratized in the third wave of democratization, and have maintained the unity of their respective states. Democratization has assisted them in containing the secession problem and maintaining state unity.[10] This is because national elections legitimize the political unit and support the regime's claim to legitimacy. Democratic packages, such as decentralization and regional autonomy, have also accommodated secessionist demands. On the other hand, democratization processes make independence or secession much more likely to succeed, as discussed previously.

Here I would like to propose a hypothesis concerning the relationship between the pattern of Chinese democratization and the resolution of the Taiwan question. If the democratization of China is prompted by popular mobilization, Taiwan is more likely to gain its independence, as demonstrated by the case of the successful secession of Mongolia from Qing rule when the Manchu ruler's resistance against democratic reform led to a revolution from below. This is because popularly mandated democratization weakens the power of the centre and creates an opportunity for independence. If, on the other hand, democratization is imposed from above, through élite negotiation, Taiwan would not have a favourable opportunity to declare independence. Democratization from above can boost the legitimacy of the government and may even strengthen state power.

China would have a chance to unify with Taiwan if it were to follow Linz and Stepan's (1997) model of sequential democratic reform: state-wide election preceding provincial election, followed by the negotiation of an autonomy statute with Tibet and a confederal arrangement with Taiwan. China would risk disintegration, however, if the first competitive election were at the provincial, not nation-wide level. In the USSR, democratization started on the periphery with the Baltic states, rather than the centre. Thus, the centre and Gorbachev had no legitimate authority to manage the identity problem; and democratization in the republics assisted secession. The result was disintegration (Linz and Stepan, 1997:34, 381–84). In fact, Chinese leaders seem to have already learnt some lessons from this sequence. In 1993, "multiple-candidate" elections were held for provincial leaders by ballots in regional "parliaments" in a few provinces, including Zhejiang and Guizhou, where officially designated candidates for governors were voted down. After learning this, the central leaders feared that they would lose control of provincial leaders if they were elected competitively; thus the central leaders made the decision that multiple candidate elections for provincial leaders should be stopped.

Moreover, one immediate effect of Chinese democratization would be that Chinese dissidents, particularly those who do not care about the Taiwan issue or who would willingly let Taiwan gain independence, could freely express their views. Thus, the myth that there is an indisputable consensus on unification might be shattered. There would be competitive political parties, and the emergence of pro-Taiwan and anti-Taiwan parties or social groups. The dominant party would be likely to be a pro-unification party. Under plural and competitive politics, it might be speculated that either some democrat members or some members of the government might strike a political deal with Taipei that would support its independence claim, in exchange for support from Taiwan. If this were done quickly and wisely, peace would be ensured. Historically, Sun Yat-sen made such a secret deal with Japan on Northern China in the 1910s (Jansen, 1967) and Boris Yeltsin supported and encouraged the Baltic States to secede in order to gain power over his rival, Gorbachev, in 1991.

In short, a Chinese democrat will argue for Chinese democratization on the grounds that if China seeks to democratize itself at a national level, it has a chance to build a democratic federal or confederate system facilitating reunification with Taiwan. By contrast, a Chinese nationalist will argue against Chinese democratization on the grounds that it is likely to facilitate the independence of Taiwan.

Conclusion

This chapter has identified and proven the effects of democratization on the resolution of the identity question. Democratization tends to lead to an acceptance of the referendum principle in settling the identity question, as demonstrated in the cases of Norway/Sweden, Spain/the Basque region and the Philippines/Mindanao. The change in power structures facilitated by the democratization process has allowed opposition parties coming to power to offer some sort of solution to the identity question, as demonstrated by the collapse of the Soviet Union. The competition for political power has also pressed governments to find ways to resolve the identity question, as shown by the case of Indonesia.

Through the notion of "asymmetric effect," the chapter identifies and explains why democratization in general favours independence rather than unification. This helps us to understand why Beijing resists a democratic approach to the Taiwan question.

Notes

1. In the case of Bangladesh, secession was a long process. Bengali became an official language together with Urdu in the 1950s. Bangladesh demanded a level of autonomy in 1954, then a loose federal system in 1966, and finally secession in 1971, in the wake of the Awami League's victory with a 75 percent vote in the 1970 December election.
2. The membership of the Social Democratic Party increased from 3,000 in 1889 to 5,600 in 1892, 10,000 in 1895, 67,000 in 1905. The number of representatives in the Riksdag grew likewise, from 1 in 1896 to 4 in 1902, 13 in 1905 (Scott, 1977:432).
3. However, the Basic Law of the Federal Republic of Germany (FRG) had two legal provisions enabling reunification: Articles 23 and 146. Article 23 provides that German states can simply accede to the Federal Republic and, therefore, East Germany or individual states can simply announce they are joining the West (Sung, 1994:263; Nelan, 1990:12).
4. I make a conceptual distinction between the maintenance of the existing national unity and the reunification of different sections, states, countries and societies into one political community, and focus on the latter rather than the former. It should be acknowledged that democratization programmes have contributed

to the unity of nation-states in the Philippines, Spain and other countries. Also, there are regional differences. East Asia has seen two cases of unification (China-Hong Kong and the two Vietnams), but no secession since 1974. Moreover, I leave out the controversial question concerning the European Union, which can be interpreted as either reunification or federation.

5. Experiences of democratization in Eastern Europe served as an example which influenced the unification of the Yemens by pushing the Marxist government of the former People's Democratic Republic towards reunification and democratization. Nevertheless, the reunification took place in 1990, prior to the national election in 1993, and this sequence of events should not lead us to over-estimate the role of democratization in promoting unification in Yemen.

6. For historical aspects of the Moro secessionist movement, see Tan, 1990:71–82.

7. According to Julian Kuo, a member of the Formosa Faction, interdependence between Taiwan and Mainland China will be the best protection for Taiwan. By contrast, the New Tide Faction promoted a strategy similar to President Lee Teng-hui's "no haste, be patient" policy, and said there is no need for cross-negotiations because the U.S. will protect Taiwan. And Hsu Yang-ming, of the Justice Alliance Faction, urged Taiwan to abandon its so-called "one China" policy and use its name when it bids for membership in the United Nations (V. Sheng, 1998c:2).

8. However, Chinese nationalists distrust the U.S. and wonder whether it will support the unification project when China moves towards democratization. They think that divide-and-rule is the best strategy for the U.S. to maintain its strategic position in East Asia.

9. Tien asks the question whether the PRC must democratize in order to appeal to the newly democratic Taiwan, or whether real negotiation requires prior democratization or federalism on the mainland.

10. Other factors such as the stability of a democratic regime, international relations and diplomatic efforts, also come in to play.

References

Derbyshire, J. and I. Derbyshire (1996), *Political Systems of the World*. New York: St. Martin's Press.

Dunbar, R. and R. Bresser (1997), "Appreciating Cultural Differences: The Case of German Reunification," *Administration and Society*, 29:440–70.

Engbarth, D. (1998), "Beijing Talks Get Nod from Taiwan Party," *The Australian*, 17 February.

Far Eastern Economic Review (1997a), 6 February, p. 13.

Far Eastern Economic Review (1997b), 3 July, p. 13.

Glaessner, G. J. (1992), *The Unification Process in Germany: From Dictatorship to Democracy*. London: Pinter.

Habermas, J. (1996), "National Unification and Popular Sovereignty," *New Left Review*, 219(September–October):3–13.

He, Baogang (2001), "The National Identity Problem and Democratization: Ruston's Theory of Sequence," *Government and Opposition*, 36(1):97–119.

Heraclides, A. (1991), *The Self-determination of Minorities in International Politics*. London: Frank Cass and Company Limited.

Huntington, S. (1996), "Democracy for the Long Haul," *Journal of Democracy*, 7 (3):24–29.

Jacobs, B. (1997), "China's Policies Towards Taiwan." Presented at Taiwan Update 1997: Taiwan, Hong Kong and PRC Relations, Brisbane.

Jansen, M. (1967), *The Japanese and Sun Yat-sen*. Cambridge: Harvard University Press.

Johnston, A. (1993), "Independence through Unification: On the Correct Handling of Contradictions across the Taiwan Straits," *Contemporary Issues*, No. 2.

Linz, Juan J. and Alfred Stephan (1996), *Problems of Democratic Transition and Consolidation: Southern Europe, South America, and Post-Communist Europe*. Baltimore and London: The Johns Hopkins University Press.

Lu, Myra (1998), "KMT Wins Taipei, Bolsters Its Majority in Legislature," *The Free China Journal*, 11 December, p. 1.

—— (1999), "DPP Opts not to Revise Wording of Platform," *The Free China Journal*, 8 January, p. 2.

Moon, E. and J. Robinson (1997), "Past Trends Show Election Results not so Surprising," *The Free China Journal*, 5 December, p. 5.

Nelan, B. (1990) "East Meets West at Last," *Time*, 135:12.

Scott, Franklin D. (1977), *Sweden: The Nation's History*. Minneapolis: University of Minnesota Press.

Sheng, Lijun, (1998), "China Eyes Taiwan: Why Is a Breakthrough So Difficult?" *The Journal of Strategic Studies*, 21(1):65–78.

Sheng, V. (1998a), "DPP Election Win May Unite Opposition Forces," *The Free China Journal*, 15:2.

——. (1998b), "DPP's Mainland Policy Exemplifies Party's Maturity," *The Free China Journal*, 27 March, p. 7.

——. (1998c), "DPP's Mainland Policy Sparks Intraparty Clash," *The Free China Journal*, 16 January, p. 2.

Stepan, A. (1997), "Toward a New Comparative Analysis of Democracy and Federalism: Demos Constraining and Demos Enabling Federations." Paper presented at IPSA XVII World Congress, Seoul.

Stewart, C. (1998), "Poll Keeps Secession Alive," *The Australian*, 2 December, p. 9.

Sung C. Y. (1994), "The Lessons of United Germany for Divided Korea." In Young Whan Kihl (ed.), *Korea and the World*, Boulder: Westview Press, Inc., pp. 261–77.

Tan, S. (1990), "The Moro Secessionist Movement in the Philippines." In R. Premdas, S. Samarainghe and A. Anderson (eds.), *Secessionist Movements in Comparative Perspective*. London: Print Publishers, pp. 71–82.

Tien, H. M. (1994), "Toward Peaceful Resolution of Mainland-Taiwan Conflicts: The Promise of Democratization." In E. Friedman (ed.), *The Politics of Democratization: Generalizing East Asian Experiences*. Boulder: Westview Press, pp. 185–201.

———. (1997), "Taiwan's Transformation." In L. Diamond, M. Plattner, Y. H. Yun, and H. M. Tien (eds.), *Consolidating the Third Wave Democracies: Regional Challenges*. Baltimore: Johns Hopkins University Press, pp. 123–61.

Tiglao, R. (1996a), "Moro Reprise: New Muslim Campaign Unsettles Mindanao Peace Treaty," *Far Eastern Economic Review*, 160(1):22.

———. (1996b), "Peace in His Time: Ramos-Misuari Accord has Structural Flaws," *Far Eastern Economic Review*, 159(36):24–26.

Appendix: New Member States in the UN

1974–1996

New State	Year	State type	Direc-tion	Parent state	State type	S-Auto	S-Dem	War	Mode of establishment
Andorra	1993	ED	D	France/ Spain	LD/LD	0	8.5	0	R
Angola	1976	ED	A	Portugal	A/D	9	0	1	War
Antigua & Barbuda	1981	LD	D	Britain	LD	0	10	0	PV
Armenia	1992	AN	D	USSR	A/D	2.7	4	1	War/R (99.31%)
Azerbaijan	1992	AN	A	USSR	A/D	5	1	1	War/R (99.58%)
Bangladesh	1974	ED	A	Pakistan	A/D	1	4	1	War
Belize	1981	LD	D	Britain	LD	0	10	0	NS
Bosnia Herzegovina	1992	ED	A	Yugoslavia	A/D	3	2	1	War/NS/R
Brunei Darussalam	1984	AB	A	Britain	LD	0	10	0	UN Resolution
Cape Verde	1975	ED	D	Portugal	A/D	9	0	0	NS Decolonization
Comoros	1975	ED	D	France	LD	0	8	0	R
Croatia	1992	ED	A	Yugoslavia	A/D	3	2	1	War/R/UN Settlement
Czech Republic	1993	ED	D	Czecho-slovakia	A/D	0	10	0	PV
Djibouti	1977	ED*	D	France	LD	0	8	0	Some violence, NS
Dominica	1978	LD	D	Britain	LD	0	10	0	NS Decolonization
Eritrea	1993	NS	A	Ethiopia	A/D	8	0	1	War, R (99. 8%)
Estonia	1991	ED	D	USSR	A/D	0	8	0	R (77.73%)
Georgia	1992	ED*	D	USSR	A/D	0	8	0	R (90.08%)
Grenada	1974	LD	D	Britain	LD	0	10	0	NS Decolonization
Guinea-Bissau	1974	ED	A	Portugal	A/D	9	0	1	War/NS/R
Kazakhastan	1992	AN	A	USSR	A/D	0	8	0	Vote for independence
Kyrgystan	1992	ED	D	USSR	A/D	0	8	0	PV
Latvia	1991	ED	D	USSR	A/D	0	8	0	R (73.68%)
Lithuania	1991	ED	D	USSR	A/D	0	8	0	R (90.47%)
Marshall Islands	1991	LD	D	US	LD	0	10	0	R

New State	Year	State type	Direc- tion	Parent state	State type	S- Auto	S- Dem	War	Mode of establishment
Fed. States Micronesia	1991	LD	D	US	LD	0	10	0	R
Mozambique	1975	ED	A	Portugal	A/D	9	0	0	NS
Namibia	1990	ED	D	South Africa	A/D	2	7	1	War/UN Settlement
Palau (or Belau)	1994	LD	D	US	LD	0	10	0	R (64%)
Papua New Guinea	1975	LD	D	Australia	LD	0	10	0	NS Decolonization
Republic of Moldova	1992	ED	D	USSR	A/D	0	8	0	Conflict, PD, R (95.4% 1994)
Saint Kitts & Nevis	1983	LD	D	Britain	LD	0	10	0	PV
Saint Lucia	1979	LD	D	Britain	LD	0	10	0	NS
St. Vincent & Grenadines	1980	LD	D	Britain	LD	0	10	0	NS
Samoa	1976	LD	D	New Zealand	LD	0	10	0	R
Sao Tome e Principe	1975	ED*	D	Portugal	A/D	9	0	0	NS
Seychelles	1976	ED*	D	Britain	LD	0	10	0	NS
Slovakia	1993	ED	D	Czecho- slovakia	A/D	0	10	0	PV
Slovenia	1992	ED	D	Yugoslavia	A/D	3	2	1	War/R(89%)/NS
Solomon Islands	1978	LD	D	Britain	LD	0	10	0	NS
Suriname	1975	ED	D	Netherlands	LD	0	10	0	NS
Tajikistan	1992	AN	A	USSR	A/D	0	8	0	PV
Republic of Macedonia	1993	ED	D	Yugoslavia	A/D	6	0	0	R(75%)/PD
Turkmenistan	1992	AN	A	USSR	A/D	0	8	0	R(94.1%)/PD
Uzbekistan	1992	AN	A	USSR	A/D	0	8	0	PV/R(98.2%)
Vanuatu	1981	LD	D	Britain/ France	LD/LD	0	9	0	Some violence; NS
Zimbabwe	1980	NS	A	Britain	LD	0	10	0	NS

Abbreviations

State types

AB — Absolutist
AN — Authoritarian Nationalist
A/D — Authoritarian state, then democratized

ED — Emerging Democracy; with*, in transition
LD — Liberal Democracy
NS — National Socialist

Direction

A — Autocratized
D — Democratized

Mode of Establishment

R — Referendum (approving rate in parentheses)
PD — Parliamentary Declaration
PV — Parliamentary Vote
NS — Negotiated Settlement
0 — No war
1 — War

Score of Regime

S-Auto stands for the score of autocracy
S-Dem stands for the score of democracy

Sources:

1. J. Denis Derbyshire and Ian Derbyshire, *Political Systems of the World*. New York: St. Martin's Press, 1996.
2. Joel Krieger (ed.), *The Oxford Companion to Politics of the World*. Oxford & New York: Oxford University Press, 1993.
3. Banks, A. Day and T. Muller, *Political Handbook of the World 1997*. New York: CSA Publications, 1997, pp. 1154–57.
4. J. David Singer and Melvin Small, "Correlates of War Project: International and Civil War Data, 1816–1992" (computer file). Ann Arbor, Michigan: Inter-university Consortium for Political and Social Research (distributor), 1994.

Data Explanation

The data concentrate on those new states established through secession or independence movements which have been recognized by the UN since 1974. The reason for choosing 1974 is that it has been identified by Samuel Huntington as the year in which the third wave of democratization began. This will allow me to assess the impact of democratization in relation to the question of national identity during that period. Specifically, the data records the year new member states were admitted by the UN, the nature and direction of the regime of independent states and their parent-states at that time, and the mode of establishment of the independent states. Portugal, Pakistan, Yugoslavia, Czechoslovakia, the USSR and Ethiopia are all classified as both authoritarian and democratizing states, because they were authoritarian states in the first instance, then democratized. Being "parent-states," they are statistically accounted for several times in accordance with the number of their "offspring" independent states being entered in the data. Only instances of indisputably successful transition to independent statehood are examined, thereby forcing me to exclude the cases of the Basques in Spain and Mindanao in the Philippines. This is regrettable because, in both cases, there is much useful information relating to the issue of how the national identity question can be managed through democratization. Also excluded are the Republic of Korea (1991), DPR Korea (1991) and Vietnam (1977) because they are not new states established through secession or independence; as well as the independent principality of Liechtenstein (1990), the independent protected state of Monaco (1993) and the independent republic of San Marino (1992). Since the study focuses specifically on referenda associated with the secession and independence of individual states, the 1991 USSR Union Referendum in which most Soviet aligned countries voted on the question of preserving or disbanding the Union, is not included. The data are drawn from three key reference books as well as Polity III data. Banks, Day and Muller's book lists the UN membership, and Derbyshire's book categorizes each state as liberal democracy, emergent democracy, absolutist, authoritarian nationalist, national socialist or communist, and records whether struggles or movements for independence involved war. The records of wars have been checked with the ICPSR War Data. What is called a "mini civil war" in Georgia is not included in my data because it was Georgia that looked to Russian force to crush the Abkhazi secessionist forces who had defeated the Georgian army in 1992.

12

Asia-Pacific Urbanism under Globalization

Yue-man Yeung

During the last two decades of the twentieth century, rapid economic growth spearheaded by globalization and urbanization changed the face of Asia, to such an extent that some politicians and observers were euphoric about the growing importance of Asia in world affairs and wealth generation/accumulation. They sanguinely predicted the advent of the Asian Century, or in a more restricted sense the Pacific Century, with a new century and millennium. The sudden onset of the Asian financial crisis in 1997 has since markedly dampened such sentiments, although the speed with which most Asian countries recovered from the upheaval has taken many shrewd analysts by surprise. What was set in train by two decades of socio-economic transformation in Asia has apparently not been set back unduly by the financial meltdown, especially in the urban-regional scene.

This chapter is aimed at laying out the main elements that have significantly affected the nature and pace of urban-regional change in Pacific Asia which has, in turn, led to revolutionary societal and cultural changes in how governments are run, how businesses are transacted and how people lead their lives. Pacific Asia is used here to denote East and Southeast Asia, or the western Pacific rim inclusive of the countries stretching from the Korean Peninsula to Indonesia. The chapter is divided into four sections. The first section simply examines the demographic background of the prospect of urban transition against global trends. It sets the stage for better understanding of the urban dynamics in Asia as the basis for societal transformation. Second, the heightened role of cities in the global economy is highlighted, given the accelerating processes of globalization that have impacted on the region, as in other parts of the world. Third, the emergence of mega-cities and world cities is outlined, drawing parallels with other regions. Finally, cities and their immediate regions have been adjusting and responding to pressures that have been brought to bear on them by new opportunities and challenges arising from globalizing influences. This section touches on some emerging urban forms and urbanism in the region.

Urban Transition and the Urban Century

If population projections by the United Nations (UN) are accurate, the world will cross the historic threshold of having more than half of its population living in cities within a decade. To be more specific, by 2010, 52 percent of the world population will be urban, having increased from 49.7 percent in 2005 (UN, 1998:89). The twenty-first century is, therefore, an urban century and this is what sets it apart from the twenty centuries that have gone before it. For the first time in human history, more people will live in cities than the countryside and the urban situation will become more pronounced as the century unfolds.

In the second half of the twentieth century, population explosion and rapid urbanization were two related processes that dominated the majority of developing countries. Where these processes were accompanied by rapid economic growth, the emergence of many developing countries having successfully transformed themselves occurred worldwide. The newly industrializing countries in the developing world have now become a force to be reckoned with. Within Asia, the postwar transformation of Japan from a defeated nation to the world's second largest economic power is widely viewed as the first economic miracle, followed by the emergence of the Four Little Dragons of Hong Kong, South Korea, Singapore and Taiwan, the so-called second-tier tigers of Malaysia, Thailand and Indonesia, and lately China. In all these countries, cities and their immediate regions have been important development platforms that effectively helped launch them on their trajectory of rapid socio-economic transformation.

As we preview the urban century, not only will the world become increasingly urban but also the urban population will be more and more concentrated in the developing world. In 2000, 76.1 percent of the population in the developed world lived in cities, as compared with 40.5 percent in the developing world. However, the former only accounted for 31 percent of the world's urban population of 2.89 billion, with the developing world accounting for the balance of 69 percent. In 2010, 2020 and 2030, the developed world's share of the world's urban population will gradually decrease to 26, 22 and 19 percent, respectively, whereas the developing world's share will progressively increase to 73, 77 and 80 percent, respectively. At the same time, the level of urbanization will continue to grow in both parts of the world (UN, 1998).

It is thus abundantly clear that within the increasingly urbanized world of the new century, the bulk of the growth in urban population will occur in developing countries. Within the developing world, Asia stands out because of its being the largest as well as the most populous continent. In 2000, 47.9 percent of the world's urban population is accounted for by Asia. As Table 12.1 shows, between 1950 and 1995, Asia as a whole more than doubled its level of urbanization, from 15 to 33 percent, with a large degree of sub-regional uniformity, noting also Western Asia's more advanced status. In the next 30 years, the projected levels of urbanization suggest that across Asia, the potential for a sizeable urban transition is real. The transition has already taken into account the more subdued rates of urban growth that have been projected for different sub-regions of Asia.

Table 12.1 Percentage of Population Residing in Urban Areas in Asia, 1950, 1975, 1995 and 2030

	1950	1975	1995	2030
East Asia	15	22	33	54
South-central Asia	13	19	33	57
Southeast Asia	15	22	33	55
Western Asia	27	48	68	82
Asia	15	22	33	54

Source: UN (1998), p. 13.

Table 12.2 indicates the projected urbanization trends for Pacific Asia by individual countries. Many of the countries have achieved levels of urbanization over the past 30 to 40 years which developed countries took more than a century to accomplish. The region's urbanization experience is consequently compressed and telescoped, often bypassing some stages of urban development in Western countries. In the next 30 years to 2030, most countries in Pacific Asia, especially in East Asia, will be at comparable levels of urbanization to developed countries. Indeed, because of their geography and peculiar space-economy, Japan, the two Koreas, Macau and Brunei Darussalam will be overwhelmingly urban. Even China will increase by more than 20 percentage points in its level of urbanization by 2030. As a result, the implications for the transfer of population across sub-regions and cities and from countryside to city are tremendous. Already since 1984, the relaxation of controls on the household registration system has

Table 12.2 Percentage of Population Residing in Urban Areas in Pacific Asia, 2000 to 2030

	2000	2010	2020	2030
East Asia	40.6	47.7	53.7	59.1
China	34.3	42.3	49.1	55.2
N. Korea	62.8	66.7	71.0	74.7
Hong Kong, China	95.7	96.4	96.8	97.2
Japan	78.9	80.9	83.2	85.3
Macau	98.8	99.0	99.1	99.2
Mongolia	63.5	68.4	72.4	76.0
S. Korea	86.2	91.2	92.7	93.6
Southeast Asia	36.9	43.5	49.4	55.0
Brunei Darussalem	72.2	76.9	80.1	82.6
Cambodia	23.5	29.7	36.2	42.8
East Timor	7.5	8.4	11.1	15.0
Indonesia	40.2	48.9	55.4	61.0
Laos	23.5	29.5	36.0	42.6
Malaysia	57.3	63.6	68.5	72.5
Myanmar	27.7	33.4	40.0	46.6
Philippines	58.6	65.5	69.9	73.8
Singapore	100.0	100.0	100.0	100.0
Thailand	21.6	26.2	32.5	39.1
Viet Nam	19.7	22.1	27.3	33.7
Asia	37.6	43.6	49.6	55.2

Source: UN (1998), p. 91.

progressively witnessed a huge exodus of rural population towards the coastal cities and regions of the order of 80 to 110 million. Another 100 million rural surplus inhabitants have been estimated to be ready for movement in the foreseeable future (Yeung, 2000b).

With the magnitude of urban-regional change that has been seen in Pacific Asia over the past two to three decades, the age-old dichotomy between urban and rural sectors has come under scrutiny and debate. Under the influence of industrialization and improvements in transport and communication, the rural-urban divide has become increasingly blurred (McGee, 1998). Indeed, in the age of globalization where telematics and information technology largely neutralize distance and save time, the very idea of what is urban and rural has to be reconceptualized. This will provide food for thought for statisticians in data collection traditionally categorized into rural-urban groups and for politicians in how effectively to meet the needs of their constituents where former administrative divisions no longer make sense. There are many challenges that await cities and their citizens alike in the urban century that has just dawned.

Cities in the New Global Economy

Since the 1980s, the world economy has changed, rapidly and fundamentally, in its nature, operating modes, and relationships among countries and cities. These changes have been driven by several emerging megatrends that have led to global structural adjustments. These trends have been described elsewhere (Lo and Yeung, 1998:2–7), but for the purpose of this chapter, a short recapitulation will suffice.

First, the price of oil and other primary commodities began to collapse in the early 1980s, owing in large measure to the long-run decline of material input in production in industrially advanced economies. The role of primary resources has diminished in importance. Countries in Africa and Southeast Asia which have traditionally depended on the export of primary commodities for their national incomes have been badly hit. Consequently, capital movements rather than trade in goods and services have become a new engine of growth in the new global economy (Drucker, 1987:21).

Second, capital movements, especially those of foreign direct investment (FDI), have become a new indicator of growth. In this respect, the Plaza Accord of 1985, with the resultant dramatic appreciation of the Japanese yen against the US dollar, has had a vast impact on the pattern of FDI, with countries in Pacific Asia being some of the major gainers. Currencies were realigned and FDI from Japan increased by leaps and bounds in the Asia-Pacific region and other parts of the world. Then in 1986 and 1987, the currencies in South Korea and Taiwan also sharply appreciated. The effect, similar to that of the Japanese yen appreciation, was to force industries in these countries to relocate offshore in order to stay competitive in the international market. The outcome of these currency realignments was a vast increase in capital movements within Pacific Asia. Countries and cities in the region have become more tightly embedded in a web of economic relationships, indeed interdependence, whose long-term consequences are profound (Yeung and Lo, 1996).

Third, technological change which has set the limits of structural change has entered forcefully into the new global economy since the late 1980s. The range and speed of innovations in microelectronics and communications have been breathtaking. The cluster of new innovations in computers, electronics and telecommunications, new materials, biotechnology and robotics has been facilitating production processes, speeding up and revolutionizing business transactions, and permitting creativity. In fact, the new microelectronics "chip" technology is resource-saving and maximizes diseconomies of scale and flexibility in production, in contrast to the Fordist mode of production with its emphasis on mass production and heavy capital outlay (Lo, 1994). A new era of telecommunications, information technology and widened opportunity is generally considered to have arrived.

These mega-trends that operate worldwide affect countries and regions in different ways. The relative decline of major cities and regions in industrially advanced countries has been observed by many scholars (Soja, 1987; Lo and Yeung, 1998). Concomitantly, certain developing countries and cities, in particular those in Pacific Asia, have stood to benefit handsomely in this new regime of open competition and free trade (Yeung, 2000c). The new global economy generates notably uneven effects: While it offers newfound opportunities to some cities and countries, it also marginalizes others. For all, however, the internationalization of production, finance, banking and services, coupled with cheap labour and advances in telecommunications and information technology, has minimized the importance of boundaries in deciding where to locate production plants (Friedmann, 1986). A borderless economy has become a distinctive feature of the new global economy.

In the new global economy, characterized by a new international division of labour, increasing digitalization and greater service intensity, the role of cities has been accentuated. The transactional environment in cities of today is becoming increasingly different from that of the past because of recent technological innovations and the ascendance of digitalization, which can be a source of major transformation of society. Saskia Sassen (1997) has submitted that electronic space (E-space) has emerged not simply as a means of transmitting information, but as a major new theatre for capital accumulation and the operation of global capital. A new economic geography is in the making in which centrality and power are being reconstituted by new technologies and globalization. Cities not located in cyberspace and digital highways are not able to partake of the new opportunities offered by the information age. The spatial correlates of centrality in the emerging economic system revolve around flows of capital, goods, information and people. The network society has emerged as a new phenomenon of the contemporary world (Castells, 1996; Yeung, 2000c).

Traditionally, cities have been seats of civilization and vitality. At the current stage, R.V. Knight (1989) has summed up their new roles well:

Given the nature and power of the global forces that are now shaping them, all cities must redefine their role in the context of the expanding global society. Global cities ... will not be determined by locational or geographical considerations but by their capacity to accommodate change and provide continuity and order in a turbulent environment. (p. 326)

The challenge to all cities is hence to plan for their future and for global or world cities (to be dealt with in the next section) to provide leadership for positive change and advance in a changing world.

From Mega-City to World City

At the beginning of the twentieth century, there were only 11 cities with over a million inhabitants. A century later in 2000, the world had approximately 400 "million" cities, of which at least 145 were located in Asia. For much of the twentieth century, it was fashionable to measure the size of urban agglomerations by way of the "million" status. As urban population grew rapidly in the postwar period, the concept of the mega-city began to be used in the 1980s.

What constitutes a mega-city is variable, depending on time and who defines it. Even within the United Nations, for example, 8 million was used as the initial threshold (Chen and Heligman, 1994; UN, 1995:6) but was recently replaced by 10 million (UN, 1998:23). This highlights the arbitrariness of the measure and there is nothing sacrosanct or objective about it. Whatever it is, there is little doubt that when a city is designated mega, it is a gigantic concentration of urban population that comes with its opportunities as well as challenges.

On the basis of the 8 million threshold, the world had 23 mega-cities in 1995, of which 13 were in Asia. In 2000, 9 of the largest 15 cities in the world were in Asia (and 4 in East Asia). By 2015, the dominance of developing countries in the distribution of mega-cities will be conspicuous, with Asia accounting for 16 of the world's 26 (Table 12.3). This clearly shows the prominence of Asia, especially Pacific Asia, in the worldwide distribution of urban population, reinforcing the demographic profile that was outlined in a previous section. It should be mentioned that, worldwide, the largest cities in many countries began to show signs of slowing down in population growth in the 1980s, compared with the previous two decades. Also, the dire projection of super-large cities growing to 30 to 40 million, as was once predicted for Calcutta and Mexico City, did not materialize. In

Table 12.3   Distribution of Mega-cities, 1975, 1995 and 2015

Region	1975	1995	2015
World	5	14	26
Less developed regions	3	10	22
Africa	0	1	2
Asia*	1	5	16
Latin America and the Caribbean	2	4	4
More developed regions**	2	4	4
Northern America	1	2	2
Japan	1	2	2

* Excluding Japan
** Including Japan
Source: UN (1998), p. 23.

fact, less than 5 percent of the world's population lived in mega-cities in 1990 (UNCHS, 1996).

Mega-cities are products of the latter stages of the twentieth century. They are important by virtue of the sheer size of their population, and concentration of economic, political and technological power. Yet many such cities in developing countries do not have the experience, resources or expertise to deliver modern and efficient management. Consequently, problems related to land-use conflicts, under-provision of basic urban services (such as water supply, electricity, solid waste collection, housing, etc.), urban poverty, and law and order have figured prominently on the policy agenda and management of these cities. These problems are so overwhelming that it is not uncommon to find that policy-makers and planners develop an ingrained bias against large cities. Controlling metropolitan growth has become a common goal in some Asian cities (Yeung, 1986) and China has been careful in avoiding the growth of its large cities while giving official blessing to the growth of small- and medium-sized cities. There is an ongoing debate on the size of cities and its relation to economic growth, urban pathology and cultural regeneration (Hamer, 1994). Mega-cities, nevertheless, continue to fascinate scholars and policy-makers alike and they constitute a subject of growing academic and policy discourse in Asia (Ginsburg et al., 1991; McGee and Robinson, 1995; Stubbs and Clarke, 1996; Yeung, 1997).

With accelerating globalization over the past two decades, attention has been focused on another type of city — world cities. World cities are a class apart from others, simply because of the critical functions they perform that drive the global economy, or that would have a worldwide impact in a non-economic sense. Of course, economic globalization affects our lives more directly and can be identified as five sub-processes. These are the globalization of finance, production, knowledge, transnational business and state power (Thrift, 1994). A recent study has concentrated on the emerging world cities in Pacific Asia and reaffirmed their growing stature and new functions against the background of global economic restructuring (Lo and Yeung, 1996). Many political leaders in the region have aspirations for their cities to become world cities and to play a larger role in the global economy in the new digital age. In this respect, the increasingly massive investment of city governments in preparing themselves and improving their infrastructure, upgrading facilities and embracing hi-tech can be viewed as part and parcel of the world city formation process. Japan and the Four Little Dragons in Pacific Asia have been preparing themselves particularly well to meet the challenges of the future (Yeung and Lo, 1998; also Chapter 5). The new generation of mammoth and state-of-the-art airports in Singapore (Changi), Osaka (Kansai), Hong Kong (Chek Lap Kok) and Shanghai (Pudong) testify to the massive sums these governments are prepared to invest in their future. The drive for hi-tech development has apparently re-energized Hong Kong's stagnant economy since 1997. The headline-catching cross-region takeovers and mergers by Pacific Century CyberWorks in 2000 have done much to enhance Hong Kong's bid as a regional centre of information technology and telecommunications.

Saskia Sassen (1991) has identified four key functions for world cities, namely, as command posts in the organization of the global economy, as key locations for finance and specialized services, as sites of production and innovation in leading industries, and as markets for products and innovations produced. Indeed, advanced producer services may be employed as indicators of world city formation. Guided by this perspective, a recent study has focused on four key services — accounting, advertising, banking and law — to measure a city's global capacity or worldcityness (Beaverstock et al., 1999).

On the basis of 122 cities in the world studied, Pacific Asia has come out rather well. Of the ten cities which score the highest (*Alpha world cities*), three (Tokyo, Hong Kong and Singapore) are in Pacific Asia. If Australasia is included in this sub-region, as in this exercise, 14 world cities of the first 3 ranks are located in Pacific Asia and highly comparable with the Americas, which have 18 world cities (Figure 12.1). The distribution of world cities reinforces the triad of world economic development, with the tripolar

Figure 12.1 The World According to GaWC

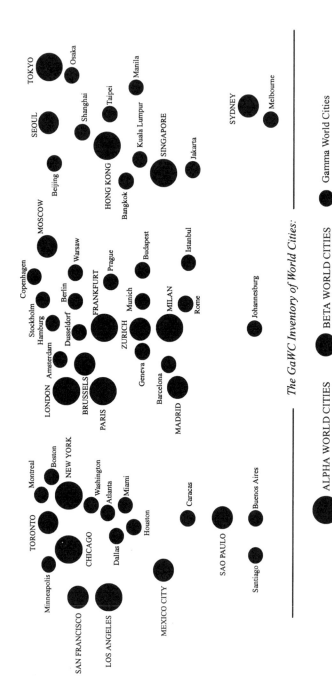

The GaWC Inventory of World Cities:

ALPHA WORLD CITIES   BETA WORLD CITIES   Gamma World Cities

Note: GaWC stands for Globalization and World Cities Research Group.
Source: Beaverstock et al. (1999).

concentration of economic power in North America, Europe and Pacific Asia. The overwhelming concentration of world cities in the northern hemisphere is also noteworthy.

Cultural globalization is as important as economic globalization. Emerging global culture includes as one of its most visible aspects popular culture, especially that produced in the West. The spread of Western popular culture can be traced to the growth of mass communication, the increase in global organizations and the revolution in long-distance transportation (Patterson, 1994). World cities are, consequently, sites of global spectacle, such as the Olympic Games, the World Cup and rock concerts. In this respect, Tokyo has fared exceptionally well among the world cities, in part the result of its huge population size and its ability to showcase global spectacle and hence play a part in the globalization of popular culture (Short et al., 1996). In fact, cities in Japan overtly compete for global attention through the hosting of international design expos (Nagoya), food festivals (Sapporo), flower expositions (Osaka), science expositions (Tsukuba) and the World Exposition (Seto, near Nagoya, in 2005) (Douglass, 1998:18). Other cities in Pacific Asia have also been successful as sites of world spectacle. Seoul has hosted the Asian and Olympic Games and will co-host with Tokyo the next World Cup. Similarly, Hong Kong succeeded in sealing an agreement with Disneyland in 1999 to open its second theme park in Asia, after Tokyo, with an opening date set for 2005. Beijing also has won its bid to host the Olympic Games in 2008.

Emerging Urbanism and Urban Forms

Apart from world cities that have thrust themselves on to the urban scene in Pacific Asia over the past two decades, there have been other emerging spatial forms that have transformed cities and their surrounding regions, in response to globalization processes that have impinged on them. The urban way of life consequent upon these changes has also adapted to new constraints and conveniences.

One of the most visible urban forms that has emerged from the recent processes of globalization and urbanization is what has been called mega-urban regions or extended metropolitan regions (EMRs) centred around large or mega-cities. Integrated rural-urban economic growth may stretch anywhere from 50 to 100 km from the city centre. This new form of urban-region reconfiguration is often not well managed by traditional urban structures. Terry McGee and others have documented this phenomenon in different parts of Pacific Asia (Ginsburg et al., 1991; McGee and Robinson, 1995; Macleod and McGee, 1996). Briefly, an EMR epitomizes a fast growing city responding to the challenges and opportunities of the global economy and the increasingly integrated and stable rural hinterland. Rural populations around an EMR tend to be stable, without being unduly attracted by the city to migrate, but they take up more non-farm jobs and have realized appreciable increases in personal income. Overall, the experience of EMRs in Pacific Asia is that it is the urban fringe areas, where land-use controls are less stringent and opportunities for development more open, that have grown the fastest in terms of population and physical change. There is a high degree of similarity in how land-use change, economic growth and population increase have occurred in Jabotabek (Jakarta and its surrounding townships), metropolitan Bangkok and Metro Manila (Yeung, 1998a).

If the EMR is viewed as a form of suburbanization, it has begun to occur in large Chinese cities as well. A recent study has shown that, based largely on the experience of Beijing, suburbanization is a process that emerged in the mid-1980s. Unlike what Western cities have gone through, suburbanization in Chinese cities is largely a passive and organized process, motivated by the decentralization of mainly state-owned industrial enterprises seeking cheaper land, having to restructure themselves or being forced to leave the city because of their polluting nature. At the present stage, suburbanization has involved primarily population and industries. About 90 percent of the population found in the suburbs belong to regular *hukou* (i.e., registered households), but the proportion of in-migrants has been increasing rapidly. The phenomenon of ethnic villages on the outskirts of Beijing testifies to the active process of self-help or spontaneous settlement by new migrants, with Zhejiang Village and Xinjiang Village being notable examples (Zhou and Meng, 2000).

A second urban-regional form capitalizing on comparative advantage and free trade as characteristics of the new global economy is a sub-regional co-operative entity involving contiguous territories of several countries. Popularly known as growth triangles, the participating territories are characterized by varied factor endowments and dovetailed complementaries, preparing them well to compete in the world market. Two of the best working growth triangles in the region are the Southern China Growth Triangle and the SIJURI Growth Triangle. The former evolved soon after China adopted its open policy and economic reforms in 1978 and involved Hong Kong, Taiwan and the southern provinces of Guangdong and Fujian. The latter networks Singapore with Johor in southern Peninsular Malaysia and the

Riau Islands of Indonesia in a "triangle of growth." Beyond these two proven successful co-operative designs, other growth triangles are at different stages of implementation in the region (Yeung, 2000c).

As urban and regional development intensifies, the coalescence of a number of cities and their intervening regions into urban or development corridors is often a natural process. The best developed urban corridor in Pacific Asia is centred around Beijing-Seoul-Tokyo (BESETO), transcends national boundaries and encompasses five mega-cities (Beijing, Tianjin, Seoul, Tokyo-Yokohama, Osaka-Kobe, each with a population of over 10 million inhabitants). It is an awesome concentration of political, economic and financial power (Choe, 1998). Other urban corridors may be more deliberately planned, as the one between Fuzhou and Xiamen, which has effectively speeded up the transformation of the southeastern part of Fujian province (Chu and Yeung, 2000). Urban and regional development in Pacific Asia, given the trends that have been reviewed earlier, will continue to intensify across countries and sub-regions. Not surprisingly, some scholars envisage the entire coastal area from the Korean Peninsula to Java centred on Jakarta becoming a continuous urban or development corridor some time later in the present century.

The macro urban-regional changes that have been lightly sketched above go hand in hand with equally fundamental changes within cities themselves — the way they are governed, how new technologies have changed urban life, and how humane they can be to people.

To begin with, one must note the growing application of new technologies in the planning of urban areas, often involving public-private partnerships and competitions. Kenneth Corey (1997) has highlighted the cases of Malaysia and Singapore in having successfully applied information technology (IT) and telecommunications in transforming their urban landscape. Malaysia's IT policies, articulated from the highest level of government, consist essentially of Vision 2020. By developing high technology, Malaysia aspires to be a fully-developed country by 2020, being able to develop a scientific, innovative and producer society. The development plan, relying on science, hi-tech and IT, consists of four major parts: (1) landmark mega-construction projects such as the Petronas Twin Towers in Kuala Lumpur, (2) the new Kuala Lumpur International Airport (KLIA) that was opened in 1998, (3) a new administrative capital, Putrajaya Bandar Bistari, planned as an intelligent city to spearhead the new Multimedia Super Corridor, and (4) the development of the Johor Information Infrastructure in Johor Bahru, directly across from Singapore. Singapore, perhaps apart from Japan in Asia, was the earliest country to state publicly in 1968 that it would depend on science and technology to drive national development. The present development represents the fourth generation of IT public policy implementation. Its IT2020 vision is to have IT for the masses, in government, in support of industry, and as an export industry.

IT has now become increasingly a part of urban life, where business transactions, information dissemination, entertainment, data gathering, etc. are transmitted over the Internet. The urban society is fast becoming a network society, with flows of ideas, money and information travelling almost instantaneously within a city and across the world. The rise of the network transnational corporation is an especially significant phenomenon, as evidenced by the active participation and sizeable investment of Hong Kong firms in the countries of the Association of Southeast Asian Nations (ASEAN) region (H. Yeung, 1998).

Over the past two decades, a conjuncture of several fortuitous factors has led to countries in Pacific Asia having realized rapid economic growth. Income per capita has increased by several orders of magnitude in almost every major city in the region. The increase in Chinese cities has been most spectacular, with income per capita in the Pearl River Delta, for instance, having grown fivefold between 1980 and 1990. As a result, the rise of the urban middle class is widespread in the region. This has led, in turn, to changes in consumer tastes and the spatial reconfiguration of land uses. Shopping centres, for example, have become a common urban institution across the region. In Jabotabek, 45 large retail shopping centres had been constructed by 1995, 24 of which came into being after 1990. Shopping centres in Metro Manila draw not only affluent residents and tourists but also shoppers from nearby provinces (Yeung, 1998a). The shopping centre as an emergent institution makes cities in Pacific Asia similar to Western cities in the built environment and character. In fact, many Asian shopping centres have been designed and developed by Western architects. This, together with the spatial rearrangement of land uses over the city, has caused, at least world cities in Southeast Asia, to converge on the model of the Western city. In addition, the middle class experience in the perceived deterioration of personal security is common to North America and Southeast Asia, as H. W. Dick and R. J. Rimmer (1998:2317) have depicted:

> Gated residential communities, condominiums, air-conditioned cars, patrolled shopping malls and entertainment complexes, and multi-storeyed offices are the present and future world of the insecure middle class in Southeast Asia.

Another dimension of change in cities in Pacific Asia relates to the changing relationship between the government and the governed in many countries. The toppling of the Marcos regime in 1986 and of the Suharto government in 1998, the public disgrace of two former Korean presidents, direct election of the president in Taiwan since 1996, and the introduction of direct election in Hong Kong since the early 1980s are milestones signposting the shifting political panorama in the region. They mark the increasing aspirations of the people to participate in governance, and greater demands for democracy and for transparency of public policy. The very idea of urban governance is in flux because many of the existing institutions born of a former era and in different circumstances are not adequate in meeting the emerging demands of the people. Urban governance in Southeast Asia has been found to be increasingly democratic and dynamic, largely as a response to the interaction of external and internal forces bearing on its urban centres. In this respect, the role of non-governmental organizations (NGOs) has been critical and civil society is emerging as a force recognized by the authorities (Porio, 1997; also Chapter 10). Urban governments in Pacific Asia increasingly have to confront the challenges of the information age, where decisions taken in the economic, financial and cultural domains are often not entirely within their control. Cross-border crime, massive speculative financial flows and unwelcome cultural influences are some examples urban governments of today have to deal with on a regular basis. Urban governance in this sense is occasionally in a state of siege.

Concluding Remarks

Globalization and the rise of mega-urban regions in Pacific Asia during the past two decades have made it plain that, notwithstanding the salutary effects these have engendered on societies, the experience has been volatile. Volatile globalization had a poignant meaning when severe vicissitudes of monetary flows led to the global stock market collapse in 1987 and the Asian financial crisis in 1997. At the same time, globalization has also had a marginalizing influence between cities and countries, as well as within cities. Enhanced social and economic polarization has been found in some cities in the region consequent upon accelerating globalization since the 1980s. Urban poverty remains a daunting problem amid growing prosperity in the cities in Pacific Asia (Yeung, 1999). One has to be aware of the pros and cons of globalization (Yeung, 1998b).

The challenges to decision-makers, planners and administrators in the information age are as numerous as the new opportunities that beckon them on. One challenge is the need for cities to be regionally and globally competitive, as open and keener competition will come with globalization. Embracing hi-tech is an obvious development strategy, but the government must develop the requisite human resources, education and fiscal policy and sharpen its competitive edge. The changing roles of cities must be recognized and governments concerned must invest sufficient resources so that they can carry out their enhanced roles.

Cities of the future will have more freedoms and more constraints. Greater freedom will be extended to individuals and institutions because they will be networked electronically. Wired interactions will supplement face-to-face contacts. This will also affect urban lifestyles as people can work at home, shop by computer and travel with smart cards. The well heeled are likely to have property and business interests in several cities or countries, and the family to be similarly dispersed, out of preference. Citizens in these cities are prone to "think globally and act locally." Indeed, social organizations and political institutions face the challenge of having to capture the loyalties of people who are oriented in highly diverse ways (Yeung, 2000a). Urban governance in such a fluid and shifting milieu is especially challenging, as apart from having to serve the local constituents, the administration has to deal with multinational corporations in the sharing of power. Urban governments need to devolve power to local units and adopt a flexible approach to involve talents in civil society. In reshaping the global society, Asians through human empowerment will be in a stronger position to challenge the heretofore near monopoly of power by the West over the symbolic grounding of global civilization, that is, making meaning of the symbols, myths, dreams and theories by which human beings live (Woodside, 1996:16).

Above all, Pacific-Asian cities of the future will have to improve their liveability, in health, education, the environment, and more generally the quality of life. Indeed, the developmental problematique may have to be reconceptualized, taking into account the fast pace of change, the pervading influence of new technologies and the growing salience of civil society. The question of liveability of our cities should be raised alongside that of their sustainability. It has been contended that some of the existing patterns of development are not sustainable in the long run, economically, environmentally and culturally. Against this backdrop, the prognosis is for the Asia-Pacific region to continue to grow at a healthy pace in the foreseeable future and, with the world's growth centre likely to gravitate further towards the Pacific, leaders in the region must rise to the urban challenge.

References

Beaverstock, J. V., P. J. Taylor and R. G. Smith (1999), "A Roster of World Cities," *Cities*, 16(6):445–58.

Castells, Manuel (1996), *The Rise of the Network Society*. Oxford and New York: Blackwell.

Chen, Nancy Yu-ping and Larry Heligman (1994), "Growth of the World's Megalopolises." In Roland Fuchs et al. (eds.), *Mega-City Growth and the Future*. Tokyo: United Nations University Press, pp. 17–31.

Choe, Sang-chuel (1998), "Urban Corridors in Pacific Asia." In Lo and Yeung (eds.), *Globalization and the World of Large Cities*, pp. 155–73.

Chu, David K. Y. and Y. M. Yeung (2000), "Developing the 'Development Corridor'." In Y. M. Yeung and David K. Y. Chu (eds.), *Fujian: A Coastal Province in Transition and Transformation*. Hong Kong: The Chinese University Press, pp. 203–26.

Corey, Kenneth E. (1997), "Digital Dragons and Cyber Communities: The Application of Information Technology and Telecommunications Public Policies and Private Partnerships to the Planning of Urban Areas," *International Journal of Urban Studies*, 1(2):184–96.

Dick, H. W. and R. J. Rimmer (1998), "Beyond the Third World City: The New Urban Geography of South-east Asia," *Urban Studies*, 35(12):2303–21.

Douglass, Mike (1998), "East Asian Urbanization: Patterns, Problems and Prospects." Discussion paper, Asia/Pacific Research Center, Stanford University.

Drucker, Peter F. (1987), *The Frontiers of Management*. London: Heinemann.

Friedmann, John (1986), "The World City Hypothesis," *Development and Change*, 17:69–83.

Ginsburg, Norton, Bruce Koppel and T. G. McGee (eds.) (1991), *The Extended Metropolis: Settlement Transition in Asia*. Honolulu: University of Hawaii Press.

Hamer, A. M. (1994), "Economic Impacts of Third World Mega-Cities: Is Size the Issue?" In Roland Fuchs et al. (eds.), *Mega-City Growth and the Future*. Tokyo: United Nations University Press, pp. 172–91.

Knight, R. V. (1989), "City Building in a Global Society." In R. V. Knight and G. Gappert (eds.), *Cities in a Global Society*. Newberry Park: Sage, pp. 326–34.

Lo, Fu-chen (1994), "Current Global Adjustment and Shifting Techno-economic Paradigm on the World City System." In Roland Fuchs, *Mega-City Growth and the Future*. Tokyo: United Nations University Press, Chapter 4.

Lo, Fu-chen and Yue-man Yeung (eds.) (1996), *Emerging World Cities in Pacific Asia*. Tokyo: United Nations University Press.

——— (eds.)(1998), *Globalization and the World of Large Cities*. Tokyo: United Nations University Press.

Macleod, Scott and T. G. McGee (1996), "The Singapore-Johore-Riau Growth Triangle." In Lo and Yeung, *Emerging World Cities*, pp. 427–64.

McGee, T. G. (1998), "Globalization and Rural-urban Relations in the Developing World." In Lo and Yeung (eds.), *Globalization and the World of Large Cities*, pp. 471–96.

McGee, T. G. and Ira Robinson (eds.) (1995), *The Mega-Urban Regions of Southeast Asia*. Vancouver: UBC Press.

Patterson, O. (1994), "Ecumenical America: Global Culture and the American Cosmos," *World Policy Journal*, 11:103–17.

Porio, Emma (1997), *Urban Governance and Poverty Alleviation in Southeast Asia*. Manila: Ateneo de Manila University.

Sassen, Saskia (1991), *The Global City: New York, London, Tokyo*. Princeton: Princeton University Press.

——— (1997), "Electronic Space and Power," *Journal of Urban Technology*, 4(1): 1–17.

Short, J. R., Y. Kim, M. Kuus and H. Wells (1996), "The Dirty Little Secret of World Cities Research: Data Problems in Comparative Analysis," *International Journal of Urban and Regional Research*, 20(4):697–717.

Soja, Edward W. (1987), "Economics Restructuring and the Internationalization of the Los Angeles Region." In Michael P. Smith and Joe R. Feagin (eds.), *The Capitalist City*. Oxford and New York: Blackwell, pp. 178–98.

Stubbs, Jeffry and Giles Clarke (eds.) (1996), *Megacity Management in the Asia and Pacific Region*. Two volumes. Manila: Asian Development Bank.

Thrift, N. (1994), "Globalization, Regulation, Urbanization: The Case of the Netherlands," *Urban Studies*, 31(3):365–80.

UN, Department for Economic and Social Information and Policy Analysis (1995), *World Urbanization Prospects: The 1994 Revision*. New York: United Nations.

UN, Department of Economic and Social Affairs (1998), *World Urbanization Prospects: The 1996 Revision*. New York: United Nations.

United Nations Centre for Human Settlements (UNCHS) (1996), *An Urbanizing World: Global Report on Human Settlements 1996*. Oxford: Oxford University Press.

Woodside, Alexander (1996), "The Empowerment of Asia and the Weakness of the Global Theory." In Alexander Woodside et al., *The Empowerment of Asia: Reshaping Global Society*. Vancouver: Institute of Asian Research, UBC, pp. 9–31.

Yeung, Henry Wai-chung (1998), *Transnational Corporations and Business Networks*. London and New York: Routledge.

Yeung, Yue-man (1986), "Controlling Metropolitan Growth in Eastern Asia," *Geographical Review*, 76(2):125–37.

—— (1997), "Geography in the Age of Mega-cities," *International Social Science Journal*, 151:91–104.

—— (1998a), "Globalization and Southeast Asian Urbanism." Paper presented at ISEAS 30th Anniversary Conference held in Singapore, 30 July – 1 August.

—— (1998b), "The Promise and Peril of Globalization," *Progress in Human Geography*, 22(4):475–77.

—— (1999), "Urban Poverty Alleviation in the Age of Globalization in Pacific Asia." Background paper prepared for the World Bank *World Development Report 2000*. Presented at the World Bank — Foundation for Advanced Studies in International Development of Japan Workshop held in Tokyo, 26–27 May.

—— (2000a), "Globalization and the New Urban Challenge." Keynote address presented at the South Asia Urban and City Management Course organized by the World Bank Institute in Goa, India, 9 to 21 January.

—— (2000b), "Migration in China under Openness and a Marketizing Economy." Paper presented at the third meeting of the Urban Population Dynamics Panel of the Committee of Population, U.S. National Research Council held in Mexico City, 24–26 February.

—— (2000c), *Globalization and Networked Societies: Urban-Regional Change in Pacific Asia*. Honolulu: University of Hawaii Press.

Yeung, Yue-man and Fu-chen Lo (1996), "Global Restructuring and Emerging Urban Corridors in Pacific Asia." In Lo and Yeung (eds.), *Emerging World Cities*, pp. 17–47.

—— (1998), "Globalization and World City Formation in Pacific Asia." In Lo and Yeung (eds.), *Globalization and the World of Large Cities*, pp. 132–54.

Zhou, Yixing and Meng Yanchun (eds.) (2000), *Suburbanization in Beijing and Relevant Policies*. Beijing: Scientific Press (in Chinese).

13

APEC's Prospects as an International Organization

Andrew Elek

Since its establishment in 1989, the Asia-Pacific Economic Cooperation (APEC) process has established itself as a significant international organization in the Asia-Pacific region. The diversity of its participants, from both shores of the Pacific, has led to the emergence of a new model of voluntary international economic co-operation, quite distinct from the treaty-driven options adopted in Western Europe and the Americas.

This chapter describes the origins of APEC, its early successes and the difficulties encountered in the late 1990s. This experience suggests the need to broaden the focus of co-operation beyond trade policy. The time has come to adopt an integrated, comprehensive strategy for co-operation — sharing the region's rich and diverse experience and expertise in order to enhance each other's capacity to design and implement progressively more efficient economic policies. Such capacity-building can foster a growing sense of community of interests and help all Asia-Pacific economies realize their full potential for sustainable growth.

Economic Co-operation in the Asia Pacific

As early as the 1960s, thinkers and statesmen foresaw the need for better communications among the governments and peoples of the region (Elek, 1991). At that time, intra-regional trade and investment links were not well developed, despite the enormous potential created by the very different resource endowments of Asia-Pacific economies.

Market forces were beginning to boost these economic links and the region's governments shared an interest in enhanced living standards and technological capability. At the same time, the great diversity of the region, including great disparities in productivity and widely different political as well as economic systems, meant that there was little sense of community. Very limited knowledge of each other's policy environment constrained economic exchange. More effective means of communications were needed to seize the opportunities for international trade and investment created by the complementarity of Asia-Pacific economies, as well as to anticipate the inevitable stresses of closer interdependence.

Objectives

The basic objective of economic co-operation in the Asia Pacific is a conservative one: to sustain the conditions needed for continued rapid economic development and mutually beneficial economic integration in East Asia and across the Pacific (Garnaut, 2000). The annual series of Pacific Trade and Development (PAFTAD) conferences, which commenced in the late 1960s, led to a progressively clearer and shared understanding of the ingredients of sustainable development. These included:

1. sound macro-economic management to create a predictable domestic environment to attract both domestic and international investment;
2. the capacity and willingness to accept major structural changes to allow economies to adapt to their evolving patterns of comparative advantage, as higher productivity is reflected in higher earnings;
3. confidence in a predictable international economic environment which is to allow specialization in line with comparative advantage, by limiting the risks of increasing interdependence.

The third of these appeared to be the most appropriate basis of early co-operation. Firstly, it was the least intrusive of sovereignty in terms of setting domestic economic policies. Secondly, by the 1980s, it became evident that the future of the GATT-based system of international trade could no longer be taken for granted. United States leadership was fading and the predictability of trans-Pacific trade was threatened by protectionist harassment of successful exporters to North America. Hence the Seoul APEC Declaration (clause 1) defined APEC's objectives as:

1. to sustain the growth and development of the region for the common good of its peoples and, in this way, to contribute to the growth and development of the world economy;
2. to enhance the positive gains, both for the region and the world economy, resulting from increasing economic interdependence,

including by encouraging the flow of goods, services, capital and technology;

3. to develop and strengthen an open multilateral trading system in the interest of Asia-Pacific and all other economies;
4. to reduce barriers to trade in goods and services among participants in a manner consistent with GATT principles, where applicable, and without detriment to other economies.

The first of these stresses the conservative objective of sustaining progress, while explicitly stressing the outward-looking, global as well as regional objectives of economic co-operation. The others stress the potential benefits of interdependence.

APEC did not set out to be merely yet another regional trading arrangement. Asia-Pacific governments wanted to develop and strengthen the global trading system, not just to promote trade among participants.[1] At the same time, the final objective acknowledges that if APEC participants expected to have a constructive influence on the global trading system, they needed to be able to set positive examples in terms of reducing impediments to trade and investment. This led to an early emphasis on promoting free and open trade and investment in the Asia-Pacific region.

Style of Co-operation

Experience of international co-operation in the Asia Pacific pointed towards an approach based on the guiding principles of openness, equality and evolution. These were the principles of two successful institutions which created the foundations for APEC, namely the Association of Southeast Asian Nations (ASEAN) and the Pacific Economic Co-operation Council (PECC).[2]

1. **Openness** required non-discrimination and transparency in trade and economic policy as well as to extended participation.
2. **Equality** implied that activities needed to be of mutual benefit to all participants and recognized the ongoing rapid transformation in the structure of economic and political power in the region.
3. **Evolution** of the process of regional co-operation recognized the need for a gradual, step-by-step, pragmatic and sustained approach to co-operation based in consensus-building and voluntary participation (Drysdale et al., 1998).

In a region containing many newly independent nation states, most governments have no intention of ceding sovereignty to any new regional organization. That ruled out the formal treaty-based approach taken in Western Europe. APEC needed to be voluntary, driven by growing consensus about shared interests.

Asia-Pacific co-operation was not built on a foundation of a traditional "free trade area," where border barriers to trade are eliminated among participants, but not against other trading partners. A traditional trading arrangement, focusing on border barriers to trade in goods, was seen to be no longer sufficient to facilitate economic integration. It was also essential to address the problems of needless divergence or lack of awareness of domestic economic policies and practices.[3]

Moreover, it would be quite impractical to undertake regional trade liberalization in the Asia Pacific by means of a conventional discriminatory free trade area of the kind sanctioned by the GATT/WTO.[4] Negotiating such an arrangement would be highly divisive and delay the process of liberalization it was supposed to promote. It would corrode the objective of community-building and lead to the exclusion of major players inside the region (such as China and Vietnam) as well as outside (Elek, 1995).

Even if feasible, a discriminatory free trade area would not be desirable. The trading interests of East Asian and the Pacific economies extend beyond their own region, especially to Europe. Intentional discrimination against the rest of the world would serve to justify selective retaliation against successful exporters, especially East Asian economies.

Fortunately, the traditional free trade area approach is not necessary to reduce obstacles to international exchange in the Asia Pacific. Most Asia-Pacific economies have been reducing their barriers to trade and investment voluntarily and unilaterally in recent decades (PECC, 1996). Therefore, APEC can promote the objective of free and open trade and investment simply by encouraging Asia-Pacific governments to maintain and accelerate this process.

Hence the approach of open regionalism adopted by APEC: setting targets for facilitating and liberalizing both trade and investment, then encouraging each other to make the policy decisions needed to approach these targets, without any attempt to discriminate among trading partners.

APEC's Early Years

The APEC process progressed rapidly after the inaugural meeting of Ministers from 12 Asia-Pacific economies. A comprehensive work programme was agreed by 1990. In 1991, APEC's non-formal structure made it possible to include all three Chinese economies (China, Taiwan and Hong Kong).[5] A modest central secretariat was set up in 1992. APEC leaders, mostly heads of government, met for the first time in 1993.[6] At only their second meeting, in 1994, they were able to make a political commitment to eliminating barriers to trade and investment by no later than 2010/2020.[7]

APEC has taken a very broad view of free and open trade and investment. The 1995 Osaka Action Agenda indicates that this will involve the elimination of all border barriers to trade and investment and the reduction of all other impediments to international economic transactions. The 15 components of the Osaka Action Agenda include co-operation to reduce the costs and risks of international commerce caused by inadequate communications, partly due to infrastructure constraints, inadequate information about opportunities for exchange and uncertainty about future policies, as well as divergent approaches to many domestic economic policies.

The Osaka Action Agenda also set out the principles which would guide the many decisions APEC governments need to make to progress towards free and open trade and investment. These principles give indivi-dual governments a high degree of flexibility to set the sequence of reforms to achieve their 2010/2020 deadlines for free and open trade and investment.[8]

All APEC governments submitted their initial Individual Action Plans (IAP) and agreed on a series of Collective Action Plans (CAP) in 1966. These action plans have been updated each year, with extensive reviews of reform programmes among APEC officials. These reviews do not involve negotiations. They are designed to create "peer pressure" on all governments to undertake further reforms, recognizing that a reasonably rapid pace of reform is needed to sustain confidence in APEC's voluntary process of co-operation.

This process, which has come to be termed concerted unilateralism, has proved reasonably effective. There has been considerable progress in trade liberalization — continuing a trend towards "opening to the outside world" in the Asia-Pacific region. The (unweighted) tariff rate of APEC economies has been lowered by almost half between 1988 and 1998. Independent reviews of IAPs indicate that all APEC participants are on track towards their commitments to eliminate tariffs by the agreed target dates (PECC, 1996).

There has also been substantial progress in terms of reducing other costs and risks of international commerce. APEC (2000) sets out a substantial list of achievements, ranging from harmonized customs procedures, increasing the scope of mutual recognition of standards, agreed principles for more transparent and competitive government procurement, and reducing impediments to international business travel. The Economic Committee of APEC has estimated that two-thirds of the welfare gains from trade and investment liberalization and facilitation (TILF) to date are due to such facilitation measures.

To sum up, APEC was able to generate a substantial momentum of co-operation in its early years, while evolving a distinctive approach to undertaking the roles and functions which are common to all international organizations. Since then, the process has encountered problems. Against the recent background of serious short-term economic crises in several East Asian economies, there has been considerable questioning of APEC's prospects.

APEC's Challenges in 2000

Like any other international organization, APEC will always face new challenges in terms of deciding:

1. the scope or breadth of co-operation;
2. the depth of co-operation on particular issues;
3. the extent of wider participation.

In principle, as set out in the first of the four Seoul APEC Declaration objectives, APEC is designed to promote all potential forms of economic co-operation in order to sustain the growth and development of the region. In practice, the process has focused on trade and investment liberalization and facilitation. Even among the many opportunities for TILF, dispropor-tionate attention has been devoted to liberalizing border barriers to trade in goods. Consequently, APEC has tended to be viewed as yet another regional trading arrangement, with its effectiveness measured by the narrow criterion of reducing tariffs against trading partners.

Deepening Trade Liberalization

APEC governments have continued to reduce tariffs rapidly since the establishment of APEC. Moreover, in some important instances, the progress can be attributed to the framework provided by APEC and its Bogor vision.

Indonesia's substantial deregulation and trade liberalization measures of May 1995 and June 1996 were undertaken in order to implement Indonesia's own commitments to the Bogor Declaration which it had championed. In the Philippines, after several decades of failing to implement liberalization strategies, the Philippine Congress supported the Ramos' programme of radical liberalization in the lead-up to the 1996 Manila meetings (Garnaut, 2000). China used the opportunity of the 1995 APEC meetings to announce a 40 percent reduction in average tariffs. Following the Asian financial crisis, several governments included commitments to further liberalization in programmes of structural adjustment agreed with the World Bank and the IMF.

APEC has also begun to act collectively to promote progress in the WTO. At their November 1996 meeting, APEC leaders endorsed a collective agreement to free trade in information technology (IT) products. That was followed, in December 1996, by a broader WTO-wide commitment. APEC also provided a forum for members to prepare for the next round of WTO negotiations. There was extensive consultation in the lead-up to the late 1999 meeting of Trade Ministers in Seattle. APEC leaders endorsed a consensus approach to the scope of negotiations at the September 1999 Auckland meetings.

Despite these constructive early outcomes, APEC has come to be seen as ineffective in terms of promoting trade liberalization. Critics and sceptics have argued that the APEC process, as such, has not made any distinguishable contribution to the trade liberalization that has occurred. APEC governments have reduced their trade barriers:

1. by taking unilateral decisions according to their own perceived self-interest;
2. by fulfilling obligations to liberalize made in the Uruguay Round of GATT/WTO negotiations;
3. as part of structural adjustment programmes agreed in order to secure support from the IMF and the World Bank, especially in the aftermath of the economic crises of 1997–1998.

However, it is frequently asserted that these moves could not be unequivocally attributed to APEC, since they were not the result of negotiations among APEC participants.[9] Moreover, APEC has yet to make any distinctive contribution to liberalizing any "sensitive sectors," such as agriculture in

East Asia and North America, or textiles in North America and Australia. For these reasons, APEC's value has remained in question, as have the prospects of meeting the 2010/2020 Bogor targets for free and open trade and investment.

Some of these criticisms are easily countered. Firstly, they underestimate the importance of a broad long-term commitment to reject protectionism. This commitment proved valuable during the recent economic crises. Despite severe balance of payment problems, there was no backtracking on the trend towards liberalization of trade in goods.[10]

Secondly, the critics ignore significant decisions to liberalize a wide range of tariffs, listed above, which were made explicitly to demonstrate commitment to their APEC commitments.

Thirdly, there is considerable long-term advantage to be gained from liberalizing currently relatively less sensitive sectors. Recent decisions of APEC governments, including their collective leadership in liberalizing the information technology sector, is of considerable future benefit; such initiatives can prevent the emergence of "sensitive sectors" of the twenty-first century.

On the other hand, to realize the Bogor vision of free and open trade and investment, APEC governments will also need to tackle the sectors which are already sensitive.

Tackling the Sensitive Sectors

Catalyzing the 1996 WTO-wide agreement to liberalize trade in information technology products encouraged a follow-up. At the 1997 Vancouver meetings, it was agreed to work towards "early voluntary sectoral liberalisation" (EVSL) of 15 more sectors, with the first nine to be agreed in 1998.[11]

By early 1998, the "V" had disappeared from EVSL and the process turned into a GATT-style trade negotiation. By November, 16 out of 18 APEC participants had agreed on concerted action in terms of trade liberalization, facilitation and technical co-operation for 7 out of the 9 sectors nominated.[12] Despite this progress, almost all the reporting about trade liberalization at the Kuala Lumpur meeting focused on the refusal by Japan — already a large importer of fisheries and forest products — to open these particular markets to a greater extent. Very little attention was paid to the much more significant positive outcome — that all APEC participants, including those in deepest short-term crisis, continued to implement and improve their voluntary IAPs for trade liberalization.

The disappointment with EVSL demonstrated the limitations of voluntary co-operation. In sectors where the short-term political costs outweigh the long-term potential gains from improved economy-wide performance, liberalization is regarded as a "concession" to others. Once reforms are perceived in this way, it becomes necessary to negotiate binding agreements which inflict comparable political pain on all those involved.

As demonstrated by the 1988 experiment with EVSL, APEC has no comparative advantage in such negotiations. APEC governments can still meet their commitment to free and open trade and investment by 2010/2020, but liberalization of sensitive sectors will need to be dealt with in the WTO, which is designed to deal with such issues. But it will not be easy to deal with these sectors, even in the WTO.

APEC's efforts to forge consensus in the lead-up to the 1999 Seattle WTO meeting were somewhat undermined when APEC representatives adopted differing positions at that meeting. They will need to work harder and more coherently to revive the prospect of multilateral liberalization of the hardest sectors.

Promoting Future Trade Liberalization through APEC

APEC's first ten years of experience with trade liberalization points towards a patient and realistic approach to promoting future liberalization, aware of the comparative advantage of voluntary co-operation, while accepting its limitations.

Asia-Pacific governments remain committed to a long-term strategy for "opening to the outside world." At the same time, it is only realistic to expect that short-term political imperatives will cause some selective departures from openness. Part of APEC's liberalization challenge is to deal with such aberrations, ideally by 2010/2020. An even more important part of the challenge is to ensure that they remain aberrations, rather than early symptoms of a more general retreat into protectionism.

Regular reviews of the IAPs of APEC governments remain crucial. Positive peer pressure can continue to lead to further liberalization of less sensitive sectors and prevent any retreat in the relatively more difficult areas. It is, therefore, encouraging to note that APEC leaders have reaffirmed the central role of IAPs and concerted unilateral liberalization within APEC's drive towards free and open trade and investment. An increasing number of APEC governments have voluntarily invited detailed peer reviews of their IAPs.

APEC governments have also learned some other useful lessons from the EVSL experience. It is now recognized that it does not matter whether market-opening decisions are taken unilaterally for domestic reasons, or to implement WTO commitments or are included in IMF programmes. APEC's objective is to sustain the momentum of "opening to the outside world," not to demonstrate that such opening is directly due to the existence of APEC.

It has also been accepted that APEC economies need to strengthen their confidence and capacity to deal with the hardest aspects of trade liberalization. Reductions of border barriers are the last stage in a political decision-making process. They need to be preceded by an acceptance that the costs protection of selected sectors exceed its benefits, and finding other more efficient policy options to meet the objectives (such as employment objectives) of existing border barriers.

The APEC process makes it possible to share the experience of how some governments have been able to make politically difficult decisions; how the earlier objectives of protection have been met by other means; and how liberalization has contributed to economy-wide improvements in efficiency and growth.

If perceptions are changed and alternatives to protectionism are found, then decisions to reduce tariffs need not require intensive negotiations. Conversely, in the absence of work to change perceptions, governments may agree to "concede" lower tariffs in the course of negotiations, then find alternative means to block competition from imports.

Broadening the Scope of Co-operation

Alongside such a multi-faceted approach towards trade liberalization, Asia-Pacific governments also need to promote other broader aspects of economic co-operation as well as managing the consequences of the increasing diversity of APEC participants.

Facilitating Trade and Investment

The ever-expanding range and sophistication of international economic transactions makes it essential to deal with the correspondingly wider and more complex impediments to them. As the APEC Business Advisory Council (ABAC) has consistently pointed out, most of the day-to-day costs and risks of international commerce in the Asia Pacific are not due to border barriers, but to the lack of consistency and/or transparency of many technical, legal and administrative regulations of international economic transactions (ABAC, 1997, 1998).

Unlike the dismantling of border barriers to protect uncompetitive sectors, there is a widely shared interest in facilitating both trade and investment. Options for reducing the costs of international commerce are perceived as positive-sum games. There is no need for negotiations, so voluntary co-operation is very well suited to promoting facilitation. The effective constraint is the capacity to design and implement co-operative arrangements.

For example, the financial crisis highlighted the desirability of well-structured bankruptcy procedures to sort out the after-effects of financial shocks. Co-operative policy development can help each economy identify the type of bankruptcy legislation and procedures suited to each of the Asia-Pacific economies, drawing on the experience of others. But once new procedures are regulated, there is an even greater human resource development challenge to ensure that new institutions are staffed by competent people. Similar institutional and human resource capacity constraints arise in all sectors. They can all be eased by exchange of information, experience, expertise and technology among APEC participants.

For most options to facilitate trade or investment, the more economies involved, the greater the benefits to all of them. Therefore, it makes sense to encourage region-wide involvement from the outset. However, it would be counter-productive to insist that all APEC participants be involved in every specific initiative for co-operation.

For these reasons, APEC's Osaka Action Agenda contained an explicit provision, sometimes called the "21-x" provision, for some Asia-Pacific economies to set examples of co-operative arrangements which can be applied region-wide once their benefits become clear.

Such flexibility can promote early progress, but also carries some risks. Initiatives by some APEC economies to facilitate trade or investment could sow the seeds of division and confusion if these arrangements neglected, or damaged, the interests of others. Partly for these reasons, the EU has chosen to insist that all members are involved in all but a few arrangements for deeper economic integration in Europe. That option is not available in a process of voluntary co-operation. APEC needs to devise a more sophisticated strategy, outlined below, to manage its diversity.

Economic and Technical Co-operation

From the outset, co-operation among Asia-Pacific economies was expected to deal with far more than international trade and investment. By 1991, APEC working groups had commenced exchanging information, identifying shared interests and options for co-operative activities in ten aspects of economic development. The Committee on Trade and Investment (CTI) was not established until 1993, but its work on TILF soon overshadowed other work. The Osaka Action Agenda relegated economic and technical co-operation (ECOTECH) to a separate and secondary endeavour of APEC.[13]

There have, nevertheless, been some constructive developments. 1996 saw the start of a more serious effort to provide a conceptual and operational framework for economic and technical co-operation. APEC leaders adopted the Manila Declaration on an Asia-Pacific Economic Cooperation Framework for Strengthening Economic Cooperation and Development. That declaration set out the objectives, guiding principles and priorities for promoting economic and technical co-operation, defining a model of co-operation based on mutual respect as well as mutual benefit.

The nature of co-operation promoted by APEC is different from "foreign aid;" that is, transfers of funds from donors to clients, often conditional on some surrender of political sovereignty. Instead, the new model seeks to take advantage of the enormous scope for co-operation by sharing the region's richly diverse resources of information, experience, expertise and technology for the benefit of all Asia-Pacific economies.

An ECOTECH sub-committee of APEC senior officials was established in 1997 to co-ordinate the economic and technical co-operation efforts. Clearer understanding of the nature of such co-operation has identified four separate strands, namely:

1. policy development, such as the exchange of information or expertise and the design of potential co-operative activities;
2. technical co-operation, such as specific programmes to upgrade expertise, institutional capacity or technological capability;
3. infrastructure-building, especially where additional capacity can benefit several Asia-Pacific economies; and
4. economic policy co-ordination to help overcome short-term macro-economic or balance of payment problems.[14]

The first of these, co-operative policy development, has been taking place since the establishment of APEC, with useful results. Co-operative policy development work by officials, particularly in the Committee for Trade and Investment (CTI), has underpinned APEC's progress towards trade liberalization to date and will be needed to sustain progress. The Bogor Declaration and its vision for free and open trade and investment would have remained no more than a vision in the absence of valuable work by the CTI and senior officials to define the guiding principles for progress, then to formulate, implement and update IAPs for trade liberalization and co-operative arrangements to facilitate trade and investment.

Such policy development work parallels what the OECD is promoting in a very different context. However, the Asia Pacific has chosen an evolutionary approach which is less bureaucratic, less expensive and less centralized. Rather than creating a large new bureaucracy, APEC committees and working groups are being encouraged to draw on existing networks such as the PECC and APEC Study Centres.

APEC governments and their private sectors are also co-operating to provide the economic infrastructure, ranging from ports, telecommunications and power generation to sewerage facilities, which will be needed to sustain rapid growth. The bulk of investments in such infrastructure will need to be financed with private risk capital. Region-wide co-operation is already helping to gather and disseminate information on best practices for policies to facilitate large-scale private investment in economic infrastructure.

Turning to economic policy co-ordination, APEC was painfully slow to react as the East Asian financial crisis deepened dramatically soon after APEC leaders met in Vancouver in late 1997. Nevertheless, by November 1998, there was a worthwhile set of initiatives for economic and technical co-operation to help overcome the crisis.

APEC Finance Ministers had set up the Manila Framework for addressing the problem and many APEC governments contributed to IMF-led rescue packages for several economies in crisis. In addition, Japan established a US$30 billion fund to support economic recovery. This was followed, at the Kuala Lumpur meetings, by an initiative announced by the U.S. and Japan, in conjunction with the World Bank and the Asian Development Bank, to contribute a further US$10 billion.[15]

To help avoid a recurrence of the crisis, APEC leaders have agreed to adopt internationally recognized principles for financial sector management and supervision. The work of Finance Ministers has become more closely connected to the rest of the APEC process. From 2000, they as well as

Foreign and Trade Ministers, will be making a direct input to the gatherings of APEC leaders.

Several technical co-operation programmes to enhance the capacity to put such principles into practice have been launched by APEC governments as well as by multilateral development agencies during 1998. Examples include an IMF-Singapore Regional Training Institute and an Australian initiative to improve capacity for economic governance.

More generally, it has been recognized that the massive effort needed to build institutional capacity and expertise for better financial sector management is just one aspect of the many opportunities for technical co-operation among Asia-Pacific economies. But it is in this aspect of ECOTECH that APEC is finding it difficult to define its potential contribution.

Several hundred activities have been proposed by APEC committees and working groups, mostly involving the exchange of information and expertise. Some of these are already under way, with some being supported by the private sector as well as by existing development agencies. Nevertheless, the total number of potential activities is growing more rapidly than the small number being implemented. A sense of frustration and several misunderstandings persist.

There are widely varying and incompatible expectations about the nature of the co-operative activities which could be promoted collectively by APEC governments and about how these could be financed and implemented. That is being compounded by an inadequate appreciation of the current and potential role of existing agencies, including the existing development agencies of several APEC governments (such as the United States Agency for International Development (USAID)), multilateral development agencies (such as the Asian Development Bank (ADB)) and the role of the private sector. As in the case of trade liberalization, a misplaced attempt is being made to isolate activities for which APEC can claim credit.

APEC as a Catalyst for Economic and Technical Co-operation[16]

APEC leaders and officials have a comparative advantage in designing options for economic and technical co-operation which can draw on information, experience, expertise and technology from throughout the region and make it available widely to many Asia-Pacific economies. But that does not mean that APEC, as such, can expect to implement all these good ideas.

Compared to the business sector, or to Asia-Pacific governments, the APEC process has very modest funds at its disposal. These can be used to fund, at most, a small proportion of the many economic and technical co-operation opportunities it has already identified. Ideas emerging from the APEC process can act as a catalyst for intensifying economic and technical co-operation, provided APEC can evoke a positive response to such new ideas from the business/private sector and from Asia-Pacific governments.

For example, within the Manila Framework for financial sector co-operation, a multi-year programme of technical co-operation is well under way to strengthen capacity for financial sector management. But this has not been reflected in any marked expansion of APEC's budget or bureaucracy. Multilateral agencies and existing bilateral development agencies have mounted programmes for institution-building and training throughout the region.

Rather than seeking to isolate APEC's direct contribution to financing and implementing physical technical co-operation projects, APEC should concentrate on its comparative advantage to complement the work of others. APEC can draw on many potential sources of support, public and private, to help ensure that more opportunities for technical co-operation to boost the growth potential of the region are taken up.

Widening Participation in APEC — Managing Diversity

Several years ahead of the North American Free Trade Agreement (NAFTA), APEC was the first attempt to forge a new type of co-operation among developing as well as developed economies. The number of member economies has expanded from 12 to 21 between 1989 and 1997 and the corresponding increase in diversity is posing some difficulties.[17]

The diversity of membership means that, typically, some APEC governments will enter into co-operative arrangements to facilitate trade or investment ahead of others. Consultations among APEC governments can help ensure that co-operative arrangements which involve some of them take full account of the interests of all members and encourage others to join when they perceive the benefits of doing so.

A successful example has been provided by arrangements to harmonize passport/visa procedures. These were pioneered by three APEC governments, with others joining later. But without adequate care in the design of initiatives to facilitate trade or investment, arrangements among some APEC economies could damage the interests of others.

At their 1999 meeting in Auckland, APEC Ministers called for guiding principles for arrangements to facilitate trade and investment. It would be desirable to design these in a way which could provide guidance to any co-operative arrangements which involve some, but not necessarily all, members of APEC. If well-designed, such principles could deal with the full range of issues raised by the need to manage the diversity of the APEC process.

Sub-regional Economic Co-operation

Another symptom of diversity is that most Asia-Pacific economies are involved in various forms of co-operation, either among sub-groups of APEC participants, or with the rest of the world, particularly with Europe.

One example is the emerging caucus among East Asian economies. The informal, but now regular, meetings of leaders of ASEAN with those of China, Korea and Japan provide useful opportunities to exchange views on the many economic issues where East Asians have justifiable, shared concerns.[18]

A different symptom of the diversity of Asia-Pacific economies is their recently renewed tendency to seek new links, either bilaterally or with existing sub-regional arrangements, like ASEAN. This reflects a desire for closer economic relations with particular neighbours as well as the wish to move more rapidly than APEC-wide co-operation.[19]

In principle, these initiatives can provide useful precedents for subsequent APEC-wide co-operation. However, early discussions suggest that most of the new links are expected to be built on the basis of traditional "free trade areas," which poses several problems.

One of these concerns is that particularly sensitive sectors, such as agriculture of clothing, may be excluded from such arrangements. Since the Uruguay Round has brought (or is bringing) these sectors under normal GATT/WTO rules, excluding these would violate Article XXIV. That would weaken respect for the international trading system and damage prospects for APEC economies to exercise collective leadership in future WTO negotiations.

Consistency with the letter of the WTO is not sufficient to ensure that new sub-regional arrangements will not undermine the cohesion of APEC. It is widely accepted that the WTO provisions which are used to justify discriminatory trade arrangements are quite ambiguous. Even if all sectors were liberalized and no new barriers were raised against other economies, there would still be some diversion of economic activity away from Asia-Pacific economies not involved, leading to potential tensions within APEC.

If the liberalization schedules for such discriminatory arrangements were at least as rapid as the commitment by APEC leaders to eliminate all trade barriers by 2010 or 2020, then any short-term trade diversion would be strictly temporary. On the other hand, if the Bogor commitments are expected to be met, then the free trade area aspects of such new arrangements are also somewhat superfluous. There is reason for concern that the suddenly renewed interest in any new, potentially discriminatory, trading arrangements reflects the fact that APEC governments are no longer serious about the Bogor commitments which were made, in more and more cases, by their predecessors in office.

All of the new initiatives under consideration are expected to deal with matters well beyond border barriers to trade and investment, such as the mutual recognition of standards or harmonization of administrative procedures. Once again, these arrangements could set positive examples for subsequently wider arrangements for facilitation. However, agreements to facilitate trade or investment which are built upon the foundation of a discriminatory trading arrangement are considerably more likely to generate new forms of discrimination. There would be a serious risk that they might divert economic activity away from other APEC economies.

WTO provisions for sub-regional economic co-operation are scarcely relevant to many of these new issues. APEC participants need to devise and agree on some principles for sub-regional trading arrangements which can avoid needless tensions and inefficient diversion of trade or investment in the Asia-Pacific region.

Links to the Rest of the World

The above concerns also apply to the links between APEC economies and others. As membership expands, more and more participants are likely to have interests in links to the rest of the world which are quite comparable, if not stronger, than to other APEC economies — for example, Russia's trade links to the rest of Europe are far more intensive than to Asia-Pacific economies. If APEC economies form "free trade areas" with the EU, they may well discriminate against their APEC trading partners relative to European economies.

New efforts to promote closer economic integration do not need to be built around discriminatory trading arrangements. For example, the new

Transatlantic Economic Partnership (TEP) between the EU and the U.S., which was initiated in late 1998, does not propose yet another "free trade area." Traditional issues of reducing border barriers to trade are left to the WTO, so the TEP focuses on tackling problems caused by regulatory barriers which, as the proponents of the new partnership state, "are now the main obstacle to transatlantic business."[20]

The TEP process, to be implemented over several years, sets the stage for a large number of co-operative arrangements to facilitate trade and investment between the EU and the U.S.; for example, by:

1. lowering technical border barriers to trade in goods in the context of shared commitments to high health, safety and environment standards;
2. widening mutual recognition of testing and approval procedures by progressive alignment of standards;
3. reducing impediments to trade in agriculture by closer scientific co-operation to set appropriate mutually recognized regulations;
4. facilitating access to public procurement markets, including by enhancing the compatibility of electronic procurement information and government contracting systems (European Commission, 1998).

The EU and U.S. emphasize their commitment that all of their new co-operative arrangements will conform fully to their international and, in particular WTO, obligations and that the TEP will not create new barriers to third countries. Nevertheless, considerable care will be needed to avoid damage to the interests of other APEC economies.

Even if no explicit new barriers are raised against third partners, it will be very difficult to avoid some diversion of economic activity. In many cases, such diversion can only be avoided by others if they can become full parties to any co-operative arrangements set up between the EU and the U.S. To protect their interests, APEC economies should seek assurances that their interests will be adequately protected.

Principles for Managing Diversity

A set of principles which could deal with these problems of "variable geometry" raised by APEC's diversity have been recommended by Drysdale et al. (1998). Those guiding principles propose that all new co-operative arrangements involving APEC economies should:

1. be consistent with existing APEC and WTO commitments;

2. be transparent;
3. avoid introducing new forms of discrimination, either among products or producers from different economies;
4. provide for, and encourage, accession by others.

Consistent with the voluntary nature of the APEC process, such principles would not be binding. However, in line with the broad principle of open regionalism, APEC governments should be prepared to respond positively to constructive suggestions from other economies on how such arrangements could be adapted to take better account of the interests of all economies.

As APEC gathers momentum, participants will become increasingly aware of the need to ensure that co-operative arrangements among some participants are indeed capable of subsequent region-wide application. More attention will be paid to avoiding the proliferation of arrangements which fragment, rather than integrate, regional markets. That is likely to lead to the adoption of principles along these lines. Once adopted, such principles will also serve as a useful framework for the design of co-operative arrangements involving both APEC and non-APEC economies.

Looking Ahead

The diversity of APEC calls for creative solutions. Agreement on principles which help assure that all co-operative arrangements involving any APEC economies take full account of the interests of all other APEC participants is an urgent imperative to preserve the integrity and coherence of the process. To foster a sense of community among developed and developing members, APEC also needs to shift from its current pre-occupation with trade policy issues and adopt a more integrated strategy for co-operation.

Integrating ECOTECH and TILF

The recent financial crisis has reminded everyone in the region to attend to the foundations of sustainable rapid growth. The experience of 1997 and 1998 demonstrated that opportunities for economic co-operation in the Asia Pacific extend well beyond issues of trade and investment. APEC has to broaden its horizons and seize more opportunities for capacity-building in the region.

The ongoing task for APEC is to strengthen the capacity of all Asia-

Pacific economies to increase their productive resources and to allocate them in an increasingly efficient way. It is becoming evident that co-operation which improves the ability of Asia-Pacific governments to reduce impediments to trade and investment is just one important part of this potential co-operative effort. Such a perception can end the recent, artificial distinction between TILF and ECOTECH.

A more integrated approach can emerge by realizing that all aspects of the APEC process are forms of capacity-building. Harking back to the primary objective stated in the 1991 Seoul APEC Declaration, APEC should be viewed as a co-operative process to enhance the capacity of Asia-Pacific economies:

> ... to sustain the growth and development of the region for the common good of its peoples and, in this way, to contribute to the growth and development of the world economy.

Sharing information, experience and expertise among Asia-Pacific economies can help all regional governments to design and implement more efficient policies to promote all aspects of economic development, including policies on international trade and investment.

Better Policies for Better Markets

To a large extent, more efficient policy-making is a matter of making markets more efficient and more competitive. One aspect of creating strong competitive markets is to eliminate inefficient distinctions between domestic and international supplies of products. In this context, TILF can be seen as just one part of the task of designing and implementing better policies for better markets. APEC's objective of progressively deeper integration of Asia-Pacific economies requires attention to the structure of all markets, domestic as well as international.

As noted by Vautier and Lloyd (2000):

> ... removing all market access restrictions which impede cross-border trade in goods and services does not assure non-discriminatory access for foreign supplies if other policies, including domestic regulations, discriminate against them.

Genuinely free and open trade and investment can only be achieved as part of a broader strategy to encourage and enable APEC governments to adopt better policies for better markets. The broad challenge for APEC is to encourage and enable all Asia-Pacific governments to improve the functioning of all markets.

Drawing on a set of competition principles developed by the PECC between 1995 and 1999 (PECC, 1999), APEC leaders have endorsed a set of principles for strengthening market structures (APEC, 1999). Strengthening the functioning of markets has been adopted, by consensus, as a priority for APEC. This is expected to be pursued by encouraging progressively closer adherence to guiding principles of:

1. comprehensiveness in the sense of dealing with all markets and all aspects of competition;
2. non-discrimination/competitive neutrality among all sources of supply, international as well as domestic;
3. transparency; and
4. accountability.

Revising policies towards such principles requires precise definition of objectives, allocating policy tools to these objectives, refining relevant regulations and legislation, then building institutional capacity to administer them. The capacity to pursue such a complex process can be considerably enhanced by economic and technical co-operation among Asia-Pacific economies. Co-operative policy development and technical co-operation can help all governments to improve the workings of their markets by helping them to:

1. identify inconsistencies between current policies and agreed principles and objectives;
2. understand the motives for such inconsistencies;
3. demonstrate the cost of inconsistencies;
4. identify more efficient and coherent policies;
5. develop the capacity to implement such policies.

Asia-Pacific governments can help each other to take these steps, voluntarily, based on a correct perception of their own self-interest, making all of their markets, international as well as domestic, more transparent and less discriminatory.

Facilitating trade or investment is part of a technically complex task of moving towards more efficient ways to manage markets. Implementing co-operative arrangements for facilitation, such as administering compliance to mutual recognized standards, is not a matter of adversarial negotiations. Facilitation, like most reforms, is essentially a challenge for co-operative policy development, to design more compatible approaches to economic regulations and administrative procedures, followed up by technical co-operation to create the capacity to implement such policies.

Patient co-operative policy development is also needed to provide a firm foundation for trade liberalization. As discussed earlier, Asia-Pacific economies can usefully share their experience in order to enhance each other's capacity to meet national objectives without need for protectionism. In other words, capacity-building through economic and technical co-operation is not an alternative to trade liberalization, but an essential means for making it possible.

An Integrated Strategy for APEC

As well as enhancing the prospects for facilitating and liberalizing trade and investment, capacity-building is also the key ingredient of economic co-operation among Asia-Pacific economies to:

1. strengthen financial markets;
2. develop economic infrastructure;
3. boost technological capability; and
4. develop human resources.[21]

This points towards an integrated strategy for APEC. Co-operative efforts of all its working groups and activity can encourage and enable Asia-Pacific economies to continue to strengthen their economic policy framework in order to enhance their available productive resources and promote their efficient allocation. This can be achieved by means of a combination of co-operative policy development and technical co-operation, with particular emphasis on human resource development and institution-building.

It would be desirable to set some priorities among the many options for capacity-building. Possible candidates include:

1. strengthening financial sectors;
2. promoting progressively closer adherence APEC's Principles for Competition and Deregulation;
3. sectoral analysis to help demonstrate the significant long-term net benefits of reducing impediments to trade in key sectors such as financial services, air and maritime transport, iron and steel products and foodgrains.

Once such programmes are endorsed by APEC leaders, they can invite APEC governments, regional and multilateral development banks as well as the business/private sector to mobilize resources to finance the technical co-operation programmes jointly identified by APEC and to make arrangements for their ongoing implementation.

ABAC has already indicated how the business sector can support APEC's ECOTECH agenda by establishing a Partnership for Equitable Growth (PEG). The PEG is to serve as a new framework to encourage business participation in technical co-operation activities. APEC leaders should continue to encourage such innovative contributions.

APEC governments should be encouraged to include their commitment to promote specific aspects of the priority technical co-operation programmes endorsed by APEC leaders as a significant part of their Individual Action Plans (IAPs). This would emphasize the organic link between the policy reform aspects and ECOTECH aspects of promoting progress towards the Bogor vision of free and open trade and investment. Where possible, APEC governments should be encouraged to promote technical co-operation projects jointly: Their contributions to such co-operative activities could be included as part of APEC's Collective Action Plans (CAPs).

It is also important to note that APEC governments are, collectively, well placed to direct regional and multilateral development banks to take up significant components of long-term human resource development and institution-building programmes endorsed by APEC leaders.

Conclusion

Economic co-operation in the Asia Pacific is facing many challenges. With patience and goodwill, all of these can be met. APEC's regular meetings of senior regional officials, ministers and leaders provide valuable channels of communication. These make it more likely that policy formation in all Asia-Pacific economies will be better informed by developments elsewhere in the region and policy-makers are more likely to choose options which facilitate regional integration and avoid needless adverse side effects on other economies.

The experience of APEC's first decade has confirmed that its participants, particularly from East Asia, continue to have no interest in ceding powers of regulation or enforcement to any new regional organization. APEC will remain a voluntary process, which helps its members to seize opportunities to realize mutual benefits, rather than expecting them to act against their perceived self-interest.

In all aspects of co-operation, it will be important to have realistic expectations. A strong sense of community has yet to emerge, so major breakthroughs on socially and politically sensitive issues should not be expected each year.

At the same time, a growing sense of community, mutual trust and mutual respect can be nurtured by broadening the scope of co-operation. The best way to discover new shared interests is to co-operate in the many areas where the opportunity for mutual benefit has already been perceived. Much can be done to realize the full potential of all Asia-Pacific economies for sustainable growth by sharing the richly diverse sources of information, experience and expertise available in the region. That will enhance the capacity to design and implement more effective economic policies.

The time has come for APEC to end its recent pre-occupation with traditional trade liberalization and adopt a more integrated strategy for capacity-building in Pacific Asia.

Notes

1. Drysdale (1988) proposed regional economic co-operation in the Asia Pacific with the primary objective of defending and enhancing a rules-based multilateral trading system, underpinned by the GATT.
2. The PECC, established in 1980, is a forum of business people, government officials and academics which evolved from PAFTAD.
3. The need for a new approach has been demonstrated by the evolution of economic co-operation in Western Europe. The EU had achieved free internal trade by the late 1960s, but a much broader effort to co-ordinate economic policies needed to be implemented, largely from 1985 to 1992, to create anything like an integrated market.
4. Article XXIV of the GATT contains a loophole from the fundamental principle of non-discrimination in Article I. This exemption allows groups of economies to discriminate against others, provided they enter into a formal agreement, subject to GATT scrutiny, to eliminate all border barriers to trade in substantially all goods within a well-defined time limit (typically 10 years). The General Agreement on Trade in Services (GATS) agreed in 1994 contains a similar loophole.
5. Taiwan participates as Chinese Taipei. Since 1997, Hong Kong has participated as Hong Kong, China.
6. Taiwan is represented by a senior economic minister at leaders' meetings. That

was also the case for Hong Kong up to 1997. Since then, Hong Kong is normally represented by its Chief Executive.

7. The target dates for eliminating all obstacles to trade and investment are 2010 and 2020 for developed and developing member economies of APEC, respectively.

8. Drysdale et al. (1998:111–13) set out and explain the significance of the guiding principles of the Osaka Action Agenda as well as early progress in terms of facilitating and liberalizing trade and investment.

9. See Bergsten (1997) and Lloyd (1999). Even APEC governments' collective commitment to free trade in all information technology products has been dismissed as unimpressive, partly because it had been preceded by trans-Atlantic discussion aimed at a similar result and partly because information technology was an "easy sector" to liberalize.

10. Even in Malaysia, which imposed some limited additional controls on capital flows, there was no question of additional protection of sectors of production.

11. The nine sectors were: environmental goods and services, fish and fish products, toys, forest products, gems and jewellery, chemicals, energy, medical equipment and instruments and telecommunications mutual recognition arrangements.

12. Mexico and Chile did not participate in the EVSL exercise as they are already committed to a schedule for eliminating border barriers across the board.

13. See Elek and Soesastro (1999) for a more detailed account of the problems of promoting economic and technical co-operation within APEC.

14. This classification first appears in FDC (1998).

15. More recently, the Auckland meetings of APEC provided an opportunity for several member economies to form a "Friends of Papua New Guinea" group. This group has committed itself to help a new government in Papua New Guinea to cope with an inherited, short-term macro-economic crisis. This group of APEC governments is now making a substantial contribution in support of reform programmes agreed by PNG with the international financial institutions.

16. The following paragraphs draw on FDC (1998).

17. In 1989, APEC was launched by ministers for 12 Asia-Pacific economies, namely, the then six members of ASEAN (Brunei Darussalam, Indonesia, Malaysia, the Philippines, Singapore and Thailand), together with Australia, Canada, South Korea, Japan, New Zealand and the United States. China, Taiwan and Hong Kong joined in 1991, with the non-formal nature of APEC permitting the simultaneous inclusion of their economies, finessing issues of sovereignty. Mexico and Papua New Guinea were admitted in 1993, Chile in 1994, then Peru, Russia and Vietnam in 1997.

18. This process is usually termed the ASEAN(10+3) process.

19. Examples include a potential Japan-Korea free trade area, close links between Australia, New Zealand and ASEAN, and a possible free trade arrangement for trade in services between Australia and Japan.

20. See Elek (1998) for a more detailed assessment of the implication of the TEP for the APEC process.
21. For further details, see Elek and Soesastro (1999).

References

ABAC (1997), *APEC Means Business: Call To Action*. Report to APEC Leaders. APEC Secretariat, Singapore.

—— (1998), *APEC Means Business: Restoring Confidence, Regenerating Growth*. Report to APEC Leaders. APEC Secretariat, Singapore.

APEC (1999), *APEC Principles to Enhance Competition and Regulatory Reform*. Auckland, November.

—— (2000), *Getting Results for Business*. APEC Secretariat, Singapore.

Bergsten, C. F. (1997), "APEC in 1997: Prospects and Possible Strategies." Paper prepared for a conference at the Institute for International Economics, Washington D.C., 14–15 April.

Drysdale, P. (1988), *International Economic Pluralism: Economic Policy in East Asia and the Pacific*. New York: Columbia University Press.

Drysdale, P., A. Elek and H. Soesastro (1998), "Open Regionalism: The Nature of Asia Pacific Integration." In P. Drysdale and D. Vines (eds.), *Europe, East Asia and APEC: A Shared Global Agenda?* Cambridge: Cambridge University Press.

Elek, A. (1991), "Asia Pacific Economic Cooperation (APEC)." *Southeast Asian Affairs 1991*. Singapore: Institute of Southeast Asian Studies.

—— (1995), "APEC beyond Bogor: An Open Economic Association in the Asia-Pacific Region," *Asian Pacific Economic Literature*, 9(1):1–16.

—— (1998), "Open Regionalism Going Global: APEC and the New Transatlantic Economic Partnership." *Pacific Economic Papers*, No. 286. Australia-Japan Research Centre, December.

Elek, A and H. Soesastro (1999), "ECOTECH at the Heart of APEC: Capacity-building in the Asia Pacific." The Foundation for Development Co-operation, Brisbane.

European Commission (1998), *The Transatlantic Economic Partnership: Action Plan*, November (available at http://europa.eu.int/comm/dg01/1109tep.htm).

The Foundation for Development Cooperation (FDC) (1998), "Forging New Partnerships: Economic and Technical Co-operation and the APEC Process." Report of meetings and recommendations to APEC and ABAC, Kuala Lumpur, 2 December 1997 and 10 August 1998.

Garnaut, R. (2000), "APEC Ideas and Reality: History and Prospects." Paper presented at Pacific Trade and Development (PAFTAD) 25 Conference, Osaka, June. To be published in proceedings of PAFTAD 25 edited by Ippei Yamazawa.

Lloyd, P. J. (1999), "APEC and the WTO." Paper presented at Pacific Economic Co-operation Council Trade Policy Forum 1999. Auckland, June.

PECC (1996), *Milestones in APEC Liberalization: A Map of Market Opening Measures by APEC Economies*. Singapore: PECC Secretariat.

—— (1999), "Principles for Guiding the Development of a Competition-driven Policy Framework for APEC Economies." Report of Trade Policy Forum Competition Principles Project. Singapore.

Vautier, K. M. and P. J. Lloyd (2000). "The Competition and Deregulation Policy Areas in APEC." Paper presented at Pacific Trade and Development (PAFTAD) 25 Conference, Osaka, June 1999. To be published in proceedings of PAFTAD 25 edited by Ippei Yamazawa.

Contributors

YUE-MAN YEUNG is Professor of Geography, Director of the Hong Kong Institute of Asia-Pacific Studies (HKIAPS), Head of Shaw College and Director of the Shanghai-Hong Kong Development Institute, The Chinese University of Hong Kong. His wide-ranging research interests have recently focused on China's coastal cities, South China, globalization and Asian cities. He has published extensively, including, as co-editor or author, *Emerging World Cities in Pacific Asia* (1996), *Shanghai* (1996), *Globalization and the World of Large Cities* (1998), *Guangdong* (1998), *Fujian* (2000) and *Globalization and Networked Societies* (2000).

JOSE V. ABUEVA is Professor Emeritus of Political Science and Public Administration at the University of the Philippines. He has published extensively on Filipino politics, public administration and political leadership, and democratization. He was Visiting Professor at the City University of New York and Yale University in the 1960s and worked at the United Nations University from 1977 to 1987 when he returned to serve as President of the University of the Philippines (1987–1993). During the presidency of Ms. Corazon Aquino, Abueva served as Chairman of the Joint Legislative-Executive Bases Council that planned the alternative uses of the military bases and military camps prior to the departure of U.S. military forces from the Philippines.

FANNY M. CHEUNG received her B.A. from U. C. Berkeley, and her Ph.D. from the University of Minnesota. She is currently Professor of Psychology at The Chinese University of Hong Kong. She founded the Gender Research Programme at the University, which has been turned into the Gender Research Centre under HKIAPS. Her research interests include gender issues, violence against women, Chinese psychopathology and personality assessment. Between 1996 and 1999, Professor Cheung was on leave from the University to serve as the full-time founding chairperson of the Equal Opportunities Commission in Hong Kong.

FREDERIC C. DEYO is Professor of Sociology at the State University of New York, Binghamton and Visiting Professor in the Department of Applied Social Studies at the City University of Hong Kong.

ANDREW ELEK is the international economic policy consultant and Research Associate of the Australia-Japan Research Centre, Australian National University.

BAOGANG HE graduated with a Ph.D. from Australian National University. He is a former Reader (or Associate Professor) at the School of Government, the University of Tasmania, Hobart, Australia. He is currently a Senior Research Fellow in East Asian Institute, National University of Singapore. Dr. He is the author of *The Democratisation of China* and other books, and has published numerous journal articles.

CHARLES K. KAO is an eminent scientist and educator, with an illustrious career spent in the United Kingdom, the United States and Hong Kong. His pioneering work in engineering has earned him the sobriquet "father of optical fibre." He is the recipient of numerous prestigious awards, including the Ericsson Prize conferred by the Swedish King, the Japan Prize conferred by the Japanese Emperor and the Draper Prize from the President of the United States. Formerly Vice-Chancellor of The Chinese University of Hong Kong, he is currently Chairman and CEO of ITX Services Ltd.

SIU-KAI LAU is Professor and Chairman, Department of Sociology, and Associate Director, HKIAPS, both at The Chinese University of Hong Kong. Professor Lau's research interests are Hong Kong's social and political development as well as comparative politics. He is the author of *Society and Politics in Hong Kong* (1982), co-author (with Kuan Hsin-chi) of *The Ethos of the Hong Kong Chinese* (1988), and many articles published in international journals. Professor Lau is also a public intellectual actively involved in Hong Kong affairs.

EMMA PORIO is Professor and Chairman of the Department of Sociology and Anthropology at the Ateneo de Manila University. For the past 15 years, she has been doing research on urban/rural poverty, children, governance and civil society.

YUN-WING SUNG is Chairman and Professor in the Department of Economics, and Co-director of the Hong Kong and Asia-Pacific Economies Research Programme, HKIAPS at The Chinese University of Hong Kong. He is editor of *Asian Economic Journal*, book review editor of *Pacific Economic Review*, and corresponding editor of *Asian Pacific Economic Literature*. He has published extensively on the Chinese and Hong Kong economies in international journals and books, including *The China-Hong Kong Connection* (1991), *Hong Kong and South China: The Economic Synergy* (1998) and others.

SHAOGUANG WANG is Associate Professor of Political Science at The Chinese University of Hong Kong, who obtained his LL.B. at Peking University and his Ph.D. at Cornell University. He taught at Tijiao High School, Wuhan, from 1972 to 1977, and at Yale University from 1990 to 2000. He has authored five books and co-authored six books. The most recent publication is *The Political Economy of Uneven Development: The Case of China* (1999).

HENRY WAI-CHUNG YEUNG, Ph.D., is Associate Professor at the Department of Geography, National University of Singapore (NUS). He is a recipient of NUS Outstanding University Researcher Award 1998 and Institute of British Geographers Economic Geography Research Group Best Published Paper Award 1998. He is the author of *Transnational Corporations and Business Networks* (1998), editor of *The Globalisation of Business Firms from Emerging Markets*, two volumes (1999) and co-editor of *Globalisation and the Asia Pacific: Contested Territories* (1999), and *The Globalisation of Chinese Business Firms* (2000). He has over 35 research papers published in internationally refereed journals.

Index